4 95

THE
ALLERGY
DISCOVERY
DIET

THE
ALLERGY
DISCOVERY
DIET

A Rotation Diet
for Discovering
Your Allergies
to Food

JOHN E. POSTLEY, M.D.

WITH

JANET M. BARTON

DOUBLEDAY

NEW YORK LONDON TORONTO SYDNEY AUCKLAND

Published by Doubleday, a division of Bantam Doubleday Dell Publishing Group, Inc., 666
Fifth Avenue, New York, New York 10103

Doubleday and the portrayal of an anchor with a dolphin are trademarks of Doubleday, a
division of Bantam Doubleday Dell Publishing Group, Inc.

> The practice of medicine requires individual questioning and examination for
> accurate diagnosis. This book is a nutritional approach to the relief of chronic
> problems which have already been evaluated by your own physician. Do not
> attempt to use this book as a substitute for a physician's personal evaluation of
> new symptoms or any change in old symptoms. Such symptoms could have serious
> and dangerous causes. If in doubt, see your physician again before embarking on
> this course.

Library of Congress Cataloging-in-Publication Data

Postley, John E.
    The allergy discovery diet : a rotation diet for discovering your allergies to food / by
John E. Postley with Janet M. Barton.—1st ed.
        p.   cm.
    Includes index.
    ISBN 0-385-24682-X
    1. Food allergy—Diet therapy—Popular works.   2. Food allergy—
Diagnosis—Popular works.   I. Barton, Janet M.   II. Title.
RC588.D53P67   1990
616.97'5075—dc20   89-32056
                                                                CIP

To Elaine and Tony

Acknowledgments

We would like to thank Stephanie Young, whose ability to organize our thoughts and assistance in getting them down on paper were an invaluable aid in the writing of this book. The quality and professionalism of her contribution is greatly appreciated.

This book would not have been written save for the energy and counsel of Julian Bach. He encouraged the project when it was an embryonic thought and he nurtured it during its development, giving generously of his time and wisdom. May its success reflect the enthusiasm of his involvement.

Above all, we thank our editor at Doubleday, Karen Van Westering, for her expert and creative guidance. Her talents as writer and editor combine elegance and excellence of literary judgment as well as amazing command of detail; she taught us how to transform a manuscript into a good and useful book. Karen added literal flavor besides; it was her delicious notion to add fruit essence to Allergy Discovery Diet herbal teas.

We owe thanks also to Judy Kern at Doubleday, for providing editorial finishing touches, and to the many patients and friends, Sally Mandel and Doris Flax in particular, who contributed invaluable gifts of time and helped us enormously by testing recipes and the Allergy Discovery Diet plan as it evolved. Our loving thanks go to our families for their support, and especially to Sam McNicol, who inspired our collaboration.

Lastly, we are grateful to Ralph S. Blume, M.D., and Jack Weissman, M.D., for their helpful review and suggestions concerning parts of the manuscript.

Contents

PART I

✳

ABOUT THE ALLERGY DISCOVERY DIET

1   What Is the Allergy Discovery Diet?   *3*

2   Why the Allergy Discovery Diet Works   *15*

3   Who Should Try the Allergy Discovery Diet?   *21*

4   Making the Allergy Discovery Diet Work for You   *42*

5   The Practical Aspects of the Allergy Discovery Diet   *61*

PART II

✳

THE ALLERGY DISCOVERY DIET COOKBOOK

The Elimination Phase

DAY 1   *76*

DAY 2   *85*

DAY 3   *98*

DAY 4   *108*

DAY 5   *120*
DAY 6   *132*

The Reintroduction Phase

DAY 7   *142*
DAY 8   *152*
DAY 9   *165*
DAY 10   *174*
DAY 11   *184*
DAY 12   *198*
DAY 13   *211*
DAY 14   *223*
DAY 15   *236*
DAY 16   *249*
DAY 17   *262*
DAY 18   *274*
DAY 19   *287*
DAY 20   *298*
DAY 21   *309*
DAY 22   *325*

APPENDIX   *339*

REFERENCES FOR APPENDIX   *359*

GENERAL REFERENCES   *362*

INDEX   *363*

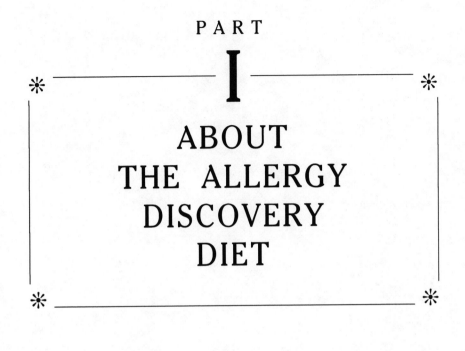

PART

I

ABOUT THE ALLERGY DISCOVERY DIET

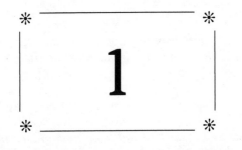

What Is the Allergy Discovery Diet?

A turgid swelling of her stomach was making Diana feel constantly "lumpy" and uncomfortable. The young interior designer was even more troubled by the puffiness beneath her eyes that made her look tired and older than her thirty-nine years. Diana consulted a succession of doctors about her problems, but nothing they prescribed seemed to help. It looked like plastic surgery was the only solution for the pouches under her eyes.

❋

Larry was afraid to shake hands anymore; business associates and even friends recoiled at the sight of his psoriasis-covered palms. "It looks like I've got some horrible, contagious disease," he explained. Psoriasis on the soles of his feet made walking torturous.

❋

Heartburn and diarrhea troubled Miguel so constantly that he munched on antacid tablets all day long, trying to ease his discomfort. Miguel knew that corn did not agree with him, but even though he took care to avoid it, his intestinal problems persisted. The many gastroenterologists he consulted could offer no cure for his unrelenting suffering.

❋

Blinding headaches and painful canker sores threatened the promising fashion career of twenty-year-old Nancy. When one of her "killer" headaches struck, the busy young dress designer had a hard time meeting deadlines and keeping appointments. Her unexplained attacks of pain became a serious handicap as she tried to keep up in the competitive New York market.

✳

Hospitalized four times for endometriosis, severe dysmenorrhea, lower back spasms, headaches and numbness in one arm, Rachel had lived with pain for years, but it was taking its toll. The steady decline of her health began to drain Rachel's spirit as well as her physical vitality, eroding her will to get better.

✳

"I just feel so worn out all the time," said Priscilla. Having two small children explained some of Priscilla's fatigue, but considering her history of sound physical health, her lack of energy was extreme. "Even a good night's sleep doesn't help; I still wake up tired. I can barely get through the day." Exhaustion was ruining Priscilla's enjoyment of life and the fun of caring for her children.

✳

Despite the wide variation of these complaints, the foregoing case histories from my files have more in common than one might expect. Thousands of patients visit their doctors every day with similarly puzzling symptoms that appear to defy diagnosis. Pinning down the exact cause of headaches, joint pains and swellings, stomachaches, diarrhea, skin rashes, bloating and intestinal inflammations, even under-eye pouches, can be a long and frustrating process for physicians and patients alike.

Frequently, I have found that the source of mysterious symptoms is an allergic reaction to food. Such was the case in each of the preceding stories. Diana, Larry, Miguel, Nancy, Rachel and Priscilla all were suffering adverse reactions to familiar, everyday foods.

The notion of food allergies is not new. As long ago as Hippocrates, food has been suspected as a possible root of disease. The old adage, "one man's meat is another man's poison" is never truer than when dealing with food sensitivities, and ancient though the notion is, the fact that food affects people in different ways still frustrates modern doctors as they attempt to treat food-related illness.

As science struggles to come up with the facts, there are some who have made food allergies trendy, touting them as the simple, clear-cut cause of everything from obesity to backaches and schizophrenia. Beware of those who claim to have all the answers. Food allergies are complex and extremely individual. Fortunately, recent medical research has provided new understanding about the human immune system and its role in allergic reactions, so that personal sensitivities to foods can be discovered, and eventually controlled.

What Are the Symptoms of Food Allergy?

Allergic reactions to foods may involve any organ of the body, but in general, the skin, respiratory tract, gastrointestinal tract and cardiovascular systems are most often affected. In my experience, I have found food allergies to be at the root of headaches, stuffy noses, sinus problems, canker sores, sore throats, swollen glands, coughs, asthma, heart palpitations, syndromes of alternating tension and fatigue, muscular chest pains, heartburn, acid indigestion, stomach pain, cramps, bloating, diarrhea, constipation, urinary frequency, urinary burning, urinary hesitancy, vaginal irritation, rectal itching, arthritis, joint stiffness and swelling, psoriasis, hives, itching and welts.

The following survey is the questionnaire I use with patients who come to me with complaints that seem to confound diagnosis. Take a moment to read through the list. If one or more of your unresolved physical problems is described on this checklist, you owe it to yourself to see if what you are eating is to blame for your discomfort and pain.

Before proceeding, I would caution that food allergies are not the only possible cause of mysterious symptoms. Food-allergic reactions are caused by the body's immune system, but there are other, nonimmunologic ways that food and food-related substances can make you sick. Food toxicity, or poisoning, is a good example. In this type of reaction, the poisoned or contaminated food (such as salmonella-infected chicken for example) acts directly upon the body's physiology, without involving the immune system. Food intolerance is also a physiologic problem which does not concern the immune system. Lactose intolerance is a familiar example, suffered by people whose bodies lack the enzyme necessary for breaking down the principal carbohydrate in milk. Sucrase deficiency describes a lack of the enzyme responsible for metabolizing the complex molecules in cane sugar.

Salicylate sensitivity is another nonimmunologic reaction which sometimes causes allergy-like symptoms. Acetylsalicylate (ASA) is the active ingredient in aspirin and often aggravates chronic skin conditions in people who are sensitive to salicylates. Salicylates are also suspected of causing hyperactivity in children. Pharmacologic food reactions describe the body's responses to substances other than food but which are ingested like foods, such as drugs and food additives. Adverse pharmacologic reactions sometimes involve the immune system, but often do not.

*

SYMPTOM QUESTIONNAIRE

Do you often have headaches? Do they occur at a particular time of day or following a certain meal?

Do you have itchy eyes? Red eyes? Puffy eyes? Crusting of the eyelids?

Do you have flaking skin in or behind your ears?

Do you often have a stuffy nose? Swelling inside the nose? Post-nasal draining? Sinus headache pressure?

Do you get sore throats? Swollen glands? A tickle in your throat?

Do you frequently get canker sores in your mouth or have a burning sensation on your tongue?

Do you have a cough, wheezing or bronchial mucus production even if you don't smoke?

Do you get sudden attacks of rapid or forceful heartbeat when you are just sitting still?

Do you get heartburn? Acid indigestion? Nausea?

Do you frequently have gas, stomach or abdominal distention or bloating?

Do you get blemishes on your face despite frequent washing?

Are you troubled by abdominal cramps, diarrhea or constipation? Do you find mucus in your stool?

Do you find you experience periods of urinary frequency, burning or discomfort, even when your doctor finds no evidence of infection?

Do you have severe, painful menses?

Do you suffer unexplained pain in the prostate area?

Do you have periodic pain, stiffness or swelling of the joints? Do you have general swelling of the hands, feet or face?

Do you experience hives? Skin rashes? Welts? Blotches? Where do these most often occur?

Finally, there are anaphylactic reactions to foods. Anaphylactic reactions are allergic in nature because they involve the immune system, but these are such virulent, violent reactions, caused by the release of a special class of antibody called IgE, that they deserve to be thought of as a breed apart. Peanuts made headlines in 1986 when a restaurant chili thickened with peanut butter caused an anaphylactic reaction in a Brown University coed. As a result of her allergic response, the young woman died.

Such dramatic reactions to common foods are not the subject of this book. My focus is not the fatal allergic reactions, but the chronic upsets caused by foods which undermine the quality of life for so many people. If you've got an acute allergy to a food, chances are you know it—your body lets you know in no uncertain terms. The young Brown student knew she was allergic to peanuts, but had no idea chili would be thickened with peanut butter. If you know you are allergic to a food, avoid it while following the Allergy Discovery Diet plan. There's no need to retest for it. Substitutions are allowed on the Allergy Discovery Diet and the proper way to custom fit the diet to your needs is outlined in Chapter 4.

Nonfood elements in your home or work environment might also be the source of your health problem, stimulating your body to overreact. One of my patients, for example, complained that a violent fit of sneezing overtook him each morning at the breakfast table. Was it the orange juice, Roger wondered? The eggs or oatmeal? In time, we discovered that the offending agent was the ink in Roger's early morning paper, and not his breakfast at all.

Similarly, your headache or raw-looking rash may be an allergic reaction to something other than food, such as pollen, for example, or the new paint and carpet in the living room. Another possibility is that you are a victim of a kind of medical mathematics. Like all symptoms of illness, symptoms of allergy are manifestations of the immune system at work as it fights harmful agents which have entered the body. Very often it is not one, but several different sorts of intruders which cause this overexertion of the body's disease-fighting mechanism. For example, if you have only a slight sensitivity to milk, you might be able to drink milk and suffer no ill-effects, but if you drink milk out in the garden when the air is full of pollen and you're just getting over a cold, the overstimulation of your immune system as it struggles to neutralize the pollen, the viral infection and finally, the slight irritation caused by the milk might "add up" to be more than your body can bear. The milk has pushed your body beyond its threshold for adverse reactions. Like a simmering pot, your "healthy" chemical balance "boils over," and you suffer an allergic reaction to milk which can take any number of uncomfortable forms.

The purpose of the Allergy Discovery Diet is to help you determine if food sensitivities are triggering your symptoms of illness and/or allergy. After only a few days on the plan (when you've completed the Elimination Phase) you will know if your problem is food-related. Then, by reintroducing suspect foods in the single-file, rotating pattern described by the second phase of the Allergy Discovery Diet, you will be able to identify the specific foods to which you are sensitive. This scheme of eliminating food antigens from your body and then reexposing yourself to them singly and in rotation is the basic strategy of the Allergy Discovery Diet.

There is a corollary to the reintroduction aspect of the diet however, and it is extremely important that you keep it in mind throughout your use of the Allergy Discovery Diet. Suspect foods should be reintroduced in SMALL amounts. If you have food allergies, any one of the foods featured in the Reintroduction Phase may be a hazardous substance as far as your body is concerned, no matter how wholesome and innocuous its reputation. Although the Elimination Phase of the Allergy Discovery Diet quiets your immune system, bringing your food allergies under control and making you feel better, be aware that it has also increased your level of guardian antibodies. Even tiny amounts of food antigens to which you are allergic can therefore cause severe adverse reactions because your body will be hypersensitive to them. Such intense reactions can result in a dramatic return of allergy symptoms, headache, wheezing abdominal pain, or diarrhea.

Even if you decide, after trying the diet, that food allergy is not the cause of your complaint, you will benefit from knowing your unique responses to foods. Food is meant to do more than nourish and sustain the body. It should comfort and delight the soul as well, and a proper diet is essential to moods of optimism and well-being. Solid new evidence (such as research conducted by the American Academy of Allergy and Immunology) indicating that millions of people suffer adverse reactions to food each day makes it clear that "eating right" demands a personal definition for each one of us. The Allergy Discovery Diet will help you learn how your body in particular reacts to different foods.

I do not, however, want to give the impression that food allergies are simple and easy to define. They are not. If you are allergic to wheat, for example, eating wheat may give you a stuffy nose. The nasal congestion may then be complicated by a sore throat which has resulted from not being able to breathe through your nose. This is an instance of food allergy causing a primary symptom (the stuffy nose) and a secondary, consequential symptom (the sore throat).

Another obstacle in the way of identifying specific allergies to food is that there are no predictable equations such as "corn = asthma" or "onion = rash" which will reliably apply to all people. The same bottle of wine may give one person a rash and another a migraine headache. Once individual reactions to foods have been established, however, they will recur true-to-form. That is one reason why the Allergy Discovery Diet is so successful. The symptom caused by your allergy to a food may be personal and even unusual, but it will at least happen consistently so that you can learn to recognize and avoid it.

As many of my patients discover as they follow the diet, the onset of allergic responses to foods can be erratic. Reactions can be instantaneous, striking immediately after the ingestion of food, or they can be delayed, sometimes not surfacing or making themselves felt until hours later, when the food has been fully digested.

To complicate the problem further, there is currently no medical test for allergies that can accurately identify an allergy to food. Blood and skin-patch (or skin-"scratch") procedures analyze the antibodies in the blood. The reason for this is that many allergy-causing substances (such as the kind that cause hay fever) can be identified according to the type of antibodies the body pours into the bloodstream as it tries to defend against them. Unfortunately, the sort of food-allergic reactions the Allergy Discovery Diet is designed to detect involve a special class of antibody which even the most modern, state-of-the-art allergy tests do not detect.

While cytotoxic testing (mixing blood with food) or sublingual testing (placing extracts of suspected foods under the tongue) probably won't do you any harm (like testing your fondness for butter by holding buttercups under your chin), neither will they do much to enlighten you about your sensitivities to foods.

The nutritional bottom line is that while space-age medicine has been striving to build a better food-allergy mousetrap, the only really dependable method of detecting your food allergies is low-tech and do-it-yourself: a meticulous, bite-and-swallow observation of your diet. With the help of the Allergy Discovery Diet you will be able to keep such a vigil and succeed in finding out which foods (if any) are causing your symptoms.

Food Allergies and Me

My interest and involvement in food-related illnesses is both professional and personal. As a doctor, my special interest is adult asthma, which is indirectly caused or "mediated" by allergies. Through working with particularly difficult cases, I learned that patients did not always respond to treatments in the ways I expected. As a result, I have learned to look beyond traditional categories and theories, keeping an open mind toward creative treatments to help my patients get better.

Then, figuratively and literally, the enigma of food allergies hit home. My wife Elaine began to suffer "strange" symptoms that apparently could not be diagnosed. We had only been married a year and a half when she had her first experience. It was 1968 and I was a medical intern. Elaine had just begun law school. As an intern, I practically lived at the hospital, and a little after seven one morning, Elaine called me on the ward where I was doing rounds. She was feeling very unwell, very dizzy, she told me. I was alarmed—Elaine was never sick and never called me at the hospital.

I said it sounded like a case of hyperventilation. "Breathe into a paper bag," I advised her.

An hour later, I got a call from a very irate Elaine. My advice had failed her, she fumed. She was feeling worse and wanted to see a real doctor right away!

I arranged for her to see a professor of mine who diagnosed Elaine as having labyrynthitis (an inflammation of the inner ear). He prescribed an antihistamine, which helped clear her symptoms.

Why a medication for allergies? I asked. My professor replied that he had no idea why it was effective, but it worked. The practice of medicine is occasionally a mysterious expertise, he observed, an application of unexplained relationships between cause and effect.

Two years passed and we moved from New York City to Washington, D.C. Elaine transferred law schools, became pregnant with our son, John, and began to get frequent headaches and a stuffy nose. I attributed her problems to the pressures of a heavy academic schedule and the physical stresses of pregnancy. It did not occur to me to connect her symptoms with our frequent outings to the ice-cream parlor where Elaine indulged her passion for vanilla ice cream with chocolate sauce.

After completing my tour of duty as a doctor in the U.S. Public Health Service, we returned to New York City. I began my residency and Elaine joined a law firm. Those busy years were punctuated by severe and recurrent bouts of sinus infection and headache for Elaine. It was easy to blame the many germs little John brought home from school for her problems, instead of the late night bowls of ice cream with chocolate sauce Elaine ate when she was too busy working to stop for dinner.

The situation became critical. Elaine felt ill almost all the time, sometimes so seriously that she spent whole weekends in bed with a heating pad on her head, trying to recuperate enough to return to work on Monday morning.

Determined to find a way to ease her suffering, I submitted Elaine to endless examinations, trying to puzzle together her test results with what I knew about asthma and bronchitis.

At last, I discovered similarities between the tissues of Elaine's lungs and sinuses which indicated that one particular irritant (or irritants which strongly resembled each other in molecular structure) was responsible for the inflammation.

I studied and began experimenting, looking for irritants that might be the key to Elaine's illnesses. My reading covered a wide variety of fields, and I was struck by how often immunologists, allergists and other medical specialists hypothesized that food was to blame (at least in part) for the afflictions they described. I began to track the relationships between foods and such symptoms as migraine headaches and joint stiffness. Very soon I realized that the only way to empirically discover (that is, demonstrate in a reliable, observable way) the precise, if any, foods troubling Elaine was to make a list of suspect ingredients and test them one by one.

My initial list of foods was meager and Elaine was skeptical the idea would work. She felt that the stresses of her job and illness were quite enough. Following this "crazy" diet struck her as the proverbial back-breaking straw.

I argued persuasively, agreeing to follow the diet with her, to keep her company. I would plan all the menus, I promised. Even do all the shopping. Reluctantly, she agreed.

This was the beginning of haunting supermarkets and health food stores, poring over the labels on hundreds of foods. I studied every can and bottle in our kitchen cupboards at home as well, trying to compose a complete list of all the "hidden" additives in Elaine's normal diet which might be the source of her troubles. For Elaine and me, reading food labels was an eye-opening experience. We were shocked to learn, for example, that the supposedly healthful, "light" salt I had so virtuously purchased a few months before was anything but "light," laden down not only with sugar and cornstarch, but a mouthful of unpronounceable chemicals like "sodium silicoalumi-nate." Elaine's favorite brand of "plain vanilla" ice cream listed no fewer than five lines of additives. This was a very unplain concoction, we discovered. It had been thickened with calcium carrageenan, xanthan and guar gums, had its protein level boosted with whey concentrate and sodium caseinate and its sweetness heightened by corn syrup and corn sugar (dextrose). It had been emulsified by sodium stearoyl lactylate and polysorbate 60 and its taste mysteriously enhanced with "manufactured flavors." Even the creamy color of Elaine's beloved treat did not escape the additive-adders; it had been intensified with the help of "Yellow 5" and "artificial caramel." Shuddering, Elaine emptied the carton of ice cream into the sink. Awareness that she had been consistently consuming "Yellow 5" was enough to thoroughly alarm her. Like most besotted parents, we had been devouring books and magazine articles on the care and feeding of our offspring ever since Johnny's birth, and we had read numerous studies linking the artificial colors found in commercially prepared foods with inability to concentrate, hyperactivity and learning disabilities in young children.

Even the most humble of commercially prepared foods may contain any number of additives, natural or otherwise. Packed into our favorite, innocent-looking bouillon cubes for instance, were disodium inosinate and guanylate, BHA and citric acid, onion powder, sugar and cornstarch again, and that darling of the U.S. food packaging industry, "natural and artificial colors and flavors." But the label that really took the additive cake was one on a box of nondairy frozen dessert pops. Leading off its multilined list of ingredients were "adipic acid" and "fumaric acid." These were necessary, the label explained, "for tartness." Two words later, the confused confection justified a need for yet another additive: "trisodium citrate" in order to "control" the acidity the first two had just finished whipping in.

Through trial and error, we learned. There were indeed certain foods that precipitated Elaine's "infections," namely dairy products and chocolate. This amazed us; Elaine had been eating these foods all her life without suffering adverse reactions. We assumed that some manufactured, obscure new additive must be causing Elaine's troubles, but our scrutiny of her diet proved us wrong. Elaine's experience is a vivid example of the kind of food allergy that is the subject of this book; acquired sensitivity to one or more familiar foods resulting from prolonged and repeated exposure to those foods. Food allergies like Elaine's involve overstimulation of the immune system, and my years of treating people with health problems has taught me that such sensitivities are extremely common and yet often go undetected, causing unnecessary discomfort and sometimes serious illness. The Allergy Discovery Diet realizes my goal of providing everyone with an effective method of detecting food sensitivities and working out new diets to avoid them.

For Elaine, this meant no more bowls of vanilla ice cream with chocolate sauce, but as intervals of health began outlasting those of illness (and three inches vanished from her hips and waistline) she considered the trade-off well worthwhile.

The excitement and relief I felt at finding answers to Elaine's problems were a powerful stimulus to translating what we had learned into professional help for my patients. Eventually, the Allergy Discovery Diet was born—a personalized, scientifically organized elimination/reintroduction/rotation diet plan.

What's Old Is New Again

The idea of a diet therapy for food allergy is not a new one, but in my review of previous works, I realized no one plan had all the answers. The idea of an "elimination diet" in which the patient goes on a strict diet that eliminates most suspected allergy-causing foods has been around in various forms at least since the 1913 tract *The Dietetic Therapy of Urticaria*. But all these earlier diets had a couple of weaknesses:

• They each depended on an extremely limited, monotonous repetition of foods, and
• They lacked a "rotation" aspect, which would allow the patient to discover if any hypoallergenic foods (foods least likely to provoke an adverse reaction) were personal troublemakers. There is no list of foods, no matter how limited, that proves allergy-free to everyone.

Deeper digging into the literature led to the discovery of Dr. Herbert Rinkel's *Rotary Diversified Diet.* This work, published in the 1940s, did set forth a food rotation concept. Dr. Rinkel proposed eating a single food at each meal. For four days, that food would not be eaten again. The idea of rotation was a good one, but Dr. Rinkel's diet had some shortcomings:

• It was highly unrealistic to ask people to eat a single food item at a meal,
• A delayed reaction to a food from breakfast could be misinterpreted as an immediate reaction to a food at lunch (and so on) and
• The proposed elimination method consisted of an unrealistic schedule of fasting.

Finally, after analyzing numerous books written by the mothers of very allergic children, I realized that a book with updated science was needed for adults who might not have the time nor the cooking skills of these very dedicated mothers.

The Allergy Discovery Diet is my attempt to answer this need. It incorporates the features of elimination, rotation and reintroduction in a structured program of simple recipes, using everyday foods. There's even a shopping list to guide you in stocking up.

I began suggesting this dietary approach to some of my patients, supplying them with handwritten copies of the diet. Those early trials proved to me that the scientific principles of the plan are sound and that the regime is easy to follow. I am grateful to all my patients who volunteered as Allergy Discovery Diet guinea pigs because it was their comments, their suggestions and above all, their commitment to keeping careful records of their reactions that helped refine the diet into the practical, successful plan it is today.

Many of my cases have had happy endings. The puffiness under Diana's eyes and the distention in her stomach eased when she stopped eating wheat, cheese and milk. Milk was a problem for Priscilla, too, and Nancy's headaches and canker sores ceased when she avoided soy and ferments like vinegar and wine.

Larry's psoriasis disappeared completely when he stopped eating tomatoes, and we cured Miguel's gastrointestinal woes when we discovered that his antacid tablets were laced with cornstarch.

Rachel, we eventually discovered, was severely allergic to a number of foods (primarily dairy products) and mildly allergic to others. Taking her Allergy Discovery Diet food diary to her nutritionist, Rachel now follows a permanent diet that excludes the foods to which she is sensitive, keeps her feeling energetic and prevents the return of her complaints.

It is gratifying to me to think that the Allergy Discovery Diet has helped all of these individuals to better understand and listen to their bodies, and to rediscover the blessings of good health.

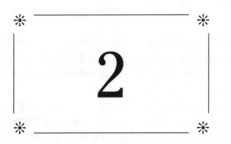

Why the Allergy
Discovery Diet Works

The Allergy Discovery Diet works because it makes good scientific as well as common sense.

The Scientific Basis

As I've said, science is a long way from explaining everything about allergies, but the basic mechanics are known. Symptoms of allergy are caused by the overstimulation of your immune system as it tries to protect you against disease. Essentially, your body wants to stay healthy, and so it is wary of any new or "foreign" substances that enter in. Dispassionate as an airport metal detector, your immune system assumes the worst of all newcomers. The instant it senses a "foreign" presence, it disperses antibodies throughout the bloodstream, ordering them to disarm the potentially hazardous particles before they can do harm.

This defensive functioning of your immune system goes on inside you all the time, usually so quietly that you do not perceive it, but occasionally, the mechanism gets carried away. Picture the ice maker in your home freezer going berserk, spewing forth such an excess of cubes that they create havok in the freezer, icing things over and clogging things up.

Why do some foreign particles (technically called "antigens") overexcite your immune system while others do not? When antigens, such as those in harmful bacteria and viruses, plainly threaten your health, it is easy to see why the immune system becomes alarmed and overstimulated, flooding your system with antibodies so that you soon have a fever and feel "sick."

In the case of food allergies, however, the reason is not so clear. Why do some normally nutritious foods pass through the body very tractably, orderly as a line of friendly foreigners through Customs, while others do not? What makes the antigen in celery for example, overexcite one person's immune system until he is struck with a terrible headache, while most people can eat celery with no problem at all? The answer is that we simply don't know. Considering that each individual food and each human being has a special, personal chemistry, however, perhaps these questions are not so difficult after all. It is easy to believe that a commingling of so many chemically idiosyncratic compounds will sometimes have unpredictable results.

Antigens and Antibodies, Close Up and Personal

Antigens, or "allergens," are tiny parts of larger substances like viruses, bacteria, pollen and foods. In foods, the antigens are distinctively shaped protein or carbohydrate molecules which, in combination with other kinds of molecules, which make up the substance of the food. When you consume antigens in your super burger or favorite breakfast cereal, these edible intruders stimulate your body's production of antibodies in defense. Like heat-seeking missiles, the antibodies quickly target their antigen prey. Buckling together like well-matched wrestlers, the antibodies and antigens grapple to immobilize each other.

Antibodies, like antigens, are also molecules. They are produced by special cells known as plasma or B-cells, located in bone marrow, lymph nodes or along the mucosal lining of the lungs, sinuses, intestinal or genital tracts.

Once manufactured, antibodies become part of the body's weapons arsenal, ready to do battle at any time. The body is capable of producing five different classes of antibodies, depending upon the nature of the antigens it is called upon to demobilize. The class of antibody most often involved in food-allergic reactions is called IgA. Over time, as you repeatedly eat a food which disagrees with you, your body builds up massive stores of IgA antibodies, readying itself to blast the enemy at the next encounter. This overstimulation of antibody production is the first stage of food-allergic response.

Antibodies are uniquely equipped to tackle antigens and take them out of play. Each antibody molecule has two ends. One of these ends can recognize a matching region or special shape on an antigen where it can take hold and perfectly fit. Picture a key fitting its lock, gelatin its mold or Cinderella's foot donning its custom-fitted slipper.

By locking on to antigens and holding fast, antibodies deactivate antigens and keep them from doing possible damage.

How Food Allergy Causes Illness

Precisely how many people suffer allergic reactions to foods is not known, but food allergies have become an undisputed fact of life for both adults and children worldwide. We do know that food-related illnesses have increased dramatically since the turn of the century. Modern food-manufacturing techniques are unquestionably a large part of the problem allergists and nutritionists say, because of the ways in which "simple" foods are commercially processed and packaged in complex combinations, or worse, within a welter of additives intended to color and flavor, "stabilize," or "preserve," "aid in dissolving," "prevent from caking," sweeten without fattening or purge of caffeine.

Even antibodies can become confused as they try to respond properly to the multitude of "hidden" substances we take in as part of our foods. The antigens in food substances, artificial or natural, often resemble one another, especially when foods or food additives belong to the same generic group, such as peanuts and cowpeas, for example. Someone who has developed an allergy to peanuts, for instance, might experience the same allergic reaction to cowpeas, even after eating the very first pea, long before the immune system has had time to produce a buildup of anti-cowpea antibodies. Mistaking the antigens in cowpeas for those in peanuts, the individual's body launches a whole squad of anti-peanut antibodies at the cowpea invaders and a "peanut attack" of food allergy results. This type of allergic response is called a cross-reaction. Bewildered antibodies explain how it can happen.

As it goes about the business of processing antigens in foods, the human body is designed to tolerate low levels of antibody-antigen skirmishing. Habitually eating a particular kind of food which chemically clashes with your body, however, overstimulates your immune system into producing an enormous store of antibodies which it can then release at the merest lip-smack of the problem food. What is more, if you are suffering from an adverse reaction to pollen or to a bacterial or viral infection at the moment you eat the problem food, your bloodstream will already contain a high concentration of antibodies in response to the pollen or infection. The additional release of food-related antibodies into your blood may be more than your body's "threshold" for allergic reactions can allow.

Such an overabundance of antibodies can cause food-allergic reactions in a number of ways. The first we might term "the blitz." When the trouble-causing food is eaten, huge numbers of hoarded-up antibodies link together with an equal number of antigens. The pairs (called "immune complexes") then snowball into chemical bombshells which the body deploys into the bloodstream in such excessive numbers that the function of sensitive systems such as circulation, digestion and respiration, is threatened.

The blitz phenomenon has been well documented in studies with those allergic to cow's milk and eggs. Upon ingestion, there is a measurable increase in immune complexes (consisting of antibodies plus lactalbumen and ovalbumen, the principal proteins of milk and egg) in the bloodstream.

If too large a mass of these antigen-antibody pairs attaches to a particular body tissue, the results can be catastrophic. Kidney failure (uremic poisoning) is one life-threatening example. Vital pores in the capillaries of the kidney can become clogged by the adherence of immune complexes, inhibiting the flow and filtering of blood. The mere presence of these immune complexes produces local inflammation and swelling, further disrupting kidney function.

Inflammatory arthritis and a host of different sorts of skin irritations (including the rash seen in measles) are other instances of immune complex assault.

Another of food allergy's principal tactics is to press innocently bystanding cells into turncoat action against the body. Once again, immune complexes are the ringleaders, corrupting cells or even cell fragments into serving as middlemen, or "mediators" to provoke an allergic attack. Combining with a normally harmless mast cell or platelet (cell fragment), the immune complex upgrades it into a hematological time bomb until the swollen cell at last erupts, exploding chemical belligerents like histamine and serotonin into the blood. Histamine controls the flow of fluids in the mucosal tissues of the body and when it is released into the bloodstream during a food-allergic response, the victim of the food allergy might experience itching or cramping of the genital or intestinal tracts, tearing eyes or a runny nose.

Fortunately, immune complexes have a definite lifespan and the body eventually rids itself of them. One recognized mechanism begins when immune complexes attach to the surface of red blood cells. The blood cells are then "cleansed" by passage through the liver and spleen. Certain types of liver cells also play a role in clearing immune complexes from the circulation. Of course, the most foolproof method of banishing food-related immune complexes from the bloodstream is to stop eating the irritating food. The first phase of the Allergy Discovery Diet is designed to help you do just that. If your health problem is caused by a buildup of immune complexes in reaction to a food, you will purge your body of the trouble-causing complexes by following the Elimination Phase diet. The disappearance of your symptoms will be proof that you do indeed suffer from food allergies, and you will be ready to begin the next phase of the Allergy Discovery

*

Diet and unmask the particular culprit foods by re-exposing yourself to them in small amounts.

The "adherence" and "cell-mediated" mechanisms described above are just two of the ways in which allergies to foods cause discomfort and disease. Researchers suspect that there are others, as yet undiscovered.

The Common Sense Basis of the Allergy Discovery Diet

Suppose for a moment that for the last few weeks you've been troubled by a puffiness around your eyes. The only recent change in your lifestyle you can think of is that you've become very fond of a new whole-wheat bread; in fact, you've been eating it a lot for the last few months. The mystery is, wheat bread has never given you problems before, and you've been eating it all your life. Wondering if some special ingredient in this particular wheat bread is responsible for the unattractive puffiness around your eyes, you read the list of ingredients on the bread label, hoping to recognize a likely suspect.

The bread, however, contains an astounding number of foodstuffs and additivies: whole-wheat-flour, water, fresh yeast, salt, soybean oil, dextrose, malt, soy flour, "dough conditioner" (whatever that is) including fungal amylase, sodium stearoly-2 lactylate, calcium propionate ("to maintain freshness"), cracked wheat berries and sesame seeds.

How can you possibly discover which of these foods or chemicals is irritating the sensitive skin tissues around your eyes? Could it be the soy flour or the sesame seeds, you wonder? Or the "dough conditioner" perhaps, plumping up your face like a punched-up dough?

Labels like the one above are not unusual and underscore the point that most foods in the modern diet contain multiple ingredients and hidden foods. It is a point worth repeating. Commercially processed and packaged foods, with all their resulting combinations and additives, are unquestionably part of the reason it is so difficult to identify specific allergies to foods.

Returning to our example of the whole-wheat bread and its confusing amalgam of chemicals and foods, the only logical way to detect which particular ingredient in the bread is giving you puffy eyes would be to first clear your body of the unknown substance, and then test your tolerance of each ingredient, separately and in rotation, so that you could recognize a pattern of allergic response. What is more, you would test your tolerance of each ingredient warily, keeping in mind that your immune system has been enjoying a brief vacation while you cleansed your system of food irritants. Your body is in a vulnerable state after any elimination diet and even a slight exposure to an allergenic food might provoke a hypersensitive reaction. These common sense principles of cleansing the bloodstream of food antigens, then isolating foods and gently reintroducing them in rotation are the fundamental axioms of the Allergy Discovery Diet.

Before the age of refrigeration and freezing, freeze-drying, hydroponic growing and chemical preserving, human beings naturally ate foods in rotation, depending upon the hunting or fishing season and the crops ripening in the garden or the field. Eating in this way, following new menus of single-ingredient foods according to the length of the growing season and the availability of fish or game, people allowed their bodies ample time to clear immune complex buildups caused by adverse reactions to foods. Recognizing personal allergies to foods was much easier than it is today, as foods were eaten in patterns of simple combinations (or even in isolation) and only at certain times of the year. Food additives and chemically adulterated soils constitute a significant change in the modern diet, and pose special problems for people today suffering with allergies to foods.

As one writer recently observed, it is sometimes "wise and not weak to be willing to learn from what has come before." So it is with food allergies, when the eating habits of past decades offer a good-sense strategy for solving a health problem of contemporary times.

3

Who Should Try the Allergy Discovery Diet?

Everyone stands to benefit from trying the Allergy Discovery Diet, even if one doesn't think one has food allergies. You may have heard of the new discipline called "PNI" (psychoneuroimmunology), which hypothesizes that thoughts and emotions can help or hinder the body in its fight against disease. Many of my patients, whether or not they have food sensitivities, ask if there are certain foods that are guaranteed to make them feel their best or to enhance the healing process when they get sick. These are not easy questions to answer. The study of the effects of neuropeptides (molecules secreted by nerve cells) on the immune system is in its infancy, so that cause and effect relationships between food sensitivities and mental attitudes cannot be quantified. We do know, however, that the phenomenon is real. Our moods and consequently our will to live and be well are strongly affected by what we eat. Since each of us has a personal food-reactive chemistry, learning which foods produce the most positive states of mind is important knowledge each individual should acquire for him or herself. You owe it to yourself to feel the strength and optimistic energy that are the special euphoria of good health. And you can, by learning the specific foods that are your nutritional natural highs.

As we've seen, the immune system is on twenty-four-hour duty. Each time you eat, fresh platoons of antigens are introduced into your body. Even when you're feeling fine, your immune system is busy fending off the potentially harmful effects of these antigens by producing retaliatory antibodies. Everyone has a personal threshold for tolerating such immuno-warfare, but when that threshold is crossed, allergic reactions—painful, worrisome, annoying—can result.

The Allergy Discovery Diet can help you keep on the right side of the threshold through careful diet choices. By discovering the foods that overwhelm your body's tolerance for immune-system activity, you can develop new dietary habits to avoid or moderate your intake of them.

The Prime Suspects

All foods are potentially allergenic, that is, capable of causing an unhealthy reaction. But some foods are more allergenic than others. After researching the medical literature on the subject of food allergies and comparing those findings with my own clinical experience, I have compiled a list of fifteen "hyperallergenic" or particularly troublesome foods. Read about each food—even if you don't consider yourself a great consumer of soy or yeast products for example. You may be surprised, as several of the foods on this list are common constituents of many prepared and processed foods.

Let's examine these chief suspects one at a time, in the order that you'll be testing your sensitivity to each as you follow the Reintroduction Phase of the Allergy Discovery Diet.

CITRUS

For those of us who grew up believing that orange juice is as wholesome as sunshine, mistrusting the citrus family doesn't come easy. One or more of this clan—oranges, grapefruit, tangerines, limes, lemons, tangelos, clementines, even kumquats and ugli fruit—probably appear on everyone's list of favorite fruits. What could be more emblematic of health and vitality than a morning glass of orange juice or a summertime sip of lemonade? Assumptions like these proved dangerous for college freshman Douglas M.

Douglas had not had an easy time with his asthma—repeated stays in the hospital, athletic activity restrictions and learning problems resulting from the distractions of illness. His mother, who accompanied him on his first visit to me, supplied details Douglas had been too young to remember—a perpetual stuffy nose as a baby that made it hard for him to take a bottle, violent sudden bronchial spasms that required ambulance rides to the emergency room, side effects from drugs used to treat the asthma, including such serious bouts of nausea and diarrhea that Douglas subsisted on prescribed liquid diets for days at a time.

Food was the reason Douglas' regular doctor referred him to me. Over the years Mrs. M. told me, she had learned that food had something to do with Douglas' susceptibility to asthmatic attacks.

"Chocolate, and eggs and fish were obvious," said Mrs. M. "All of them made him sick right away. But except for those, it was hard to

✳

tell. I knew there were other troublemakers because in spite of avoiding chocolate, and eggs and fish, Doug still had attacks of asthma."

Douglas' mother had heard of elimination diets, but she was afraid to put her young son on one. "He was a growing boy and I was worried he'd end up with malnutrition. The best I could do was keep track of the foods that did agree with him. "Doug lived on milk, peanut butter and American cheese," she concluded.

I applauded Mrs. M. for her good judgment. The nutritional needs of children are great and it would have been unwise to deliberately deny any nourishing food unless an allergy was clearly indicated.

Since he was now fully grown, it was safe for Douglas to follow the Elimination Phase of the Allergy Discovery Diet, and he began the plan during his first few weeks at college. Life in a dormitory naturally restricted Douglas' nutritional freedom of choice, but the Allergy Discovery Diet offers a sufficiently broad selection of foods to allow many permissible personal options. One morning Douglas called me from school. He sounded terrible—so audibly asthmatic I was worried. Douglas, however, was exhilarated.

"It's citrus!" he wheezed. "I felt fine on the diet until this morning. Asthma's been better than usual all last week. This morning I had orange juice. Big glass . . ." The allergic reaction was making Douglas so breathless it was hard for him to talk. ". . . spasm started one hour later!"

The severity of Douglas' attack illustrates the wisdom of following this basic rule during the Reintroduction Phase: eat only a small amount of the suspect food at the first meal of the day and then wait three to four hours before eating it again. If you experience symptoms, do not eat the food again; choose a substitute food from Recovery Day (Day Twenty-two) menus instead. If no reaction occurs, continue to test your sensitivity to the food for the rest of the day by eating it in moderate amounts.

CORN

Corn and its derivatives have a number of aliases on prepared food labels, including maltodextrin, maize and dextrose, which is corn sugar. Corn is also lurking in some unlikely products and places such as aspirin, baking powder, breath sprays, carbonated drinks and antacids. Technically, not all of these are "foods," but all are ingested orally and thus gain access to the body.

As you'll remember from Chapter 1, Miguel unknowingly aggravated his heartburn and diarrhea, not by eating the wrong foods, but by attempting self-medication with an antacid. Aware that he might have a sensitivity to corn, Miguel ate only a small amount of popcorn to test his suspicions on the appropriate day during the Reintroduction Phase of the Allergy Discovery Diet. Within two hours he experienced cramps and diarrhea, and when he called me to report his reaction, I told him his symptoms were proof enough of an allergy to corn, and not to eat any more corn that day. Corn was clearly an instigator of Miguel's intestinal discomforts, and yet Miguel insisted that even before today's proof of his sensitivity, he had made a point of avoiding corn and corn products. The mystery deepened as Miguel continued on the Reintroduction Phase of the diet, for he experienced no further adverse reactions. Why had he been so constantly troubled by symptoms of corn allergy even though he hadn't eaten corn? I found the answer by checking the inert ingredients of Miguel's favorite antacid. It contained cornstarch as a binder and Miguel had been constantly re-exposing himself to his primary allergen every time he took the antacid to quell the very symptoms they caused.

CHICKEN

The danger of eating chickens (or their raw eggs) that are infected with salmonella bacteria has been a hot news topic in recent months, and though food allergy is not the heart of this issue, the hazard to your health is real and worth a brief review. Unless thoroughly cooked, contaminated chickens and the eggs they lay can cause severe gastroenteritis in human beings. Symptoms of salmonella include fever, diarrhea, vomiting, abdominal cramps and headache. Salmonella can be serious, even fatal, and a doctor should always be consulted if signs of infection result from eating undercooked chicken or eggs.

It is impossible to tell if a chicken or raw egg is contaminated just by inspecting it in the grocery store, but the good news is that you can protect yourself and those for whom you cook even if the chicken or eggs you buy are carriers of the bacteria. It's important to use only the freshest eggs. To check if an uncooked egg is fresh, place it in a pan of cold water. If it sinks, it's fresh; if it floats, discard it. Always chill fresh eggs and chicken (in small amounts if possible) immediately after bringing them home, and freeze any of the meat you do not intend to use within two days. Scrub your hands and any dishes, utensils or kitchen surfaces that have come in contact with the raw chicken or eggs, and when it comes time to prepare the food, cook both the chicken and eggs thoroughly, so that the chicken meat is no longer pink and the eggs are set and no longer "runny." Sufficient cooking of even contaminated chickens and eggs destroys salmonella bacteria and will prevent you from getting the disease.

As we have seen, food allergies call for a different type of defensive antibody than do bacterial infections, so that someone with an allergy to chicken will get sick from eating the meat even if it is uncontaminated and fully cooked. Like all food allergies, individual sensitivities to chicken can surface in almost any form—anything from skin rashes to bronchial constriction, but the symptoms can also be almost identical to the gastroenteritis seen in salmonella infection. In fact, if someone with a sensitivity to chicken should eat undercooked, contaminated chicken in the bargain, the consequences could be harrowing. In such a situation, immune-system activity shifts into overdrive as the body mass-produces one type of antibody to counter the chicken antigens, and another to assail the salmonella bacteria. The body-boggling tangles of antibody/antigen complexes that result from such overstimulation of the immune system cause obstructions and disruptions of normal cell functions throughout the body.

Allergy to chicken does not necessarily indicate allergy to eggs as well. This point is a nice illustration of how adverse reactions caused by food allergy differ from those caused by food bacteria such as salmonella. If a chicken is infected with salmonella, its eggs will be contaminated as well, and you could get sick from eating either food. But in the case of food sensitivities, even within a given species, animal products are not generally cross-reactive. The antigens in chicken which cause food allergy, for example, are a different shape from those which cause egg allergy, so that the immune system does not respond equally to both types of antigens. In fact, many people who cannot eat eggs can enjoy chicken with no problem, and vice versa.

If following the Allergy Discovery Diet reveals that you have an allergy to chicken, read food labels carefully before buying prepared foods for even a commodity as forthright as chicken can be a "hidden" food. Keep in mind that chicken might be an undercover agent in any food containing "animal products," including soups, bouillons, broths, hamburger or tuna "helpers," baked goods (including desserts) or dry baking mixes that contain animal shortening and any prepared stews or casseroles. After learning from the Allergy Discovery Diet that she had an allergy to chicken, one of my patients was astounded to discover that chicken had been masquerading in her favorite brand of chocolate frosting.

OATS

For some people, "feeling their oats" means painful muscles and joints, gasping for air or blossoming out in itchy patches of skin. Although oats are rarely a primary allergen, sensitivity to oats has been shown to exacerbate allergy-mediated conditions such as eczema, asthma and arthritis. If improperly stored, whole-grain oats can also sprout a fungus to which many people are allergic. Then there is the Peril of the Warehouse Pests—like any stockpiled grain, oats are at risk of becoming contaminated by such unsavory agents as worms, rodent droppings or bits of the rodents themselves. Symptoms of allergy to impurities include diarrhea, nausea and vomiting.

Once the backbone of the hearty winter breakfast, oats have come back into fashion. With an eye to its impeccable nutritional credentials (oats are high in protein and the natural, soluble fiber that helps lower blood cholesterol levels), its good flavor and all-purpose flour abilities to coat, thicken and bind, food manufacturers have produced a new tide of oat products—oat bran and flake cereals, oatmeal cookies, cakes, breads and granola bars and oat-based baking mixes. Oat bran has a new identity as a weapon against illnesses such as heart disease and cancer and with all good intentions, food producers have begun adding it to a number of prepared foods and mixes.

If the Allergy Discovery Diet indicates that you are sensitive to oats, read labels carefully before eating commercially prepared foods such as these:

- any bakery products, including croutons, doughnuts, pretzels, ice-cream cones, piecrusts and crackers
- cereal-based beverages
- any baking mixes, including breading mixtures, stuffings and cracker crumbs
- breaded frozen fish or meats
- cold cuts like bologna and salami, hot dogs, sausages and any other meats to which fillers or extenders have been added
- any cereal to which extra bran has been added
- pastas and noodles to which bran has been added
- all candy bars, breakfast and granola bars and trail mixes

EGGS

Almost magically able to produce life or sustain it, eggs hold a place in human history that borders on the mystical. Inexpensive, nutritious and extremely versatile, eggs have been used by cooks for centuries to enrich, lighten, thicken and bind ingredients in recipes of all kinds. But eggs are world-renowned allergens as well, causing a multitude of adverse reactions—everything from hives and blistering skin to indigestion, migraine headaches, rhinitis, and bronchial constriction so severe that sufferers cannot breathe. In fact, allergy to eggs is so often extreme it is usually recognized in infancy, at a child's first introduction to the food. Milder sensitivities or those acquired later on in life are less easy to identify. Most modern diets include some prepared foods, and in commercial preparations, eggs are nutritionally hard to avoid; both whites and yolks are used extensively in almost every category of processed food.

✳

In the case of salmonella, it matters whether the chicken came before the egg; eggs can become contaminated with the bacteria as they grow within infected hens. Remember that as with salmonella-tainted chicken, eggs containing salmonella bacteria are safe to eat as long as they have been thoroughly cooked so that the bacteria is destroyed. You can also take precautionary action by buying only clean, fresh eggs that have been properly refrigerated and are free of cracks. At home, chill both uncooked eggs and any egg-containing leftovers thoroughly and avoid recipes containing raw or undercooked eggs such as mayonnaise, ice cream and Caesar salads.

What doesn't matter is whether you eat yolks or whites; both can carry salmonella bacteria and both can cause allergic reactions. Rich in protein, vitamins and iron, with 274 milligrams of cholesterol and 5 grams of fat, egg yolk seems the most likely perpetrator of adverse reactions, but egg white can be an evil-doer too, despite its healthy status as calorie-, fat- and cholesterol-free. Albumin contains a trouble-causing protein called ovomucoid as well as histamine-releasing agents which can cause acute allergic symptoms. If you are concerned about cutting down on eggs in general, remember that one tablespoon of oil mixed with two tablespoons of water can substitute for an egg in most baking recipes, and that starches and flours can be used instead of egg to thicken sauces, puddings and custards.

WHEAT

In addition to all the obvious places, wheat crops up unexpectedly in a veritable smorgasbord of commercial preparations—alcoholic beverages such as beer, bourbon and gin, coffee substitutes, chocolate candy, bouillon cubes, soups, mayonnaise, even fruits and vegetables that have been prepared with sauce. Needless to say, if you're sensitive to wheat, this staff of life can become the bane of your nutritional existence.

Mickey was a sixty-year-old librarian whose medical history was an interesting story of sensitivity to wheat. As a child, Mickey had suffered paralytic polio, and it left her with severe breathing troubles. Her condition stabilized during the early years of her adulthood, but lately, Mickey told me on her first visit to my office, the childhood impairment seemed to have worsened; it was harder to breathe than ever. Making life even more miserable, her digestive system had begun acting up at the same time, afflicting her with embarrassing rumblings, cramping and abdominal pain. Was it possible Mickey wondered, that some kind of food was provoking these very different complaints?

After examining her and subjecting her to my litany of questions concerning her eating habits and lifestyle, I suspected that Mickey was right. I found a great deal of mucus in Mickey's lungs, and my research concerning food allergies had taught me that food sensitivity could explain both the irritation of Mickey's digestive system and the aggravation of her old respiratory weakness as well. I explained to Mickey that the mucosal tissues of the human body (such as the lungs, tonsils, sinuses, genital and gastrointestinal tracts) possess an integrated power of immunity all their own. Like a special branch of the body's overall defensive military, certain cells within mucosal tissues serve as an elite corps. They are uniquely and closely linked by codes of communication indecipherable to medical researchers as yet, so that they are able to synchronize their protective maneuvers against antigen invasion. This is what happened in Mickey's case. As the mucosal tissues in her digestive system reacted to irritating food antigens, pumping antibodies into her stomach and intestine, they signaled the mucosal tissue in her lungs to do the same. The effect was like pouring salt on the old wounds of Mickey's polio-damaged lungs, further crippling her attempts to breathe.

At the time she consulted me, I had just begun to formalize the Allergy Discovery Diet into a practical regime, so that Mickey became one of the plan's first and thus most exciting successes. Wheat and dairy products proved to be the chief offenders in Mickey's diet, and when she stopped eating them, her abdominal and digestive troubles ceased and her lungs cleared of mucus, making it easier for her to breathe.

SOY

Soybeans are a member of the legume family. They can be ground into a flour (soy flour) or milled into a powder, known as soy powder. Soy powder is made from high-quality, washed and steam-cooked soybeans which are then finely ground and sifted to remove any remaining hulls. Because of its careful processing soy powder can be mixed with water to make a smooth "soy milk." Soy flour is made by grinding whole dry beans. It is coarser than soy powder and may contain hull material.

Tofu is soybean curd. Like the beans from which it is made, tofu is very high in protein. As you will see from the Allergy Discovery Diet recipes on Day 13, tofu is an edible chameleon. It comes in both soft and firm varieties and it can be sliced or cubed (like cheese), melted, fried, mashed, or frozen into an ice-cream-like dessert. Tofu or steamed soybeans are often served in Chinese and Japanese restaurants, as the bean is a staple of many Asian cuisines.

Soybeans are a cheap source of protein and because of their bland natural flavor and textural adaptability, they are used extensively by food manufacturers to "beef up" almost any processed food, including beef itself. Bakery goods and mixes, cereals, beverages, candies, pasta, salad dressings and mayonnaise, sandwich spreads, shortenings, oils and margarine, soups, vegetables, snack foods and frozen desserts all might contain soy or soy products. If you are sensitive to soybeans, read labels carefully before buying any commercially prepared foods.

MILK

Milk is one of the most common causes of food sensitivities. Milk-related products that should be avoided if you are allergic to milk include malted milk, condensed milk, evaporated milk, dried milk, cheese, yogurt, cream, cottage cheese, sour cream, buttermilk, cream cheese, butter, ice cream, ice milk and sherbet. Scan labels on prepared foods for the terms "whey," "milk solids" or "casein," as these are other milk compounds. Like soy, milk is an ubiquitous presence in commercially prepared foods; it is high-quality protein, mild-flavored and amenable to assuming almost any shape or form. Following are some general types of foods in which milk is often found:

- bakery items
- beverages such as cocoa mixes, shakes
- breads
- casseroles
- puddings
- salad dressings, sauces and gravies
- dips, appetizers, spreads and snack foods
- soups, stuffings
- candies, cookies, cupcakes, cakes, ice cream, whipped desserts, toppings and frostings
- au gratin dishes, mashed potatoes, scalloped dishes, rarebits, soufflés and fondues

The brief summary of Rachel's story in Chapter 1 gives some idea of how varied and severe the symptoms of milk allergy can be. All through her teens, Rachel was plagued with diverse and chronic maladies—endometriosis and severe dysmenorrhea (menstrual cramps), muscle dysfunction and incapacitating, "monster" headaches. All of these maladies were milk-induced, but for years, the cause of Rachel's afflictions went undetected. Rachel had great energy and her determination to succeed first at school and then in the highly competitive world of fashion design drove her to ignore her symptoms as best she could, distracting herself from them with work.

When he hospitalized her for the fourth time, Rachel's gynecologist came to me because of my interest in food-related illnesses. I was a last resort. Rachel was now in her early thirties, and over the years, the gynecologist had conferred with neurologists, orthopedists and psychiatrists. These specialists all diagnosed stress reactions of various sorts, but none had hit upon a permanent cure.

The gynecologist now asked if I thought food allergies could be causing Rachel's problems. I answered at once that I was eager to investigate the possibility but the Allergy Discovery Diet was still just a theory at this time, its formalization merely a twinkle in my eye, and for many weeks, my best efforts to find the underlying source of Rachel's problems were to no avail. Rachel's condition continued to deteriorate until her stomach pains and nausea grew so severe she developed an acute ulcer and was unable to keep down any food at all. Placing her back in the hospital, I dug back into my research on hypo (least allergenic) foods. Rachel's weight loss had become alarming and I was desperate to find some sort of nourishment her body would not reject. Finally I hit upon the idea of prescribing a predigested nutritional supplement used for severely debilitated patients. Much to my surprise and delight, Rachel began to get better. At first, I attributed her improvement to my novel approach to ulcer therapy. Then, when her diet was expanded to include milk, Rachel's pain recurred. That's when I saw it—the possibility that Rachel's seemingly unrelated symptoms might all be the ill-doings of a single allergy to food.

Rachel, we eventually discovered, was severely allergic to milk. Once we worked out a diet with her nutritionist eliminating all dairy products, Rachel's former vitality returned. Occasionally, the pressure of her life distracts her and Rachel forgets some prohibition. Her body, however, is quick to complain; it punished her very first transgression with a recurrence of the violent menstrual cramps she had suffered since her teens.

Marvin is another example of how milk allergy can perform within the human body like a biochemical "man-of-a-thousand-faces." Marvin was a fifty-year-old businessman under my care for angina. My examination also revealed a high cholesterol count, a slightly overweight condition and a mild case of psoriasis which I suspected of being food-related. I told Marvin of my suspicions, but the skin condition didn't bother Marvin much, and he wasn't a bit keen on the idea of investigating the idea by means of an elimination diet. Besides, Marvin had more pressing medical problems. An angiogram showed a critical narrowing of the arteries in Marvin's heart, and a bypass operation was required. Now "to eat or not to eat" became the question in earnest. Marvin's surgeon demanded that his cholesterol count be lowered and that he lose some weight, as both conditions were placing extra stress on Marvin's heart. I put Marvin on a strict diet, primarily eliminating all dairy products. As I'd expected, Marvin lost weight immediately and his cholesterol count dropped almost to normal, but the diet had an interesting side effect as well; the psoriasis disappeared. Marvin agreed that this was a clear indication that he was sensitive to milk and milk products, but the prospect of life without butter and sour cream frankly depressed him.

It took nearly six months for Marvin to recover sufficiently from his surgical ordeal to find the willpower necessary for serious dieting, and during this time, he gained weight, his cholesterol count rose and his mild case of psoriasis reappeared. At last it became clear that Marvin had two alternatives to avoiding a heart attack: another operation or a diet limiting his intake of high-cholesterol foods, including milk and milk products. Preferring dietary prevention to surgery, Marvin now follows a milk-free, low-fat diet and we're both happy—Marvin has a surgery-free future to look forward to and I have a trim, psoriasis-free patient with low cholesterol.

VINEGAR/FERMENTATION PRODUCTS

Wines, beers, "hard" alcohols, vinegar and its by-products (bottled sauces, dressings, condiments, olives, pickles) and yeast all belong to this category. But less obvious foods also fall under this heading. Coffee beans, tea leaves and vanilla beans are also fermented in the course of their preparation.

Technically, fermentation describes the process of converting sugar, carbohydrates and other organic acids into simpler compounds. The best known by-product of fermentation is alcohol. The action of fermentation is triggered by enzymes of various origins. If left to "ripen" at raised temperatures, many foods (especially fruits and vegetables that are high in sugar like apples, bananas or grapes) are colonized by bacteria, molds or fungi which possess the enzymes necessary for "natural fermentation" to take place. The active cultures that turn milk into yogurt are a good example of this type of fermentation.

For ease, these different sorts of ferments have been grouped together. Whether or not the human immune system responds in exactly the same way to both "natural" and "artificial" fermentation is not known. We do know, however, that both types of fermentation cause responses, sometimes in the form of allergic reactions to foods.

Whether or not something has undergone fermentation can sometimes be difficult to determine. One patient of mine, for example, reported that after eating a beef stew the day it was made, she suffered no ill-effects. However, when she reheated the stew the following day and ate it, she suffered an upset stomach and a headache. The second-day stew contained the same beef, carrots, turnips, potatoes and sweet onions as the day before, but something "fishy" had obviously happened to it overnight. Was this a case of natural fermentation, I wondered, triggered by the enzymes in the high-sugar carrots, turnips or onions? Or had the stew been improperly stored, so that microorganisms from the environment caused the conversion of sugars to alcohol? It is frustrating not to know the answer, but at least we can be alerted to the possibility that such mechanisms exist, so that those with sensitivities to fermented foods will know to avoid eating leftovers or foods held for long periods of time.

As I pointed out while discussing chickens and eggs, the different products of a single animal are not necessarily cross-reactive. Many of my patients however, report that they can drink milk and enjoy whipped cream, but they cannot eat yogurt or aged cheese without suffering adverse reactions. The key to this mystery is fermentation: both yogurt and cheese have been converted by enzymes into new organic compounds.

The subject of alcohol requires a book of its own, but this substance has such global and detrimental effects on human beings, it is appropriate to summarize the dangers involved in consuming it as a "food."

The variety of adverse reactions to wine is based on a number of factors. Most easily accounted for are the bisulfites added to halt further fermentation and stabilize the wine. These chemicals are used in varying amounts in different areas of the world.

Precise aging and fermenting techniques sometimes determine whether or not a wine will make you sick. These special processes are often the proud, closely guarded secrets of vineyard and château families, safely shuttered away from inquiring eyes. The variety in methods produces distinctive flavors and compounds. You might notice that only white or sparkling wine gives you a headache, for example, or only French reds of a certain vintage, or only a highly sweet Italian, German or American apéritif.

More than bubbles might go (painfully) to your head if you choose to drink champagne. "La méthode champenoise" involves a number of steps and more than one ingredient likely to provoke a food-allergic reaction. The cuvée, or initial blend of wines used to create champagne, is reason enough to suffer an allergic reaction because more than one variety of grapes is often used to produce a characteristic flavor. Then, both yeast and sugar are added to stimulate fermentation. You are thus imperiled by several of the Allergy Discovery Diet's "most wanted" culprits, all at the same time.

For Jane M., such revelations about wines proved to be the keys to her return to health. Her problem was incapacitating headaches. They began, Jane told me, immediately following the birth of her twin sons, five years ago.

"I always used to feel so sorry for people who had migraines," Jane said ruefully. "I'd never had a headache an aspirin couldn't cure and

*

now suddenly I was getting doozies—pain so awful it made me dizzy, throwing up—the works. Suddenly people were feeling sorry for ME. The first couple of times I thought they were just from nerves and fatigue: Excedrin Headaches #1–10, all at the same time. I was a new mother, stubborn about taking care of the babies all by myself, and nursing them both to boot. I was so worried in fact, about not having enough milk, I wouldn't let anyone else give them supplemental feedings. Which of course meant nonstop nursing. Babies digest breast milk incredibly fast." For two years, Jane simply lived with the migraines, enduring them when they struck and calling upon her mother or close friends to help with the babies when she was too sick to get up.

"But now the boys are five," explained Jane the first time she came to see me. "They're in school half the day and I get plenty of rest. Life is a breeze compared to three years ago, but I'm still getting headaches more often than ever."

It was her husband, Tom, who sent Jane to see me. He'd been a patient of mine for some time, and knew of the work I was doing in food-related illnesses. Since stress and exhaustion did not seem to be the whole explanation for Jane's "sick days," Tom wondered if a recently developed food allergy might be part of the answer. She'd seen her gynecologist, an endocrinologist, even a psychiatrist, but none had been able to offer a solution. A number of drugs had been prescribed, but none succeeded in preventing the headaches. The last she'd tried in fact, only added to her problems, causing such a severe side effect of joint stiffness that Jane couldn't walk down the stairs.

Jane and I spent a long time talking about the specifics of her diet, looking for a pattern to the recurrences of migraine. The subject of wines provided the first glimmer of hope in solving the mystery of Jane's migraines. Always a wine-enthusiast, Tom's interest had expanded into a serious hobby, not so very coincidentally, some five or six years ago. He and Jane often shared a bottle at dinner.

I suggested she take careful note of each vintage Tom selected, particularly where and when each was bottled. When I explained to her that different methods of fermentation might cause some wines to affect her while others would not, Jane was eager to see if she could tolerate at least one or two certain kinds.

Jane was lucky. Within a short time she was able to determine that it was principally the age of a wine that mattered. When she drank young wines, she got a headache within hours.

I saw Jane recently at a cocktail party, almost six months after her diet discoveries. Saluting me with her glass of wine, she said, "You wouldn't approve, Dr. P. I have no idea how old this stuff is, and I'll probably regret it in the morning." Teasing aside, she went on to say that while she'd learned she could tolerate small amounts of aged wine or batch-distilled liquors, more than four ounces of any sort of alcohol promptly gave her a headache, particularly when she was tense or overtired. "At least now I know how much my head can 'stomach,'" she added, "so I can stop before I get into the danger zone."

George G. was another wine-sensitive patient. He came to me complaining of giant hives and joint swellings. The attacks were erratic—or so George thought—but they were becoming increasingly severe. Only thirty-five, basically in good condition and very active, a little diet sleuthing seemed in order as George was not a likely candidate for gouty arthritis despite the suggestion of his symptoms. To George's great relief, the antagonist in his customary diet was soon exposed. After a full trial of the Allergy Discovery Diet, it was clear that the source of George's problem was a certain wine of which he was particularly fond. Recommending that he forsake wine completely for a while to allow antigen levels to subside, I suggested substituting Irish whiskey instead, if he was determined to drink alcohol. Irish whiskey, I explained, is unique among liquors because it is distilled three times instead of the customary two. This extra round of processing removes fermentation by-products left in most other spirits, rendering it less likely than other types of alcohol to cause hangovers and other side effects. George's wife Martha was present at this interview, and while George readily agreed to the proxy-potable, Martha was overheard murmuring something about "mad scientists" as she and her husband left my office. The experiment succeeded. George remained untroubled by either hives or joint swellings as long as he refrained from drinking wine. (There is a footnote to this happy ending: in moments of weakness, George occasionally sneaks a glass or two of his beloved beverage. The results are painful and it is Martha who calls me then, beseeching me to remind George to drink only the "safe" Irish whiskey. There has been no further mention of my madness!)

Despite my advice to George, I do not recommend drinking alcohol to any of my patients. There is no "safe" beer, wine, or hard liquor. The hard fact about alcohol is that it is an addictive, dangerous drug. Drinking alcohol unbalances the body's natural chemistry, threatening every vital organ and body tissue with damage. The damage can be severe and permanent, including cirrhosis of the liver and serious diseases of the stomach, nervous system, heart and brain. Alcoholism is a well-publicized tragedy, but one does not have to be an alcoholic to be injured by its effects. In or out of an automobile, a single, moderate bout of drinking can result in a paralyzing fall or fatal accident. A pregnant woman who drinks raises her risk of having a mentally retarded or physically malformed child. The emotional life of the individual who drinks to excess is no less subject to the malignant influence of alcohol. Books, articles and talk shows abound with accounts of lives disabled by drinking—stories of broken marriages and friendships, psychological illnesses like depression and paranoia, ruined relationships between parent and child.

The next time you find yourself debating whether or not to drink alcohol, remind yourself that "intoxicate" comes from the Latin *intoxicatus* and it means "to poison."

COFFEE AND TEA

Coffee and tea have double identities. On the one hand, they are ferments—coffee beans and tea leaves are fermented early on in their processing—and on the other they qualify as drugs because they contain caffeine. Caffeine can cause addiction, or to use the pharmacological phrase "habituation," and is classified as a mild stimulant of the central nervous system.

Caffeine occurs naturally in over sixty species of plants including coffee beans, cocoa beans, tea leaves and cola nuts. Caffeine is also used in many drug compounds such as stimulants, analgesics, diuretics, cold remedies and weight control products to mask fatigue, elevate mood and constrict blood vessels to counteract pain.

Because it's easy to become addicted to caffeine, many people develop a caffeine "habit." Withdrawal symptoms include headache and lethargy—some of the very reasons you crave a cup of tea, cocoa or coffee in the morning. The Elimination Phase of the Allergy Discovery Diet calls for the elimination of caffeine from your system. If going cold turkey produces the withdrawal symptoms listed above, however, you should cut back gradually on your intake of caffeinated substances. After one cup of coffee or tea in the morning during the Elimination Phase, drink the herbal tea allowed for the day if you want something warm to drink.

CANE SUGAR

Cane sugar or common table sugar often appears on labels as sucrose. If you have a sweet tooth, the mere thought of giving up sugar may make you doubt you'll ever make it through the Allergy Discovery Diet. Fear not. There are alternatives to cane sugar—maple syrup, maple crystals, honey and fruit "sugars" among them—that will satisfy your yearnings for a sweetener.

Sensitivity to cane sugar is not uncommon, especially if it is consumed in large amounts. Nervousness, irritability, sleeplessness, sudden onsets of weakness, headaches, skin problems and puffy eyes are possible symptoms of adverse reactions to cane sugar.

CHOCOLATE

Chocolate is often packaged with a number of constituents targeted by the Allergy Discovery Diet "hit" list of highly allergenic foods. To begin with, pure chocolate naturally contains caffeine, and commercial foods which feature chocolate are often spiked with cane sugar and other additives used to stabilize, dissolve, thicken or emulsify, depending upon the food. Since products containing chocolate are so often chemical melting pots, be sure to test yourself with a pure baking chocolate or unsweetened cocoa as specified in Allergy Discovery Diet recipes. Our aim is to identify a specific allergy to chocolate, unadulterated by your reaction to incidental additives.

Imagine telling a Frenchman that he would have to give up wine and cheese! That's the task I faced with Jean-Luc, a bank executive who began to suffer from severe migraines, vomiting and stomach pain. When a neurologist, a cardiologist and a battery of tests including a CAT scan revealed no disease, I told Jean-Luc of my suspicions that he might be allergic to a food. Bracing myself for his Gallic outrage, I warned Jean-Luc that his symptoms hinted at a sensitivity to ferments and dairy products like cream, butter and cheese. Jean-Luc, however, was still in an exultant mood from hearing that all his tests for brain tumors, nerve damage and heart disease were negative, and because the attacks of migraine and vomiting were making it impossible to function normally either at home or at work, he docilely agreed to give the Allergy Discovery Diet a try. During the entire first, Elimination phase of the diet, Jean-Luc jubilantly reported that he had not experienced a moment of nausea or head pain.

In the end, I am happy to report, it was neither wine nor cheese but chocolate which proved the malefactor triggering Jean-Luc's episodes of illness and pain. Having avoided chocolate ever since following the Allergy Discovery Diet plan, Jean-Luc recently told me that he is enjoying better sleep and general health as well as freedom from the painful and handicapping manifestations of his allergy.

TOMATO

For many people, this "love apple" does not live up to its name. The antigens in raw, fresh tomatoes are proven allergy inducers. Recall Larry from Chapter 1, whose psoriasis was a result of eating fresh, uncooked tomatoes in daily plates of salad. Larry's story is a dramatic example of allergy to raw tomatoes—his palms became so blistered with red, fluid-filled patches of skin he became too embarrassed to shake hands. Even his nails were a sore sight for the eyes—thickened, pitted and peeling away from the underskin of his fingers.

Cooked tomatoes also spark allergic reactions in a great many people, but the trouble is not always caused by tomato antigen alone.

Fresh tomato sauces prepared in restaurants and pizza parlors are deliberately prepared early in the day to allow the flavor of seasonings to develop. Tomatoes are a highly perishable fruit, however, and if the temperature of the "developing" sauce is allowed to drop below a safe simmer for too long, mold spores or other enzymes are likely to cause fermentation to begin. The tomatoes in fermenting sauce thus pack a one-two punch, threatening both tomato-sensitive and ferment-sensitive consumers. A patient of mine named Delancy once had a morning-after she won't forget. The ferment responsible for her discomfort wasn't alcohol but made-to-order pizza, and her hangover took the form of a mouthful of canker sores.

PEAS AND PEANUTS

Contrary to their nutty surname, peanuts are members of the pea or "legume" food family. Technically, peanuts are oil-rich, edible seeds that just happen to have nutlike shells.

Other members of the legume family include:

- acacia
- alfalfa
- black-eyed pea (cowpea)
- broad bean (fava bean)
- carob bean (St. John's bread)
- chick-pea (garbanzo bean)
- common beans: (kidney, navy, pinto and string)
- Jack bean
- lentils
- licorice
- lima bean
- mesquite
- pea (yellow or green)
- peanut
- soybean
- tamarind
- tragacanth

The foods listed above are grouped together because they are botanically alike—that is, they are all the same type of plant, with similar traits and properties such as general structure, nutritional needs and patterns of growth. But just like members of a human family, certain legume brothers and sisters are genetically very similar, while others are almost completely unlike.

In Chapter 2, cowpeas and peanuts served as an example of foods which can cause a cross-reaction type of food-allergic response. You'll recall that the cross-reaction can occur because some of the antigens in cowpeas and peanuts are molecularly similar in shape. IgA antibodies produced by the immune system to counter peanut antigens for example, may sometimes bind themselves to cowpea antigens instead, because the antibodies "fit" into the receptor ends of both peanut and some cowpea antigens with equal ease.

As far as food-allergic cross-reactions are concerned, the legumes to avoid are the following:

- peas (including fresh green peas and dried split green or yellow peas
- peanuts
- black-eyed peas (cowpeas)

These offshoots of the legume family all bear antigens which have cookie cutter-like similarity of shape, and are thus likely to spur cross-reactive allergic reactions. Do not eat any of these foods during the Elimination Phase. You may choose any one of them to test your sensitivity on "pea/peanut" day (Day Twenty) during the Reintroduction Phase, but remember to protect yourself against the possibility of a severe reaction by eating a small amount of the suspect legume early in the day and then waiting three to four hours before eating it again. If you suffer no ill-effects after the initial, cautious exposure, you may safely continue with the menu for Day Twenty by eating moderate amounts of the recipes you prepare.

Cross-reactions between peas/peanuts with any other of their legume relatives are virtually unknown. IgA antibodies can apparently distinguish the antigens of these other legumes from those of peanuts and peas.

ONIONS AND CHIVES

Leeks, onions, chives, shallots, aloe and sarsaparilla are all the somewhat unlikely members of the lily family. The worst troublemakers in the group are garlic, onions, chives and shallots—all are harshly acidic. Many of you who eat raw onions and know you'll "pay for it" later—typically with burping, gas and heartburn—should take note. You may actually be experiencing mild allergic symptoms that you don't have to live with.

One patient of mine has an interesting onion story to tell. Tony's favorite childhood meal had always been a hamburger crowned with a thick slice of raw onion. As he got older, however, Tony found that his onion hangovers (upset stomach and indigestion) began to hurt more than they used to. His potential for suffering seemed to be growing, so that even handling or smelling the pesky little bulbs gave

✻

him sinus headaches and feverish chills. Reluctantly admitting to himself that raw onions had become too much for him, Tony gave them up.

The symptoms, however, did not go away, and finally Tony came to me, worried that the persistence of his maladies signaled serious disease. But Tony's profession provided the clue. He was a cooking teacher, given to sampling his students' culinary classwork, and it turned out that many of these edible assignments were heavily laced with onions. Whenever classroom creations contain onions, Tony now relinquishes his role as official taster. He has been able to control the symptoms of his allergy to onions ever since.

ADDITIVES

In terms of the Allergy Discovery Diet, the working definition of an additive is any nonfood substance added to common foods (foods derived from vegetable or animal sources) during preparation and packaging. Adverse interactions between the body and chemical additives are sometimes caused by the immune system, but just as often, they are not. The body's normal, protective function of anti-peristalsis (when your digestive track literally shifts into reverse, making you vomit) is one example of a nonimmunologic mechanism which often operates without immune system intervention. The production of stomach acid is another; by secreting digestive juices like hydrochloric acid, bile salts and glycoproteins, the body prevents harmful organisms from penetrating the small intestine. As most of us unfortunately know from personal experience, too much stomach acid can cause gastrointestinal problems, but it is not always the immune system which causes the troublemaking excess.

Preservatives are perhaps the single largest subdivision of chemical food additives. Some of these chemical compounds are manufactured while others are naturally derived from common foods. Manufacturers of perishable foods understandably make frequent use of FDA-approved preservatives to prolong the shelf, dairy case or freezer life of packaged foods. Recent medical studies proving that millions of people are sensitive to chemical preservatives have slowed the trend, however, and the ground swell of consumer demand for additive-free foods continues to grow.

The Allergy Discovery Diet can help you learn if you are sensitive to the chemical additives used so prevalently today by restaurants, fresh-produce markets and manufacturers of processed foods. If following the Allergy Discovery Diet relieves your symptoms but does not indicate an allergy to any of the fifteen "suspect" foods, there is a good chance that your problems are caused by "hidden" additives in your normal diet. The following chart describes some common addi-

COMMON ADDITIVES

ADDITIVE	FOODS INVOLVED	PURPOSE	SYMPTOMS
Aspartame (Nutra-Sweet)	Diet soft drinks, Low-cal foods	Sugar substitute	Headaches
Azo Dyes: Especially FD&C Yellow Nos. 5 & 6	Fruits, vegetables, dessert mixes, frozen foods, drugs	Coloring agent	Hives, bronchial congestion, hyperkinesis (hyperactivity, esp. in children)
Benzoates, BHA/BHT	Crackers, baked foods, dry mixes, candies, dry cereals	Preservative	Headaches, hyperkinesis (hyperactivity, esp. in children), skin irritations
Cobalt acetate	Beer	Improver for head of beer	Fatigue, weakness
Emulsifier "ME18"	Margarine & shortenings	Prevents spattering during frying	Skin irritations, swelling
Glutamate: especially monosodium glutamate (MSG)	Chinese foods, canned soups, stews, sauces & gravies, snack foods (peanuts, pretzels, chips, etc.)	Flavor enhancer	"Chinese restaurant syndrome" (headache, facial pressure, chest pain, tingling sensations)
Methyl paraben	Cake icing, drugs, prepared foods	Anti-bacterial agent to retard mold growth	Burning sensation of mouth, lips, mouth sores, nausea, diarrhea
Nitrates & Nitrites	Processed meat & fish, meat & fish soup mixes & bouillons	Color developer, preservative	Nausea, vomiting, cyanosis (blueness of lips & fingertips), blood pressure disorders, headache, vertigo
Phenolphthalein	Candy, cakes, laxatives	Coloring agent	Vomiting, diarrhea
Potassium bromate	Bread, cake, foods baked in dough	Dough conditioner	Nausea, vomiting, cramps, diarrhea
Sulfites (including bisulfites and sulfur dioxide)	Fresh fruits & vegetables, canned or fresh seafood, dried fruits & vegetables, avocado dip, soft drinks, fruit juices, cider, beer, wines, sausages, potato chips	Preservative	Asthmatic wheezing, flushing, hypotension, tingling sensations
Vegetable gums (karaya, arabic, & tragacanth)	Puddings, ice cream, whipped toppings	Thickeners	Skin irritations, respiratory problems

*

tives, where and why they are most often added and the symptoms they frequently cause. Do not buy any food containing these additives while following the Allergy Discovery Diet. After the diet, read food labels carefully to avoid these compounds when you return to a diet of your own design.

Additives do not affect everyone. Some people are naturally more susceptible than others to additive side effects, depending upon their individual body chemistries. However, my concern is not whether everyone is fated to having adverse reactions to additives, but whether YOU are suffering reactions. That is what the Allergy Discovery Diet is all about—discovering your personal sensitivities.

4

Making the Allergy Discovery Diet Work for You

Before You Begin

It's a good idea to consult your personal physician before starting any special diet. The Allergy Discovery Diet is no exception. Make an appointment for a physical exam so that you'll have a professional assessment of your current state of health. You might even ask your doctor to look over the diet itself. This is especially important for those individuals already following prescribed diets, such as for heart disease or diabetes. The recipes were written using salt as a seasoning, but this can be eliminated and the other seasonings used alone.

You may want to delay starting the diet if you're suffering from an acute illness—a cold, the flu, a viral infection—or if you've recently undergone surgery or severe trauma.

Since anything you ingest might affect your immune system, scan the following list of items to see if any apply to you. If you take any one of them on a regular basis, they must be considered part of your normal "diet" and therefore potential allergy-inducers:

• Prescription medications—Medicines are not above threatening you with antagonistic antigens. Many medicines contain sugar to help camouflage bitter taste, starches (especially wheat and corn) to bind powders into pills, sulfites as preservatives or artificial coloring agents. Any one of these foods or additives may produce symptoms in susceptible people. However, the decision to change medications or to stop them temporarily is one that should be made only upon the advice of a medical doctor. Under no condition should you endanger your health by practicing medicine upon yourself!

• Over-the-counter medications—If you're in the habit of taking drugstore or "health food" medications, it's a good idea to make a list of them and show it to your doctor. Pain relievers such as aspirin and acetaminophen, ibuprofen, antihistamines, decongestants, cough/cold remedies, antacids and laxatives all fall within this category. So do the various "herbal remedies" sold by natural food and health food stores. Your physician can help you assess your need for such products and suggest alternatives if a preparation seems capable of kindling an adverse food reaction.

For example, if you are accustomed to using a laxative, you should switch from the stimulant type while following the Allergy Discovery Diet. Laxatives of this sort are identifiable by their listed active ingredients: phenolphthalein, cascara or senna. Saline-type laxatives are also undesirable adjuncts to the Allergy Discovery Diet. The active ingredients in saline laxatives are sodium, potassium or magnesium salts. The Allergy Discovery Diet features lots of fiber-rich fresh fruits and vegetables, but if you need something to relieve constipation while on the diet, substitute a bulk-forming agent for either a stimulant or saline type. Bulk-forming agents work by "exercising" the bowel with natural, nonnutrative plant fibers such as cellulose, bran or psyllium seed. During the first, or Elimination stage of the diet, you may use powdered psyllium seed as a bulk agent. Rice bran is also allowable on any day which features rice as the grain for the day. During the second, Reintroduction phase, you may use unprocessed, unsweetened wheat, rice, oat or corn bran, according to the grain allowed for the day. Use psyllium seed on any day when no grain is allowed. Throughout the diet, you may use the oil allotted for the day as a natural laxative agent by adding an extra tablespoonful or two to recipes. Eat as many raw fruits and vegetables as you can (leaving skins on if possible) to reap the full benefit of their natural fiber. Minimizing cooking times of both fruits and vegetables will guarantee intenser flavors and preserve vitamin and fiber content. Drinking water will help keep your personal "plumbing" running smoothly too—tap, bottled or seltzer.

• Vitamins—If you are currently taking a multivitamin or an assortment of single-nutrient vitamins from a health food store, you should stop taking them before going on the Allergy Discovery Diet. Vitamins invariably contain nonvitamin elements. Even if your brand is labeled "corn-free," "wheat-free" or "sugar-free," it may contain yeast (a ferment) that can trigger symptoms. The emphasis on fresh foods in the Allergy Discovery Diet menus provides plenty of vitamins and minerals, naturally, the way nature intended you to eat them.

Allergy Discovery Diet Dividends: Weight Loss and Lower Cholesterol—This is not a reducing diet; portion sizes (and calorie intake)
are left to individual discretion. But if you are looking to lose a little
weight, you will be happy to hear that almost everyone who follows
the diet reports weight loss as a serendipitous result. I boast no magic
formula. But in light of the mounting evidence that deprivation dieting
is doomed to result ultimately in weight gain, an eating plan that
allows three full meals (including dessert), plus snacks as well, can
only contribute to a feeling of satisfaction instead of the gnawing
hunger which eventually defeats even the most determined dieter. If
you've been in the habit of quaffing a beer or two every evening, or
drinking cocktails and wine, losing a few pounds on the Allergy
Discovery Diet will be easy for you. Drinking alcohol is fattening to
begin with, but the crowning blow is that it artificially stimulates your
appetite so that you're lured into eating more than you need.

Limited amounts of cholesterol are necessary for good health, and
it is carried in the bloodstream in envelopes called lipoproteins.
There are two types: "good," or HDL, cholesterol; and "bad," or LDL,
cholesterol, which can clog arteries and lead to stroke or heart attack
if present in excessive amounts. In contrast, "good" HDL cholesterol
seems to break up fatty deposits in the bloodstream and helps the
body clear itself of too much LDL. A glance at the Allergy Discovery
Diet Food Charts (see pages 53–59) explains why "bad" LDL cholesterol levels drop for many who follow the regime. The major portion
of the diet's "allowed foods" are plant foods—fruits, vegetables, grains
and legumes—and thus are completely cholesterol-free. More, these
foods are high in the soluble fiber that helps reduce levels of the
"bad" LDL cholesterol linked to stroke and heart disease. Plant foods
are rich in minerals and vitamins besides, and are so satisfying that
they lessen the craving for high-fat side dishes and snacks. In a
cholesterol-free nutshell, the Allergy Discovery Diet is good food, and
good food is the fuel of good health.

Special note for children and pregnant women—The Allergy Discovery Diet is perfectly safe; it consists of fresh, wholesome foods
combined and rotated in a careful order. However, the diet was
designed for use by basically healthy, fully grown adults, and does
not necessarily fulfill the special dietary requirements of children and
pregnant women, with their exceptional needs for nutrients like high-
quality protein, calcium and iron.

If you suspect your child of having food allergies, however, you can
adapt the Allergy Discovery Diet to help you track how individual
foods do or do not agree with your child's chemistry. Feed your child
his or her accustomed foods (or the foods prescribed by your pedia-

*

trician)—just take care to observe the Allergy Discovery Diet's number-one commandment and do not offer any food that has been processed or packaged with additives. Then, arrange the foods into "sets" or patterns ("set one" might be beef, carrots, peaches and rice, for example; "set two": lamb, squash, bananas, oats, etc.). Alternate these food "sets" according to the Allergy Discovery Diet's principle of a four-day rotation. Using the two basic concepts of single-ingredient foods consumed according to a scheduled rotation will help you identify any specific foods that disagree with your child.

For centuries, mothers have recognized the wisdom of using a serial approach as they present new foods to their babies. And manufacturers of baby foods are beginning to catch on. Both Beech-Nut Stage One and Gerber First Foods products are now prepared as single-ingredient foods, expressly to help in the prediction of food allergies and sensitivities. For this reason, and because the preparations offer pure, wholesome shortcuts to puréeing fruits, meats and vegetables, both these commercial food lines are permissible in Allergy Discovery Diet recipes and "Diet Express" menus.

It is with great excitement that I offer you the Allergy Discovery Diet as a new instrument to help solve the health problem troubling you. I wish you luck, and above all, a future of good health.

Putting the Plan into Action

One of the best ways to prepare for and maximize the benefits of the Allergy Discovery Diet is to heighten your awareness of your present eating patterns (including aftereffects): what you eat, when you eat it, and how it affects you. This seems to be a simple request, but to the contrary, I find that most of my patients are extremely absentminded eaters. Many apparently suffer a kind of eating amnesia—to the point of having not the least idea what they ate for breakfast. (Excuses often include being too distracted by the kids or the morning paper to notice, or too sleepy to care.) To help raise your consciousness about your own eating habits and the symptoms they arouse, I've devised the following questionnaire, which is similar to the one I use to evaluate patients with suspected food allergies. Be honest with yourself as you answer—"idealizing" your habits to make you look good on paper won't help you sort out your food allergy problems.

EATING PATTERNS

What do you eat for breakfast?

What did you eat for breakfast this morning?

Do you eat breakfast at home, on your way to or at work?

What do you eat for breakfast on weekends?

Do you often each brunch on weekends? What do you eat?

What do you drink with breakfast? How much?

Do you eat anything between breakfast and lunch?

Do you regularly take a coffee break?

Do you generally eat lunch in your office or out of the office?

Do you eat alone or with customers/friends?

Do you brown bag it from home? How often?

What do you usually eat for lunch?

What did you eat for lunch today?

What did you drink with lunch?

How often do you drink beer, wine or alcohol at lunch?

Do you snack in the afternoon or when you get home from work?

What do you snack on?

Do you generally have a cocktail? What kind?

Do you usually eat dinner at home or at a restaurant? Is it usually the same restaurant(s)?

Do you order take-out food for dinner? What kind? Do you always use the same take-out restaurant?

What did you eat for dinner last night?

What do you have for dessert?

Do you eat as you watch television?

Do you eat a bedtime snack?

Do you avoid eating foods because they cause digestive problems? List any foods you feel are too rich for you.

Do you take vitamins? When do you take them?

What kinds and which brands of vitamins do you take?

Do you regularly use laxatives, antacids, decongestants, appetite suppressors, aspirin/aspirin substitutes? How often and how many do you usually take?

Do you use breath mints? Which brand?

Do you use cough drops? Which brand?

Do you use dietetic candy? Which brand?

Do you chew gum? Which brand?

Do you use breath sprays? Which brand?

Do you use mouthwash? Which brand?

How to keep and interpret a food diary—After spending some time answering the questionnaire, you'll be more aware of how to analyze your eating habits to detect your allergies to foods. The next step is to begin a food diary of what and how you eat. For three or four days before starting the Elimination Phase—while you are still following your normal diet—write down when and how your symptoms occur, your regular snack and mealtime schedules, and any foods you eat with particular frequency. This prediet list of food-allergy clues will help make diagnosis of your food sensitivities even more precise as you follow the diet and test your reactions to specific foods.

Starting with Day One of the Elimination Phase and throughout the Reintroduction Phase, keep a more detailed account of your "food day"; write down exactly what you eat, when and where you eat it, and how you feel each day. Be conscientious; good detective work will help you single out the foods causing your symptoms, particularly if those symptoms seem to strike unpredictably. A written record is a very helpful way of "seeing" a pattern of food-related symptoms.

A few diary-keeping tips:

• Buy a small, spiral-bound notebook for your diary (see page 48). You should carry your diary with you at all times, to record meals and any symptoms as they occur.

• Don't depend on your memory—write down everything you consume and any noteworthy reactions immediately. Use abbreviations or your own brand of shorthand, but remember what everything means!

• List each food in multi-ingredient dishes. For example, if you made puffed millet cereal for breakfast according to an Allergy Discovery Diet recipe which also included oranges and honey, don't just enter the recipe title, "Puffed Millet Cereal." Write "Puffed Millet

Cereal, chopped oranges, honey" instead. If you're sensitive to citrus, it might be twenty-four hours before your body reacts to the chopped oranges in the cereal and by then, you'll have forgotten when and if you ate oranges unless you've got it written down. As your teachers used to say in school, "BE SPECIFIC!" This will make playing diet detective easier so that you can connect symptoms with particular foods.

SAMPLE FOOD DIARY

MEAL	TIME	FOOD/AMOUNTS	SYMPTOMS/COMMENTS
BREAKFAST	7 A.M.	o.j., 1 sm. glass honey-millet cereal (safflower oil, millet, honey) mint tea (mint, lemon, honey)	woke up with head/chest stuffiness
SNACK	11 A.M.	orange frappe (oranges, clementines, honey) millet crunch (millet cereal, pignoli (pine nuts), safflower oil, honey, fresh orange)	sinus congestion, worse about an hour after b'fast
LUNCH	1 P.M.	grilled salmon (marinade: safflower oil, lemon juice, sea salt, chervil), avocado aspic (gelatin, carrot juice, avocados, orange, lemon juice, carrot) lemon dressing (lemon peel, lemon juice, sea salt, safflower oil, chervil) iced tea (mint tea, orange juice, honey, mint)	
"COFFEE BREAK"	4 P.M.	carrot spritzer (carrot juice, honey, o.j., seltzer, mint sprig) fresh tangerines, glass of water	breathing raspy ½ hr. ago, skin on face, patchy, red
DINNER	7 P.M.	orange spritzer (o.j., seltzer, honey) seared swordfish (swordfish steak, sea salt, safflower oil, okra, zucchini, chervil) carrot salad (shredded carrots, lime-mint dressing [safflower oil, lime juice, honey, chopped mint]) broiled grapefruit (grapefruit, honey) w/ scoop of orange freeze (oranges, o.j.)	wheezing on way home from work, patches of skin on face itchy
NIGHTCAP	10 P.M.	hot tea (mint tea, o.j., honey, sprig of mint) millet crunch (see "snack" 11 A.M.)	

• When planning meals throughout both phases of the diet, remember to note any foods to which you suspect or know you are allergic. In the case of a known allergy, do not eat the food; choose a substitute food and then eat only that particular substitute whenever the problem food is called for in the diet. If sensitivity is merely suspected, test your tolerance of the food, but remember to eat it in SMALL amounts.

A Detailed Look at the Elimination Phase

The first days of the Elimination Phase of the Allergy Discovery Diet are designed to clear your system of the antigens causing your allergic symptoms. During the Elimination Phase, you will be eating only hypoallergenic foods—foods to which you are least likely to be allergic. The Allergy Discovery Diet roster of these hypoallergenic foods is based upon analysis of many medical articles, papers and reports. This body of evidence represents the work of doctors and medical researchers all over the world and it details the frequency with which allergic reactions have been found to cause various symptoms and complaints (see Appendix for documentation). The Allergy Discovery Diet inventory of hypoallergenic foods includes:

tapioca	beef	thyme	maple sugar
celery	lima bean	banana	carrot
mustard	parsley	spinach	nutmeg
rosemary	clove	olive oil	coconut
peach	rice	potato	rhubarb
turnip	artichoke	navy beans	canola oil
sage	veal	cinnamon	amaranth
lentils	gelatin	millet	green beans
zucchini	pear	cucumber	honey
kasha	tuna fish	basil	beets
pork	chick-peas	apple	ginger
sesame	lamb	oregano	melon
bean sprouts	carob	cranberry	turkey
rose hip	escarole	pumpkin	squash

The Elimination Phase diet quiets your immune system's activity level below your body's threshold for allergic reactions so that specific sensitivities will be easier to identify as foods are reintroduced in the second phase of the diet.

Clinical studies, including extensive testing with my own patients, indicate that in most cases it takes six to ten days for the body to "wash out" antigens and recover from the effects of allergic symptoms. Therefore, the first six days of the Allergy Discovery Diet represent the Elimination Phase. I hesitate to call this period "Week One," as you may have to repeat part or all of the six-day cycle if your symptoms are unusually persistent and your body needs more time to rout all enemy antigens. You will know when your body has successfully cleared itself when your symptoms (skin rash, headache, stomach pain, etc.) disappear. But if your malady worsens after the first six days, it is possible that you are allergic to one of the hypoallergenic foods featured on the diet. Repeat the Elimination Phase in this case, taking careful note of your reactions each day. Then, once you have identified the allergy-provoking food, choose an appropriate substitute from the list of allowed foods for Day Twenty-two (Recovery Day) and repeat Days One, Two and Three, using the new pinch-hitter you have selected. If you discover that you are allergic to bananas (Elimination Phase, Days One and Five), for example, you can choose fresh plums from Recovery Day instead. As you continue on the Allergy Discovery Diet, remember to replace bananas with plums each time bananas appear in the Allergy Discovery Diet program. Recovery Day foods are hypoallergic for most people, and have been chosen to provide you with an "emergency" list of hypoallergenic foods not used during the Elimination Phase.

As you might guess from reading through its list of foods, the Elimination Phase is a particularly mild and system-soothing health regimen. It is a well-balanced, wholesome diet, and if you are severely food-allergic, you can follow it for up to fifteen days while you wait for your symptoms to clear. If the therapeutic effects of the Elimination Phase do not relieve your complaint after fifteen days, however, it is unlikely that your problem is food-related and there is no need to proceed to the Reintroduction Phase. You can be confident seeking another kind of medical remedy. Bring your copy of the Elimination Phase diet to your doctor and discuss your reactions; your experience with the Elimination Phase represents a thorough investigation of the possibility that your illness is nutritionally based, and its findings will help your doctor decide what other kinds of treatment you need. As I've said, there may be factors other than food contributing to your allergic reaction, but at least, by concentrating on the foods research has shown to be the most hypoallergenic, food is one variable that can be erased from the allergy equation.

Three features of the Allergy Discovery Diet are particularly important to keep in mind. They are:

1. Only single-ingredient foods are used—that is, foods processed and packaged without additional chemicals or food substances.

✳

2. Foods are presented on a FOUR-DAY rotating basis: no food is used twice within a THREE-DAY period to allow clearance of immune complexes from the body.

3. Foods on the Allergy Discovery Diet hyperallergenic list should be reintroduced in small amounts.

I've dubbed these three axioms my dietary golden rules. Living by them as you follow the Allergy Discovery Diet is fundamental to reaching the goal of identifying your allergies to foods.

A Detailed Look at the Reintroduction Phase

Now come the "discovery days" of identifying the foods causing your immune system to overexercise. Take a moment first, though, for self-congratulations. No diet regimen is the world's greatest form of entertainment. Your perseverance throughout the Elimination Phase deserves some admiring words. My concern about your need for relief from your symptoms inspired the Allergy Discovery Diet, but it is your allergy, your pain, and ultimately, your initiative that will determine the effectiveness of the plan.

Chapter 3 outlined the fifteen hyperallergenic foods on the Allergy Discovery Diet roll call—those foods I have found most likely to be triggering your symptoms of food allergy. They are:

Day Seven . . . citrus
Day Eight . . . corn
Day Nine . . . chicken
Day Ten . . . oats
Day Eleven . . . egg
Day Twelve . . . wheat
Day Thirteen . . . soy
Day Fourteen . . . milk and milk products
Day Fifteen . . . vinegar, ferments
Day Sixteen . . . coffee/tea
Day Seventeen . . . cane sugar
Day Eighteen . . . chocolate
Day Nineteen . . . tomato
Day Twenty . . . pea/peanut
Day Twenty-One . . . onion/chives

The order in which these fifteen foods are presented is intentional and important. Each "new" food is worked into the rotation schedule begun during the Elimination Phase of the diet so that different combinations of foods are presented each day.

Biochemically, the Elimination Phase has primed your body for an allergic reaction. Much like someone stepping from a dark room out into dazzling sunlight, your body emerges from the Elimination Phase with a heightened sensitivity to irritating allergen. Any one of the fifteen foods you are about to reintroduce into your diet might stage a dramatic response so remember to make the debut of each a cameo performance.

Identifying your allergens takes a bit of detective work. Individual "suspect" foods headline each day during the Reintroduction Phase, but there are other foods in the supporting cast, rounding out the menus. How can you tell which one is causing your symptoms?

Let's say you experience your symptom, a migraine headache, on Day Nine. How can you be sure it's chicken you're reacting to (chicken is the chief suspect for the day) and not the banana? If you read through the diet, you'll notice that foods are arranged in different combinations each day. If you had no adverse reaction after eating banana on Day One, for example, and nothing happens on Days Fifteen and Twenty, when you eat bananas again, it is unlikely that banana is causing your problems on Day Nine. If on the other hand, you get a reaction on each of those days, you can feel reasonably sure that bananas are not your cup of fruit.

The Allergy Discovery Diet's three-week duration allows you time for working out offending foods by process of elimination. Three weeks is a long time, and that is why keeping a food diary is so important—instead of trying to remember when or if you experienced symptoms, all you have to do is flip through your notes to find out. Remember from Chapter 1 that while symptoms of allergy are individual, predicated by the special character of each person's unique body chemistry, once your symptoms of food allergy assume a certain form (chocolate gives you headaches, for instance, and tomatoes give you hives) they will recur consistently, so that you can correctly correlate causes and effects.

If you already know your sensitivities to certain foods—that citrus fruits make you very sick—do not eat them. Heightened sensitivity following the Elimiation Phase can cause severe reaction. If you have doubts about a certain food, exaggerate the Allergy Discovery Diet principal of reintroducing foods in small amounts until you confirm or disprove the suspected allergy.

Everyone who discovers food sensitives during the Reintroduction Phase of the Allergy Discovery Diet naturally experiences allergic symptoms. If these reintroductions are managed in small amounts (especially when allergies are suspected) suffering is kept to a minimum.

*   *   *

FOOD CHART: ELIMINATION PHASE

	DAY ONE	DAY TWO	DAY THREE	DAY FOUR	DAY FIVE	DAY SIX
GRAIN	None	Rice	Millet	Kasha	None	Rice
PANCAKE	Lima bean	Potato	Amaranth/Lentil	Chick-pea	Lima bean	Potato
FRUIT	Bananas	Coconut Peaches	Pears	Apples	Bananas Cranberries Melon Plantains	Coconut Peaches
VEGETABLES	Carrots Celery Lima beans Parsley	Alfalfa sprouts Artichokes Navy beans (white) Potatoes Rhubarb Squash Turnips	Cucumbers Green beans Lentils Yellow squash Zucchini	Bamboo shoots Beets Celery Chick-peas Spinach Sweet potatoes	Artichokes Bean sprouts Escarole Lima beans Mustard greens Pumpkin	Cucumbers Green beans Kidney beans Parsley Potatoes Rhubarb Squash
MEAT	Lamb	Veal	Whitefish/tuna/salmon	Pork, lamb	Turkey	Beef/Duck
SALAD DRESSING	Mustard	"Mayo"	Green beans	Oregano	Mustard	Tarragon
HERB TEA	Clove	Cinnamon	Mint	Ginger	Rose hip	Chamomile
SHORTENING	Olive oil	Puritan oil	Safflower oil	Sesame oil	Olive oil Nyalat	Puritan oil
SEASONING	Mustard Nutmeg Rosemary	Sage	Basil	Oregano Ginger	Mustard Thyme	Nutmeg Tarragon
SWEETENER	Banana flakes (purée)	Peach flakes (purée)	Honey	Apple butter Apple flakes	Maple crystals Maple syrup	Peach flakes (purée)
OTHER	Tapioca	Gelatin Potato starch Rice bran	Potato starch	Carob Sesame seeds Psyllium seed	Tapioca	Potato starch Rice bran

FOOD CHART: REINTRODUCTION PHASE

	DAY SEVEN (Citrus)	DAY EIGHT (Corn)	DAY NINE (Chicken)	DAY TEN (Oats)	DAY ELEVEN (Egg)	DAY TWELVE (Wheat)
GRAIN	Millet	Corn	Kasha	Oat	Millet	Wheat
PANCAKE	Amaranth/Lentil	Corn	Lima bean	Oat	Amaranth/Lentil	Wheat
FRUIT	Clementines Grapefruit Lemons Limes Oranges Tangerines	Apples	Bananas Melon	Papayas Pears	Coconut Peaches	Apples Cranberries
VEGETABLES	Avocados Carrots Green beans Lentils Okra	Broccoli Cauliflower Corn Sweet potatoes Water chestnuts	Alfalfa sprouts Beets Celery Chick-peas Kidney beans Lima beans Pumpkin Spinach	Eggplant Lettuce Parsley Pink beans Yellow Squash Zucchini	Asparagus Bamboo shoots Lentils Rhubarb	Carrots Turnips
MEAT	Whitefish/tuna/ salmon	Lamb	Chicken Rock Cornish Game Hen	Veal	Eggs (Pork or Whitefish/Tuna/Salmon)	Lamb
SALAD DRESSING	Chervil	Basil	Beet Tahini	Mustard	Egg mayo	Rosemary
HERB TEA	Mint	Cinnamon	Ginger	Rose hip	Mint	Clove
SHORTENING	Safflower oil	Corn oil Nyafat	Sesame	Olive oil	Sunflower oil	Safflower oil
SEASONING	Chervil Saffron	Basil Cinnamon Mace Rosemary	Ginger	Mustard	Oregano	Nutmeg Rosemary

SWEETENER	Honey	Apple flakes (purée) Corn syrup (Karo Light)* Maple syrup	Banana flakes (purée)	Pear flakes (purée)	Maple crystals Maple syrup	Apple flakes (purée) Honey
OTHER	Arrowroot Gelatin Pignoli (pine nuts) Psyllium seed	Corn bran Sunflower seeds	Carob Sesame seeds	Gelatin Oat bran	Potato starch flour Psyllium seed Sunflower seeds	Baking soda Wheat (miller's) bran

*Pure high-fructose corn syrup is very hard to find. Karo syrup can be used as long as you are aware that it contains vanilla, a fermented product.

FOOD CHART: REINTRODUCTION PHASE

	DAY THIRTEEN (Soy)	DAY FOURTEEN (Milk)	DAY FIFTEEN (Vinegar/Ferments)	DAY SIXTEEN (Coffee/Tea)	DAY SEVENTEEN (Cane Sugar)	DAY EIGHTEEN (Chocolate)
GRAIN	Rice	Kasha	Oat	None	Rice	Corn
PANCAKE	Soy-Rice	Chick-pea	Oat	Amaranth/Lentil	Lima bean	Corn
FRUIT	Bananas Blueberries Melon	Peaches	Dates Figs Pears Prunes Raisins	Apples Pineapples	Bananas Coconut Cranberries	Cherries Peaches
VEGETABLES	Broccoli Kidney beans Spinach Squash	Bamboo shoots Cauliflower Celery Chick-peas Green beans Sweet potatoes Watercress	Beets Black beans Cucumbers Lettuce Mushrooms Olives Potatoes Zucchini	Avocados Bean sprouts Carrots Lentils Pumpkin Turnips	Celery Endive Lima beans Spinach	Asparagus Beets Corn Pink beans Rhubarb Zucchini
MEAT	Turkey	Beef	Lamb	Whitefish/Tuna/ Salmon	Chicken	Veal
SALAD DRESSING	Dill	Tahini	Vinegar	Mustard	Ginger	Dill
HERB TEA	Cinnamon	Ginger	Mint	Coffee/Tea	Ginger	Mint
SHORTENING	Puritan oil Soy oil	Butter Sesame oil	Sunflower oil	Safflower oil	Nyafat Olive oil	Corn oil
SEASONING	Dill Thyme	Ginger Summer savory	Basil Mint Nutmeg	Cinnamon Fennel Mustard	Ginger Thyme	Dill Nutmeg Mint

SWEETENER	Banana flakes (purée)	Maple crystals / Maple syrup / Peach flakes (purée)	Beet sugar / Date sugar / Pear flakes (purée)	Honey	Light brown sugar / Cane sugar / Unsulphured light molasses	Beet sugar / Maple crystals / Maple syrup / Syrup (Karo syrup)
OTHER	Rice bran	Cottage cheese / Cream / Gelatin / Milk / Sesame seeds / Sour cream / Yogurt	Baking powder / Beer / Oat bran / Potato starch / Psyllium seed / Sunflower seeds / Vanilla / White grape juice / Wine / Yeast	Arrowroot / Tapioca	Carob / Milk / Rice bran / Sunflower seeds	Baking soda / Cocoa (unsweetened) / Corn bran / Gelatin / Peach flakes (purée)

FOOD CHART: REINTRODUCTION PHASE

	DAY NINETEEN (Tomato)	DAY TWENTY (Pea/Peanut)	DAY TWENTY-ONE (Onion/Chives)	DAY TWENTY-TWO (Recovery Day)
GRAIN	Kasha	Millet	Oat	Barley
PANCAKE	Chick-pea	Amaranth	Oat	Italian flatbread
FRUIT	Apples Papayas Pineapple	Bananas Coconut Cranberries Melon	Mangoes Peaches Pears	Apricots (fresh) Chestnuts Hearts of palm Mammees Plums
VEGETABLES	Chick-peas Cucumbers Lettuce Sweet potatoes Tomatoes	Alfalfa sprouts Black-eyed peas Carrots Green beans Lentils Peas Snow peas Spinach Water chestnuts	Artichokes Chives Garlic Leeks Lima beans Onions Parsley Potatoes (white) Squash Watercress Zucchini	Collards Eggplant Kale Kidney beans (white) Wax beans
MEAT	Lamb	Pork or Whitefish/ Tuna/ Salmon	Turkey	Frogs' legs Rabbit
SALAD DRESSING	Tahini	Ginger	Mustard	Marjoram Sorrel Plum vinagrette Vinegar
HERB TEA	Cinnamon	Ginger	Mint/Rose hip	Anise

SHORTENING	Sesame oil	Peanut oil	Sunflower oil	Puritan oil
SEASONING	Cinnamon Mace Oregano	Ginger Summer Savory	Chives Mint Mustard Nutmeg Sweet Basil Thyme	Anise Marjoram Sorrel
SWEETENER	Apple butter Apple flakes (purée)	Banana flakes (purée)	Honey	Barley malt sugar Palm sugar
Other	Buckwheat flour Buckwheat pasta Psyllium seed Tapioca Yam noodles or threads	Peanuts Peanut butter	Arrowroot Pignoli (pine nuts) Poppy seeds Rice bran Sunflower seeds	Arrowroot Gelatin

After the diet—After completing the twenty-one days of the combined Elimination and Reintroduction Phases, take some time to assess your status.

Anyone who follows the Allergy Discovery Diet must be prepared to accept the fact that it might not cure your symptoms. The diet does accomplish a detailed, scientific analysis of your reactions to the most common causes of food allergy, however, so if your specific complaints persist after a full trial of the Allergy Discovery Diet, you can feel confident that you've thoroughly explored the possibility that your health problem stems from allergies to foods. Whatever the outcome of your investigation, your experience of the Allergy Discovery Diet will be time well spent. You will know a great deal more than you did before about how you are affected by different foods, and it is more than likely that you will feel fitter, trimmer and more energetic than you did three weeks ago, as a result of following a diet of wholesome, additive-free foods.

The best-case scenario (one that the overwhelming majority of my patients experience) is that your symptoms will disappear during the Elimination Phase and you will now be able to associate any reappearances with one or more foods. The next step is to take your copy of the Allergy Discovery Diet menus and your food diary with notes on your reactions to your doctor or nutritionist. In consultation with a professional, you can work out a permanent diet plan which accommodates your nutritional needs as well as your newly discovered allergies.

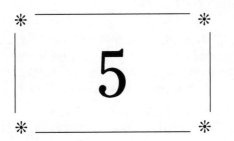

5

The Practical Aspects of the Allergy Discovery Diet

The Allergy Discovery Diet has been "reality-tested"; my patients have put it to work and lived with it in their homes, offices—even their schools. Thanks to their constructive suggestions and criticisms, the Allergy Discovery Diet plan is usable, flexible and—it works.

Your Choice of Menus

One aspect of that practicality is the Allergy Discovery Diet's menu design. For those who may be cooking for a family or friends there is the Regular Track; recipes in this category employ conventional cooking methods and moderate investments of time. The Diet Express is the fast lane of the diet, for the days you're only cooking for one, don't feel like cooking or just don't have the time. Use the tracks interchangeably, alternating by meal, by day or by week, depending on your preferences and constraints of time.

Recipe Choices

Each day of the diet also offers a selection of recipes to choose from, so that you can plan meals to suit your mood and appetite. If you're ravenous at breakfast-time on Day Six for example, you might fill up on Potato Pancakes. Or, if hearty meals in the morning are too much for you, "breakfast light" on puréed peaches and a bowl of puffed rice cereal instead. Don't feel obliged to eat every dish on the menu for every meal—it's what you eat that matters, not how much, especially as you venture into the Reintroduction Phase of the diet and begin to test your reactions to suspect foods.

Food Choices—How to Substitute Foods

The Allergy Discovery Diet has a good deal of built-in elasticity to allow for personal food preferences—flexibility is one of the main reasons why the Allergy Discovery Diet has been so successful with so many people. If you don't eat red meat or you know you are allergic to wheat for example, you don't have to go hungry. Throughout the diet, whether during the Elimination or Reintroduction Phase, you may choose a substitute food when a daily menu calls for something you don't like or can't eat. Eating specific foods in consistent rotation is essential to using the regime successfully, but you can tailor the diet to include your own allowable "deputy" choices. If you decide to make substitutions in either phase of the diet, be sure to follow these three principles of replacement:

1. Observe a four-day rotation of foods.
2. Be consistent in substitutions. Once you choose a replacement food, think of it as the permanent "understudy" for the unacceptable food throughout the diet: replace the undesirable food with the same understudy food each time.
3. Do not eat any food during the Elimination Phase that is targeted for reintroduction during the second phase of the Allergy Discovery Diet: citrus, corn, chicken, oats, egg, wheat, soy, milk, vinegar, ferments, coffee/tea, cane sugar, chocolate, tomato, pea/peanut, onion/chives.

As an example, let's revise six days of the diet for someone who doesn't eat fish.

Look at the Food Chart for the Elimination Phase (Days One through Six). You will see that lamb is allotted to Day One, veal to Day Two, whitefish, tuna or salmon to Day Three, pork or lamb to Day Four, turkey to Day Five, and beef or duck to Day Six. Since you don't eat fish you need an alternate food for Day Three.

Suppose you decide to substitute duck for fish. First, check the Reintroduction Phase menus to make sure duck is not among the foods featured for reintroduction. Then, cross out duck on Day Six and replace it with veal, so that a four-day rotation of veal is preserved. Now, pencil in duck to replace fish on Day Three. Your personalized version of the Elimination Phase now follows this scheme:

✳

Day One . . . lamb
Day Two . . . veal
Day Three . . . duck
Day Four . . . pork
Day Five . . . turkey
Day Six . . . veal

Your customized scheme observes all three principles of replacement because you have:

scheduled all meats according to a four-day rotation.
picked a replacement food that is not slated for reintroduction in the second phase of the diet.
been consistent in your substitutions.

Note that you would continue this individualized food schedule throughout the rest of the diet. Notice too, that each day of the Allergy Discovery Diet allows a high-protein "bean for the day," so that you can always satisfy your appetite and nutritional requirements for protein (about 50 grams per day, according to the dietary standards set by the U.S. Food and Drug Administration) by substituting a one-half-cup serving of beans for each four-ounce serving of fish or meat. Because they are rich in complex carbohydrates, beans in moderate amounts are a satisfying, energy-boosting comfort food in the bargain, and supply a health-benefiting average of two grams soluble fiber per serving.

The Allergy Discovery Diet cookbook is designed to make the diet's rules and regulations clear and easy to observe. The cookbook follows a day-by-day format, presenting each day as an individual unit, complete with a list of the foods permitted for the day, menus and accompanying recipes. When you choose a substitute food, pencil it in above the food you want it to replace in the Food Chart for the day, so your "understudy" will be easy to remember.

Special Situations

What if you have to travel on business during the course of the Allergy Discovery Diet? Or take a guest out to a meal? What if you're the family cook and don't relish the idea of having to make two separate dinners? The Allergy Discovery Diet regime is pliable enough to adjust to any of these demands.

If you have to eat in a restaurant, simply consult the Allergy Discovery Diet list of allowable foods for the day and order only those foods. Ask that meats and fish be plainly broiled (hold the marinades and butter) and that vegetables be steamed or boiled. Restaurants are much more sympathetic to individual dietary needs now than in the past—many even offer special "low-cal" or "heart-saving" menus for diet-conscious patrons. Even in the most cosmopolitan restaurants, your requests will be respected.

What to Do If You "Blow" It

If you go off the Allergy Discovery Diet (inadvertently or otherwise) by eating a food that is not on the daily roster of allowable foods, what do you do? Don't berate yourself, but at the same time, don't reason that since you've already strayed from the Allergy Discovery Diet straight and narrow, you might as well go whole-hog and eat anything that takes your fancy.

If you are in the Elimination Phase, it's a good idea to extend the phase another three days to ensure maximum clearance of any immune complexes. If you are in the Reintroduction Phase, continue on the program at the very next meal, making sure you test yourself with the food scheduled for reintroduction. Then, if you experience symptoms that day or the next, repeat the specific day of your transgression (minus the transgression itself!) at the end of the phase. This repetition will reveal whether your symptoms were provoked by the food slated for reintroduction or by the misdemeanor-food you ate instead.

What to Do If You Have a Severe Reaction

The chances of suffering a severe reaction are greatest during the Reintroduction Phase, when you might forget to reintroduce a hyper-allergenic food in small amounts and eat enough of it to cause a flare-up of your symptoms. If this should happen early in the day, after breakfast on Day Twelve for example (an hour after you polish off two bowls of wheat cereal), you should continue to eat all foods allowed on Day Twelve, minus the offending wheat, to give your symptoms time to subside. Then, as long as you are clear of symptoms by the next morning, you should follow the plan for Day Thirteen, as scheduled.

But if your hyperreaction does not occur until the middle of the night, or even early the next morning, so that it is impossible to test yourself against a new hyperallergenic food, then you need a "day off" from the Allergy Discovery Diet so that you can recover from symptoms before recommencing the program. Day Twenty-two (Recovery Day) is designed for this purpose; it is a custom-made holiday from the Allergy Discovery Diet which allows you to interrupt the diet

✳

without destroying its overall food rotation schedule. Reading through the list of foods slated for Day Twenty-two, you will notice that except for Puritan oil, none of the foods listed are used on any other day of the diet, so that you can eat them without disrupting the rotation of foods you have been following so far. Moreover, all Recovery Day foods are hypoallergenic for most people and thus eating them helps clear your body of irritating antigens.

Day Twenty-two is the spare tire of the Allergy Discovery Diet, an emergency elimination day. Resorting to its bill of fare in the event of a severe reaction should alleviate your symptoms and allow you to resume the diet within twenty-four hours. As they say in sports, however, the best offense is a strong defense: remember to reintroduce hyperallergenic foods in small amounts and avoid the suffering and complication of acute reactions! (For discussion of how to use Recovery Day during the Elimination Phase, see A Detailed Look at the Elimination Phase, Chapter 4.)

When Brand Names Matter

It is rarely important to buy and eat only certain brands of foods while on the Allergy Discovery Diet. All that really matters is that foods are pure and free of additives. In fact, many major food chains offer house "generic" brands of common foods such as oils, grains and cereals, yogurt, cottage cheese, applesauce, canned and frozen vegetables and juices. As long as these products are processed without additional ingredients, they are fine, thrifty choices. Just be sure to read the labels carefully before you buy.

There are times, however, when knowing a brand name helps. Most foods on the Allergy Discovery Diet are "normal" and ordinary, but a few are generally unfamiliar, and my patients who served as subjects for the Allergy Discovery Diet recommended that brand names be suggested for unusual items, so that you'll know a name to ask for if you can't find the food on the market shelf. Following are the foods my patients voted "hardest to find," with brand names to help you locate them:

amaranth flour—Arrowhead Mills
beet sugar—White Satin
buckwheat pasta—Westbrae
canned turkey and chicken—Swanson
canola (rapeseed) oil—Puritan oil
carrot juice—Hollywood or Bugs Bunny
cold-water wheat crackers—Bent's
dry mustard—Coleman's

frozen rabbit—Pel-Freeze
kasha (buckwheat)—Wolff's
nyafat (liquid or hydrogenated cottonseed oil)—Rokeach
oat bran cereal—Quaker or Mother's
potato meal—Streit's or Goodman's
potato starch flour—Swan's
puffed millet cereal—El Molino
quick-cooking barley—Mother's
rapid-rising yeast—Fleischmann's
rice flour—Goya
sea salt—Diamond (in kosher section)
pure sesame oil—Ka-Me (or use the oil which rises to the top of a
   can of tahini)
tahini (sesame "butter")—Joyva
soybean margarine—Old Stone Mill
soy powder—Fearn's
sparkling white grape juice—Catawba

Baby Foods and the Discovery Diet

"Fast" food, whether restaurant or home-prepared, has become a necessity as well as a modern mealtime style, and it is primarily for this reason that the Allergy Discovery Diet lists some Beech-Nut, Heinz and Gerber baby foods among recipe ingredients. Both Beech-Nut Stage One and Gerber First Foods offer users of the Allergy Discovery Diet a source of instant meat, vegetable and fruit purées— all single-ingredient and additive-free. Just take care to note that the diet specifies using the Stage One and First Foods product lines— Gerber Beginner foods and Beech-Nut Stage Two and Table Time foods sometimes combine a number of foods or contain additives such as citric acid to retain color. Because the Gerber First Foods product line does not offer as many different foods as the Beech-Nut Stage One series, and because First Foods are prepared in extremely small amounts, recipes in the Allergy Discovery Diet cookbook specify use of Beech-Nut Stage One products. First Foods are fine to use instead; you will just have to buy twice as many jars.

Heinz dehydrated peaches, bananas and apples have been crystallized down to their essences—they are pure fruit sugar, and substitute for cane sugar in Allergy Discovery Diet recipes. The other important plank in the Allergy Discovery Diet policy of using baby foods is that the foods are particularly easy to digest. One of the most if not the most frequent symptom of food allergy is gastrointestinal distress. Heinz, Beech-Nut Stage One and Gerber First Foods are prepared and processed expressly to treat sensitive digestive systems gently (cereals are precooked for example, and juices have been processed to reduce acidity). These products may have been made for babies, but they are food-perfect for adults on the Allergy Discovery Diet, especially during the Elimination Phase.

Shopping

The Allergy Discovery Diet represents a new way of eating and, practically speaking, a new way of shopping. To keep the plan as economical and convenient as possible, we've drawn up a composite list of staple foods that can be purchased the first week and used throughout the diet. The key to shopping efficiently for the diet is to decide how many days you want to prepare for, and then read through the recipes intended for those days (including Night-Before Preparation Tips). As you select recipes, note which cuts of meat and fish you want and if fruits and vegetables should be fresh. Estimate the amounts of foods to buy (depending upon how many people you are cooking for) and you're ready to go shopping.

Where to Find the Foods You Need

With the goal of making the diet easy to follow, we have used familiar, supermarket stock whenever possible. Large supermarket chains carry nearly all the ingredients used in the Allergy Discovery Diet cookbook recipes; some of these whopper markets even contain boutique-like aisles devoted entirely to "health" foods.

The trend toward supermarket production of generic foods makes these big stores a silent partner in our attempt to prescribe easily affordable, available foods. Look for fruits, vegetables, tuna, and chicken packaged under the supermarket's own brand label. Such products are often prepared without additives, and you will find very little difference in quality from comparable, name-brand ingredients, at much lower cost. The frozen foods section of a large market is another place to find generic-brand foods permissible on the diet. Again, many chains freeze fruits and vegetables without added ingredients, and charge less than name-brand producers. Water-pack canned foods can be found in the "diet" section of supermarkets, although these items will carry the cost of their specialty status.

A few ingredients on the Allergy Discovery Diet are especially hard to locate; they are listed below under "A Trip to the Health Food Store." Health is the fashion in many of these elegant little shops— the fun of browsing through them and cooking your exotic "finds" will outweigh any inconvenience of your trip.

A Trip to the Health Food Store

The following foods are not generally carried by supermarkets. (As you read through the recipes in the Allergy Discovery Diet cookbook, you will find that most of these ingredients are optional.) In addition to the items below, most health food stores offer a full selection of puffed cereals, fresh or water-packed fruits and vegetables, seeds, nuts, spices, herb teas and pure fruit juices, yogurt, soy and tofu products, cheeses and some meats.

1. *Sweeteners*
   beet sugar
   date sugar
   palm sugar
   barley malt sugar
   maple crystals

2. *Flours*
   amaranth
   chick-pea
   sesame
   barley

3. *Whole Grains*
   whole-wheat berries
   millet

4. *Pasta*
   buckwheat pasta

5. *Margarines*
   safflower oil margarine
   soybean margarine

6. *Fruits and Vegetables*
   carob
   unsweetened dehydrated banana chips
   unsweetened shredded coconut

✳

The Allergy Discovery Diet Shopping List

STAPLES TO HAVE ON HAND THROUGHOUT THE DIET

1. *Meats and Fish* (water-pack canned or jarred)
   tuna
   salmon
   turkey
   chicken (such as Swanson brand)
   Beech-Nut Stage One or Gerber First Foods veal, lamb, turkey, beef

2. *Fruits* (water-pack canned, frozen or jarred)
   peaches
   pears
   applesauce, plain apple butter
   rhubarb
   cranberries (frozen)
   melon balls
   pumpkin (unsweetened)
   Beech-Nut Stage One peaches, pears, applesauce, bananas
   Heinz dehydrated peach, pear, apple and banana flakes (purée)
   unsweetened dehydrated banana chips

3. *Vegetables* (dried, water-pack canned or frozen)
   artichoke hearts
   asparagus
   dried beans: chick-peas, green, lentils, limas, navy, kidney, white, pink, black
   water-pack beans: lentils, pink, black, white kidney
   frozen beans: limas
   carrots
   green peas (frozen)
   snow peas (frozen)
   beets
   potatoes (water-pack, white)
   pumpkin
   spinach
   turnips
   corn on the cob (frozen)
   bean sprouts
   bamboo shoots
   water chestnuts (canned or frozen)
   butternut squash (optional)

zucchini
Beech-Nut Stage One or Gerber First Foods carrots, spinach, beets, sweet potatoes, squash, green beans

4. *Cereals*
puffed rice
puffed millet
cream of rice
Beech-Nut Stage One rice cereal

5. *Grains*
white rice (regular or quick-cooking)
kasha
millet

6. *Flours*
rice
chick-pea (home-ground from dried chick-peas)
lima bean (home-ground from frozen limas)
amaranth
potato starch flour
potato starch such as Goodman's brand
arrowroot (in spice section)
sesame (home-ground from seeds)
lentil (home-ground from dried lentils)

7. *Pasta*
buckwheat pasta (oriental food section—Japanese)
rice sticks (oriental food section)
yam noodles (oriental food section)

8. *Crackers*
plain rice cakes
plain rice crackers (look for rice flour and water only crackers in the oriental section of markets; Ka-Me is one good brand).

9. *Oils and Shortenings*
sunflower
safflower
olive, light olive
Puritan (canola/rapeseed oil)
nyafat (liquid or hydrogenated cottonseed oil)
sesame
soy

✳

10. *Sweeteners*
   honey
   maple syrup
   maple crystals (usually health food store item)
   Heinz fruit sugars (see "Fruits" above)

11. *Herbs and Spices*
   cinnamon (stick and pure powdered)
   ginger (fresh ginger root or pure powdered)
   mint (fresh or dried leaves)
   cloves (whole)
   nutmeg (fresh or dried leaves)
   tarragon (fresh or dried leaves)
   summer savory (fresh or dried leaves)
   basil (fresh or dried leaves)
   fennel (fresh or dried leaves) and fennel seeds
   oregano (fresh or dried leaves)
   rosemary (fresh or dried leaves)
   thyme (fresh or dried leaves)
   dill
   dry mustard (Coleman's)
   mustard seeds (whole)*
   sage
   sea salt
   anise seeds (whole)

*On days when mustard is allowed, fill a pepper mill with whole mustard seeds; season meals to taste with freshly ground mustard, as you would with pepper.

12. *Herbal Teas†*
   plain mint
   plain cinnamon
   chamomile (any brand, no other ingredients)
   rose hip
   plain ginger
   plain clove

†Remember that most of these "teas" are easy to make at home with your own spices and hot water, but if you buy commercial brands, be sure they contain only herbs: no real tea.

13. *Plain Juices and Waters*
   mineral water (sparkling and noncarbonated)
   pear juice (pure juice such as After the Fall brand)
   apple juice (plain)

carrot juice
celery juice

14. *Miscellaneous*
tahini
gelatin (unflavored)
carob (powdered, usually a health food store item)
sunflower seeds
pignoli (pine nuts)
sesame seeds
tapioca (granulated, quick-cooking)
baking soda
canned unsweetened coconut milk
psyllium seed
rice bran
shredded unsweetened coconut
olives
potato meal

PART

II

THE ALLERGY DISCOVERY DIET COOKBOOK

To Every Day, There Is a Food

Successful use of the Allergy Discovery Diet depends upon eating only certain foods each day, and so a reminder of what to eat headlines each day's menus. Don't feel you must follow menu listings to the letter, however; if you feel like having the melon scripted for breakfast for lunch instead, the alteration is fine. Nor are you required to eat certain amounts of food; this is not a weight-loss diet. If a Diet Express breakfast menu suggests puffed rice cereal, for example, eat as much or little cereal as you like. As I have cautioned, the Allergy Discovery Diet's only restriction on quantities to be eaten applies to the fifteen hyperallergenic, or "suspect," foods featured in the Reintroduction Phase of the diet. Initial reintroductions of suspect foods should always be eaten in small amounts, in case of severe reaction.

The cookbook is offered as a convenience and general guide; its purpose is to provide you with ready-made menus and recipes using only the foods "allowed" for the day according to the Allergy Discovery Diet plan. If none of the recipes appeal to you on any given day, however, it is perfectly all right to make up recipes of your own. Just be sure to use only the foods listed as "allowed" on the menu for the day. Above all, the cookbook is designed for flexibility, like the Allergy Discovery Diet itself. For this reason, serving amounts are not always specified for menu items that don't require detailed recipes, such as plain apple juice, especially on the Diet Express. As long as you are not reintroducing a suspect food for the first time, you may eat as little or as much of any menu item as you like.

Flexibility is also the reason for the cookbook's two tracks, Regular and Express. Alternate between the Regular and Express tracks as you like, depending on your needs, and use frozen or canned items interchangeably. When menu items are identical (no "express" version needed), refer to the Regular Track for recipes. Just remember to reduce ingredient amounts and microwave cooking times by one half, if you need only one or two servings.

Plan Ahead

Before you set out for the market, read ahead in the cookbook, marking the items and amounts of food you'll need as you select recipes. Remember to note suggested "Night-Before Preparation Tips" and adjust the recommended amounts to be prepared according to which recipes you plan to make.

Microwaving

Microwave directions are included when microcooking saves considerable amounts of time and produces recipes of comparable quality to recipes cooked by conventional methods. Microwave versions in the Allergy Discovery Diet cookbook were tested in microwave ovens that operate on 600 to 700 watts. Cooking times are approximate, however, as microwave ovens vary according to manufacturers' specifications.

DAY 1
✳

THE ELIMINATION PHASE

ALLOWED FOODS:
Tapioca, lima beans, bananas, carrots, celery, parsley, lamb, mustard, cloves, olive oil, nutmeg, rosemary

MENU	REGULAR	DIET EXPRESS

BREAKFAST	Lima Bean Pancakes
	Banana Tapioca Cereal
	Banana-Carrot Breakfast
	  Pudding
	Lima Bread
	Clove Tea
		Banana Tapioca Cereal
		Banana-Carrot Breakfast
		  Pudding
		Clove Tea

SNACK	Carrot Juice Frappe	Carrot Juice Crunchy Limas
LUNCH	Minestrone Lamburgers	Quick Soup Brown-Bag Lamb Pâté
DINNER	Lamb Chops Herbed Lima Beans Shredded Carrot Salad with Mustard Dressing Baked Bananas with Carrot Syrup Banana Shake	Quick Lamb Stir-Fry Shredded Carrot Salad with Mustard Dressing Broiled Banana

BULK AGENT: None

*

R E G U L A R   T R A C K

BREAKFAST

Lima Bean Pancakes

*   SERVES 4

1 (10-ounce) package frozen lima beans (do not thaw)
1 teaspoon olive oil
1 cup (approximate) water
Olive oil for greasing skillet

Process the frozen lima beans 1 cup at a time in a blender or processor until they resemble cornmeal in texture about 1 minute. Scrape ground beans into a bowl. Add oil. Add enough water to make lima bean batter pourable but still thick. Grease a skillet thoroughly with oil. Heat the skillet until it is hot (beads of water will "dance" on a properly heated skillet). Using 2–3 tablespoons for each pancake, drop batter onto the hot skillet. Cook pancakes until lightly browned on one side, 2–3 minutes. Turn pancakes and brown on other side until cooked through, 1–2 minutes. Top with Beech-Nut Stage One bananas mixed with a dash of nutmeg.

Banana Tapioca Cereal

*   SERVES 4

²/₃ cup granulated quick-cooking tapioca
2½ cups water
2 large, ripe bananas, peeled and well mashed

Combine tapioca and water in a saucepan. Heat until boiling, stirring continually. Simmer 2 minutes over low heat. Stir in banana, cook over lowest heat 2 minutes more. Cool 15 minutes.

Banana-Carrot Breakfast Pudding

*   SERVES 4

4 jars Beech-Nut Stage One bananas
4 jars Beech-Nut Stage One carrots
2 bananas, peeled and sliced

Combine all ingredients. Can be served warm or chilled.

Lima Bread

✳ SERVES 4

1 (10 ounce) package frozen lima beans (do not thaw)
1 tablespoon olive oil
Sea salt (optional)
Water

Preheat oven to very hot, 500° F.

Process frozen limas in a food processor or blender (1 cup at a time) until beans are well ground. (They will be slightly flaky, roughly the texture of uncooked cornmeal.)

Place processed beans in a mixing bowl. Add oil, salt, if desired, and just enough water to bind beans. Do not add too much water, or bread will be mushy, more like bread pudding. Ideal batter is pourable, but thick.

Grease a cookie sheet with oil.

Spread batter in a thin, even layer on cookie sheet. Turn oven (gas or electric) to broil. Place cookie sheet about 6 inches from source of heat and broil bread until it begins to brown around the edges, about 5 minutes.

Immediately turn off stove. Leaving bread in oven, close door. Allow bread to "crisp" in cooling stove, about 15–20 minutes. Remove and serve. For a more textured, less crisp bread, remove bread immediately from stove after broiling.

Clove Tea

✳ SERVES 1

3 whole cloves
¼ teaspoon nutmeg
1 cup boiling water
Heinz banana flakes to taste

Place cloves and nutmeg in a small piece of cheesecloth. Gather edges of cloth and secure with threat to make a "tea bag." Steep in boiling water 2–4 minutes. Add dried banana flakes to sweeten.

❋

SNACK

Carrot Juice Frappe

❋   SERVES 1–2

½ cup crushed ice
1 (12-ounce) can plain carrot juice
2 medium bananas, peeled and sliced
¼ teaspoon nutmeg

Place all ingredients in a blender. Blend on highest speed 1 minute.

LUNCH

Minestrone

❋   SERVES 4

1 (10-ounce) package frozen lima beans
1 teaspoon chopped fresh parsley
3 stalks fresh celery, chopped
2 fresh carrots, pared and sliced
1 teaspoon olive oil
6 cups water
Sea salt to taste

Sauté beans, parsley, celery and carrots in olive oil 2 minutes. Add water and salt. Simmer 20–30 minutes, or until beans are tender.

MW—Heat (H) lima beans in ¼ cup water 5–9 minutes, until tender. Stir in remaining ingredients, except salt. Microwave (H) until hot, about 4–5 minutes more. Season to taste with sea salt.

Lamburgers

❋   SERVES 4

1 pound ground lamb (shaped into 3–4 patties)
¼ teaspoon each sea salt and ground rosemary

Preheat broiler.
   Sprinkle patties with sea salt and ground rosemary. Press seasoning into meat and broil 2 inches from heat 3–5 minutes, turning once.

MW—4 patties (H) 5–8 minutes

Turn patties halfway through cooking time and season after cooking with sea salt.

DINNER

Lamb Chops

✳   SERVES 4

4 loin or shoulder lamb chops
1 teaspoon ground rosemary
Sea salt to taste

Season chops lightly with rosemary. Broil thick chops 3–4 inches from heat, 3–5 minutes each side. Thin shoulder chops may be pan-broiled 2–3 minutes over high heat, turning once. Season with sea salt after broiling.

Herbed Lima Beans

✳   SERVES 4

1 (10-ounce) package frozen lima beans
Water
¼ cup minced fresh celery
1 tablespoon olive oil
½ cup minced fresh parsley
1 teaspoon ground rosemary
¾ teaspoon sea salt

Cook beans in 2 inches boiling water in covered pan 15 minutes over low heat. Drain and keep warm. Sauté celery in skillet in hot oil until tender but not browned. Add remaining ingredients, simmer, covered, 10 minutes. Toss beans with herb oil before serving.

Shredded Carrot Salad with Mustard Dressing

✳   SERVES 4

4–6 large fresh carrots
Mustard Dressing (recipe follows)

Pare and shred carrots to make about 3 cups shredded carrot. Toss with mustard dressing and serve.

Mustard Dressing

MAKES 1 CUP

2–3 teaspoons dry mustard
¼ cup water
¾ cup olive oil
Sea salt to taste
Fresh parsley, minced

Mix mustard with water. Add olive oil and mix well. Add sea salt and fresh, minced parsley to taste. Shake well before using or blend in a blender until smooth and thick.

Baked Bananas with Carrot Syrup

SERVES 4

2 large, ripe bananas, peeled
2 tablespoons grated, pared fresh carrots
2 tablespoons Beech-Nut Stage One bananas
2 tablespoons plain carrot juice
1 teaspoon grated nutmeg
Light olive oil

Preheat oven to 350° F.

Cut 4 pieces of foil, each 4×6 inches. Cut bananas in half lengthwise, and place each half on a piece of foil. In a small bowl, mix the grated carrots, Beech-Nut Stage One bananas, carrot juice and nutmeg and spoon over the banana halves. Sprinkle bananas VERY LIGHTLY with olive oil. Place on a baking sheet and bake 5–8 minutes; if bananas are really ripe, they will cook in about 5 minutes.

MW—Prepare bananas as above, but use plastic wrap or waxed paper instead of aluminum foil. Microwave (H) 2–3 minutes.

Banana Shake

SERVES 1

1 jar Beech-Nut Stage One bananas
4 ounces cold mineral water
Nutmeg (optional)

Mix bananas and mineral water. Sprinkle with nutmeg if desired.

DIET EXPRESS

BREAKFAST

Banana Tapioca Cereal
(See Breakfast, Regular Track)
✳

Banana-Carrot Breakfast Pudding
(See Breakfast, Regular Track)
✳

Clove Tea
(See Breakfast, Regular Track)
✳

SNACK

Carrot Juice
✳
SERVES 1

> *6–8 ounces plain carrot juice, chilled*
> *Heinz banana flakes to taste*
> *2 ounces mineral water, chilled*

In a tall glass, mix carrot juice with banana flakes until juice is sweetened to taste. Add mineral water and stir briskly to produce a frothy blend.

Crunchy Limas*
✳
SERVES 1

> *1 (10-ounce) package frozen lima beans or butter beans*

MW—Rinse the frozen beans briefly under cold water until they are separated. Drain in a colander and dry completely on paper towels. Spread ½ cup limas on a dry microwave-safe paper towel and place

✳

them on a dish or platter. Microwave (H) 10 minutes, until limas are crunchy. Rotate dish every 2 minutes, unless microwave oven has a carousel, self-rotating dish.

*Note: To prepare more servings (see Day Twenty-one, Snack, Regular Track), repeat procedure for each serving.

LUNCH

Quick Soup

✳
SERVES 1

½ cup thawed frozen lima beans
1 jar Beech-Nut Stage One carrots
½ cup thawed frozen sliced carrots
1 tablespoon water
1 jar Beech-Nut Stage One lamb
Sea salt to taste
Hot water or plain carrot juice

MW—In a microwave-safe dish, cook (H) lima beans and carrots in 1 tablespoon water 5–8 minutes. Stir in lamb. Microwave (H) until hot (about 2 minutes). Season to taste with sea salt and thin with water or carrot juice as desired.

Brown-Bag Lamb Pâté

✳
SERVES 1

1–2 jars Beech-Nut Stage One lamb
1 teaspoon olive oil
Dry mustard
Sea salt
2 stalks fresh celery, cut in sticks
1–2 fresh carrots, pared and cut into sticks

Blend lamb with oil to make a smooth pâté. Season pâté to taste with dry mustard and sea salt. Chill. Serve with stalks of fresh celery and carrot sticks.

DINNER

Quick Lamb Stir-Fry

✻   SERVES 1–2

  ¾ pound fresh lamb (uncooked) from leg or shoulder chops
  1 tablespoon olive oil
  1 (10-ounce) package frozen sliced carrots
  2 stalks fresh celery, chopped
  1 teaspoon sea salt
  1 teaspoon dry mustard
  1 teaspoon ground rosemary

Cut lamb into slivers and sauté in oil over medium heat for 2 minutes. Add vegetables and seasoning. Simmer, covered, for 5–10 minutes. Stir, correct seasonings and serve.

Shredded Carrot Salad
(See Dinner, Regular Track)

✻

Mustard Dressing
(See Dinner, Regular Track)

✻

Broiled Banana

✻   SERVES 1–2

  1 ripe banana, unpeeled
  Nutmeg
  Heinz banana flakes
  Light olive oil

Slice banana lengthwise, do not peel. Sprinkle with nutmeg, banana flakes and oil. Broil 4–6 inches from heat until surface of banana "carmelizes" (begins to brown). Serve.

NIGHT-BEFORE PREPARATION TIPS
FOR DAY 2

1. Make Peach Sorbet: Allowing 1 jar per serving, empty as many jars Beech-Nut Stage One peaches as you think you will need into a freezer container with a lid. Freeze overnight to use as instant sorbet in beverages or desserts. As dessert, allow to soften 15 minutes in the refrigerator before serving as sorbet.

2. If you wish, you may soak 1 pound of dried white navy beans overnight, for use in Autumn Soup.

DAY

2

THE ELIMINATION PHASE

ALLOWED FOODS:
Rice, potatoes, coconut, peaches, artichokes, white navy beans, rhubarb, squash, alfalfa sprouts, turnips, veal, cinnamon, Puritan oil, sage, gelatin

MENU	REGULAR	DIET EXPRESS
BREAKFAST	Fresh Coconut Hot Cream of Rice Cereal or Beech-Nut Stage One Rice Cereal Potato Pancakes Peach-Rice Pancakes Cinnamon Stick Tea	Fresh Coconut Rice Cereal with Peaches Cinnamon Stick Tea
SNACK	Rice Cakes Cinnamon-Peach Shake	Rice Cakes Peach Spritzer
LUNCH	Autumn Soup Vealburgers Risotto with Vegetables Coconut-Peach Dessert Quick Peach Whip Peachy Iced Tea	Veal Pâté on Rice Cakes Fresh Coconut with Peach Sauce Peachy Iced Tea

DINNER	Veal Chops with Jerusalem
	  Artichokes
	Baked Acorn Squash
	Boiled Rice
	Alfalfa Sprout-Rhubarb Salad
	with "Mayo" Dressing
	Peach Sorbet
		Veal Chops with Jerusalem
		  Artichokes
		Sweet and Sour Squash
		Quick Rice
		Fresh Fruit Cocktail

BULK AGENT: Rice bran

REGULAR TRACK

BREAKFAST

Fresh Coconut
✳   SERVES 4

1 medium coconut

Using a hammer, split a medium-size ripe coconut in half. Discard the liquid inside; this is not coconut milk. (Naturally occurring coconut milk comes from green coconuts.) Score the ripe coconut meat with a sharp knife and break off pieces from each half of the hard coconut shell. Serve raw, or shred as needed in today's recipes.

Coconut Milk

After sectioning a ripe coconut as above, remove coconut meat from pieces of hard shell. Chop meat into bite-size pieces and then place in bowl or large measuring cup. Cover meat with 2 cups boiling water. Cover the bowl or measuring cup and allow the coconut to stand at least 20 minutes. Strain and chill the resulting "milk" for use during the day. Makes 2 cups.

MW—Chop coconut. Microwave (H), covered, in ¾ cup water until boiling. Stir, cover and microwave (M) 10 minutes, stirring every 5 minutes. Strain.

Note: Canned unsweetened coconut milk is available at most Thai grocery stores in 12-ounce or 14-ounce size. One good brand is Stanfood.

Hot Cream of Rice Cereal
✳   SERVES 4

2 cups water or coconut milk (see recipe above)
Dash sea salt
⅓ cup plain farina cereal (cream of rice)
Cinnamon (optional)

Salt water or milk and heat to boiling. Add cereal slowly, stirring constantly. Return to boil, reduce heat and cook until desired thick-

✳

ness. Sprinkle with cinnamon, if desired. Serve with fresh, sliced peaches, Heinz peach flakes, or Beech-Nut Stage One strained peaches.

MW—Combine water and cereal (do not add salt) in a 4-cup container. Cover and cook (H) 2–3 minutes until boiling. Stir, cover and microwave (L) 2–3 minutes more, or until cereal is thickened.

Beech-Nut Stage One Rice Dry Cereal

✳   SERVES 1

Make desired amount of cereal by adding Coconut Milk (see recipe above) or water to achieve preferred thickness. Sweeten to taste with Beech-Nut Stage One peaches or Heinz peach flakes. Sprinkle with cinnamon, if desired. Can be served hot or cold.

Potato Pancakes

✳   SERVES 4–6

*2 cups plain potato meal or equivalent amount raw
     potatoes, peeled, grated and well drained*
Dash sea salt
½ cup potato starch flour
2 teaspoons Puritan oil plus oil for greasing skillet
2 cups water (approximate)

If using potato meal, sift dry ingredients together and place them in a mixing bowl. Stir in oil and add water until batter is thick but pourable. (If using fresh potatoes, stir salt, potato starch flour and oil evenly into grated potatoes and add water until mixture holds together.) Grease a skillet with oil. Heat skillet until it is hot but not smoking. Using 2–3 tablespoons for each pancake, drop batter onto hot skillet. Cook pancakes until browned on one side (about 2–3 minutes). Turn and brown until cooked through, 2–3 minutes more. Top with Beech-Nut Stage One peaches.

Peach-Rice Pancakes

✳   SERVES 4

2 cups plain rice-cake crumbs (about 4 large cakes)
½ cup Heinz peach flakes
1 tablespoon Puritan oil plus oil for greasing skillet
Water

Place rice-cake crumbs in a large mixing bowl. Add peach flakes and oil to rice-cake crumbs. Stir in enough water to make a thick, muffin-like batter.

Grease a skillet with Puritan oil. Heat the skillet over medium-high heat until it is hot but not smoking. For each pancake, drop batter (2–3 tablespoons) onto hot skillet. Flatten and spread slightly with a spatula to form a medium-sized pancake. Cook until one side of cake is crisp and brown (about 2–3 minutes). Turn the cake and brown until it is crisp and can be lifted easily from the skillet. Top pancakes with Beech-Nut Stage One peaches.

Cinnamon Stick Tea

✳   SERVES 1

> 1 cinnamon stick
> 6–8 ounces boiling water
> Heinz peach flakes

Break the cinnamon stick into several pieces and steep them for 3–4 minutes in an 8-ounce mug of water. Remove pieces of cinnamon stick and sweeten to taste with Heinz peach flakes.

SNACK

Rice Cakes

✳

Cinnamon-Peach Shake

✳   SERVES 1

> 1 jar Beech-Nut Stage One peaches
> ½ cup chunks peeled, ripe fresh peaches or 4 ounces plain
>   frozen peaches such as Big Valley brand
> ¼ cup Coconut Milk (see Breakfast, Regular Track)
> ¼ teaspoon ground cinnamon
> 1 ice cube, crushed

Place all ingredients in blender or processor and blend until smooth.

＊

LUNCH

Microwave conversion tips for cooking soups:

1) Reduce liquid by one fourth (except when cooking dried peas, beans, rice or lentils).
2) Reduce salt and seasoning by one half. Correct seasoning after cooking.
3) Cut dense vegetables (carrots, potatoes, etc.) in thin slices or cubes. Cube less tender meats.
4) Cook milk-based soups in deep containers to avoid boil-overs.

Autumn Soup

＊ SERVES 4–6

1 pound dried white navy beans
Water to cover
3 quarts cold water
2–3 meaty veal bones (rib or neck)
1 cup frozen turnips
1 cup fresh or frozen rhubarb chunks
Beech-Nut Stage One veal (optional)
Sea salt to taste
Ground sage to taste

Pick over and wash beans. Cover with water in a large pot or kettle and boil beans 2 minutes. Remove from heat, cover, and soak 1 hour before cooking. (Beans may also be soaked in cold water to cover overnight.) Rinse beans and place in pot with 3 quarts cold water and veal bones. Bring to boil and add vegetables. Simmer over very low heat or in preheated 200°F. oven (covered) 4 hours. Skim soup. Cut meat from bones and add to soup. Thicken with Beech-Nut Stage One veal, if desired. Season soup to taste with sea salt and ground sage.

Vealburgers

＊ SERVES 4

1 pound ground veal
1 teaspoon ground sage
Puritan oil
Sea salt

Mix ground veal with sage (¼ teaspoon per burger) into 4 patties. Drizzle lightly with oil. Grease a skillet lightly with oil and heat until hot. Pan-broil patties over medium heat, 3–5 minutes each side. Season to taste with sea salt. Serve with rice cakes and Risotto with Vegetables (below).

(If desired, make a quick "gravy" by stirring 1 jar Beech-Nut Stage One veal into pan juices left after broiling. Season to taste with sea salt (thin with water if desired) and pour over rice.

Risotto with Vegetables*

SERVES 4

4 tablespoons Puritan oil
1 stalk fresh rhubarb, scrubbed and minced
1 cup arborio rice
3 cups water
1 turnip, trimmed, peeled and coarsely chopped
1 Jerusalem artichoke, scrubbed, trimmed and thinly sliced
1 yellow squash, scrubbed, trimmed and coarsely chopped
2 teaspoons ground sage
Sea salt to taste

*Preparing this recipe in a microwave oven is particularly recommended; texture of cooked short-grain rice is enhanced by the microwave process, and minimal stirring is required. To prepare the rice by conventional methods, follow package directions, using water, Puritan oil and sea salt.

MW—In a 10-inch microwave-safe casserole or soufflé dish, stir oil and rhubarb together and cook (H) about 3 minutes. Add rice and stir to coat with oil. Cook (H) 3–4 minutes more. Add water, stir, and cook uncovered about 9 minutes (H). Add turnip, artichoke, squash and sage, stir and cook uncovered (H) 9 minutes. Remove casserole from the oven and allow to stand uncovered for 5–8 minutes, until rice has absorbed liquid in the casserole. Stir, salt to taste and serve.

Coconut-Peach Dessert

SERVES 4

1 envelope Knox unflavored gelatin
¼ cup cold water
1 cup boiling water
2 jars Beech-Nut Stage One peaches
1 cup chopped fresh or frozen peaches
½ cup shredded unsweetened fresh coconut (shell removed; optional; see Breakfast, Regular Track)

Soften 1 envelope Knox unflavored gelatin by sprinkling gelatin over ¼ cup cold water and allowing it to stand 1 minute. Add 1 cup boiling water and stir until gelatin is dissolved. Add 2 jars Beech-Nut Stage One peaches. Stir thoroughly. Chill until consistency of unbeaten egg white. Add 1 cup chopped fresh or frozen peaches and, if desired, ½ cup shredded fresh coconut. Stir and chill until set.

Quick Peach Whip

SERVES 4

1 envelope Knox unflavored gelatin
½ cup cold water
2 jars Beech-Nut Stage One peaches
1 cup chopped fresh or frozen peaches (optional)
¾ cup shredded unsweetened fresh Coconut, shell removed;
*   optional; see Breakfast, Regular Track)*

In a small, deep saucepan, soften 1 envelope Knox unflavored gelatin by sprinkling gelatin over ¼ cup cold water and allowing it to stand 1 minute. Beating with electric or hand beater, bring gelatin to boil, adding remaining ¼ cup water a few drops at a time. Remove from heat and continue beating until light and fluffy. Combine with 2 jars Beech-Nut Stage One peaches. If desired, stir in chopped peaches and top with shredded coconut. Serve at once.

Peachy Iced Tea

SERVES 1

Mix 1 jar Beech-Nut Stage One peaches with ¾ cup strong Cinnamon Stick Tea (see Day Eight, Breakfast, Regular Track, for recipe). Pour over ice.

DINNER

Veal Chops with Jerusalem Artichokes

SERVES 4

2 large Jerusalem artichokes, scrubbed
4 tablespoons Puritan oil
Sea salt
Fresh or ground sage
4 large veal chops
1–2 tablespoons water

Slice artichokes thinly (do not peel). In 2 tablespoons oil, sauté artichokes until tender, stirring often, 5 minutes. Transfer to bowl, sprinkle with sea salt and crushed fresh or ground sage. Keep warm.

In same skillet, heat remaining oil and brown chops on both sides (2 minutes each side). Add artichokes, cover and cook over low heat until chops are tender, about 25 minutes. Remove chops from pan. Add 1–2 tablespoons water to pan and heat, scraping loose all brown particles. Pour over chops and serve.

MW—Place sliced artichokes uncovered in browning dish (or 1-quart microwave casserole) with 2 tablespoons oil. Microwave (H) 4–6 minutes, stirring after 2–3 minutes. Remove artichokes from dish and season with sage, but not salt. Add remaining 2 tablespoons oil to browning dish, add 2 chops and microwave (H) uncovered 2 minutes. Turn chops over and microwave (H) 2 minutes more. Remove and keep warm. Repeat with remaining 2 chops. Place all 4 chops in a large microwave casserole, add artichokes and 2 tablespoons water. Microwave (L) loosely covered 5 minutes. Turn chops, stir artichokes and microwave (L) 5–8 minutes, until chops are barely pink when cut with a knife, and artichokes are tender. Season to taste with sea salt.

Baked Acorn Squash

✳   SERVES 4

2 acorn squash
4 teaspoons Puritan oil
Ground cinnamon
Sea salt

Preheat oven to 350° F.

Cut 2 acorn squash in half and spoon out and discard seeds. Arrange halves, cut side up, in baking dish. Drop 1 teaspoon oil into each half. Sprinkle each half lightly with cinnamon and pinch of sea salt. Bake 40 minutes or until tender when pierced with fork.

MW—Prepare squash as above, omitting salt. Place on microwave-safe baking dish. Cover with waxed paper or plastic wrap, leaving vent, and microwave (H) 7–10 minutes or until squash halves are tender. Season with sea salt.

Boiled Rice

* S E R V E S   4

2 cups water
1 tablespoon Puritan oil
Sea salt
1 cup rice

Bring water, oil and a pinch of sea salt to boil in saucepan. Add rice, stir, cover and cook over hot water or very low heat 15–20 minutes.

Note: Minute brand or supermarket generic brand quick rices may also be used. Make according to package directions, using Puritan oil and sea salt.

Alfalfa Sprout-Rhubarb Salad with "Mayo" Dressing

* S E R V E S   4

½ cup fresh or frozen rhubarb chunks
Water to cover
2 cups alfalfa sprouts (washed and dried)
1 Jerusalem artichoke, scrubbed and sliced
"Mayo" Dressing (recipe follows)
Sea salt

Place ½ cup fresh or frozen rhubarb chunks in saucepan. Add water to cover and simmer until tender, 8–10 minutes.

MW—Place rhubarb in shallow bowl with 2 tablespoons water. Microwave (H) 2 minutes.
   To make rhubarb vinegar, remove rhubarb from pan, reserving cooking water. To make a mock vinegar of juice left from cooking the rhubarb, mince or press rhubarb to extract as much juice as possible and add the juice to the reserved cooking liquid. Add sea salt to taste. Reserve cooked rhubarb and rhubarb "vinegar."
   Combine alfalfa sprouts, sliced Jerusalem artichoke and reserved cooked rhubarb in a salad bowl. Chill while preparing "mayo" dressing. Toss chilled salad ingredients with dressing. Correct seasoning to taste and serve.

"Mayo" Dressing

✳   MAKES 1–1½ CUPS

1 envelope Knox unflavored gelatin
½ cup cold water
⅓ cup (approximate) Puritan oil
¼ cup rhubarb "vinegar" (reserved from Alfalfa Sprout-
*   Rhubarb Salad above)*
Sea salt

In a small, deep saucepan, soften 1 envelope Knox unflavored gelatin by sprinkling gelatin over ¼ cup cold water and allowing it to stand 1 minute. Beating with electric or hand beater, bring gelatin to boil, adding ¼ cup more water a few drops at a time. Remove from heat and continue beating until light and fluffy. Add Puritan oil, a few drops at a time, until whip is consistency of mayonnaise. Add rhubarb "vinegar" and sea salt to taste.

Peach Sorbet
(See Night-Before Preparaton Tips for Day Two)

✳

DIET EXPRESS

BREAKFAST

Fresh Coconut
(See Breakfast, Regular Track)

✳

Rice Cereal with Peaches

✳

1 cup puffed rice cereal or ½ cup Beech-Nut Stage One rice
*   cereal*
Coconut Milk (see Breakfast, Regular Track)
Beech-Nut Stage One peaches, Heinz peach flakes or 1 fresh
*   peach, washed, and chopped*

Mix puffed rice cereal or Beech-Nut cereal with coconut milk and peaches until cereal is desired consistency and sweetened to taste.

✳

Cinnamon Stick Tea
(See Breakfast, Regular Track)

✳

SNACK

Rice Cakes

✳

Beech-Nut Stage One peaches
2 large plain rice cakes

Spread peaches on rice cakes as desired.

Peach Spritzer

✳   SERVES 1

1 jar Beech-Nut Stage One peaches
4–6 ounces chilled mineral water
Heinz peach flakes
Crushed ice or 1 ice cube

Combine peaches with mineral water. Sweeten to taste with Heinz peach flakes. Serve over ice. (Blend in blender for a thicker drink.)

LUNCH

Veal Pâté on Rice Cakes

✳   SERVES 1

1 jar Beech-Nut Stage One veal
1 teaspoon Puritan oil
Sea salt
Ground sage
Plain rice cakes or plain rice crackers

Combine veal with oil. Season to taste with salt and sage and chill if possible, to blend flavors. Spread on rice cakes or crackers.

Fresh Coconut with Peach Sauce

✳ SERVES 1

⅓ cup (approximate) Heinz peach flakes
Water or Coconut Milk (see Breakfast, Regular Track)
¼ teaspoon ground cinnamon
1 cup chunks Fresh Coconut (shell removed; see Breakfast,
*   Regular Track)*

Mix Heinz peach flakes with water or coconut milk and cinnamon until of desired sweetness and consistency for dipping. Chill or heat sauce as desired and serve as dip with chunks of coconut. Note: Use 1 jar Beech-Nut Stage One peaches as sauce, heated or chilled, if you prefer. Omit peach flakes and water. Add cinnamon to taste, as above.

Peachy Iced Tea
(See Lunch, Regular Track)

✳

DINNER

Veal Chops with Jerusalem Artichokes
(See Dinner, Regular Track)

Sweet and Sour Squash

✳ SERVES 1

1–2 jars Beech-Nut Stage One squash
1 teaspoon frozen, minced rhubarb
2 teaspoons Beech-Nut Stage One peaches
¼ teaspoon ground cinnamon

MW—Empty squash into a microwave-safe bowl. Stir in minced rhubarb, peaches and cinnamon. Cover loosely and microwave (H) 1 minute or until hot. Stir, correct seasonings and microwave (H) until hot.

✻

Quick Rice

✻

1 cup water
Dash sea salt
1 teaspoon Puritan oil
1 cup quick-cooking plain rice

Bring water, salt and oil to boil in small, deep saucepan. Add rice (in equal amount to water used), stir and remove from heat. Cover and allow to stand 5 minutes. Fluff with a fork and serve.

Fresh Fruit Cocktail

✻

4 ounces frozen sliced peaches or 1 fresh peach, sliced
4 ounces Fresh Coconut (see Breakfast, Regular Track),
*   shell removed, cut into chunks*
3 teaspoons Heinz peach flakes
¼ teaspoon ground cinnamon
¼ cup (approximate) mineral water

Combine peaches and coconut in a bowl. Sprinkle with peach flakes and cinnamon. Add mineral water to moisten. If using fresh peaches, chill in freezer 5 minutes before serving.

NIGHT-BEFORE PREPARATION TIPS
FOR DAY 3

1. To make Instant Hot Millet Cereal in the morning, parboil raw millet: Bring 1 cup water to a boil in a small saucepan. Stir in ½ cup raw, washed millet. Simmer 10 minutes, covered, stirring occasionally. Remove from heat, transfer to a container with a cover, and refrigerate overnight.

MW—Combine ½ cup raw, washed millet and 1 cup water in a microwave container with a cover. Bring to boil (H) 2–3 minutes. Stir, re-cover and microwave (L) 10 minutes more, stirring after 5 minutes. Stir, cover and refrigerate.

2. Make On-the-Double Pear Sorbet: Allowing 1 jar per serving, empty as many jars Beech-Nut Stage One pears as you think you will need into a freezer container with a lid. Freeze overnight to use as instant sorbet in beverages or desserts. As dessert, allow to soften 15 minutes in the refrigerator before serving as sorbet.

DAY **3** THE ELIMINATION PHASE
✳

ALLOWED FOODS:
Millet, potato starch, amaranth, lentils, pears, cucumbers,
green beans, zucchini, yellow squash, tuna fish, whitefish,
salmon, mint, safflower oil, basil, honey

MENU	REGULAR	DIET EXPRESS
BREAKFAST	Pear Juice	Pear Juice
	Millet Breakfast Pudding	Puffed Millet Cereal with Fresh
	Amaranth Pancakes	Pears
	Mint Tea	or Instant Hot Millet Cereal
		Mint Tea
SNACK	Cucumber-Mint Frappe	Pear Shake
LUNCH	Grilled Fresh Tuna	Brown-Bag Six-Hour Salad
	Zucchini Soup	Fresh Pear
	Pear Iced Tea Special	Pear Iced Tea Special
DINNER	Stuffed Sole	Broiled Whitefish
	Cucumber Salad	Green Bean Purée
	Zucchini Dressing	Fresh Zucchini Sticks
	Pear Spritzer	On-the-Double Pear Sorbet
	Baked Pears	or Pear Float

BULK AGENT: None

REGULAR TRACK

BREAKFAST

Pear juice
Not nectar; pure juice such as After the Fall brand
✳

Note: If you cannot find pure pear juice for today's recipes, thin 1 jar
Beech-Nut Stage One pears with 4 ounces water as a substitute (yields
8 ounces pear juice).

✳

Millet Breakfast Pudding

✳
SERVES 4

½ cup raw millet
1½ cups water
¼ teaspoon sea salt
¼ cup honey
½ cup chopped fresh pears
Safflower oil for greasing pan

Preheat oven to 350°F. Bring millet, water and salt to a boil in a saucepan. Remove from heat and add honey and pears. Pour into a 1-quart casserole or pie plate greased with oil. Cover and bake one-half hour. Serve warm.

Amaranth Pancakes

✳
SERVES 4

2 cups amaranth flour*
2 cups (approximate) water
1 tablespoon safflower oil plus oil for greasing skillet

Mix the amaranth flour, water and oil together until a smooth, thick but pourable batter is formed. Thoroughly grease a skillet with oil. Heat the skillet over medium-high heat until it is hot but not smoking.

Using ½ cup for each pancake, pour the batter onto hot skillet. Cook pancake until bubbles appear on surface and underneath side is browned, about 1 minute. Turn and cook until other side is browned and pancake is cooked through, about 1 minute more. Top with honey or Beech-Nut Stage One pears.

*Amaranth flour behaves very much like wheat flour in this recipe. If you cannot find amaranth flour, grind 2–3 cups dry lentils in a processor until ground into flour. Sift the lentil flour twice before using to ensure a smooth-textured pancake. When you have ground and sifted enough dry lentils to make 2 cups flour, proceed with recipe as above. Top with honey or Beech-Nut Stage One pears.

Mint Tea

✳
SERVES 1

1 teabag commerical mint herbal tea
1 cup boiling water
honey to taste

Steep teabag in boiling water. Sweeten with honey to taste.

✳

SNACK

Cucumber-Mint Frappe

✳ SERVES 1

1 fresh cucumber, peeled, halved and seeded
4 leaves fresh mint
2–3 teaspoons honey
1 ice cube, crushed
Heinz pear flakes (optional)

Purée cucumber in blender or processor until smooth. Add 3 mint leaves, honey and ice and purée again until smooth. Garnish with remaining mint leaf. Correct sweetness with additional honey or Heinz pear flakes if desired.

LUNCH

Grilled Fresh Tuna

✳ SERVES 4

2 (½ pound) tuna steaks, each 1 inch thick
½ cup safflower oil
½ teaspoon sea salt

Marinate steaks 1 hour or more in a mixture of oil and salt.
    Preheat barbecue or broiler.
    Grill tuna over charcoal or in broiler 6 inches from source of heat, basting well with oil marinade. Cook a total of 8–10 minutes, turning once.

MW—Brush steaks with oil. Arrange in microwave baking dish with thickest parts to outside of dish. Microwave for a total of 5 minutes per ½ pound of fish. Turn over after half of cooking time. Let stand 2 minutes. Note: For moist fish, cover with waxed paper while cooking. For drier surface, elevate on rack in baking dish and do not cover.

Zucchini Soup

SERVES 4

6 small fresh zucchini, trimmed and cubed or shredded or 1
    (20-ounce) bag frozen chopped zucchini
Sea salt
3 tablespoons safflower oil
1½ cups water
2 jars Beech-Nut Stage One green beans
2 tablespoons crushed fresh basil

Place zucchini in a colander, sprinkle with salt and allow to drain for about 20 minutes, reserving liquid. In a large soup pot or Dutch oven, sauté zucchini in oil 5 minutes. Add reserved water, 1½ cups additional water, simmer 10 minutes. Purée in a blender or food processor. Return half the purée to pot; refrigerate remaining for use at dinner (see Zucchini Dressing, Regular Track). Add green beans to purée in pot. Season to taste with sea salt and basil. Reheat over medium heat until hot. This soup can also be served cold.

MW—In a large, microwave-safe casserole, cook (H) zucchini in oil 1 minute. Stir, microwave 1 minute more. Cook (L), covered, 5 minutes. Stir. Cook (L) 4 minutes. Purée and continue as above, reheating (H) in microwave oven ½ minute.

Pear Iced Tea Special

SERVES 1

6 ounces strongly brewed commercial mint herbal tea
4 ounces plain pear juice
Honey to taste
Crushed ice
1 sprig fresh mint
1 (2-ounce) scoop On-the-Double Pear Sorbet (see Night-
    Before Preparation Tips for Day Three)

Mix tea with pear juice. Sweeten to taste with honey and pour over ice. Garnish with a spring of fresh mint and a scoop of pear sorbet.

DINNER

Stuffed Sole

*8 skinless fillets of sole (or other lean whitefish), each
     approximately the same size, about 1¼ pounds total
     weight*
Sea salt to taste plus 1 teaspoon
1 cup cooked millet*
1 tablespoon potato starch flour
4 tablespoons safflower oil
*10 ounces fresh zucchini, chopped or 1 (10-ounce) package
     frozen chopped zucchini*
¼ cup water

Preheat broiler.

Place 4 fillets, skinned side up, on a flat surface. Sprinkle with sea salt.

Blend millet, potato starch and ½ teaspoon salt in a bowl. Center equal portions of this filling on top of fillets placed on a flat surface. Smooth the filling over the fillets, leaving a slight margin around it.

Sprinkle remaining fillets with remaining ½ teaspoon salt. Arrange them, skinned side down, over the filling. Press lightly around the sides

Rub the bottom of a flameproof baking dish with half the oil. Arrange stuffed fish over it. Scatter zucchini around the fish. Brush fillets and zuccchini with remaining safflower oil. Add ¼ cup water.

Place under broiler about 7–8 inches from heat. Broil, but watch closely to prevent burning. Turn baking dish so that the fish and zucchini broil evenly. Total broiling time is about 6–8 minutes. (If, during broiling time, liquid in dish completely cooks away, add a little water.

MW—Prepare fish as above, omitting all salt, in a 14-inch microwave glass or ceramic baking dish. Cover and cook (H) 8 minutes. Fish is done when white and opaque. Separate flakes near center with a fork to test that it is fully cooked. Do not overcook. Sprinkle with salt after cooking.

*To make cooked millet: Add ½ cup millet to 1 teaspoon safflower oil in a skillet. Toast gently over low heat until millet is golden. Remove from heat. Bring 1 cup water to boil in a deep saucepan, add ½ teaspoon more oil, add millet and stir thoroughly. Cover and simmer over low heat until water is absorbed, 15–20 minutes.

Cucumber Salad

SERVES 4

2 medium, fresh cucumbers
Zucchini Dressing (recipe follows)

Pare and slice cucumber and place in a salad bowl. Toss with zucchini dressing and serve.

Zucchini Dressing

MAKES ABOUT 1 CUP

¾ cup zucchini purée (reserved from Zucchini Soup, Lunch,
    Regular Track)
⅓ cup safflower oil
Ground basil
Sea salt

Combine reserved zucchini purée and ⅓ cup safflower oil. Season to taste with basil and sea salt. Blend in a blender until thick and smooth.

Pear Spritzer

SERVES 1

6 ounces plain pear juice
1 teaspoon honey
2 ounces sparkling mineral water
Crushed Ice
1 sprig fresh mint

Mix pear juice with honey. Stir in 2 ounces sparkling mineral water and pour over ice. Garnish with a sprig of fresh mint.

Baked Pears

SERVES 4

2 large fresh pears, halved and cored
Safflower oil for greasing pan plus 1 tablespoon oil

1 tablespoon crushed fresh mint
4 teaspoons honey

Preheat oven to 350°F.
Place pear halves cavity side up in a baking dish greased with safflower oil. Mix mint and honey. Place a teaspoon in each pear cavity. Sprinkle lightly with remaining 1 tablespoon safflower oil.
Bake 30 minutes, until tender when pierced with a fork, and lightly browned on top.

MW—Prepare pears as above. Microwave (H), covered, 10–15 minutes, re-arranging pears in dish after ½ cooking time.

DIET EXPRESS

BREAKFAST

Pear Juice
(See Breakfast, Regular Track)

✳

Puffed Millet Cereal with Fresh Pears

SERVES 1

✳

1 cup puffed millet cereal
1 jar Beech-Nut Stage One pears
Water or plain pear juice
1 fresh pear, washed, but not peeled
Honey to taste (optional)

Pour puffed millet into a bowl. Thin Beech-Nut Stage One pears with a little water or plain pear juice and pour over cold cereal. Slice pear and add to cereal. Sweeten with honey, if desired.

Instant Hot Millet Cereal

SERVES 1

✳

½ cup parboiled millet (see Night-Before Preparation Tips
    for Day Three)
¼ cup (approximate) water or plain pear juice
Honey to taste

Combine parboiled millet and liquid and heat to boiling. Add more water or pear juice to moisten if cereal seems dry and continue cooking (stirring occasionally) over low heat until millet is tender, about 5–10 minutes, depending on "crunchiness" desired. Add honey to taste. Top with sliced fresh pear.

MW—Heat (H) parboiled millet until hot, 1–2 minutes. Stir in ⅓ cup water or pear juice. Continue cooking (L) covered until millet is tender, 5–10 minutes. Add honey to taste. Top with sliced fresh pear.

Mint Tea
(See Breakfast, Regular Track)

SNACK

Pear Shake

SERVES 1

1 ripe fresh pear or 1 jar Beech-nut Stage One pears
¼ cup plain pear juice
1 ice cube, crushed
1–2 teaspoons honey
2 leaves fresh, mint, crushed
1 sprig fresh mint plus 1 sprig for garnish (optional)

Peel and core a fresh, ripe pear and chop it into chunks. Place in a blender with pear juice, ice cube, honey and crushed fresh mint. Blend 30 seconds at highest speed. Add a fresh sprig of mint for garnish, if desired.

LUNCH

Brown-Bag Six-Hour Salad

SERVES 1

½ cup chopped fresh green beans (washed and trimmed) or
  ½ cup chopped frozen green beans
Sea salt
Ground basil

1 small fresh zucchini, scrubbed and sliced
1 (3-ounce) can water-pack salmon, drained and well
    picked over for cartilage and bone
1 small chopped fresh yellow summer squash (washed)
1 jar Beech-Nut Stage One green beans
1 tablespoon safflower oil

Line the bottom of a plastic or well-chilled thermal container with the beans. Sprinkle with sea salt and basil. Add one layer each of zucchini, salmon and squash, sprinkling each layer very lightly with salt and basil.

Mix Beech-Nut Stage One green beans with safflower oil, and salt and basil to taste. Spread over top of salad and refrigerate until lunchtime. Toss just before eating.

Note: Pack puffed millet cereal in a plastic bag to toss on top of salad for a crunchy topping.

Pear Iced Tea Special
(See Lunch, Regular Track)

✳

DINNER

Broiled Whitefish
✳   SERVES 1

4–6 ounces whitefish such as sole, flounder or perch, filleted
1 teaspoon safflower oil
Ground basil and sea salt to taste

Preheat broiler. Drizzle fillets with oil and sprinkle with basil. Broil 4–6 inches from heat, 2–3 minutes each side. Correct seasoning after cooking with sea salt to taste.

Green Bean Pureé
✳   SERVES 1

2 jars Beech-Nut Stage One green beans
Sea salt to taste

In a small saucepan, heat 2 jars Beech-Nut Stage One green beans with sea salt to taste. Serve as side dish.

MW—Remove lids from jars. Heat (H) 15 seconds. Watch for boil-overs unless you remove the beans to a larger microwave-safe bowl or casserole.

Fresh Zucchini Sticks

✳   SERVES 1

1 medium fresh zucchini
Sea salt to taste

Scrub a medium-size zucchini, trim it and cut into strips. Sprinkle with sea salt.

On-the-Double Pear Sorbet

✳   SERVES 1

Soften frozen Beech-Nut Stage One pears (see Night-Before Prepara-tion Tips for Day Three) in refrigerator 10–15 minutes before eating. Sprinkle with crushed fresh mint if desired for extra flavor.

Pear Float

✳   SERVES 1

Add 1 tablespoon sorbet to a tall glass containing 6 ounces of plain pear juice (see Pear Juice, Breakfast, Regular Track) and 2 ounces of sparkling mineral water. Garnish with a sprig of fresh mint.

NIGHT-BEFORE PREPARATION TIPS
——— FOR DAY 4 ———

1. For "instant" hot kasha cereal in the morning: Place ½ cup raw, washed and picked over kasha in a dish with a cover. Add 1 cup boiling water, stir, cover and refrigerate overnight. In the morning, reheat the kasha to boiling, adding a little water or plain apple juice to moisten. (Kasha will have absorbed water overnight.) On Day Four, use for Diet Express breakfast.

2. Make Apple Sorbet: Allowing 1 jar per serving, empty as many jars Beech-Nut Stage One applesauce as you think you will need into a freezer container with a lid. Freeze overnight to use as instant sorbet in beverages or desserts. As dessert, allow to soften 15 minutes in the refrigerator before serving as sorbet.

DAY 4

THE ELIMINATION PHASE

ALLOWED FOODS:
kasha, chick-peas, apples, beets, celery, spinach, bamboo
shoots, sweet potatoes, pork, lamb, oregano, ginger,
sesame, carob

MENU	REGULAR	DIET EXPRESS
BREAKFAST	Apple Juice Hot Kasha with Apple and 　Ginger Chick-pea Pancakes or Socca Ginger Herbal Tea	Apple Juice Hot Instant Kasha with Apple 　and Ginger Ginger Herbal Tea
SNACK	Apple-Ginger Iced Tea Special	Apple Juice Spritzer
LUNCH	Sparerib Soup Fresh Apple with Carob 　Fondue	Hearty Quick Soup Brown-Bag Lamb Pâté or Apple-Nutter Sandwich Ginger Tea Special
DINNER	Chops with Ginger Baked Sweet Potatoes Fresh Spinach Salad with Beet or Tahini Dressing Baked Apple	Pork Chops with Apple and 　Celery or Broiled Lamb Chops Quick Sweet Vegetable Purée Fresh Spinach Salad Applesauce or Apple Sorbet Apple-Carob Clusters

BULK AGENT: Psyllium seed

REGULAR TRACK

BREAKFAST

Apple Juice

Hot Kasha with Apple and Ginger

SERVES 4

2 cups water
*1 cup raw kasha (washed and picked over)**

*

> *1 cup plain unsweetened smooth or chunky-style*
> *applesauce or 1 large fresh apple, washed, cored and*
> *chopped, but not peeled*
> *Ground ginger to taste*

Bring water to boil in a large saucepan or top of a double boiler. Stir kasha into boiling water. Cook over low heat or boiling water 20–30 minutes.

Mix in applesauce or chopped raw apple. Add a pinch or 2 of ground ginger and serve warm.

*Note: As kasha has a very strong flavor, try mixing it in equal proportions with plain unsweetened applesauce (smooth or chunky) for a milder-tasting cereal.

Chick-pea Pancakes

*   SERVES 4

> *2 cups chick-pea flour**
> *1 tablespoon sesame oil plus oil for greasing skillet*
> *2 cups (approximate) water*
> *Dash sea salt (optional)*

Mix the chick-pea flour with 1 tablespoon oil and enough water to make a thick but pourable batter. (Add a dash of sea salt, if desired).

Thoroughly grease a skillet with oil. Heat skillet until it is very hot, but not smoking.

Using ½ cup for each pancake, pour the batter onto hot skillet. Cook pancakes until browned on one side, 2–3 minutes. Turn pancakes and brown on the other side about 1 minute, or until cooked through. Top with apple butter, tahini or applesauce.

*If you cannot find chick-pea flour, it is very easily made at home in a food processor. Using a steel blade, process 1 cup dried chick-peas until fully ground into flour, about 5 minutes at highest speed. Repeat with second cup. Be sure to sift the chick-pea flour well if smooth-textured pancakes are desired. Less sifting produces a grainier-textured pancake.

Socca (Italian Flatbread)

*   SERVES 4

This recipe is adapted from M. F. K. Fisher's recollections, "In Nice, Snacking in the Flower Market," *New York Times Sunday Supplement,* "The Sophisticated Traveler," 1986.

*

*1 cup chick-pea flour**
1 cup water
2 tablespoons sesame oil plus oil for greasing cookie sheet
1 teaspoon sea salt
Sesame seeds (optional)

Preheat oven broiler.

Combine flour, water, oil and salt in the bowl of a food processor and process 2 minutes on high power, using steel blade. Scrape bottom and sides of bowl. Process until very smooth. If beating mixture by hand, beat vigorously and then pour batter through a sieve before cooking.

Pour batter onto a cookie sheet or pizza pie platter oiled with sesame oil, spreading batter very thin. Sprinkle with sesame seeds, if desired.

Place cookie sheet 6–8 inches from source of heat. Watch carefully, as flatbread broils very fast. Prick air bubbles with a long fork as they form in the dough. Total cooking time is 3–5 minutes. (Watch for edges to turn brown.) Serve half of the cooked bread warm from the oven to eat with kasha. Wrap remaining flatbread in aluminum foil to serve with lunchtime recipe for Sparerib Soup.

*If you are using homemade chick-pea flour (see Chick-pea Pancakes recipe above), sift flour before using.

Ginger Herbal Tea

* SERVES 1

1–2 teaspoons ground ginger
2 tablespoons chopped apple peel from a fresh, washed
    apple
6 ounces boiling water
Heinz apple flakes, plain apple juice or beet sugar to taste

Wrap ground ginger and apple peel in a piece of cheesecloth. Gather edges of cloth together to make a "tea bag." Secure with thread. Steep the bag in 6 ounces boiling water until tea is of desired strength. Sweeten to taste with Heinz apple flakes, apple juice or beet sugar.

SNACK

Apple-Ginger Iced Tea Special

SERVES 1

6 ounces strongly brewed Ginger Herbal Tea (see recipe
    above)
2 ounces plain apple juice
2 ounces mineral water
1 (2-ounce) scoop Apple Sorbet (see Night Before
    Preparation Tips for Day Four)

Allow tea to cool or chill quickly over ice. Combine tea, apple juice
and mineral water. Top with a scoop of apple sorbet.

LUNCH

Sparerib Soup

SERVES 4–6

5 cups water
2 pounds meaty pork spareribs or lamb riblets, cut into 3-
    inch pieces
¼ cup dried chick-peas
¼ cup raw kasha (washed and picked over)
½ cup chopped fresh celery
Sea salt to taste
Ground oregano to taste

Bring water to a boil in a wide-bottomed soup pot. Add ribs and
chick-peas. Lower heat, partially cover and simmer slowly 1½ hours.
Remove meat to a shallow baking dish. Degrease soup with a large
spoon, as the broth will be quite fatty.

Add kasha to soup and cook, covered, at a slow boil for 30 minutes.
Add celery and season to taste with sea salt and oregano. Simmer 20
minutes more.

Preheat oven to 350°F.

While soup is cooking, place meat in the oven to crisp and brown.
Serve ribs in a separate dish at the table, along with soup and Socca
bread reserved from breakfast.

Fresh Apple with Carob Fondue

✳ SERVES 4

4 tablespoons Heinz apple flakes or beet sugar
2 tablespoons (scant) carob powder (use carob sparingly as
it has a slightly bitter taste)
¾ cup plain apple juice
4 fresh apples, washed, cored and sliced, but not peeled

Combine apple flakes or beet sugar with carob powder in a saucepan. Over very low heat, stir in apple juice, a few tablespoons at a time, until very smooth, and the consistency of chocolate syrup. Heat until hot. Pour into a bowl. Dip fresh slices of apple into hot fondue.

DINNER

Chops with Ginger

✳ SERVES 4

¾ cup sesame flour or chick-pea flour (see Chick-pea
Pancakes, Breakfast, Regular Track) or crushed puffed
millet cereal
1 teaspoon ground dried ginger
½ teaspoon sea salt
4 (1-inch-thick) pork chops or shoulder lamb chops or 4
lamb shanks
Sesame oil for greasing skillet, about 1 tablespoon
⅓ cup plain apple juice

Preheat oven to 250°F.

Combine flour or crushed cereal with ½ teaspoon ginger and ½ teaspoon sea salt in a paper bag; add chops or shanks and toss to coat. Heat oil in skillet until hot and brown meat on all sides. Arrange meat in a baking dish. Sprinkle with remaining ginger and bake 1 hour. Skim fat, add apple juice and heat until bubbling hot.

MW—Prepare meat as for oven baking (above), omitting salt. Heat (H) a microwave browning dish 4 minutes. Add 1 tablespoon oil to cover bottom of dish and brown meat, one piece at a time, 1 minute each side. Transfer meat to a 2-quart microwave-safe glass or ceramic casserole. Sprinkle with remaining ginger, add apple juice, cover and cook on roast setting 30 minutes. If your microwave does not have a roast setting, place a glass of water in the oven with the casserole and

✳ ───────────

cook on high power. If you do not have a carousel-type microwave oven, rotate dish every 10 minutes, rearranging meat pieces in the casserole each time. Season to taste with sea salt.

Baked Sweet Potatoes

✳   SERVES 4

4 fresh sweet potatoes, scrubbed
8 teaspoons tahini or plain apple butter
Ground ginger and sea salt to taste

Preheat oven to 400° F.

Pierce potatoes with a fork and bake 1 hour until tender. Split hot potatoes and place a teaspoonful of tahini or plain apple butter on each half. Sprinkle with ginger and sea salt to taste.

MW—Scrub potatoes and pierce with fork. Cook (H) 20–24 minutes (allow 5–6 minutes per potato). After cooking, proceed as above.

Fresh Spinach Salad

✳   SERVES 4

1 pound fresh spinach, carefully washed, trimmed, and torn
*   into bite-sized pieces*
1 (8-ounce) can bamboo shoots, drained, or 1 cup fresh
*   bamboo shoots (washed)*
¼ cup cooked or water-pack canned chick-peas
Beet Dressing or Tahini Dressing (recipes follow)

Combine spinach, bamboo shoots and chick-peas in a salad bowl. Toss with beet dressing or tahini dressing.

Beet Dressing

✳   MAKES 1 CUP

1 jar Beech-Nut Stage One beets
3 ounces sesame oil
Sea salt, beet sugar or ground ginger to taste
Plain apple juice (optional)

Combine beets with oil and mix well. Season to taste with sea salt, beet sugar or ginger. Thin with a little apple juice, if desired.

Tahini Dressing

✳ MAKES 1 CUP

½ cup tahini
½ cup plain apple juice
Ground ginger and sea salt to taste

Combine tahini and apple juice. Mix well. Season to taste with ginger and sea salt.

Note: If oil has risen to the top of tahini, stir to recombine before making dressing.

Baked Apple

✳ SERVES 4

4 large fresh baking apples
Sesame oil for greasing baking dish
4 tablespoons plain apple butter
Ground ginger

Preheat oven to 400° F.
  Core apples and place in a small baking dish oiled with sesame oil. Place 1 tablespoon apple butter in the center of each apple. Sprinkle with ginger and bake for 30–40 minutes.

MW—Prepare apples as directed above. Cover, leaving vent, with waxed paper and microwave (H) 4–6 minutes for each apple cooked.

DIET EXPRESS

BREAKFAST

Apple Juice
(See Breakfast, Regular Track)
✳

Hot Instant Kasha with Apple and Ginger

✳ SERVES 1

½ cup presoaked kasha (see Night-Before-Preparation Tips
for Day Four)
Hot water or plain apple juice (optional)

*

¼ teaspoon ground ginger
Plain unsweetened applesauce, Heinz apple flakes or 1 fresh
   apple, washed, cored and chopped, but not peeled

Stirring frequently, reheat the presoaked kasha on top of the stove. Thin with a little hot water or apple juice, if desired. Stir in ground ginger. Sweeten to taste with applesauce, Heinz apple flakes or fresh, chopped apple.

MW—Stir precooked kasha, adding a little water or apple juice to moisten. Cover and microwave (H) 1 minute until hot. Kasha will be crunchy. If more tender cereal is desired, add about ⅓ cup more liquid and continue cooking (L) a few minutes more, stirring every minute. Stir in ginger and sweeten to taste.

Ginger Herbal Tea
(See Breakfast, Regular Track)

*

SNACK

Apple Juice Spritzer

*

SERVES 1

6 ounces plain apple juice
2 ounces sparkling mineral water
1 scoop Apple Sorbet (see Night-Before Preparation Tips for
   Day Four)

Mix apple juice wth sparkling mineral water. Add a scoop of apple sorbet.

LUNCH

Hearty Quick Soup

*

SERVES 1–2

1 (10-ounce) package frozen chopped spinach
½–1 cup water or celery juice
1–2 jars Beech-Nut Stage One lamb
½ cup well drained canned yam noodles or threads
   (optional)

½ cup bamboo shoots
Sea salt and ground oregano to taste

Cook spinach over low heat in saucepan in ½ cup water or celery juice until hot, stirring often. Thicken with lamb and add remaining water or celery juice until soup is of desired consistency. Add yam noodles or threads and bamboo shoots and cook until hot. Season to taste with salt and oregano.

MW—Cook spinach (H) 4 minutes, covered, in 2 teaspoons water or celery juice. Add remaining ingredients except salt and yam noodles or threads until soup is of desired thickness. Heat (H), covered, 2–3 minutes until hot. Stir in yam noodles, heat (H) 30 seconds more. Season to taste with sea salt.

Brown-Bag Lamb Pâté

✳   SERVES 1

1–2 jars Beech-Nut Stage One lamb
Sea salt and ground oregano to taste
1 tablespoon sesame oil

Blend all ingredients and chill, if possible, before eating. Spread on celery sticks or Socca bread (see Breakfast, Regular Track).

Apple-Nutter Sandwich

✳   SERVES 1

Socca (see Breakfast, Regular Track)
1–2 tablespoons tahini
1–2 tablespoons plain apple butter

Spread pieces of socca bread with equal amounts tahini and apple butter to make this mock "PB&J" sandwich.

Note: If you did not have time to make socca bread, spread tahini and apple butter on celery sticks or slices of raw apple instead.

Ginger Tea Special

✳   SERVES 1

6 ounces strong Ginger Herbal Tea (see Breakfast, Regular
    Track)
Ice cubes

2 ounces plain apple juice
Beet sugar or apple flakes

Chill tea by pouring over ice cubes. Combine tea with apple juice. Sweeten to taste with beet sugar or apple flakes. Note: This drink may also be served hot; on the stove, heat tea and apple juice together to boiling in a saucepan, or in the microwave, heat in a microwave-safe mug (H) 1–2 minutes. Sweeten to taste with beet sugar or apple flakes.

DINNER

Pork Chops with Apple and Celery

SERVES 1–2

2–4 thin loin pork chops
Ground oregano
Sesame oil for greasing skillet
½ cup plain apple juice
1 small fresh apple, washed, cored and sliced, but not
*   peeled*
1 stalk fresh celery, sliced
1 tablespoon plain apple butter

Rub chops with ground oregano. In a skillet lightly greased with sesame oil, brown chops on both sides over high heat. Add apple juice. Cover, reduce heat to very low and cook slowly until chops are almost tender, about 15 minutes. Add apple and celery, stir and cook slowly a few minutes more. Remove chops, apples and celery and keep warm on a platter. Add apple butter to the skillet and stir, scraping up all the browned bits clinging to the skillet bottom. Pour over chops and serve.

Broiled Lamb Chops

SERVES 1–2

4 double loin lamb chops (each at least 1 inch thick)
1 tablespoon (approximate) sesame oil
Ground oregano
Sea salt to taste

Preheat broiler. (It should be very hot.)
Brush chops with sesame oil and rub with oregano. Broil on a rack about 2 inches from heat. Broil both sides, cooking a total of 10 minutes for rare, 15 for medium, 20 for well done. Transfer to a warm platter and season to taste with sea salt.

Quick Sweet Vegetable Purée

*

> ½ cup plain unsweetened applesauce
> 1 jar Beech-Nut Stage One sweet potatoes
> Ground ginger and sea salt to taste

Combine applesauce and sweet potatoes. Season to taste with ground ginger and salt. Heat in a saucepan until hot.

MW—Combine applesauce and sweet potatoes. Season to taste with ground ginger and salt. Heat (H), covered, until hot, about 2 minutes per cup of purée.

Fresh Spinach Salad
(See Dinner, Regular Track)

*

Applesauce

*

> 2 cups plain unsweetened applesauce

Apple Sorbet
(See Night-Before Preparation Tips for Day Four)

*

Apple-Carob Clusters

*

> 1 cup tahini, mixed well to incorporate oil
> ¼ cup (scant) carob powder (use carob sparingly as it has
>   a slightly bitter taste)
> 1 cup (approximate) plain apple butter
> Pinch ground ginger
> 1 large sweet fresh apple (such as Delicious variety) peeled,
>   cored and chopped
> Sesame seeds

Mix together the tahini, carob powder, apple butter and ginger until well combined. Test for sweetness. If a sweeter taste is desired, add a little more apple butter. Fold in fresh apple until mixture is combined. Generously sprinkle a large sheet of waxed paper with sesame seeds. Roll tahini-apple mixture by teaspoonfuls into sesame seeds until clusters are completely coated. In a single layer, place clusters in a covered container or ice-cube tray lined with waxed paper and chill in the refrigerator.

NIGHT-BEFORE PREPARATION TIPS
FOR DAY 5

1. Scoop out balls of fresh, ripe cantaloupe, crenshaw or honeydew melon (or a combination of all) and freeze overnight in a plastic container for "instant" sorbet additions to cold drinks and desserts, if desired.

2. Roast turkey for Brown-Bag Turkey Salad or Brown-Bag Deviled Wingettes: Combine 1 tablespoon dry mustard, 2 teaspoons sea salt and enough olive oil to make a thick paste. Brush over 2 fresh turkey wingettes (or drumsticks) or 1 1–2 pound fresh turkey breast. Roast turkey pieces or breast in a 375° F. oven, 20 minutes per pound.

Cool. Wrap turkey in plastic wrap or aluminum foil and refrigerate. On Day Five, use for Diet Express lunch.

3. Make Maple-Dipped Frozen Bananas: Dip 2 peeled, firm, ripe bananas in maple syrup. Coat completely. Line an ice-cube tray with waxed paper. Place coated bananas on waxed paper, cover and freeze overnight. Serves 2. Use for Day Five, Lunch, Regular Track.

DAY 5

✳

THE ELIMINATION PHASE

ALLOWED FOODS:
Tapioca, lima beans, plantains, bananas, cranberries, melon, artichokes, bean sprouts, escarole, pumpkin, turkey, mustard, mustard greens, rose hip, olive oil, nyafat, thyme, maple syrup

MENU

	REGULAR	DIET EXPRESS
BREAKFAST	Melon Fondue Maple-Sweetened Tapioca Lima Bean Pancakes Rose Hip Tea	Half Melon Instant Hot Tapioca with Bananas Rose Hip Tea
SNACK	Roasted Pumpkin Seeds Melon-Banana Smoothy	Banana Chips
LUNCH	Escarole-Turkey Soup Turkey-Banana Crumble Maple-Dipped Frozen Bananas or Cranberry-Banana Pudding	Brown-Bag Turkey Salad or Brown-Bag Deviled Wingettes or Brown-Bag Turkey Pâté Instant Pumpkin Pudding Rose Hip Spritzer
DINNER	Turkey Bake or Turkey Burgers Baked Plantains or Bananas Escarole-Artichoke Salad with Mustard Dressing Honeydew Granité Rose Hip-Cranberry Spritzer	Broiled Turkey Breast Frozen Artichoke Hearts Escarole-Bean Sprout Salad Honeydew Melon

BULK AGENT: None

REGULAR TRACK

Note: Canned, water-pack turkey such as Swanson brand may be used in any Day Five recipe calling for cooked turkey. Drain turkey before using.

BREAKFAST

Melon Fondue

✳ SERVES 4

1 honeydew, crenshaw or persian melon, or 2 cantaloupes
Maple syrup or maple crystals

Slice melon, pare and cut into chunks. Dip individual pieces of fruit into maple syrup or maple crystals.

Maple-Sweetened Tapioca

SERVES 4

4 tablespoons granulated, quick-cooking tapioca
2 cups water
Dash sea salt (optional)
½ cup maple crystals or maple syrup

Sprinkle tapioca over water in a small saucepan and allow to stand 5 minutes. Add salt and bring to boil, stirring constantly. Remove from heat and pour into a bowl. Cool slightly before serving. Sweeten with maple crystals or maple syrup to taste.

MW—Sprinkle tapioca over water in a large, shallow, microwave-safe bowl and allow to stand 5 minutes. Stir and microwave (H) to boiling, about 2 minutes. Remove from oven, and stir. Serve warm with maple crystals or syrup and a dash of salt as above.

Lima Bean Pancakes

SERVES 4

2 (10-ounce) packages frozen lima beans (do not defrost)
2 teaspoons olive oil plus oil for greasing skillet
1 cup (approximate) water

Empty the lima beans into a blender or processor and process them until they are ground to resemble cornmeal in texture (about 1 minute). Scrape ground limas into a bowl. Add 2 teaspoons oil and enough water to make lima bean batter pourable but still thick. Grease a skillet thoroughly with oil. Heat the skillet until it is hot (beads of water will "dance" on a properly heated skillet). Using 2–3 table-spoons for each pancake, drop batter onto the hot skillet. Cook pancakes until lightly browned on one side, 2–3 minutes. Turn pan-cakes and brown on the other side until cooked through, 1–2 minutes. Top with Beech-Nut Stage One bananas.

Rose Hip Tea

SERVES 1

1 tea bag pure rose hip tea
1 cup boiling water
Maple syrup or maple crystals to taste

Steep tea bag in boiling water until of desired strength. Add maple syrup or crystals to sweeten to taste.

SNACK

Roasted Pumpkin Seeds
✳   SERVES 4

> 1 ripe fresh pumpkin (about 3 pounds)
> ½ teaspoon sea salt
> 2 teaspoons olive oil

Preheat oven to 250° F.

Remove seeds from pumpkin, enough to make 2 cups seeds. Cover pumpkin halves with plastic wrap and refrigerate for later use in preparing Turkey Bake (see Dinner, Regular Track). Clean the seeds thoroughly and dry with paper towels. In a skillet, sprinkle seeds with salt and sauté them in olive oil until all seeds are coated with oil. Place seeds on a nonstick baking sheet and bake 30–40 minutes. Crisp on paper towels.

MW—Combine clean, dry seeds with oil in a shallow, microwave-safe bowl. Do not cover seeds. Microwave (H) total of about 5 minutes, stirring every minute. Seeds will be light brown and crisp as they cool. Season to taste with sea salt.

Melon-Banana Smoothy
✳   SERVES 1

> 1 cup melon chunks or balls*
> ½ ripe banana, peeled
> 1 ice cube, crushed

Purée melon and banana in blender or food processor. Add ice and continue to blend until smooth.

*If using prefrozen melon balls (see Night-Before Preparation Tips for Day Five), omit ice cube.

LUNCH

Escarole-Turkey Soup

✳   SERVES 4

Note: If you plan to microwave this dish, substitute 1 (10-ounce) package frozen artichoke hearts for the whole artichokes

4 small artichokes, trimmed and stems removed
2 teaspoons sea salt
2 teaspoons ground thyme
4 large turkey wings
1½ quarts water
1 (8-ounce) can bean sprouts with water
2 cups coarsely shredded escarole (carefully washed and
    dried)
Hot olive oil or nyafat for dipping artichokes, seasoned to
    taste with ground thyme and sea salt, about ½ cup per
    serving

In a soup kettle or large casserole, place artichokes, 2 teaspoons salt, 2 teaspoons thyme and turkey wings in water. Bring to boil and simmer, covered, until wings are tender, about 1 hour. Remove artichokes, drain and keep warm. Remove wings and de-bone meat, discarding fatty skin and bones. Skim excess fat from broth. Add turkey meat, sprouts with water and escarole to broth, and simmer a few moments. Correct seasonings with additional thyme and sea salt. Serve artichokes separately with hot olive oil or nyafat seasoned with thyme and salt for dipping.

MW—Place wings in a 4-quart round, covered microwave-safe casserole and cook on roast or (L) setting until juices run clear when wings are pierced with a fork, about 10–15 minutes (cook 6 minutes per pound). Allow to stand 10 minutes. Remove wings to a platter. Add frozen artichoke hearts and ¼ cup water to turkey juices in the casserole. Cook (H) in casserole, covered, 5–6 minutes. Add turkey cut from wings, bean sprouts with liquid and escarole to artichokes and turkey juices in casserole. Stir. Microwave (H) 3 minutes. Add 3 cups water, sea salt and thyme until soup is seasoned to taste. Microwave (H) 1–3 minutes until hot.

Turkey-Banana Crumble

SERVES 4

1 tablespoon light olive oil
1 pound fresh, ground turkey
1 firm banana, peeled and sliced
Sea salt and ground thyme to taste

Heat oil in a large frying pan. Add turkey and brown over medium heat. Add sliced banana and brown quickly, turning slices. Season to taste with sea salt and thyme, and serve with Lima Bean Pancakes if desired, (see Breakfast, Regular Track).

Maple-Dipped Frozen Bananas
(See Night-Before Preparation Tips for Day Five)

SERVES 4

Cranberry-Banana Pudding

SERVES 4

1 cup whole fresh cranberries (washed and picked over)
2 cups cold water
⅓ cup maple syrup or maple crystals
4–6 ounces peeled, ripe banana, blended or processed with
    a little water until thick and smooth
2 tablespoons granulated, quick-cooking tapioca

In a saucepan, cook cranberries at a slow boil in enough of the water to cover them until berries pop open (about 3 to 5 minutes, depending on ripeness of berries). Remove from heat. Stir in remaining water, maple syrup or crystals and banana. Stir to combine. Sprinkle tapioca on top and allow to sit for 5 minutes. Bring mixture to boil over moderately high heat, stirring constantly to keep from scorching on the bottom of the pan. (Lifting the saucepan an inch or two above the source of heat, or placing the saucepan in a shallow skillet of boiling water are other methods of preventing burning. Remove from heat and cool slightly. Pour into serving dishes and chill. Tapioca thickens as it cools.

Add more syrup or crystals, or fresh sliced bananas for added sweetness.

✳ ──────────────────────────────────

DINNER

Turkey Bake

✳

2 cups water
½ cup maple syrup
1½ cups whole fresh cranberries (washed and picked over)
1 (3-pound) pumpkin
½ cup olive oil
1 (2-pound) whole fresh turkey breast
¼ teaspoon each ground thyme and sea salt

Combine water and ¼ cup syrup. Stir in cranberries and let stand for 2 hours.*

Preheat oven to moderate 375°F.

Halve pumpkin, or use reserved pumpkin from Snack, Regular Track. Remove seeds and stringy portion. Cut into 2-inch diamonds. Pare each piece. Lightly grease a shallow baking dish with half the oil. Arrange pumpkin in single layer in the greased dish. Drain cranberries, reserving juice for Rose Hip-Cranberry Spritzer (see Dinner, Regular Track), and add them to the pumpkin. Drizzle remaining ¼ cup oil and ¼ cup syrup over the vegetables and toss the mixture with a spoon. Place the turkey breast on top of the vegetables, sprinkle it with thyme and sea salt and bake 15–20 minutes per pound of turkey.

MW—Prepare cranberries and pumpkin as above. Arrange in a microwave-safe casserole dish. Remove skin of turkey breast (it will not brown during microwave cooking). Place skinned breast on top of vegetables. Sprinkle with thyme. Cover casserole with microwave-safe plastic wrap (leaving vent) and microwave on roast setting (or (H) with a glass of water placed in the oven during cooking). Microwave 30 minutes. Add salt to taste after cooking.

*Cranberries can be "quick-soaked" by simmering them in a saucepan with water and syrup over direct heat for 5 minutes. Another method is to cover berries with boiling water and allow them to stand until cooled, about 20 minutes. Stir in syrup.

Turkey Burgers

❋   SERVES 4

> 1 pound ground turkey
> ½ tablespoon each ground thyme, dry mustard, minced
>   fresh mustard greens, (washed and dried)
> Olive oil
> Sea salt

Preheat broiler.

Place turkey in a large mixing bowl. Mix in thyme, dry mustard and mustard greens lightly with a fork and then shape the mixture into patties. Drizzle each patty lightly with olive oil and sprinkle with sea salt. Broil the burgers 2–3 minutes each side, 4–6 inches from source of heat.

Baked Plantains or Bananas

❋   SERVES 4

> 2 plantains or bananas
> 1 tablespoon maple syrup
> 1 tablespoon water
> 1 teaspoon light olive oil

Preheat oven to 350°F.

Cut four pieces of foil, each 4×6 inches. Peel fruit, cut in half lengthwise and place each half on a foil rectangle. In a small bowl, mix syrup and water. Spoon over fruit halves. Sprinkle each half with oil. Fold over the foil once and crimp the ends to seal. Place on a baking sheet and bake 5–8 minutes. (If fruit is really ripe, it will cook in 5–6 minutes and be very tender when pierced with a fork.)

Escarole-Artichoke Salad

❋   SERVES 4

> 1 medium head escarole
> 1 (10-ounce) package frozen artichoke hearts
> Mustard Dressing (recipe follows)

Wash leaves of a small head of escarole carefully. Dry and tear into bite-sized pieces. Place escarole in a salad bowl. Empty frozen artichoke hearts into a colander. Run hot water over hearts until thawed, about 1 minute. Allow to drain. Add artichokes to escarole. Toss with mustard dressing.

Mustard Dressing

MAKES 1 CUP

2 teaspoons dry mustard
¼ cup water
2 teaspoons chopped fresh mustard greens
1 teaspoon sea salt or to taste
¾ cup olive oil

Combine dry mustard, water and greens. Stir well. Add oil. Correct seasoning to taste with salt and dry mustard, stir and chill. Shake well before adding to salad.

Honeydew Granité

SERVES 4

½ large, ripe honeydew melon
4 ice cubes, cracked
2–3 tablespoons maple crystals or maple syrup to taste

Seed melon and scoop flesh into a blender or processor. Add 4 cracked ice cubes and 2–3 tablespoons maple crystals (or to taste). Purée, stopping twice to scrape down sides of bowl, until mixture is milky. Freeze in a bowl 1 hour, stirring after 30 minutes.

Rose Hip-Cranberry Spritzer

SERVES 1

4 ounces brewed pure Rose Hip Tea (see Breakfast, Regular
    Track)
2–4 ounces cranberry juice (reserved from Turkey Bake—
    see recipe above)*
2 ounces sparkling mineral water
Ice cubes
1–2 frozen melon balls (optional; see Night-Before
    Preparation Tips for Day Five)
Maple crystals or maple syrup

Combine tea, juice and mineral water in a glass. Add ice and melon balls. Sweeten with maple crystals or syrup to taste.

*If you did not make Turkey Bake, you can make quick cranberry juice by simmering 1 cup frozen cranberries in 1 cup water for 5 minutes over medium-high direct heat. Drain liquid and chill to use as juice.

DIET EXPRESS

BREAKFAST

Half Melon (Cantaloupe)

✳

Instant Hot Tapioca with Bananas

✳   SERVES 1

1 tablespoon granulated, quick-cooking tapioca
1 cup water
1 jar Beech-Nut Stage One bananas

Combine tapioca and water in a microwave-safe casserole. Cover and let stand 3 minutes. Microwave (H) 1 minute. Stir. Microwave 30 seconds. Stir in 1 jar Beech-Nut Stage One bananas and serve.

Rose Hip Tea
(See Breakfast, Regular Track)

✳

SNACK

Banana Chips

✳   SERVES 1–2

½ cup (approximate) maple syrup
1 teaspoon light olive oil
1 cup unsweetened dehydrated banana chips*

In a mixing bowl, whisk syrup and oil until thoroughly combined. Add bananas; stir until chips are completely coated with syrup. Cover a microwave-safe plate large enough to hold the chips in a single layer with waxed paper; spread banana chips on paper. Microwave (L), uncovered, 3–5 minutes, until syrup-coated chips are dry. Rotate dish halfway through cooking time and watch carefully to avoid burning. Do not allow chips to brown. Cool completely before serving.

*Unsweetened dehydrated banana chips are sold in many health food stores and stores that specialize in Asian cooking.

LUNCH

Brown-Bag Turkey Salad

*   SERVES 1

½ cup whole fresh cranberries (washed and picked over) or
    frozen cranberries*
¼ cup water
2–3 teaspoons maple crystals or maple syrup
¼ teaspoon sea salt
¼ cup olive oil
1 cup escarole (carefully washed, dried and torn into bite-
    sized pieces)
1 cup fresh bean sprouts (washed), or canned bean sprouts,
    drained
Cooked, sliced turkey breast (see Night-Before Preparation
    Tips for Day Five) or canned turkey, drained

In a blender or processor, combine berries, water, maple crystals or
syrup and salt. Cover and process until berries are puréed. Sieve
mixture, discard skins. Transfer to screw-top jar, add olive oil. Cover
and shake well. Chill in freezer while putting salad together.

In a thermal container, make a bed of escarole. Top with bean
sprouts and cooked turkey slices cut into julienne strips. Drizzle
dressing over all, or carry separately and pour on just before serving.
Reserve leftover turkey for snacking, or wrap in freezer wrap and
freeze for use on Day Thirteen.

*If time does not allow puréeing of cranberries, substitute canned,
unsweetened pumpkin. Sweeten ½ cup canned pumpkin to taste with
maple crystals or syrup, add 1 teaspoon olive oil, and proceed as
above.

Brown-Bag Deviled Wingettes
(See Night-Before Preparation Tips for Day Five)

*

Brown-Bag Turkey Pâté

*   SERVES 1

1–2 jars Beech-Nut Stage One turkey
2 teaspoons olive oil
Sea salt and ground thyme to taste

Fresh melon, pared and cut into chunks (1 cup)
1 cup escarole (washed, dried and torn into bite-size
*   pieces)*

Combine turkey with oil, salt and thyme. Chill. Spread on chunks of fresh melon or torn-up escarole leaves.

Instant Pumpkin Pudding

✳   SERVES 1

Canned unsweetened pumpkin
Beech-Nut Stage One bananas
Maple syrup or maple crystals to taste

Combine pumpkin and Beech-Nut Stage One bananas in equal amounts. Sweeten to taste with maple crystals or syrup. Chill if time allows and top with fresh banana.

Rose Hip Spritzer

✳   SERVES 1

6 ounces brewed Rose Hip Tea (see Breakfast, Regular
*   Track)*
2 ounces sparkling mineral water
Maple crystals or maple syrup
1 frozen melon ball (see Night-Before Preparation Tips for
*   Day Five)*
Crushed ice

Combine tea and water. Sweeten to taste with maple crystals or syrup. Add melon ball and serve over ice.

DINNER

Broiled Turkey Breast

✳   SERVES 1–2

¼ cup dry mustard
1 teaspoon sea salt
½ teaspoon ground thyme
Olive oil
1 small turkey breast, about 1 pound

Preheat broiler.

Combine dry mustard with sea salt, thyme and enough olive oil to make a thick but spreadable paste. Place turkey, skin side up, in a broiling pan. Spread with paste. Broil, 6–8 inches from source of heat, until skin of breast is well browned, about 10 minutes. Turn turkey, baste with more mustard paste, and continue browning, 10 minutes more. Turn turkey breast side up, baste with surrounding sauce, and broil a minute or 2 more, until crisped on top. Allow 15 to 20 minutes per pound, total cooking time.

MW—Skin turkey breast. Place in a shallow, wide microwave-safe casserole and spread with mustard paste. Cover loosely with waxed paper and microwave on roast setting 15–20 minutes. Rearrange breast in dish after ½ cooking time. Check for doneness by pricking breast with fork. If juices run clear (no pinkness), turkey is done.

Frozen Artichoke Hearts

SERVES 1–2

1 (10 ounce) package frozen artichoke hearts
Water
Sea salt
1 teaspoon light olive oil
Ground thyme to taste

Cook hearts according to package directions, using water and sea salt. Drain. Toss cooked hearts with olive oil to coat, and season to taste with sea salt and thyme.

Escarole-Bean Sprout Salad

SERVES 1–2

1 small head escarole
1 cup fresh bean sprouts (washed) or drained canned bean
sprouts
Mustard Dressing (see Dinner, Regular Track)

Carefully wash, dry and tear into bite-size pieces enough escarole leaves to make 1–2 cups. Add bean sprouts and dress with ½ cup mustard dressing.

Honeydew Melon

NIGHT-BEFORE PREPARATION TIPS
FOR DAY 6

1. Roast Beef (use a 1-rib [2-pound] standing rib roast or 1 [2-pound] sirloin tip roast). High Temperature Method: Preheat oven to hot 450°F. Wipe roast with a damp cloth. Rub it with sea salt. Insert a meat thermometer in thickest part of roast. Place meat in roasting pan. Cook 25 minutes and reduce heat to slow, 300°F. Cook until thermometer registers 140°F. for rare beef, 150°F. for medium-rare, 160°F. for medium, or 170°F. for well done. If not using a thermometer, cook 16–30 minutes per pound: 16–18 for rare, 18–20 for medium-rare, 20–22 medium, 26–30 for well done.

Wrap in plastic wrap or aluminum foil and refrigerate for use for Roast Beef Sandwich, Lunch, Diet Express.

2. Make Peach Sorbet: Allowing 1 jar per serving, empty as many jars Beech-Nut Stage One peaches as you think you will need into a freezer container with a lid. Freeze overnight to use as instant sorbet in beverages or desserts. As dessert, allow to soften 15 minutes in the refrigerator before serving as sorbet.

DAY 6
✳

THE ELIMINATION PHASE

ALLOWED FOODS:
Rice, potatoes, coconut, peaches, cucumbers, green beans, kidney beans, parsley, rhubarb, butternut squash, beef, tarragon, chamomile, Puritan oil, nutmeg

MENU	REGULAR	DIET EXPRESS

BREAKFAST	Fresh Coconut
	Hot Cream of Rice Cereal or
	    Potato Pancakes
	Chamomile Herbal Tea
		Fresh Coconut
		Puffed Rice Cereal or Beech-
		    Nut Stage One Rice Cereal
		Chamomile Herbal Tea

SNACK	Rice Cakes or Rice Crackers with Peaches Peach Spritzer	Rice Cakes Fresh Coconut

❋

LUNCH	Western Beef and Rice Casserole or Broiled Hamburgers Boiled Rice Peach Sorbet	Broiled Hamburgers Roast Beef Sandwich or Brown-Bag Beef Pâté Peach
DINNER	Ragout of Liver or Beef and Parsley Stew Bean and Cucumber Salad with Tarragon Dressing Fresh Peach Pie	Broiled Minute Steaks with Parsley Squash Quick Rice or Microwave Baked Potato Frozen Green Beans Peach Sorbet

BULK AGENT: Rice bran

REGULAR TRACK

BREAKFAST

Fresh Coconut

❋

For directions on preparing coconut, see Day Two, Breakfast, Regular Track.

Hot Cream of Rice Cereal

❋   SERVES 4

Follow directions for Hot Cream of Rice Cereal on Day Two, Breakfast, Regular Track, substituting nutmeg for cinnamon. Serve with peaches as suggested.

Potato Pancakes

❋   SERVES 4

2 cups potato meal (nothing added) or 2 cups raw potatoes, peeled, grated and well drained
Dash sea salt
½ cup potato starch flour
2 teaspoons Puritan oil plus oil for greasing skillet
2 cups (approximate) water

Sift dry ingredients together and place them in a mixing bowl. Stir in 2 teaspoons oil and add water until batter is thick but pourable. (If using fresh potatoes, blend salt, potato starch flour and 2 teaspoons oil into grated potatoes and add water until mixture is smooth and holds together.) Grease skillet with oil. Heat skillet until it is hot but not smoking. To make each pancake, drop several tablespoonfuls of batter onto hot skillet. Cook pancakes on one side until browned, about 2–3 minutes. Turn and cook until cooked through, 2–3 minutes more. Top with Beech-Nut Stage One peaches.

Chamomile Herbal Tea

✳ SERVES 1

1 tea bag plain chamomile tea
8 ounces boiling water
Heinz peach flakes
Nutmeg to taste

Steep tea bag in 8 ounces boiling water until of desired strength. Sweeten tea with Heinz peach flakes and nutmeg to taste.

SNACK

Rice Cakes or Rice Crackers with Peaches

✳ SERVES 1

2–3 plain rice cakes or 4–5 plain rice crackers
Dash nutmeg
1 jar Beech-Nut Stage One peaches

Preheat oven to 400° F.

Place rice cakes or crackers on a baking sheet or a sheet of aluminum foil and warm 1–2 minutes in the preheated oven. Stir nutmeg into peaches and spread on hot cakes or crackers.

Peach Spritzer

✳ SERVES 1

1 jar Beech-Nut Stage One peaches
6 ounces mineral water
1 tablespoon Peach Sorbet (see Night-Before Preparation
Tips for Day Six)

Mix peaches with mineral water. Add the sorbet and stir.

LUNCH

Western Beef and Rice Casserole

✳ SERVES 4

1 pound lean ground beef
2 tablespoons Puritan oil
½ cup chopped fresh or frozen green beans
½ cup sliced fresh or frozen rhubarb
1 cup raw rice
2 cups water
Sea salt to taste

Preheat oven to moderate, 325° F.

Brown beef in oil. Remove meat from pan, drain off excess fat and set aside. To the same pan, add beans, rhubarb and rice; cook, stirring, until browned. Add water, salt and reserved meat and bring to a boil. Pour into a 2-quart casserole and cover. Bake 45 minutes to 1 hour, or until rice is tender and liquid is absorbed.

MW—Place beef and oil in a 2-quart microwave-safe covered casserole. Microwave (H) 5–7 minutes, stirring every 2 minutes, until beef is browned. Stir in beans, rhubarb, ¾ cup uncooked, INSTANT rice and 1 cup water. Cover, microwave (H) 5 minutes, or less, until rice is tender, liquid is absorbed and casserole is hot. Season to taste with sea salt.

Broiled Hamburgers

✳ SERVES 4

1 pound ground round steak
1 tablespoon minced fresh parsley
Sea salt to taste

Preheat broiler.

Combine meat and parsley, form into 4 patties and broil 4 inches from heat, 2–4 minutes each side for medium-rare. Salt after cooking, to taste.

MW—Prepare patties as above. In a microwave-safe glass or ceramic dish loosely covered with waxed paper, cook burgers (H) 4 minutes, 2 minutes per patty, turning patties over after ½ cooking time. Season with sea salt after cooking.

Boiled Rice
(See Day Two, Dinner, Regular Track)

✳

Peach Sorbet
(See Night-Before Preparation Tips for Day Six)

✳

DINNER

Ragoût of Liver

✳   SERVES 4

⅓ cup potato starch flour or rice flour
½ teaspoon sea salt
1½ pounds beef liver
2 tablespoons Puritan oil
1½ cups water
¾ cup thinly sliced fresh or frozen rhubarb

Combine potato starch or rice flour and salt. Dredge liver with this mixture and then work flour into meat with a meat pounder. Cut liver into four individual portions. In a heavy skillet or Dutch oven, heat oil and brown meat on both sides. Combine water and rhubarb and pour over meat. Cover and either bake in a preheated 350° F oven or simmer on top of stove for approximately 1½ hours until liver is tender.

Note: This recipe works equally well with beef round steak (1½ pounds, 1 inch thick) to make Swiss Steak.

Beef and Parsley Stew

✳   SERVES 4

6 tablespoons Puritan oil
3 pounds round steak, cut into 1-inch cubes
3 large bunches fresh parsley, washed, dried and chopped
Sea salt to taste
2 teaspoons dried tarragon
Water to cover
3 cups cooked kidney beans, with liquid to cover

In a heavy, 4-quart pot or Dutch oven, heat 4 tablespoons oil, add meat and brown lightly. Add parsley and cook until parsley is dark green. Sprinkle beef and parsley lightly with salt, stir in tarragon and water to cover and cover with a lid. Simmer until meat is almost tender, 1–1½ hours. Add kidney beans and their liquid; correct seasonings with tarragon and sea salt. Reheat. Serve with boiled white rice (see Day Two, Dinner, Regular Track).

Bean and Cucumber Salad

SERVES 4

2 small fresh cucumbers, pared and sliced
10 ounces fresh green beans or 1 (10-ounce) package
*   frozen chopped green beans*
Tarragon Dressing

Place prepared cucumber in a bowl. Wash, trim and chop fresh beans or thaw frozen beans by placing in colander and rinsing with cold water. Allow thawed beans to drain while preparing tarragon dressing. Toss with chilled dressing.

Note: Cucumbers and beans can also be marinated in tarragon dressing. Combine vegetables with enough dressing to coat, cover, and refrigerate 1 hour.

Tarragon Dressing

MAKES 1 CUP

⅓ cup rhubarb "vinegar" (see Alfalfa Sprout-Rhubarb
*   Salad, Day Two Dinner, Regular Track)*
2 teaspoons crumbled fresh tarragon or 1 teaspoon dried
*   tarragon*
¾ cup Puritan oil
1 teaspoon sea salt or to taste

Combine vinegar and tarragon. Allow to stand 5 minutes. Add oil and salt to taste. Shake well. Chill if time allows before tossing with salad.

Fresh Peach Pie

SERVES 4–6

3–4 large plain rice cakes
⅓ cup Puritan oil
3–4 large fresh peaches or 20 ounces frozen sliced peaches
1 jar Beech-Nut Stage One peaches
1 teaspoon nutmeg

⅓ cup rice flour or potato starch flour
3 tablespoons Puritan oil
4 cups shredded Fresh Coconut (optional; see Day Two,
    Breakfast, Regular Track)

Preheat oven to hot 400° F.

Make rice crumb crust: Crumble enough rice cakes to make 1½ cups crumbs, combine them with ⅓ cup Puritan oil and mix thoroughly. Press mixture firmly against sides and bottom of a 9-inch pie pan, using the back of a spoon. Bake 5 minutes and cool.

Raise oven temperature to 425° F.

Prepare peaches: peel and slice enough fresh peaches to make 3–4 cups, or use frozen peaches, thawed and drained.

Assemble pie: spread fresh or thawed, drained frozen peaches in cooled piecrust. Pour Beech-Nut Stage One peaches evenly over fresh peaches, and sprinkle with nutmeg. Mix together rice flour or potato starch, oil and shredded fresh coconut, if desired. Sprinkle over fruit in pie shell. Bake in 425° F. oven 15–20 minutes, until fruit is tender and pie is lightly browned on top.

DIET EXPRESS

BREAKFAST

Fresh Coconut

✳

1 medium coconut

Split and drain coconut according to directions on Day Two, Breakfast, Regular Track. Cover and refrigerate one half of coconut for Snack later in the day. Remove meat from other half of coconut as directed on Day Two. Serve coconut pieces plain or with Beech-Nut Stage One peaches for dipping if desired.

Puffed Rice Cereal or
Beech-Nut Stage One Rice Cereal

✳   SERVES 1

1 cup puffed rice or Beech Nut Stage One rice cereal
½ cup coconut milk
Dash nutmeg (optional)

*1 jar Beech-Nut Stage One peaches, or 1 fresh peach,
    scrubbed, pit removed and sliced*

Combine cereal, milk and nutmeg. If using Beech-Nut cereal, blend until smooth. Top with peaches and serve. For directions on making coconut milk, see Day Two, Breakfast, Regular Track.

Chamomile Herbal Tea
(See Breakfast, Regular Track)

✳

SNACK

Rice Cakes

✳

Fresh Coconut
(See Day Two, Breakfast, Regular Track)

✳

LUNCH

Broiled Hamburgers
(See Lunch, Regular Track)

✳

Roast Beef Sandwich

✳   SERVES 1

*4–6 ounces roast beef (see Night-Before Preparation Tips
    Day Six), thinly sliced
⅓ cup Tarragon Dressing (see Dinner, Regular Track)
2 large plain rice cakes*

Marinate roast beef slices in ⅓ cup dressing for 15 minutes in refrigerator if time allows, or toss beef with dressing just before serving. Make a sandwich using rice cakes instead of bread slices. Wrap leftover roast beef in freezer wrap and freeze for use on Day Fourteen.

Brown-Bag Beef Pâté

✳ SERVES 1

1–2 jars Beech-Nut Stage One beef
1 teaspoon Puritan oil
1 teaspoon minced fresh parsley
Sea salt to taste
Plain rice cakes or plain rice crackers

Combine beef, oil, parsley and salt to taste. Chill if time allows. Spread on rice cakes or crackers.

Peach

✳

DINNER

Broiled Minute Steaks with Parsley

✳ SERVES 1–2

4 teaspoons Puritan oil
¼ cup finely chopped fresh parsley
1 teaspoon sea salt
2 minute or cubed steaks

Blend oil and parsley thoroughly in a large measuring cup and set aside. Heat a heavy, nonstick skillet until it is very hot and sprinkle it with sea salt. Sear meat quickly on one side, about 2 minutes. Turn and brown on other side, about 1 minute. Remove meat to a platter, drizzle immediately with parsley oil and serve.

Squash

✳ SERVES 1–2

1–2 jars Beech-Nut Stage One squash or 1 (10-ounce)
*   package frozen plain butternut squash*
1 teaspoon Puritan oil
Heinz peach flakes, nutmeg and sea salt to taste

Empty 1–2 jars Beech-Nut Stage One squash or the frozen squash into a saucepan. Add oil and heat, stirring, until hot. Add Heinz peach flakes, nutmeg and sea salt to taste.

Quick Rice

✻

Make any brand, plain precooked rice according to package directions, using Puritan oil, sea salt and water.

Frozen Green Beans

✻

Prepare any brand plain frozen green beans according to package directions, using sea salt and water.

Peach Sorbet
(See Night-Before Preparation Tips for Day Six)

✻

NIGHT-BEFORE PREPARATION TIPS
FOR DAY 7

Parboil millet for Quick Hot Millet Cereal (see Day Seven, Breakfast, Diet Express). Place ½ cup raw millet in small saucepan. Stir in 1 cup boiling water. Cover and simmer over low heat, 10 minutes, stirring occasionally. Remove from heat, transfer to a container with a cover and refrigerate overnight.

MW—Combine ½ cup raw washed millet and 1 cup water in a microwave-safe dish with a cover. Bring to boil (H), 2–3 minutes. Stir, re-cover and microwave (L) 10 minutes more, stirring after 5 minutes. Stir, cover and refrigerate.

DAY ✳ 7 THE REINTRODUCTION PHASE (CITRUS)

ALLOWED FOODS:
Millet, amaranth, lemons, limes, oranges, tangerines, clementines, grapefruit, avocados, carrots, green beans, lentils, okra, salmon, tuna, whitefish, gelatin, chervil, mint, saffron, safflower oil, arrowroot, honey, pignoli (pine nuts)

MENU	REGULAR	DIET EXPRESS
BREAKFAST	Fresh Orange Juice Honey-Millet Cereal or Amaranth Pancakes Mint Tea with Lemon	Fresh Orange or Grapefruit Quick Hot Millet Cereal Mint Tea with Lemon
SNACK	Orange-Mint Frappe Puffed Millet Crunch	Fresh Tangerines

LUNCH	Grilled Salmon
	Avocado Aspic Ring or Quick
	   Avocado Gelatin
	Lemon Dressing or Lime-Mint
	   Dressing
	Iced Tea Special
		Brown-Bag Salmon Salad
		Fresh Orange Juice or Slices
		Iced Tea Special

DINNER	Seafood Gumbo Avocado Sherbet	Seared Tuna or Swordfish Shredded Carrot Salad Quick Carrot Dressing Quick Orange Freeze or Broiled Grapefruit

BULK AGENT: Psyllium seed

REGULAR TRACK

BREAKFAST

Fresh Orange Juice
✳

Freshly squeezed juice (not from concentrate).

＊

Honey-Millet Cereal

＊
SERVES 4

2 teaspoons safflower oil
1 cup raw millet
2 cups water
¼ cup honey

In a heavy skillet, heat 1 teaspoon safflower oil. Add 1 cup millet and toast gently until grain is light tan. Bring 2 cups water to a boil in a saucepan, add remaining oil, ¼ cup honey and toasted millet. Stir, cover and simmer gently until water is absorbed, about 25–30 minutes. Serve hot in bowls, with honey to taste.

Amaranth Pancakes
(See Day Three, Breakfast, Regular Track)

＊

Mint Tea with Lemon

＊
SERVES 1

1–2 leaves fresh mint, washed and crushed or 1 tea bag
    plain mint tea
6–8 ounces boiling water
Fresh lemon and honey to taste

Steep mint leaves or tea bag in 6–8 ounces boiling water about 5 minutes. Add lemon and honey to taste.

SNACK

Orange-Mint Frappe

＊
SERVES 1–2

4 juice oranges
2 tangerines or clementines (if available)
2 ice cubes, crushed
2 teaspoons honey
1–2 Fresh mint sprigs, washed and trimmed

Squeeze oranges and tangerines or clementines by hand or in an electric juicer. (Hand method produces a richer, more filling drink.)

Add crushed ice cubes and honey. Place in blender or processor. Blend until smooth and serve over ice with a sprig of fresh mint.

Puffed Millet Crunch

SERVES 4

3 cups puffed millet cereal
1 cup pignoli (pine nuts)
3 teaspoons safflower oil
⅓ cup honey
¼ cup chopped fresh orange, including peel (wash orange thoroughly before using)

Preheat oven to 275° F.

Combine all ingredients in a bowl. Mix until cereal is completely coated with honey and oil. (Add a bit more honey if necessary.) Spread in a shallow baking pan. Bake for 30 minutes, stirring often until browned. Cool. Store in an airtight container.

MW—Combine ingredients. Spread in a thin layer on a microwave-safe glass or ceramic dish. Microwave (H) 2–3 minutes. Stir after 1 minute. WATCH CAREFULLY to prevent burning. Remove when lightly browned. Cool. Store in an airtight container.

LUNCH

Grilled Salmon

SERVES 4

½ cup safflower oil
2 tablespoons fresh lemon juice
¾ teaspoon sea salt
½ teaspoon ground chervil
4 (6-ounce) salmon steaks

Preheat broiler or barbecue.

Combine oil, lemon juice, salt and chervil to form a marinade. Marinate steaks for 2–3 hours in the refrigerator. Place steaks on a greased broiler rack or grill and cook, basting frequently with marinade, for 7–8 minutes on each side, or until salmon flakes easily with a fork.

✳

MW—Omit salt from marinade. Place marinated steaks in a microwave-safe baking dish just large enough to accommodate them. Pour marinade over steaks. Cover with waxed paper. Cook on roast setting (or [H], with a glass of water placed in oven during cooking) 12 minutes. Rotate one-quarter turn every 3 minutes. Add sea salt when done.

Avocado Aspic Ring

✳

SERVES 4-6

2 envelopes Knox unflavored gelatin
½ cup cold water
3 cups plain carrot juice
2 ripe avocados
Fresh lemon juice
1 large naval orange, peeled and cut into sections
Safflower oil for greasing mold
1 cup sliced, pared fresh carrots

In a large saucepan, soften gelatin in cold water 1 minute; heat, stirring, until dissolved. Add carrot juice, mix well and cool to room temperature. Halve avocados and remove pits. Peel the avocados and cut them into crescent slices. Sprinkle with lemon juice and chill in a covered bowl with orange sections.

Lightly grease a 10-inch (5-cup) ring mold with safflower oil (to facilitate unmolding) and then cover the bottom of the mold with a very thin layer of gelatin. Chill in freezer until set, about 15 minutes. Allow remaining gelatin to stand at room temperature. Arrange half the avocado and orange sections on top of set gelatin in mold and cover with a layer of the remaining room-temperature gelatin. Chill again in freezer until set, about 15 minutes. Arrange more avocado and orange slices around sides of mold and add a thin layer of gelatin to hold them in place. Chill again in freezer 15 minutes.

Mix remaining gelatin with carrots and leftover avocado and chopped orange slices. Turn into the mold and chill in refrigerator until firm, 1 to 2 hours. Unmold and serve with Lemon Dressing or Lime-Mint Dressing (recipes follow below).

Quick Avocado Gelatin

✳ SERVES 4–6

(use same ingredients as for Avocado Aspic Ring on page 145)

In a large saucepan, soften gelatin as in recipe above, and then dissolve completely over heat. Stir in carrot juice. Pour into a serving bowl and chill until consistency of unbeaten egg whites, about 1 hour. Meanwhile, slice avocados and sprinkle with lemon juice. Chill with orange sections and carrots. When gelatin is thickened, stir in avocado, oranges and carrots. Cover and chill until completely set about 2 hours. Unmold and serve with Lemon Dressing or Lime-Mint Dressing (recipes follow).

Note: Substitute orange juice for carrot juice for a sweeter aspic or gelatin.

Lemon Dressing

✳ MAKES ABOUT 1 CUP

1 teaspoon grated lemon peel
¼ cup fresh lemon juice
1 teaspoon sea salt (or to taste)
¾ cup safflower oil
½ teaspoon ground chervil

Combine all ingredients in a jar with a tight-fitting lid. Refrigerate and shake well before using.

Lime-Mint Dressing

✳ MAKES ABOUT 1 CUP

¾ cup safflower oil
¼ cup freshly squeezed lime juice
2 tablespoons honey
1 teaspoon finely chopped fresh mint
1 ice cube, crushed

Mix oil, lime juice, honey and mint. Place in a blender and add crushed ice cube. Blend until mixture is consistency of medium cream sauce.

✳ ———

Note: This dressing is also good in a tossed salad of sliced frozen okra (thawed), shredded carrots and cooked millet (optional). Top with puffed millet for added "crunch."

Iced Tea Special
✳   SERVES 1–2

8 ounces strongly brewed Mint Herbal Tea (see Day Eleven,
*   Breakfast, Regular Track)*
Ice cubes
4 ounces freshly squeezed orange juice
Honey
1 sprig fresh mint

Pour tea over enough ice cubes to chill it quickly. Add orange juice. Sweeten to taste with honey. Stir and add a sprig of mint for garnish.

DINNER

Seafood Gumbo
✳   SERVES 4

½ cup amaranth flour*
½ cup safflower oil
1 (10-ounce) package frozen french-cut string beans
6 cups hot water
1 (10-ounce) package frozen okra, thawed
½ teaspoon saffron
1 teaspoon sea salt
1 pound fresh cod fillet, cubed
6 ounces fresh perch fillet, cubed
Fresh lemon juice to taste

Make the roux: In a heavy 1-quart Dutch oven, combine flour and oil. Cook over medium heat until a dark, reddish-brown roux is formed, about 25 minutes.

Add green beans and stir over medium heat 10 minutes. Stir in water. Stir in okra, saffron and salt. Bring to boil, reduce heat; cover and simmer 1 hour. Add seafood. Simmer, uncovered, 5 minutes or until fish flakes easily. Correct seasonings with sea salt and lemon juice. Serve gumbo with hot millet, cooked according to breakfast directions for Honey-Millet Cereal, omitting honey. (See Day Seven, Breakfast, Regular Track, for Honey-Millet directions.)

*Arrowroot may be used instead of amaranth flour: omit making the roux. Cook green beans in ¼ cup safflower oil 10 minutes. Proceed as above. Just before correcting seasonings, dissolve ⅓ cup arrowroot in ⅓ cup fresh lemon juice and 1 tablespoon cold water. Stir into gumbo until thickened. (Arrowroot thickens before boiling; do not overcook.)

MW—In a large microwave-safe casserole, combine flour and oil. Microwave (L) covered, 4 minutes. Stir every 2 minutes. Stir in string beans, 5 cups hot water, okra, and saffron. Bring to boil (H). Cover. Cook (H) 7–10 minutes. Stir after 5 minutes. Add seafood, stir. Microwave, (H) covered, until fish is cooked, 3–5 minutes. (Cooked fish will look opaque.) Correct seasonings.

Avocado Sherbet

✳ SERVES 4–6

This recipe is adapted from *The California Heritage Cookbook* by The Junior League of Pasadena (Doubleday, 1976).

3 medium-size ripe avocados
¾ cup fresh lemon juice
1 teaspoon grated lemon rind
1½ cups honey
Lemon rind curls (optional)
4 sprigs fresh mint

Peel and pit avocados. Mash in a large bowl until pulp is formed (about 1½ cups pulp) or blend in blender or processor. Add lemon juice and lemon rind to avocado pulp. Slowly add honey, blending thoroughly. Pour into a freezer tray and freeze. Stir once during freezing. Serve in dessert dishes and garnish each serving with rind curls and sprig of fresh mint.

Note: Fresh orange or lime juice (and rinds) can be substituted for lemon, if preferred.

DIET EXPRESS

BREAKFAST

Fresh Orange or Grapefruit

❋

Quick Hot Millet Cereal

❋

SERVES 1

½ cup parboiled millet (See Night-Before Preparation Tips
for Day Seven)
½ cup orange juice or water
Honey to taste

Heat parboiled millet and orange juice or water to boiling, adding a
little more orange juice or water if millet is dry. Cook milet over very
low heat until millet is tender, about 10 minutes, stirring occasionally
and adding liquid as needed. Millet cooked by this method will retain
its texture; it will be chewy and flavorful. If a creamier cereal is desired,
continue cooking over low heat, adding liquid as needed. Sweeten to
taste with honey. Top with chopped oranges.

MW—Heat (H) precooked millet until hot, 1—2 minutes. Stir in ½
cup orange juice or water and continue cooking (L), covered, until
millet is tender, 5–10 minutes. Sweeten to taste with honey. Top with
chopped oranges.

Mint Tea with Lemon
(See Breakfast, Regular Track)

❋

SNACK

Fresh Tangerines

❋

✳

LUNCH

Brown-Bag Salmon Salad

✳   SERVES 1

 1 ripe avocado
 ¼ cup fresh lemon juice
 1 (3-ounce) can water-pack salmon, drained
 2 fresh carrots, pared and chopped
 Fresh mandarin orange sections from 3 oranges (or 4½
   ounces water-pack canned, well drained)
 ½ cup fresh or frozen okra
 ½ cup Lemon Dressing (see Lunch, Regular Track)

Split avocado and remove pit. Brush cut surfaces of avocado liberally
with lemon juice to prevent browning. Place avocado halves in a
plastic or chilled thermal container with a lid. Pick over salmon for
bone and cartilage. Toss with chopped carrots, oranges, okra and
dressing. Stuff avocado halves with mixture. Cover container tightly
and keep refrigerated until ready to eat.

Note: avocado can also be packed whole, split and stuffed just before
serving.

Fresh Orange Juice or Slices

✳

Iced Tea Special
(See Lunch, Regular Track)

✳

DINNER

Seared Tuna or Swordfish

✳   SERVES 1–2

 1 (½-pound) center-cut yellow or blue fin tuna or swordfish,
   thickly cut into 1 or 2 steaks
 1 teaspoon sea salt
 2 tablespoons ground chervil
 2–3 tablespoons safflower oil

*

½ cup frozen okra
½ cup frozen green beans

Press steaks into a mixture of sea salt and ground chervil so that surface of steaks is lightly covered. Heat a heavy sauté pan and pour half the oil into the pan. Bring to the smoking point and carefully place steaks in pan. Sear each side until dark brown and crusty, adding more oil if needed to keep fish from sticking. Sear ends well. Each side should take about 1½ minutes.

Remove steaks from pan to a platter. Lower heat to medium and add remaining oil and vegetables. Sauté vegetables until lightly browned, about 2 minutes. Return steaks to pan and cook with vegetables over low heat about 5–6 minutes more.

Note: Lime-Mint Dressing (see Lunch, Regular Track) may be served as a cold sauce with the fish.

Shredded Carrot Salad

*   SERVES 1–2

3–4 large fresh carrots
Lemon Dressing or Lime-Mint Dressing (see Lunch, Regular
  Track) or Quick Carrot Dressing (recipe follows)

Pare and shred carrots. Toss carrots with lemon dressing, lime-mint dressing or quick carrot dressing and serve.

Quick Carrot Dressing

*   MAKES ½ CUP

1 jar Beech-Nut Stage One carrots
1 tablespoon safflower oil
1 tablespoon honey
½ teaspoon sea salt (or to taste)
1 teaspoon finely chopped fresh mint

Whisk all ingredients together with a wire whisk, or process in a blender. (Blending produces a creamier dressing.)

Quick Orange Freeze

*   SERVES 1–2

1–2 cups peeled, seeded and diced fresh oranges
½ cup fresh orange juice

✳

Purée oranges in a blender or processor, gradually adding juice. Freeze in a mechanical ice-cream maker according to manufacturer's directions.

Broiled Grapefruit

✳   SERVES 1–2

One large ripe red or pink grapefruit
Honey

Preheat broiler.
    Split grapefruit. Spread surface of each half lightly with honey. Broil 4 inches from heat until top of fruit is "caramelized" and lightly brown, about 1 minute.

NIGHT-BEFORE PREPARATION TIPS
———— FOR DAY 8 ————

Make Apple Sorbet: Allowing 1 jar per serving, empty as many jars Beech-Nut Stage One applesauce as you think you will need into a freezer container with a lid. Freeze overnight to use as instant sorbet in beverages or desserts. As dessert, allow to soften 15 minutes in the refrigerator before serving as sorbet.

DAY
✳

8

THE REINTRODUCTION PHASE
(CORN)

ALLOWED FOODS:
Corn, apples, broccoli, cauliflower, sweet potatoes, water chestnuts, lamb, basil, cinnamon, rosemary, corn oil, nyafat, mace, maple syrup, sunflower seeds

MENU	REGULAR	DIET EXPRESS
BREAKFAST	Hasty Pudding	Puffed Corn Cereal with
	Corn Pancakes	Applesauce or
	Sliced Apple	Quick-Cooking Grits with
	Cinnamon Stick Tea	Applesauce
		Cinnamon Stick Tea

✳

SNACK	Fresh Popcorn or Puffed Corn Granola Apple Juice	Fresh Microwave Popcorn Apple Juice

LUNCH	Lamb-Cauliflower Soup
	Corn Cracker-Bread
	Lamburgers
	Fried Cornmeal Mush
	Applesauce
	Apple Spritzer
		Quick Lamb Pâté with Corn
		  Tortillas
		Beech-Nut Stage One Sweet
		  Potatoes
		Fresh Apple
		Iced Cinnamon Stick Tea

DINNER	Roast Leg of Lamb or
	Crown Roast of Lamb or
	Middle Eastern Style Leg of
	  Lamb
	Fresh Corn on the Cob
	Fresh Broccoli, Cauliflower and
	  Water Chestnut Salad
	Sweet Dressing
	Apple Crisp
		Broiled Lamb Chops
		Fresh Corn on the Cob
		Quick Broccoli, Cauliflower and
		  Water Chestnut Salad
		Quick Apple Cobbler
		Apple Sorbet

BULK AGENT: Corn bran

R E G U L A R   T R A C K

B R E A K F A S T

Hasty Pudding (Cornmeal Mush)

✳

SERVES 4–6

¾ cup yellow cornmeal
3 cups water
½ teaspoon sea salt
Dash ground cinnamon
Nyafat
Maple syrup or plain unsweetened applesauce

Mix cornmeal with 1 cup water. Bring 2 cups water to boil, add salt. Stir in cornmeal mixture, lower heat, and cook 10–15 minutes, stirring frequently. Add cinnamon. Serve warm with a pat of nyafat and maple syrup or applesauce. (Pudding may be started in the top half of a double boiler, then covered and placed over boiling water and steamed for half an hour. This eliminates need for frequent stirring.)

Corn Pancakes

SERVES 4–6

2 cups corn flour
2 cups (approximate) water
1 tablespoon pure corn oil plus oil for greasing skillet
Dash sea salt

Mix corn flour, water, oil and salt together into a smooth, thick but pourable batter. Grease a skillet with corn oil. Heat the skillet over medium-high heat until it is hot, but not smoking.

Using ½ cup for each pancake, pour batter onto hot skillet. Cook pancakes on one side until crisp, about 2 minutes. Turn pancakes and cook until other side is crisp and pancakes can be lifted easily from the pan, about 2 minutes more. Top with maple syrup or plain unsweetened applesauce.

Cinnamon Stick Tea

SERVES 1

1 cinnamon stick
2 tablespoons chopped apple peel from a fresh, washed
    apple
6–8 ounces boiling water
Apple juice, Heinz apple flakes or maple syrup to taste

Break 1 cinnamon stick into pieces. Place cinnamon and apple peel in a tea ball or homemade cheesecloth tea bag and steep 1–2 minutes in the boiling water. Sweeten with apple juice, Heinz apple flakes or maple syrup to taste.

SNACK

Fresh Popcorn

MAKES 4–6 CUPS POPCORN

1 teaspoon pure corn oil
½ cup plain corn for popping
½ cup nyafat, melted
Sea salt to taste

Heat oil until hot in a large, deep pot with a lid. Add popcorn, cover and cook over medium-high heat until corn begins to pop, about 5 minutes. Shake pan continually until popping stops. Remove pan immediately from heat and empty popped corn into a bowl. Drizzle hot popcorn with melted nyafat and salt to taste with sea salt.

Puffed Corn Granola

SERVES 4–6

*3 cups puffed corn cereal or fresh popcorn (see above
    recipe)
1 cup chopped, unpeeled fresh apple (washed)
½ cup sunflower seeds
1 tablespoon melted nyafat or pure corn oil plus nyafat or
    oil for greasing pan
⅓ cup maple syrup*

Preheat oven to 275° F.

Combine cereal, apple and seeds in a bowl. Heat nyafat or oil and maple syrup in a saucepan until smooth and bubbly, stirring constantly. Pour over cereal and mix well to coat, adding a little more syrup if necessary to coat cereal mixture completely. Spread in a baking pan lightly greased wth corn oil or nyafat.

Bake for 30 minutes, stirring occasionally until browned. Cool. Store in a covered container for remainder of day. Reserve ½ cup of Puffed Corn Granola for Quick Apple Cobbler, Dinner, Diet Express.

MW—Prepare cereal mixture as above. Spread on waxed paper in a wide, shallow microwave-safe dish. Cover with a sheet of waxed paper. Microwave (H) 3 minutes. Stir. Microwave (H) 1 minute more, or until syrup-shortening is absorbed. Granola crisps as it cools.

LUNCH

Lamb-Cauliflower Soup

SERVES 4

*2–4 tablespoons nyafat or pure corn oil
1 large head fresh cauliflower, washed and separated into
    flowerets or 3 cups thawed frozen cauliflower florets
Water to cover
2 jars Beech-Nut Stage One lamb
Sea salt to taste
Ground rosemary (1–2 teaspoons or to taste)
Cooked lamb cut into small chunks (optional)*

Heat nyafat or oil in large skillet and sauté cauliflower until golden brown, about 5 minutes. Add water to cover and simmer cauliflower 15 minutes.

Remove cauliflower, drain (reserving liquid) and purée in a blender or with a potato masher until smooth. Place puréed cauliflower in a large saucepan, add Beech-Nut lamb and mix well. Slowly add reserved cauliflower water until soup is of desired consistency. Season with sea salt and rosemary to taste. Add lamb chunks and heat just to boiling.

Note: This makes a rich, creamlike soup base without any dairy products or thickeners. If using cooked lamb, reserve the meat juices left from cooking the lamb and add to the soup.

Corn Cracker-Bread

✻   SERVES 4

Pure corn oil for greasing pan plus 1 tablespoon oil
2 cups corn flour
Dash sea salt (optional)
2–3 cups water

Preheat oven broiler.

Grease a baking pan or cookie sheet with pure corn oil.

In a large bowl, mix corn flour, 1 tablespoon oil and salt with 1½ cups water until completely mixed. Keep adding water, a little at a time, until mixture holds together and is a thick but pourable batter. Spread batter on cookie sheet in a thin, even layer.

Place cookie sheet about 6 inches from broiler. Broil about 5 minutes, or until edges and top of bread begin to brown. Turn off broiler and close oven door. Allow cracker-bread to continue cooking 10–15 minutes in the cooling oven. (Test bread for crispness after 10 minutes; 15 minutes produces a very crisp, firm bread-cracker when it cools.)

Lamburgers
(See Day One, Lunch, Regular Track)

✻   SERVES 4

✳

Fried Cornmeal Mush

✳ SERVES 4

2 tablespoons corn flour plus flour for coating
1 cup cooked cornmeal mush (see Breakfast, Regular Track)
1–2 teaspoons pure corn oil or nyafat (see Index)

Mix 2 tablespoons corn flour into cooked cornmeal. Pack into a 1-pound loaf-shaped container and refrigerate 1 hour or more. When ready to fry, cut cold mush into 4 slices, dust them lightly with corn flour and fry slices in hot corn oil or melted nyafat until browned on both sides, about 4 minutes. Serve with maple syrup or unsweetened pure applesauce.

Applesauce

✳

Apple Spritzer

✳ SERVES 1

2 ounces strongly brewed Cinnamon Stick Tea (see
    Breakfast, Regular Track)
4 ounces plain apple juice
Ice cubes
1–2 ounces mineral water
1 cinnamon stick
1 (2-ounce) scoop Apple Sorbet (see Night-Before
    Preparation Tips for Day Eight)

Combine tea and apple juice in a glass over ice. Add 1–2 ounces mineral water. Serve with a stick of cinnamon and scoop of sorbet as garnish.

DINNER

Roast Leg of Lamb

✳ SERVES 4–6

1 (5–6 pound) leg of lamb
Ground rosemary
Sea salt to taste

✳

Preheat oven to 300° F.

Rub leg of lamb all over with ground rosemary. Place lamb on a rack in a roasting pan, and roast, uncovered, 18 minutes per pound for well done (175° F. on meat thermometer), 15 minutes for medium (160°), 12 minutes for rare (140° F). After cooking season to taste with sea salt.

Crown Roast of Lamb

✳   SERVES 4–6

2 racks of lamb, about 2 pounds each
Ground rosemary
Sea salt
3 cups chopped, unpeeled fresh apples (washed)
1 cup crushed puffed corn cereal
1 teaspoon pure corn oil

Ask butcher to form racks into a crown roast.

Preheat oven to 350° F.

Rub roast with rosemary and sprinkle lightly with sea salt. Mix chopped apples, crushed corn cereal and oil together; stuff center of roast with mixture. Cover tips of roast with foil and roast 12 minutes per pound of meat (140° F. on a meat thermometer).

Middle Eastern Style Leg of Lamb

✳   SERVES 4–6

1 (5–6 pound) leg of lamb
Sea salt
Ground basil
8 leaves fresh basil, washed and trimmed
1 cup plain apple juice

Preheat oven to 450° F.

Rub lamb all over with sea salt and ground basil. Bake for 15 minutes, to brown. Baste the roast with juices in pan, reduce heat to 300° F., and roast 45 minutes more, basting frequently. Cover roast with 8 fresh basil leaves, add 1 cup apple juice and roast 20–30 minutes more (or until roast registers 175° F. on a meat thermometer), basting frequently.

Fresh Corn on the Cob

SERVES 4–6

6 ears fresh corn
1 teaspoon sea salt
Sufficient cold water (2 quarts) so that corn "rolls" freely at
*   boil*
Nyafat and sea salt to taste

Shuck corn, washing well in cold water. Place in a large pot with 1 teaspoon salt and enough cold water (2 quarts) so that corn will "roll" freely when water is brought to boil. As soon as water is boiling rapidly, remove pot from heat, cover, and allow corn to stand at least 10 minutes, or until ready to serve. Serve hot corn with nyafat and sea salt to taste.

MW—Wrap husked ears individually in plastic wrap or waxed paper. Microwave (H) 2–3 minutes per ear.

Fresh Broccoli, Cauliflower and Water Chestnut Salad

SERVES 4

6 ounces each fresh broccoli florets, cauliflower florets, and
*   drained canned water chesnuts*
Sweet Dressing (recipe follows)

Wash and drain vegetables; place them in a bowl. Pour sweet dressing over vegetables, toss the salad and serve.

Sweet Dressing

MAKES 1 CUP

1 jar Beech-Nut Stage One sweet potatoes
¼ cup maple syrup
¼ cup pure corn oil
Sea salt and ground basil to taste

Combine ingredients in a blender or shaker with a lid and blend or shake until thoroughly combined.

Apple Crisp

✳ SERVES 4–6

4 cups chopped, cored, unpeeled fresh apples washed
½ cup plain unsweetened chunky-style applesauce
1 teaspoon ground cinnamon
Dash mace
4 tablespoons nyafat
4 tablespoons maple syrup
2 cups puffed corn cereal, crushed

Preheat oven to 350° F.

Place apples, applesauce, cinnamon and mace in a deep-dish pie plate. Mix well.

Heat nyafat in a saucepan. Add maple syrup and puffed corn. Stir. Pour topping over apples and press down flat. Bake until apples are bubbly and top is golden brown, about 20 minutes.

Variation: Make corn puff cereal pie shell: Preheat oven to 400°F. Crumble enough puffed corn cereal to make 1 cup. Combine with 2 tablespoons nyafat, hydrogenated or liquid, and mix until well combined. Spread over botton of a pie plate. Bake 5 minutes. Cool and fill with apple filling (prepared as above). Bake until hot, about 10–15 minutes.

DIET EXPRESS

BREAKFAST

Puffed Corn Cereal with Applesauce

✳ SERVES 1

1 cup puffed corn cereal
1 jar Beech-Nut Stage One applesauce or ½ cup
    unsweetened plain chunky-style applesauce
Plain apple juice

Combine cereal and applesauce. Thin with apple juice if desired.

*

Quick-Cooking Grits with Applesauce

SERVES 1

*

1 cup water
¼ cup quick-cooking grits
Dash sea salt
Nyafat and/or plain unsweetened applesauce to taste

Bring water to a boil in a small, deep saucepan. Stir in grits, salt and cook over low heat, 2 minutes. Pour into a bowl and allow to stand until thickened to taste. Add a pat of nyafat or top with applesauce.

MW—Combine water, grits and salt in a large, shallow bowl. Microwave (H) until water boils, 1 minute. Stir, microwave (L) 1–2 minutes more, until thickened to taste.

Cinnamon Stick Tea
(See Breakfast, Regular Track)

*

SNACK

Fresh Microwave Popcorn

SERVES 1

*

¼ cup plain popping corn
Sea salt

MW—Place popping corn in a lunch bag made of heavy brown paper. Fold over the top of the bag, leaving a small vent at one corner. Microwave (H) until corn begins to pop, 2–3 minutes. Watch carefully during cooking; paper bags can catch fire if left too long in microwave ovens. Remove bag immediately after popping begins to slow. Do not leave bag in oven longer than 4 minutes. Empty popcorn into a bowl and salt to taste with sea salt.

Apple Juice

*

LUNCH

Quick Lamb Pâté with Corn Tortillas
✳   SERVES 1

> *2–3 corn tortillas*
> *1–2 jars Beech-Nut Stage One lamb*
> *½ teaspoon pure corn oil*
> *Sea salt to taste*
> *Ground basil to taste (optional)*

Preheat oven to 350° F.

Place tortillas on a baking pan or piece of aluminum foil and heat briefly while preparing pâté. Combine lamb with corn oil. Season to taste with sea salt and basil, if desired. Serve with heated tortillas.

Note: Look for tortillas made of corn flour and water only in the freezer section of the market. One good brand is Patio. (See suggestions for making corn tortillas under recipe for Wheat Flour Tortillas, Day Twelve, Breakfast, Regular Track; and also Day Eighteen, Breakfast, Regular Track).

Beech-Nut Stage One Sweet Potatoes
✳   SERVES 1

> *1–2 jars Beech-Nut Stage One sweet potatoes*
> *Cinnamon and sea salt to taste*

Season sweet potatoes to taste with cinnamon and sea salt. Heat or serve chilled.

Fresh Apple
✳

Iced Cinnamon Stick Tea
(See Breakfast, Regular Track)
✳   SERVES 1

Make cinnamon stick tea according to directions (Breakfast, Regular Track). Serve over ice and sweeten to taste with maple syrup.

✳ ───

DINNER

Broiled Lamb Chops

✳ SERVES 1

2 thick lamb chops, shoulder or loin
Ground basil
2 teaspoons melted nyafat
Sea salt

Preheat broiler (very hot).

Rub lamb with ground basil. Press in. Broil chops on a rack about 2 inches from heat. Broil both sides, cooking a total of 10 minutes for rare, 15 for medium, 20 for well done. Transfer to a plate, top each chop with 1 teaspoon nyafat, and season to taste with sea salt.

Fresh Corn on the Cob
(See Dinner, Regular Track)

✳

Quick Broccoli, Cauliflower and Water Chestnut Salad

✳ SERVES 1–2

1 (20-ounce) bag frozen combination broccoli, cauliflower
    and water chestnuts
1 recipe Sweet Dressing

Place ½ bag frozen vegetables in a colander and rinse briefly with cold water to defrost them. Place defrosted vegetables in a large bowl. Prepare Sweet Dressing according to directions for Dinner, Regular Track, toss ½ cup dressing with vegetables and serve.

Quick Apple Cobbler

✳ SERVES 1

1 large fresh unpeeled red Delicious apple, washed, cored
    and thinly sliced
Dash each cinnamon and mace
1 teaspoon maple syrup
1 teaspoon melted nyafat
½ cup Puffed Corn Granola (see Snack, Regular Track) or
    crushed puffed corn cereal

Preheat oven to 350° F.

Combine all ingredients except granola or puffed corn cereal. Toss to mix. Spread in a small baking dish. Bake 5 minutes. Sprinkle with granola or puffed corn and return to the oven for 2–3 more minutes. Serve hot.

Apple Sorbet
(See Night Before Preparation Tips for Day Eight)

✳　　　　　　　　　　　　　　　　　　　　　　　　　SERVES 1

NIGHT-BEFORE PREPARATION TIPS
FOR DAY 9

1. Presoak raw, washed and picked over kasha for Microwave Kasha with Bananas (see Day Nine, Breakfast, Diet Express): Bring 1 cup water to a boil in a saucepan. Stir in ½ cup kasha. Cover and refrigerate overnight.

2. Soak 1 cup chick-peas in water to cover overnight in refrigerator.

3. Make Frozen Bananas: Combine ⅛ scant cup carob powder (use carob sparingly, as it has a slightly bitter taste) and ½ cup beet sugar or 4 ounces banana flakes in a saucepan. Blend in about ⅓ cup hot water and bring to boil, stirring constantly. Lower heat and stir about 2 minutes, adding more water or sweetening according to taste, until syrup is smooth and consistency of thick chocolate syrup.

Cool slightly.

Peel 2 firm fresh bananas. Dip bananas in carob syrup and coat completely. Place on waxed paper and freeze until completely frozen.

4. Make Carob-Banana Frozen Dessert: In a blender or processor, combine 4 teaspoons water, 2 scant teaspoons carob powder, (use carob powder sparingly as it has a slightly bitter taste), 4 heaping teaspoons beet sugar or Heinz banana flakes. Add 2 large very ripe peeled bananas, cut into chunks. Blend until completely smooth.

Freeze dessert in a covered freezer container overnight. Allow to soften 10–15 minutes in refrigerator before serving. Top with sliced, fresh banana or melon, if desired.

✳

5. Make Banana Sorbet: Allowing 1 jar per serving, empty as many jars Beech-Nut Stage One bananas as you think you will need into a freezer container with a lid. Freeze overnight to use as instant sorbet in beverages or desserts. As dessert, allow to soften 15 minutes in the refrigerator before serving as sorbet.

DAY 9
✳

THE REINTRODUCTION PHASE (CHICKEN)

ALLOWED FOODS:
Chicken, kasha, lima beans, bananas, melon, alfalfa sprouts, beets, celery, chick-peas, kidney beans, pumpkin, spinach, sesame, ginger, carob

MENU	REGULAR	DIET EXPRESS
BREAKFAST	Hot Kasha with Bananas and Ginger Lima Bean Pancakes Ginger Herbal Tea	Microwaved Kasha with Bananas Ginger Herbal Tea
SNACK	Banana-Carob Clusters Banana Shake	Crunchy Chick-peas Watermelon Cooler
LUNCH	Chicken Livers Baked with Kasha Creamy Chicken Soup Frozen Bananas	Brown-Bag Salad Beet Dressing Fresh Bananas
DINNER	Roast Chicken with Kasha Stuffing Three-Bean Salad Beet Dressing Carob-Banana Frozen Dessert	Quick Chicken Bake Spinach Salad Tahini Dressing Quick Pumpkin-Banana Pudding

BULK AGENT: None

REGULAR TRACK

BREAKFAST

Hot Kasha with Bananas and Ginger

✳ SERVES 4

> *2 cups water*
> *1 cup raw kasha (washed and picked over)*
> *2 ripe bananas, peeled and mashed*
> *1 teaspoon ground ginger*
> *Heinz banana flakes to taste*

Bring water to boil in a large saucepan or top of a double boiler. Stir kasha into boiling water. Cook over low heat or simmering water 20–30 minutes. Stir in mashed bananas and ginger and cook until heated through. Sweeten to taste with Heinz banana flakes.

Lima Bean Pancakes
(See Day One Breakfast, Regular Track)

✳ SERVES 4

Use Beech-Nut Stage One bananas as a topping for pancakes.

Ginger Herbal Tea

✳ SERVES 1

> *2 teaspoons minced gingerroot*
> *1 cup boiling water*
> *Heinz banana flakes to taste*

Steep minced gingerroot in 1 cup boiling water about 5 minutes. Sweeten to taste with banana flakes.

✳ ——————————————————————

SNACK

Banana-Carob Clusters

✳   SERVES 4

1 cup tahini, mixed well to incorporate oil
¼ cup (scant) carob powder (use carob sparingly as it has
    a slightly bitter taste)
1 large ripe banana, peeled and mashed
1 teaspoon ground ginger
Heinz banana flakes (optional)
Sesame seeds

Mix together tahini, carob powder, mashed banana and ginger until
thoroughly combined. Taste for sweetness; add banana flakes to
sweeten, if desired. Generously sprinkle a large sheet of waxed paper
with sesame seeds. Roll tahini-banana mixture by teaspoonfuls in
seeds until clusters are coated.

In a single layer, place clusters in a covered container or ice-cube
tray lined with waxed paper and chill in refrigerator.

Banana Shake

✳   SERVES 1

1 jar Beech-Nut Stage One bananas
1 (2-ounce) scoop Banana Sorbet (see Night-Before
    Preparation Tips for Day Nine)

Combine Beech-Nut Stage One bananas with banana sorbet in a
blender. Blend until smooth and serve.

LUNCH

Chicken Livers Baked with Kasha

✳   SERVES 4

Sesame flour or buckwheat flour for dredging
1 pound chicken livers, each cut into 2–3 pieces
Sea salt
3 tablespoons sesame oil
1½ cups raw kasha (washed and picked over)

2½ cups water
1 teaspoon minced gingerroot

Preheat oven to 350°F.

Place a small amount of flour in a plastic or paper bag. Sprinkle cut-up livers with salt, add them to the flour in the bag and shake them until lightly coated. Heat 1 tablespoon of the oil in a skillet. Sauté the livers until crisp on the outside and brown, about 5 minutes. Transfer the livers to a large casserole with a cover.

Wash the kasha and drain it. Heat remaining 2 tablespoons oil in the skillet and sauté kasha 2 minutes over medium heat. Add water and gingerroot and stir well. Add to livers in the casserole and stir to combine. Cover the casserole tightly and bake 30 minutes, or until kasha is tender and liquid is absorbed. Stir with fork before serving to release steam and correct seasoning with sea salt.

Creamy Chicken Soup
✳   **SERVES 4**

1 (3-pound) chicken, cut into serving pieces
1 cup chopped celery
Water to cover
1 teaspoon sea salt
4 jars Beech-Nut Stage One chicken

Cover chicken and celery with water in a deep saucepan, add salt and bring to boil. Lower heat and simmer covered until chicken is tender, about 1 hour.

Remove chicken from stock. Strain stock and take meat from skin and bones. Chop meat and return to stock. Thicken soup with Beech-Nut Stage One chicken, using about 1 jar per 1 cup broth. Correct seasoning with sea salt.

Frozen Bananas
(See Night-Before Preparation Tips for Day Nine)
✳

DINNER

Roast Chicken with Kasha Stuffing

✳   SERVES 4

Stuffing:

> *1 cup raw kasha (washed and picked over)*
> *2 cups water*
> *½ teaspoon sea salt*
> *1 (10-ounce) package frozen chopped spinach*
> *2 tablespoons sesame oil*

Wash and drain the kasha. Bring water to boil and add kasha and salt. Lower heat, cover pan and simmer for 15 minutes, until kasha is tender and water is absorbed. While kasha is cooking, defrost the spinach and squeeze it dry by hand. Stir kasha and oil into spinach until thoroughly combined and set aside.

Chicken:

> *1 (4-pound) roasting chicken*
> *Kasha stuffing (above)*
> *1 tablespoon sesame oil*
> *½ teaspoon sea salt*
> *Dash ground ginger*
> *½ cup water*

Preheat oven to 425°F.

Stuff chicken with kasha stuffing, truss it and place in a shallow baking dish. Drizzle with sesame oil. Combine salt and ginger and sprinkle over chicken. Roast for 15 minutes at 425°F. Add water, reduce heat to 350°F. and roast 1 hour longer, basting occasionally with juices in pan, until juices run clear from chicken when pierced with a fork.

Three-Bean Salad

✳   SERVES 4

> *1 cup drained presoaked chick-peas (see Night-Before*
> *   Preparations for Day Nine)*
> *Water to cover*
> *Sea salt*
> *½ cup chopped, drained, canned water-pack beets*
> *1 cup drained, canned water-pack white kidney beans*

1 cup drained, defrosted frozen lima beans
½ cup fresh alfalfa sprouts (washed and dried)
Beet Dressing (recipe follows)

Place presoaked chick-peas in a saucepan with water to cover. Add a pinch of salt, bring to boil and simmer until peas are tender, about 30 minutes. Chill in refrigerator while preparing the rest of the salad.

Combine remaining vegetables in a salad bowl and chill while preparing beet dressing. When chilled, add chick-peas to the vegetables in the salad bowl. Toss vegetables with dressing before serving.

Beet Dressing

✻   MAKES 1 CUP

1-2 jars Beech-Nut Stage One beets
½ cup sesame oil
Sea salt and ground ginger to taste

Combine beets, oil, salt and ginger in a blender or shaker with a lid. Blend or shake well.

Carob-Banana Frozen Dessert
(See Night-Before Preparation Tips for Day Nine)

✻

DIET EXPRESS

BREAKFAST

Microwaved Kasha with Bananas

✻   SERVES 1

½ cup water
1 teaspoon sesame oil
*½ cup presoaked kasha, with any liquid that has not been
    absorbed (see Night-Before Preparation Tips for Day
    Nine)*
Dash each ground ginger and sea salt
1 jar Beech-Nut Stage One bananas
1 banana, peeled and sliced

MW—Place water in a 2-cup microwave-safe bowl or measuring cup. Heat (H) until water boils, about 1 minute. Stir in oil, presoaked kasha, ginger and sea salt. Microwave (H) 30 seconds. Stir again, and cook (L) or on defrost setting, 1–2 minutes more. Test kasha for doneness. For a more tender cereal, microwave a few minutes more (L), adding water if kasha seems dry. Stir Beech-Nut Stage One bananas into cooked cereal and garnish with fresh, sliced banana.

Ginger Herbal Tea
(See Breakfast, Regular Track)

*

SNACK

Crunchy Chick-peas
*   SERVES 1–2

1 cup drained, canned water-pack chick-peas
Sea salt to taste

MW—Empty canned chick-peas into a colander, rinse them under cold water and allow them to drain. Place drained chick-peas on a paper towel in a microwave-safe pie plate. Cover with another paper towel. Microwave (H) 8–12 minutes, until peas are crunchy. Season to taste with sea salt.

Watermelon Cooler
*   SERVES 1

1 cup chopped watermelon (seeds and rind removed)
Pinch ground ginger
1–2 ounces sparkling mineral water

Place watermelon and ginger in a blender. Blend until smooth and pour into a tall glass. Add sparkling mineral water and stir.

LUNCH

Brown-Bag Salad
✳   SERVES 1

½ cup drained, canned water-pack beets
¼ cup drained, canned water-pack chick-peas (rinsed
*   under cold water)*
½ cup fresh alfalfa sprouts (washed and dried)
1 (6-ounce) can water-pack chicken
Fresh spinach leaves, washed, dried and torn into bite-sized
*   pieces*
Sesame seeds
Beet Dressing (recipe follows)
Sea salt

Make sure vegetables and chicken are thoroughly drained before proceeding with recipe. In thermal container, layer vegetables, chicken and sesame seeds on top of dressing in the following order: beets, chick-peas, sprouts, chicken, spinach and seeds, sprinkling each layer very lightly with sea salt. Refrigerate until ready to serve. Toss just before serving.

Beet Dressing
✳   MAKES ½ CUP

1 jar Beech-Nut Stage One beets
1 teaspoon sesame oil
Sea salt and ginger to taste

Combine all dressing ingredients in a thermal or plastic container with a lid. Shake well to combine.

Fresh Bananas
✳

DINNER

Quick Chicken Bake

✳ SERVES 1

Aluminum foil, double-strength
1 cup fresh (uncooked) chicken nuggets
½ cup fresh alfalfa sprouts (washed and dried)
½ cup sliced fresh celery
½ cup frozen lima beans
1 tablespoon sesame oil
Ground ginger
Sea salt

Preheat oven to 400°F.

Tear off a large sheet of aluminum foil and fold it in half. Combine chicken nuggets, sprouts, celery, and lima beans and place them in the middle of the piece of foil. Drizzle the mixture with sesame oil and sprinkle with ground ginger and salt. Bring sides and ends of aluminum foil together and tightly seal. Place the aluminum foil "envelope" on a baking sheet and bake 10–15 minutes, until chicken is no longer pink in the middle and lima beans are tender-crisp. Serve with hot kasha.

Spinach Salad

✳ SERVES 1–2

1 pound fresh spinach
1 teaspoon sesame seeds (optional)
Tahini Dressing (recipe follows)

Wash spinach leaves thoroughly, dry and tear into bite-sized pieces. Place spinach in a salad bowl, sprinkle with sesame seeds and toss with Tahini Dressing.

Tahini Dressing

✳ MAKES 1 CUP

½ cup tahini, mixed well to incorporate oil
½ cup water
Sea salt and ground ginger to taste

Combine tahini and water in a blender or by hand. Season to taste with sea salt and ginger.

Quick Pumpkin-Banana Pudding
✳   SERVES 1–2

1 cup plain canned pumpkin
1 banana, peeled and sliced
1 teaspoon ground ginger
Heinz banana flakes to taste (optional)

Place pumpkin, banana and ginger in a blender, blend until smooth and taste for sweetness. Add Heinz banana flakes if greater sweetness is desired. Serve at once, or place in the freezer in a covered container about 15–20 minutes, until pudding is thoroughly chilled. Stir before serving.

NIGHT-BEFORE PREPARATION TIPS
FOR DAY 10

Make On-the-Double Pear Sorbet: Allowing 1 jar per serving, empty as many jars Beech-Nut Stage One pears as you think you will need into a freezer container with a lid. Freeze overnight to use as instant sorbet in beverages or desserts. As dessert, allow to soften 15 minutes in the refrigerator before serving as sorbet.

DAY 10
✳

THE REINTRODUCTION PHASE
(OATS)

ALLOWED FOODS:
Oats, papayas, pears, eggplant, lettuce, parsley, pink beans, yellow squash, zucchini, veal, mustard, rose hips, olive oil, gelatin

MENU	REGULAR	DIET EXPRESS
BREAKFAST	Pear Juice	Pear Juice
	Hot Oatmeal or Oat Pancakes	Beech-Nut Stage One Oatmeal
	Rose Hip Herbal Tea	Cereal or
		Quick-Cooking Plain Oatmeal
		Rose Hip Tea

✳

SNACK	Papaya-Pear Shake	Rice Cakes
		Fresh Papaya
LUNCH	Broiled Vealburgers	Veal Pâté with Rice Cakes and
	Veal and Zucchini Soup	Zucchini Sticks
	Pear and Oat Bars	Quick Squash-Zucchini Soup
	Rose Hip Tea Spritzer	Fresh Pear
DINNER	Veal Breast with Parsley-Oat	Sautéed Veal Chops
	Stuffing	Quick-Cooking Rice
	Ghiveciu	Pink Bean Salad
	Pink Bean Salad	Quick Mustard Dressing
	Mustard Dressing	On-the-Double Pear Sorbet
	On-the-Double Pear Sorbet	

BULK AGENT: Oat bran

R E G U L A R   T R A C K

B R E A K F A S T

Pear Juice

Not nectar; pure juice such as After the Fall brand

Note: If you cannot find pure pear juice for today's recipes, thin 1 jar Beech-Nut Stage One pears with 4 ounces water as substitute (yield: 8 ounces pear juice).

Hot Oatmeal

✳   SERVES 4

1⅓ cups plain regular oatmeal (not quick-cooking)
4 cups water
Dash sea salt (optional)
1 large fresh unpeeled pear, washed, cored and chopped

Combine oatmeal, water and salt, if desired, in a large saucepan. Bring to boil, stirring constantly. Lower heat and continue to cook, stirring, until oatmeal is of desired consistency. Stir in fresh pears. Top with Beech-Nut Stage One pears, if desired.

Oat Pancakes

✳ SERVES 4

> *2 cups plain oat bran cereal**
> *2 cups (approximate) water*
> *2 teaspoons olive oil plus oil for greasing skillet*

Mix oat bran cereal, water and oil together until a smooth, thick but pourable batter is formed. Grease a skillet with oil. Heat the skillet until hot but not smoking. Using ½ cup for each pancake, pour batter onto hot skillet. Cook pancakes 1–2 minutes on one side. Turn and cook pancakes 1–2 minutes more, until they are cooked through and can be easily lifted from pan. Top with Beech-Nut pears.

*If you cannot find oat bran cereal, you can make an acceptable substitute by processing 2 cups plain uncooked oatmeal (not quick-cooking) in a blender until well ground. Mix the ground oats with ½ cup Beech-Nut Stage One oatmeal cereal and proceed with recipe.

Rose Hip Herbal Tea

✳ SERVES 1

> *1 tea bag pure rose hip herbal tea*
> *6 ounces boiling water*
> *Plain pear juice to taste*

Place tea bag in a mug or cup. Add boiling water and steep tea until of desired strength. Add pear juice to sweeten to taste.

SNACK

Papaya-Pear Shake

✳ SERVES 1

> *1 ripe fresh papaya, peeled and seeded*
> *1 ripe fresh pear, peeled and cored*
> *1 ice cube, crushed*

Cut fruit into chunks and place in a blender or food processor. Add ice cube and blend on highest power until smooth.

LUNCH

Broiled Vealburgers

SERVES 4

1 pound ground veal
1 teaspoon dry mustard
½ teaspoon sea salt
Olive oil for greasing skillet

Combine veal with mustard and salt. Shape into 4 patties. Lightly oil a skillet with olive oil and heat until hot. Pan-broil patties on both sides until desired doneness, 5–10 minutes total cooking time.

Veal and Zucchini Soup

SERVES 4

1 tablespoon olive oil
3 pounds (4–6 large pieces) veal stew meat (with bone)
1½ cups fresh or frozen chopped zucchini (undefrosted)
½ teaspoon sea salt
1 teaspoon dry mustard
1–2 jars Beech-Nut Stage One veal
1½ cups water

Heat oil in a Dutch oven over medium heat. Add veal and brown pieces on all sides for about 4 minutes. When meat pieces are browned, reduce heat to low, add zucchini, and sauté until vegetable is softened, about 5 minutes. Stir in salt, mustard, 1 jar veal and ½ cup water. Reduce heat to very low and simmer, covered, 20 minutes. (Add more water or Beech-Nut Stage One veal, depending on thickness of soup desired. Correct seasoning with sea salt.)

Pear and Oat Bars

MAKES 2 DOZEN

½ cup cold water mixed with ¾ cup plain pear juice
3 envelopes Knox unflavored gelatin
2 cups plain regular oatmeal
1 jar Beech-Nut Stage One pears
½ cup chopped firm fresh pears (washed and cored, but not
    peeled)

Place cold water and pear juice mixture in a saucepan. Sprinkle gelatin on top and allow to soften 1 minute. Bring to boil, stirring constantly. Remove from heat and continue to stir, until gelatin is completely dissolved (about 2 minutes).

Stir in oatmeal, Beech-Nut pears and fresh pears. Pour into an 8-inch baking pan and refrigerate until firm. Cut into bars and serve.

Rose Hip Tea Spritzer
✳   SERVES 1

2 ounces strongly brewed rose hip tea
4 ounces plain pear juice
Ice
2 ounces sparkling mineral water
Heinz pear flakes (optional)

Combine tea and pear juice. Pour over ice and add 1–2 ounces sparkling mineral water. If desired, sweeten to taste with Heinz pear flakes.

DINNER

Veal Breast with Parsley-Oat Stuffing
✳   SERVES 4

Stuffing:

4 tablespoons olive oil
1½ cups chopped fresh parsley (washed and dried)
¾ cup plain regular oatmeal (not quick-cooking)
½ teaspoon sea salt
Water or plain pear juice to moisten stuffing

Heat 3 tablespoons oil in a large skillet. Add parsley and sauté 3 minutes. Add remaining 1 tablespoon oil and oatmeal and sauté 1 minute more. Mix in salt and add a little water or pear juice if stuffing seems too dry.

Veal:

1 (3-pound) veal breast, cut with a pocket
Olive oil
Dry mustard
1 cup water or water mixed with a little plain pear juice

✳

Preheat oven to moderate 350°F.

Stuff veal breast with parsley-oat mixture and close with metal skewers. Place meat on low rack in a roasting pan and brush all over with olive oil. Sprinkle with dry mustard. Add plain water or water mixed with a little pear juice to pan. Cover with aluminum foil and bake 2 hours. Uncover and bake 30 minutes more, until crisp and brown on top. Place breast on a platter. Remove rack and stir broth, scraping up browned bits clinging to the bottom. Drizzle over breast and serve.

Ghiveciu (Vegetable Casserole)

✳   SERVES 4–6

  ¼ cup olive oil plus oil for greasing casserole
  ½ teaspoon sea salt
  1 teaspoon dry mustard
  ½ large eggplant, unpeeled, washed and cubed*
  1 large zucchini, sliced in ½-inch slices
  1 large yellow summer squash, sliced in ½-inch slices

Preheat oven to 350°F.

Beat together ¼ cup olive oil, sea salt and dry mustard. Lightly oil a large casserole with olive oil. Sprinkling each layer with oil mixture, layer the eggplant, zucchini and squash. Cover tightly and bake 1 hour.

*This is the first introduction of eggplant as well as oats in the diet. While eggplant is not generally considered a potently allergenic food, adverse reaction is possible. Make careful note of any symptomatic responses.

Pink Bean Salad

✳   SERVES 4–6

  1 (16-ounce) can water-pack pink beans
  4 cups lettuce (washed, drained and torn into bite-sized
      pieces)
  ½ cup chopped fresh parsley (optional)
  Mustard Dressing (recipe follows)

Drain pink beans in a colander and then on paper towels. Place lettuce and parsley in a salad bowl, add beans and combine. Toss with Mustard Dressing.

Mustard Dressing

✳   MAKES ABOUT 1 CUP

> 2 tablespoons plain regular oatmeal (not quick-cooking)
> ⅔ cup olive oil
> 1 tablespoon finely chopped firm fresh pear (washed and
>   cored, but not peeled)
> 1 teaspoon dry mustard
> 1 teaspoon sea salt

Combine all ingredients in a jar and shake to mix well. Chill in freezer 10–15 minutes. Shake well before using.

On-the-Double Pear Sorbet
(See Night-Before Preparation Tips for Day Ten)

✳

DIET EXPRESS

BREAKFAST

Pear Juice
(See Breakfast, Regular Track)

✳

Beech-Nut Stage One Oatmeal Cereal

✳   SERVES 1

> ½ cup Beech-Nut Stage One oatmeal
> Plain pear juice (hot or cold)
> 1 fresh pear, washed, cored and chopped, but not peeled
>   (optional)

Mix oatmeal and pear juice until desired consistency. Stir in chopped fresh pear if desired.

※

Quick-Cooking Plain Oatmeal

※   SERVES 1

¾ cup water or plain pear juice
⅓ cup quick-cooking oatmeal

In a saucepan, bring water or pear juice to boil. Stir in oatmeal. Cook over low heat until desired thickness. Top with Beech-Nut pears.

MW—In a microwave-safe bowl, cook (H) water or pear juice until it boils, about 2 minutes. Stir in oatmeal. Microwave (L) 1–2 minutes, until desired thickness. Stir. Top with Beech-Nut pears.

Rose Hip Tea
(See Breakfast, Regular Track)

※

LUNCH

Veal Pâté with Rice Cakes and Zucchini Sticks

※   SERVES 1

1–2 jars Beech-Nut Stage One veal
1 teaspoon olive oil
Dry mustard and sea salt to taste
*Plain rice cakes or plain rice crackers and/or 1 small fresh
    zucchini or yellow squash, scrubbed, trimmed and cut
    into sticks.*

Combine veal, oil, mustard and sea salt until thoroughly blended and chill. Spread on rice cakes or rice crackers and/or sticks of fresh zucchini or yellow squash.

Quick Squash-Zucchini Soup

※   SERVES 1

½ cup fresh or frozen sliced yellow summer squash
½ cup fresh or frozen sliced zucchini
½ cup water plus water for thinning soup
1 jar Beech-Nut Stage One veal
Dry mustard and sea salt to taste

Cook squash and zucchini in ½ cup water over medium heat until tender, about 5 minutes. Stir in veal, dry mustard, sea salt and water until soup is of desired thickness and seasoned to taste.

MW—Combine vegetables in a microwave-safe casserole with 3 tablespoons water. Cover and microwave (H) 3 minutes, stirring after each minute. Stir in veal, sprinkle with a little mustard, and add water to desired thickness. Cover and microwave (H) until hot, 1–2 minutes more. Season to taste with sea salt.

DINNER

Sautéed Veal Chops

✷ SERVES 1–2

½ cup Beech-Nut Stage One oatmeal or plain oat bran
    cereal
1 teaspoon dry mustard
1 teaspoon sea salt
2 veal rib chops, about ½ inch thick
2 tablespoons olive oil
3 tablespoons plain pear juice plus juice for "sauce"

Combine oatmeal or oat bran cereal, dry mustard and salt in a plastic or paper bag. Place chops in bag and shake until chops are thoroughly coated. Heat oil in a heavy skillet, add meat and brown on both sides. Reduce heat to low, add pear juice, cover and cook about 20 minutes. Transfer to platter and keep warm. Add a few tablespoons more pear juice to the juices in the pan and stir, scraping up browned particles clinging to pan. Pour over chops and serve.

MW—Coat and brown chops in skillet as above. Place in a microwave-safe casserole, add pear juice, cover and microwave (H) 10 minutes, total cooking time. Turn chops after half the cooking time.

Quick-Cooking Rice

✷ SERVES 1–2

1 cup boiling water
1 cup plain quick-cooking rice*
½ teaspoon salt
1 teaspoon olive oil

✳

Pour boiling water into a casserole with a lid. Stir in rice, salt and oil, cover and let stand 5 minutes. Fluff with a fork before serving.

*You may use quick-cooking brown or white rice.

Pink Bean Salad

✳   SERVES 1–2

1 (8-ounce) can plain pink beans, drained
2 cups lettuce (washed, dried and torn into bite-sized
    pieces)
¼ cup chopped fresh parsley
Quick Mustard Dressing (recipe follows)

Place drained beans in a salad bowl. Add lettuce and parsley and toss with Quick Mustard Dressing.

Quick Mustard Dressing

✳   MAKES ABOUT ¾ CUP

1½ teaspoons dry mustard
¼ cup plain pear juice
⅓ cup olive oil
Sea salt to taste

Mix mustard and pear juice until mustard is dissolved. In a blender or with a wire whisk, blend in olive oil and sea salt to taste.

On-the-Double Pear Sorbet
(See Night-Before Preparation Tips for Day Ten)

✳

NIGHT-BEFORE PREPARATION TIPS
FOR DAY 11

Make Peach Sorbet: Empty 4 jars Beech-Nut Stage One peaches into a plastic freezer container. Cover and freeze overnight. Allow to soften 10–15 minutes in the refrigerator before serving as a sorbet. On Day Eleven, use sorbet in Peach-Egg Shake, Snack, Regular Track and as dessert for Lunch, Express Track.

*

DAY 11

THE REINTRODUCTION PHASE
(EGG)

ALLOWED FOODS:
Eggs, millet, amaranth, coconut, peaches, asparagus, bamboo shoots, lentils, rhubarb, zucchini, potatoes, pork, whitefish, salmon, tuna, mint, sunflower oil, oregano, maple syrup

M E N U	REGULAR	DIET EXPRESS
BREAKFAST	Fresh Coconut Hot Millet Cereal Eggs (cooked according to preference) Pancakes Mint Herbal Tea	Fresh Coconut with Beech-Nut Stage One Peaches Eggs (cooked according to preference) Puffed Millet Cereal with Peaches Mint Herbal Tea
SNACK	Coconut-Millet Clusters Peach-Egg Shake	Crunchy Lentils Iced Mint Tea
LUNCH	Broiled Pork Patties Millet Patties Omelet with Vegetable and Herbs Gefilte Fish Chilled Asparagus with Mayonnaise Fresh Peaches with Coconut Crème Anglaise	Brown-Bag Tuna or Salmon Salad Peach Sorbet
DINNER	Fried Flounder Barbecued Spareribs Peach and Rhubarb Fool Peach-Meringue Pie	Quick-Baked Pork Chops Pan-Fried Fish Fillets Quick-Broiled Fish Fillets Fried Asparagus 1-2-3 Soufflé Quick Maple Zabaglione Instant Peach Sorbet

BULK AGENT: Psyllium seed

✻

R E G U L A R   T R A C K

BREAKFAST

Fresh Coconut
(See Day Two, Breakfast, Regular Track)

✻

Hot Millet Cereal

✻

SERVES 4

> ¾ cup raw millet
> 3 cups water
> Dash sea salt
> 1 teaspoon sunflower oil
> 1 cup frozen peaches
> Maple syrup to taste

Place millet, water, sea salt and oil in the top of a double boiler. Stirring constantly, boil 5 minutes over direct heat. Stir in frozen peaches and cook over simmering water 45–50 minutes. (Check water level in bottom half of boiler occasionally to make sure water has not boiled away.) Drizzle maple syrup over hot cereal.

Refrigerate any leftover millet for later use in day's recipes.

Eggs
Cooked according to preference, using sunflower oil and/or sea salt.

✻

Pancakes

✻

SERVES 4

> 1 egg, beaten
> 1 tablespoon sunflower oil plus oil for greasing pan
> 2 cups amaranth (or lentil*) flour
> 2 cups (approximate) water

Mix together beaten egg, 1 tablespoon oil, flour and enough water to form a smooth, thick but pourable batter. Grease a skillet with sunflower oil. Heat the skillet until it is hot, but not smoking. Using ½ cup for each pancake, pour batter onto hot skillet. Cook pancakes 1–2 minutes, turn, and continue to cook until pancakes are cooked through and can be easily lifted from the pan, 1–2 minutes more. Top pancakes with maple syrup.

*See Day Three, Breakfast, Regular Track.

Mint Herbal Tea

✳   SERVES 1

> 1 tea bag mint herbal tea or 2 teaspoons dried mint tied
>   into a cheesecloth bag
> 6 ounces boiling water
> Maple crystals or maple syrup to taste

Steep tea bag (commercial or homemade) in boiling water 2–5 minutes, according to preference. Sweeten to taste with maple crystals or syrup.

SNACK

Coconut-Millet Clusters

✳   SERVES 4

> ¼ cup sunflower oil
> 1 fresh peach, washed, chopped and unpeeled
> 2–3 cups puffed millet cereal
> ½ cup sunflower seeds
> ⅓ cup maple syrup
> 1 cup shredded unsweetened coconut
> ½ cup maple crystals (optional)

Heat oil in a saucepan over medium heat. Add peaches and sauté 2 minutes. Remove from heat, add cereal, sunflower seeds and maple syrup. Mix so that cereal is completely coated. Drop tablespoons of the mixture into coconut and roll to coat. Refrigerate on waxed paper until completely chilled.

Note: Add ½ cup maple crystals to coconut, if desired, for extra sweetness.

Peach-Egg Shake

SERVES 1

1 large fresh egg
1 jar Beech-Nut Stage One peaches or 1 cup chopped frozen
    peaches
2 teaspoons maple crystals or maple syrup
1 ice cube, crushed (optional)
1 sprig fresh mint
1 (2-ounce) scoop Peach Sorbet (see Night-Before
    Preparation Tips for Day Eleven)

Place egg in blender. Blend on highest speed until fully beaten and frothy, about 15 seconds.

Add peaches, maple crystals or syrup and crushed ice cube. (If using frozen peaches, you may omit ice cube. Do not thaw peaches before blending.)

Blend on highest speed until shake is smooth and thick, about 1 minute. Serve with a sprig of fresh mint and a scoop of Peach Sorbet as garnish.

LUNCH

Broiled Pork Patties

SERVES 4

1 pound ground pork
1 teaspoon ground oregano
1 tablespoon potato starch flour or crushed puffed millet
    cereal
¼ teaspoon sea salt
1 egg, beaten
Sunflower oil for greasing skillet

Combine all ingredients except oil. Shape into 4 patties. Pan-broil in a hot skillet lightly greased with sunflower oil, 3–5 minutes per side, until meat is no longer pink in center of burgers.

Millet Patties

SERVES 4

1 cup chilled, cooked millet (see Hot Millet Cereal,
    Breakfast, Regular Track)
1 egg, beaten

> *1 tablespoon potato starch flour or crushed puffed millet*
>   *cereal plus additional for coating*
> *Sea salt*
> *Ground oregano*
> *2 tablespoons sunflower oil*

Combine chilled millet, egg and flour or crushed puffed millet cereal so that cooked millet holds together. Shape into 4 patties and dredge lightly in more flour or crushed millet. Sprinkle patties with sea salt and ground oregano. Heat sunflower oil in a skillet until hot and fry the patties over medium heat until they are brown and crisp on both sides, about 3 minutes per side.

Omelet with Vegetable and Herbs

✳   SERVES 4 AS APPETIZER

> *4 eggs*
> *⅛ teaspoon sea salt*
> *2 tablespoons cold water*
> *1 tablespoon ground oregano*
> *¼ cup chopped fresh bamboo shoots*
> *1 tablespoon sunflower oil*

Combine eggs, salt and water in a small bowl. Whisk until just combined (not frothy). Stir oregano and bamboo shoots into eggs, mixing well. Heat a medium-size heavy skillet over high heat. (It is ready when a small amount of cold water sprinkled over the surface sizzles and rolls off in drops.) Add oil, heat until it sizzles but does not brown. Quickly pour egg mixture into skillet. Reduce heat to medium-low. As omelet sets, loosen edge with a spatula and tilt the skillet to let uncooked mixture run under set portion.

When omelet is set (but not dry) on top, and golden brown on the bottom, fold it over to one edge of the pan. Tilt it out onto a warm serving plate.

VARIATIONS: Drained, water-packed canned salmon or shredded cooked roast pork may be added during cooking time. Sprinkle approximately 1 cup meat or fish over top of the omelet as it sets.

Gefilte Fish

✳   SERVES 4–6

> *4 pounds fish fillets (equal amounts any lean whitefish and*
>   *pike plus a small amount of carp)*
> *Heads, bones and trimmings from fish*

*

1 stalk fresh rhubarb, scrubbed and sliced
2 teaspoons sea salt
Water to cover plus ¼ cup for fish mixture
3 large eggs
2 tablespoons potato starch flour or crushed puffed millet
    cereal

Process fish fillets in blender or processor fitted with a steel blade until fish is finely ground. Remove fish to a large bowl. In a large skillet, combine heads, bones and trimmings with sliced rhubarb and 1 teaspoon salt. Add water to cover and bring to boil. Lower heat and simmer while preparing eggs. Place eggs in the blender and blend well, or whisk thoroughly by hand. Add eggs to the bowl of ground fish and blend well. Add potato starch flour or crushed millet and remaining 1 teaspoon salt. Add remaining ¼ cup water and blend well. Shape fish mixture into balls and drop into simmering fish broth. Cover and simmer gently 1 hour. Remove to a platter. Strain broth and refrigerate fish balls and broth. Serve fish with jellied fish broth.

Chilled Asparagus with Mayonnaise

*   SERVES 4

1 (10-ounce) package frozen asparagus spears
2 egg yolks
½ teaspoon sea salt
1 teaspoon ground oregano
¼ cup rhubarb "vinegar" (see Alfalfa Sprout-Rhubarb
    Salad, Day Two, Dinner, Regular Track)
2 cups sunflower oil

Rinse frozen asparagus spears under warm water until completely thawed. Drain and chill.

To make mayonnaise: beat egg yolks until thick and lemon-colored. Add salt, oregano and half the vinegar. Beat well. While still beating, start adding oil a few drops at a time, increasing amount as mixture thickens. Slowly add remaining vinegar and beat well. Chill and serve over asparagus. Refrigerate leftover mayonnaise for dinner recipes.

Fresh Peaches with Coconut Crème Anglaise

*   SERVES 4

1 teaspoon potato starch flour
¾ cup Coconut Milk (see Day Two, Breakfast, Regular
    Track)

✳

2 egg yolks
2 tablespoons maple crystals
1 teaspoon sunflower oil
4 cups fresh or frozen sliced peaches

In the top of a double boiler, whisk together potato starch flour and coconut milk until smooth. Whisk in egg yolks and maple crystals and place over moderately boiling water. Cook, stirring constantly, until thickened and smooth. Whisk in oil, blending well. Remove from heat and serve over peaches, or refrigerate and serve chilled.

MW—Mix potato starch flour, coconut milk, egg yolks, and maple crystals in a 1-quart microwave-safe glass measuring cup until completely smooth. Cover with plastic wrap or waxed paper. Microwave (H) until thick, 2–3 minutes, stirring every minute. Add oil, blend well. Serve warm or chilled over peaches.

DINNER

Fried Flounder

✳

SERVES 4

1½ pounds flounder fillets
Sea salt
2 large eggs
½ cup sparkling mineral water
½ cup crushed puffed millet cereal
1 teaspoon potato starch flour
1 cup sunflower oil

Cut fillets into 3 × 4-inch pieces. Sprinkle with salt and set aside. Separate eggs, reserving whites. Combine egg yolks, water, millet and flour. Blend thoroughly. Whip egg whites until stiff. Gently fold egg whites into batter until well mixed in.

In a deep saucepan or fryer, heat oil until hot, 375°F. Put fish into batter and shake off excess. Fry one or two pieces of fish at a time, turning with a slotted spoon when they rise to the surface of oil. Drain on paper towels and keep warm until ready to serve.

Barbecued Spareribs

SERVES 4–6

4 pounds spareribs, cut into serving pieces
2 cups sparkling mineral water
1 jar Beech-Nut Stage One peaches
1 large fresh peach chopped, or 1 cup chopped frozen
    peaches
1/2 cup frozen rhubarb chunks
1/2 cup maple crystals or maple syrup
1/4 teaspoon sea salt

Place ribs in a shallow pan. Mix remaining ingredients and pour over ribs. Marinate in refrigerator 1–6 hours, turning at least once.

Preheat barbecue or broiler.

Remove ribs from marinade. Reserve liquid. Weave ribs on a spit or long skewers, or place flat on a rack of a hot charcoal grill or broiler, about 4 inches from heat. Cook, turning frequently and brushing with marinade, until brown, about 1 hour.

Ribs may also be baked in a moderate 350°F. oven until brown and glazed. Baste frequently.

Serve with hot millet. Use mayonnaise reserved from lunch as dip.

Peach and Rhubarb Fool

SERVES 4

2 cups fresh or frozen rhubarb chunks
Water to cover
3 cups fresh or frozen peach chunks
2 eggs, separated
1/2 cup maple syrup

Place rhubarb in a saucepan and cover with water. Bring to boil, simmer 10–15 minutes. Cool and drain before blending with peaches, egg yolks and syrup in blender or processor. Purée until smooth. Pour into a saucepan and cook over low heat, stirring constantly, 4 minutes. Let cool. Meanwhile, whip egg whites until stiff. Fold fruit purée into whites and serve at once or chill in sherbet goblets.

MW—Rhubarb can also be cooked in microwave. Place rhubarb in microwave-safe bowl. Add 2 tablespoons water. Cover with waxed paper. Microwave (H) 5–10 minutes, stirring every few minutes. Cool and drain before proceeding with recipe.

Peach-Meringue Pie

3 cups sliced, peeled fresh peaches or frozen sliced peaches
2 jars Beech-Nut Stage One peaches
3 egg whites
¼ teaspoon potato starch flour
6 tablespoons maple crystals

Preheat oven to 350°F.

Combine sliced peaches and Beech-Nut peaches and empty into a 8-inch pie tin. Bake 5 minutes; cool. Raise oven temperature to 425°F. Beat egg whites until light and frothy. Add potato starch, continue beating until whites are stiff enough to hold a peak. Gradually beat in maple crystals and beat until meringue is stiff and glossy. Pile meringue lightly on cooled pie filling, spreading it until it touches the edges of pan to prevent shrinking. Bake at 425°F. until top is brown, about 5 minutes.

Note: A meringue crust (recipe follows) can be substituted for meringue topping.

Meringue Crust:

Sunflower oil for greasing 8-inch pie tin
3 egg whites (room temperature)
Dash sea salt
⅛ teaspoon potato starch flour
½ cup maple crystals
¼ cup shredded unsweetened coconut (optional)

Preheat oven to 300°F. Lightly grease a pie tin with oil. Combine egg whites, salt and potato starch in mixing bowl. Beat until foamy. Add maple crystals, 2 tablespoons at a time, beating after each addition until mixture stands in stiff peaks. Shredded coconut can be added at this point, if desired. Spoon mixture into pie tin and make a meringue shell, spreading meringue over bottom and building up the sides ½ inch above the edge of the pan, but not over the rim. Bake 50 minutes to 1 hour until toasted and dry. Cool before filling.

✳ ──────────────────────────────

DIET EXPRESS

BREAKFAST

Fresh Coconut with Beech-Nut Stage One Peaches

✳   SERVES 1

> *1 cup Fresh Coconut chunks (see Day Two, Breakfast,*
>   *Regular Track)*
> *1 jar Beech-Nut Stage One peaches*

Dip coconut chunks into Beech-Nut peaches.

Eggs
(See Breakfast, Regular Track)

✳

Puffed Millet Cereal with Peaches

✳   SERVES 1

> *1–2 cups puffed millet cereal*
> *1 fresh peach, washed, sliced and unpeeled*
> *Maple syrup*

Pour cereal into a bowl; top with fresh peaches and maple syrup to taste.

Mint Herbal Tea
(See Breakfast, Regular Track)

✳

SNACK

Crunchy Lentils

✳   SERVES 1

> *1 cup drained, canned water-pack lentils*

MW—Spread lentils on paper towels and pat dry. Place a microwave-safe paper towel on a heavy microwave-safe dish or platter, spread lentils on top and cover with another paper towel. Microwave (H) 8–12 minutes, until lentils are crunchy. Rotate plate during cooking if not on a self-rotating carousel.

Iced Mint Tea

✳   SERVES 1

> 6 ounces strong Mint Herbal Tea (see Breakfast, Regular
>   Track)
> Ice
> Maple crystals or maple syrup to taste
> 1 sprig fresh mint
> Sparkling mineral water (optional)

Pour brewed tea over ice in a tall glass. Sweeten with maple crystals or syrup, and add a sprig of mint as garnish. Sparkling mineral water may be added as well, to make a spritzer.

LUNCH

Brown-Bag Tuna or Salmon Salad

✳   SERVES 1

> 3–4 canned water-pack white asparagus spears, drained
> 1 stalk fresh rhubarb, chopped
> 1 (3-ounce) can water-pack salmon or tuna, drained
> 2 frozen asparagus spears (defrosting not necessary)
> ½ cup canned bamboo shoots, drained
> ¼ cup sunflower seeds
> Mayonnaise (see Chilled Asparagus with Mayonnaise,
>   Lunch, Regular Track, for directions)
> 1 hard-boiled egg
> 1 cup puffed millet cereal
> Salt to taste

Layer the above ingredients except egg and cereal in a thermal container in the following order, sprinkling every other layer very lightly with salt: asparagus, rhubarb, tuna or salmon, bamboo shoots, sunflower seeds. Spread mayonnaise over top layer of salad so that it forms a "seal" around the edges of the container. Chill and toss before eating. Pack egg and crushed puffed millet separately. Crumble egg and millet together and sprinkle over salad before eating.

✻

Peach Sorbet
(See Night-Before Preparation Tips for Day Eleven)

✻

DINNER

Quick-Baked Pork Chops

✻   SERVES 1–2

1 tablespoon sunflower oil
2 loin pork chops, 1 inch thick
Sea salt
Ground oregano
1–2 jars Beech-Nut Stage One peaches
Water

Preheat oven to low, 300°F. Place oil in a 2-quart casserole and heat 5 minutes in oven until hot. Meanwhile, sprinkle chops lightly with salt and oregano and press in. Brown chops briefly on both sides in the hot oil. Add 1 jar peaches mixed with ¼ cup water. Cover and bake 20–30 minutes. Check chops after 20 minutes. If too dry, add a little more water or peaches mixed with water. Stir, and continue to bake about 15 minutes.

MW—Sprinkle chops with oregano and press in. Brown chops in hot oil (omitting salt) in a skillet on stove. Place browned chops with 1 jar peaches (omit adding water to peaches) in a large microwave-safe glass or ceramic casserole. Cover and microwave (H) 7–10 minutes, turning chops every 2 minutes and adding a little water if chops are becoming too dry. Salt after cooking.

Pan-Fried Fish Fillets

✻   SERVES 1–2

1 large egg
¼ cup crushed puffed millet cereal or potato starch flour
Dash salt and ground oregano
Sunflower oil
½ pound fish fillets (trout, perch, sole, flounder or whiting),
*   skin removed*

Beat egg. In another bowl or paper bag, combine crushed millet or potato starch flour with salt and oregano. Pour sunflower oil into a heavy skillet to the depth of ¼ inch. Heat until very hot. Meanwhile, dip fillets in egg and then into seasoned flour to coat. Cook fillets in hot oil, turning once. A 1-inch thick fillet should be cooked a total of 10 minutes until fish flakes easily. Thinner fillets will take 5–7 minutes total cooking time.

Quick-Broiled Fish Fillets

＊　　　　　　　　　　　　　　　　　　　　　　　　　SERVES 1–2

½ pound fish fillets (whitefish, salmon, pike, carp, flounder,
*　　tuna, whiting), ½ inch thick*
Sunflower oil for greasing pan
2 tablespoons mayonnaise (see Chilled Asparagus with
*　　Mayonnaise, Lunch, Regular Track)*

Preheat broiler.

Place fillets in a broiler pan lightly greased with oil. Spread fillets lightly on top with mayonnaise. Broil 3 inches from source of heat until fish is browned on top and is opaque, about 5–6 minutes.

Remove fish to a platter. Scrape up browned bits and juices from cooking in bottom of pan and pour over fish before serving.

Fried Asparagus

＊　　　　　　　　　　　　　　　　　　　　　　　　　SERVES 1

1 large egg
½ cup crushed puffed millet cereal or potato starch flour
1 teaspoon each sea salt and ground oregano
Sunflower oil
3–4 spears fresh asparagus, scrubbed and trimmed of hard
*　　white stalks*

Beat egg. In a separate bowl or paper bag, combine millet or potato starch flour with salt and oregano. Pour sunflower oil into a skillet to a depth of 1 inch. Heat until very hot. Meanwhile, dip asparagus in egg and then in seasoned millet or flour. Add to hot oil and fry, turning frequently and using a slotted spoon, until spears are crisped and browned. Drain on paper towels and serve hot. Serve with mayonnaise (see Chilled Asparagus with Mayonnaise, Lunch, Regular Track).

1-2-3 Soufflé

Sunflower oil for greasing soufflé dish
⅓ cup maple crystals plus 1 tablespoon maple crystals and
more maple crystals for sprinkling on top
4 egg whites
Dash sea salt
2 jars Beech-Nut Stage One peaches

Preheat oven to 400°F.

Lightly oil the inside of a 1-quart soufflé dish, then sprinkle dish evenly with ⅓ cup maple crystals. In a medium-sized bowl, beat egg whites and salt on highest speed of an electric beater until foamy. Add 1 tablespoon maple crystals and continue beating until stiff peaks form when beaters are slowly raised. With rubber scraper or wire whisk, gently fold peaches into egg whites just until combined. Turn into soufflé dish. Sprinkle top with more maple crystals. Bake 15–20 minutes, until top of soufflé is golden brown. Serve soufflé with halved fresh peaches.

Note: Meringue cannnot be cooked in a microwave oven. Microwave power disintegrates meringue.

Quick Maple Zabaglione

3 egg yolks
3 tablespoons maple crystals
3 tablespoons Beech-Nut Stage One peaches mixed with
enough water to make ⅓ cup peach "nectar"
1–2 cups sliced fresh or frozen peaches (optional)

Beat the egg yolks, and while continuing to beat, slowly add the maple crystals and the peach-water mixture. Place mixture over boiling water and whip with a wire whisk until custard foams up and begins to thicken. Do not overcook. Serve warm in goblet glasses or over fresh or frozen peach slices.

Instant Peach Sorbet

20 ounces plain frozen sliced peaches
⅓–½ cup maple syrup
2 sprigs fresh mint, minced
1 tablespoon Beech-Nut Stage One peaches

Do not defrost peaches. Chop peaches, 1 cup at a time, and place them in a blender. Drizzle peaches with maple syrup (about ⅓ cup per cup of peaches). Add mint and 1 tablespoon Beech-Nut peaches. Blend on highest speed just until combined. Blend a little longer if very smooth sorbet is desired. Serve at once. Serve sorbet alone, or with 1-2-3 Soufflé or Quick Maple Zabaglione (see recipes on page 197). Freeze remainder for Day Fourteen.

NIGHT-BEFORE PREPARATION TIPS
—— FOR DAY 12 ——

Make Apple Sorbet: Allowing 1 jar per serving, empty as many jars Beech-Nut Stage One applesauce as you think you will need into a freezer container with a lid. Freeze overnight to use as instant sorbet in beverages or desserts. As dessert, allow to soften 15 minutes in the refrigerator before serving as sorbet.

DAY ✳ 12   THE REINTRODUCTION PHASE (WHEAT)

ALLOWED FOODS:
Wheat, apples, cranberries, carrots, turnips, lamb, rosemary, cloves, safflower oil, nutmeg, honey, baking soda

MENU

	REGULAR	DIET EXPRESS
BREAKFAST	Wheat Flour Tortillas (Pancakes) Apple Butter Hot or Cold Wheat Cereal with Honey Crème Clove Herbal Tea	Quick Hot Wheat Cereal or Cold Wheat Cereal with Honey Crème Hot Spiced Apple Juice
SNACK	Wheat Germ Crackers Carrot Juice Spritzer	Plain Wheat Crackers with Apple Butter Carrot Juice or Clove Herbal Tea
LUNCH	Scotch Broth Lamburgers with Wheat Flour Tortillas or Toasted Crackers Flummery Apple Spritzer	Lamb Pâté with Plain Wheat Flour Tortillas Quick Carrot Soup Fresh Apple

DINNER   Lamb with Turnips   One-Dish Lamb Chop Dinner
                  Wheat Berry Salad   Microwaved Baked Apple
                  Rosemary Dressing
                  Baked Apples

BULK AGENT: Wheat (Miller's) bran

REGULAR TRACK

BREAKFAST

Wheat Flour Tortillas (Pancakes)

* MAKES 1 DOZEN

This recipe is adapted from *The California Heritage Cookbook* by The Junior League of Pasadena (Doubleday, 1976).

2 cups whole-wheat or white-wheat flour plus flour for dusting
1⅓ cups (approximate) water
2 teaspoons safflower oil

Combine flour and water in a large bowl until dough is firm but not dry. Keep dough covered with a clean, damp cloth while making tortillas. On a large piece of waxed paper dusted with wheat flour, place 1 heaping tablespoonful of dough and cover it with another piece of waxed paper. With a rolling pin or thick, smooth-sided glass, flatten the ball of dough into a thin circle, as near to ⅛-inch thickness as possible. When tortilla is formed, carefully remove top piece of waxed paper. If tortilla sticks to paper, dough is too moist; knead a little more flour into remaining dough in mixing bowl before making next tortilla. Heat oil in heavy skillet until medium-hot. Place tortilla in hot skillet, paper side up. Allow tortilla to cook a few seconds, then peel paper off. Cook tortilla about 1 minute on first side. Turn and cook other side about 1 minute more. Tortilla is done when dry around the edges. Remove tortilla when cooked to a clean cloth towel. Repeat procedure until all the dough is used, stacking cooked tortillas on top of one another in the cloth towel. When all tortillas are cooked, wrap them in the towel until they are cool enough to eat. Serve tortillas hot with plain apple butter for breakfast. Refrigerate or freeze any remaining tortillas for use later on in the day with Scotch Broth and Lamburgers, if desired (see Lunch, Regular Track) and with Diet Express Lamb Pâté, if desired.

Note: Wheat-flour-and-water-only tortillas (such as Patio brand) can be found in frozen food section of some markets and in health food stores.

This recipe can also be used on Day Eight and Day Eighteen to make corn tortillas by substituting corn flour or masa harina for wheat flour, and corn oil for safflower oil.

Hot or Cold Wheat Cereal with Honey Crème

SERVES 4

Hot Cereal:

> 1½ cups water
> ½ cup regular Wheatena, farina, or cream of wheat
> Dash sea salt

Bring water to boil in a large saucepan. Stirring constantly, add cereal to water and cook over low heat until desired consistency, about 2–5 minutes. Serve with ½ cup Honey Crème (recipe follows) and/or plain, unsweetened, smooth or chunky-style applesauce.

Cold Cereal (per serving):

> 2 biscuits plain shredded wheat or 1 cup plain (or with
>   bran) spoon-sized shredded wheat or puffed wheat
>   cereal

Place cereal in bowls. Serve with ½ cup Honey Crème (recipe follows) and/or plain, unsweetened applesauce, smooth or chunky-style.

Honey Crème

MAKES 1 CUP

> 1 teaspoon all-purpose wheat flour
> ¾ cup water
> ¼ cup honey

In a small, deep saucepan, mix flour into water until smooth. Stirring constantly, heat until boiling. Stir in honey, cool slightly, and pour over cereal in desired amounts.

MW—In a 2-cup measuring cup, mix flour with water until smooth. Heat (H) until boiling, about 2 minutes. Stir in honey, cool and serve.

Clove Herbal Tea

✳   SERVES 1

3 whole cloves
2 tablespoons chopped apple peel from a fresh, washed
    apple
2–3 whole fresh cranberries (washed and picked over)
6 ounces boiling water
Honey or Heinz apple flakes to taste

Steep cloves, apple peel and cranberries in boiling water until tea is desired strength. Remove cloves; eat or remove apple peel and cranberries. Sweeten to taste with honey or Heinz apple flakes.

SNACK

Wheat Germ Crackers

✳   MAKES ABOUT 1 DOZEN

1½ cups unbleached all-purpose white flour, plus flour for
    dusting
¼ cup toasted wheat germ*, plus wheat germ for dusting
½ teaspoon baking soda
½ teaspoon sea salt
1 cup water
2 tablespoons safflower oil plus oil for greasing baking sheet

Preheat oven to 350°F.

Mix together the flour, wheat germ, soda and salt. Combine the water and oil and then mix them thoroughly into the flour mixture until a dough is formed. Oil a large baking sheet lightly with oil. Place the dough on the baking sheet and flatten it with the back of a wooden spoon or with your hand. Dust the dough with a little wheat germ and flour to prevent it from sticking as it is rolled out. Cover the spread-out dough with a large sheet of waxed paper. With a rolling pin or thick, smooth-sided glass, roll the dough very thin, as near as possible to ⅛-inch thickness. If crackers are too thick they will be chewy and more like flat bread. Remove the waxed paper and score the dough into cracker-sized squares, about 2 inches square. Prick tops with a fork and bake 8–10 minutes, until golden brown. Allow crackers to cool 5 minutes before removing them from the sheet. Cool completely on a metal rack; crackers will crisp as they cool.

*Pure, unprocessed wheat bran, such as Quaker brand, can be substituted for wheat germ to make bran crackers. Look for toasted wheat germ and wheat bran in the cereal sections of markets.

Carrot Juice Spritzer

✳   SERVES 1

> 4 ounces plain carrot juice
> Ice
> 2–4 ounces plain apple juice to taste
> 1–2 teaspoons honey to taste
> Dash nutmeg
> 1 ounce sparkling mineral water

Pour carrot juice over ice. Flavor with apple juice, honey and nutmeg to taste. Add mineral water for effervescence.

LUNCH

Scotch Broth

✳   SERVES 4–6

> ½ cup raw whole-wheat berries, rinsed and picked over
> 1 quart water for cooking berries
> 1½ pounds boneless lamb shoulder, trimmed and cut in ¼-inch cubes
> 1 meaty lamb soup bone, shank or cut from shoulder
> 1 tablespoon ground rosemary
> 5 cups water
> Sea salt
> ¾ cup diced, pared fresh carrots
> ½ cup chopped fresh turnips or chopped frozen turnips

Place berries in a large soup pot with 1 quart water. Bring pot with berries to boil on stove. Simmer, partially covered, about 20 minutes, until berries are tender but still crunchy. Drain berries and set aside.

Place lamb and soup bone in the soup pot. Sprinkle meat all over with ground rosemary and press it in. Add 5 cups water and bring to boil, turn heat to low and simmer gently, partially covered, 1 hour. Salt to taste with sea salt. Preheat oven to 200°F. Remove lamb and bone from broth. Pour broth into a bowl and skim off excess fat that has risen to the surface. Wash any scum from the pot, cut lamb from bone, and return all lamb and broth to pot. Discard bone. Add vegetables and berries. Bring soup to a boil and bake, covered, in a very slow oven, 200°F., 1 hour longer.

Serve with Wheat Flour Tortillas (reserved from Breakfast, Regular Track), Wheat Germ Crackers (see Snack, Regular Track), plain spoon-sized shredded wheat, or any commercial wheat-flour-and-water-only crackers such as Bent's or plain matzo wheat crackers.

MW—Whole-wheat berries can also be microwaved: Place berries in a 2-quart microwave-safe casserole with 1½ cups water. Cover loosely and microwave (H) 20 minutes, stirring every 5 minutes. Drain berries of any water left after cooking and set the berries aside. Omit lamb bone. Press ground rosemary into lamb. In a 2-quart, microwave-safe covered casserole, place lamb cubes, 1 cup at a time, in 1 cup water. Cover and microwave (M) 20 minutes. Remove cooked lamb and broth to a large bowl. Repeat procedure until all the lamb pieces are cooked. Skim excess fat from broth. Place carrots, turnips and reserved wheat berries in a large, clean microwave-safe casserole. Add ½ cup of the skimmed broth. Cover and microwave (H) 10–15 minutes, until vegetables are tender. Add lamb and remaining broth to casserole, cover and heat (H) until hot, about 5–10 minutes. Stir every 2 minutes. Season to taste with sea salt.

Lamburgers

※   SERVES 4

4 lamburgers, broiled (see Day One, Lunch, Regular Track)
4 plain Wheat Flour Tortillas (reserved from Breakfast,
    Regular Track) or Toasted Crackers (recipe follows)

While lamburgers are broiling, toast tortillas on a hot, ungreased skillet 15–20 seconds each side, until lightly browned but not crisped. Toasting time will depend upon heat of skillet. Place each lamburger on a hot tortilla, wrap and serve. If you are using toasted crackers, place each lamburger on one half of a cracker, top with other side and serve.

Toasted Crackers

※   SERVES 4

4 cold-water wheat crackers* such as Bent's brand
4 teaspoons safflower oil
Sea salt

Preheat broiler.
Split crackers and drizzle each side with safflower oil. Sprinkle cracker halves lightly with sea salt and broil under a hot broiler, 6 inches from heat, until tops of crackers begin to brown.

*Do not confuse cold-water wheat crackers with table water crackers. Table water crackers contain multiple ingredients.

Flummery (Cranberry-Apple Pudding)

✳   SERVES 4

> 1 cup whole fresh cranberries (washed and picked over)
> 1 cup chopped, unpeeled, cored fresh apples, washed
> 2 cups water plus ¼ cup cold water or plain apple juice
> ½ cup honey
> 3 tablespoons all-purpose wheat flour

Combine berries, apples, and 2 cups water, and cook over low heat, simmering gently, for 10 minutes. Mix honey and flour, blend in ¼ cup cold water or apple juice. Stir mixture carefully into fruit. Simmer 5 minutes more. Cool slightly and pour into a glass bowl or individual glass serving dishes. Chill thoroughly and serve very cold.

MW—Combine berries and apples with water (reduce 2 cups water to 1⅓ cups) in a glass or ceramic microwave-safe casserole and cover. Cook (H) 3–5 minutes, stirring after each minute. Blend in honey and flour as above. Cover and microwave (H) 2 minutes, stirring every 30 seconds. (If flummery is too thick, thin with up to ¾ cup water or apple juice). Proceed as above.

Apple Spritzer

✳   SERVES 1

> 6 ounces plain apple juice
> 2 ounces strong Clove Herbal Tea (see Breakfast, Regular
>   Track)
> Ice
> Honey
> 1 (2-ounce) scoop Apple Sorbet (see Night-Before
>   Preparations for Day Twelve)
> 1–2 ounces sparkling mineral water

Combine apple juice and tea; pour over ice in a tall glass. Sweeten to taste with honey and add scoop of Apple Sorbet. Add mineral water for effervescence, stir briskly and serve.

DINNER

Lamb with Turnips

*   SERVES 4

4 large fresh carrots, pared and split
2 tablespoons safflower oil
1 (4–5-pound) leg of lamb, boned
2 tablespoons ground rosemary
1 cup plain carrot juice
2 cups chopped frozen turnips or 2 large fresh turnips,
    pared and chopped
1 tablespoon all-purpose flour
¾ cup cold water
Sea salt

Preheat oven to 400°F.

Place carrots in a heavy casserole with a lid and drizzle with oil. Rub lamb with ground rosemary and place on top of carrots. Roast, uncovered, turning occasionally, until lamb is browned (about 20 minutes total cooking time). Add carrot juice, cover, reduce heat to 325°F. and braise 3–3½ hours. Baste occasionally. Add turnips 15 minutes before cooking time is over. Cover and braise until turnips are tender. Remove lamb and vegetables from juices in casserole; strain and skim fat from juices. Combine flour and ¾ cup water in a measuring cup; stir until completely blended. Stirring constantly, slowly add mixture to meat juices and bring to boil on top of the stove, until gravy is thickened. Add water as desired until gravy is desired consistency; season to taste with sea salt. Serve gravy with lamb and vegetables.

Wheat Berry Salad

*   SERVES 4

1¼ cups raw whole-wheat berries
1 cup whole fresh cranberries (washed and picked over)
1 large fresh carrot, pared and chopped
1 Golden Delicious fresh apple, washed, cored and
    chopped, but not peeled
2 quarts water
Rosemary Dressing (recipe follows)
½ cup puffed wheat cereal or plain spoon-sized shredded
    wheat

Place wheat berries in a large saucepan. Add 2 quarts water and bring to boil. Lower heat and simmer until berries are tender-crisp, about 1 hour. Add cranberries, apples and carrots during last 20 minutes cooking time.

Drain and cool while preparing Rosemary Dressing.

Toss prepared dressing with wheat berries, cranberries, carrots and apples. Top salad with puffed wheat or shredded wheat, toss to combine, and serve.

Rosemary Dressing

✳   MAKES 1 CUP

⅓ cup plain apple juice
2 tablespoons honey
1 teaspoon ground rosemary
Pinch nutmeg
Pinch sea salt
½ cup safflower oil

Place apple juice, honey, rosemary, nutmeg and salt in a blender or deep bowl. Whisk or blend until combined. Add safflower oil and whisk or blend until thick and smooth.

Baked Apples

✳   SERVES 4

4 large fresh baking apples
Safflower oil for greasing pan plus ¼ cup oil
1 cup whole fresh cranberries (washed and picked over)
4 teaspoons honey
Nutmeg

Preheat oven to 400°F.

Wash, core and pare the apples, leaving a ring or two of skin near the bottom of each apple. Grease baking pan with oil and set apples upright in pan. Fill each apple with cranberries. Drizzle stuffed apples with honey and ¼ cup oil and sprinkle them lightly with nutmeg. Bake 45–50 minutes, until apples are tender and golden brown.

✳ —————————————————————

DIET EXPRESS

BREAKFAST

Quick Hot Wheat Cereal

✳   SERVES 1

1 cup water
2 tablespoons regular Wheatena, farina or cream of wheat
*   cereal*
Dash salt

MW—Stir water and cereal together in a 2-cup microwave-safe glass measuring cup. Cook (H) until mixture boils, 1–2 minutes. Stir and cook (L) until cereal is desired consistency. Serve with Honey Crème (See Breakfast, Regular Track) and/or plain unsweetened applesauce.

Cold Wheat Cereal with Honey Crème
(See Breakfast, Regular Track)

✳

Hot Spiced Apple Juice

✳   SERVES 1

1 cup plain fresh or bottled apple juice
¼ teaspoon nutmeg
2 whole cloves

Place apple juice, nutmeg and cloves in a saucepan and bring to boil, stirring. Reduce heat and simmer 4–5 minutes. Serve in a mug.

MW—Place 1 cup apple juice in a microwave-safe mug. Add cloves and nutmeg. Stir. Microwave (H) until boiling, about 1 minute. Stir. Microwave (L) 2 minutes more.

SNACK

Plain Wheat Crackers with Apple Butter

✳ SERVES 1

> 1 cold-water wheat cracker* such as Bent's brand or plain
>   matzo wheat crackers (amount depends on size of
>   matzo)
> 1/2 cup plain apple butter

Preheat oven to 400°F.

Split cold-water cracker, if used. Place on aluminum foil and heat briefly in hot oven, about 2 minutes. Spread hot crackers with apple butter.

*Do not confuse cold-water wheat crackers with table water crackers. Table water crackers contain multiple ingredients.

Carrot Juice

✳ SERVES 1

> 6 ounces plain carrot juice
> Ice
> Honey to taste
> Dash nutmeg

Pour carrot juice over ice, sweeten to taste with honey and add a dash of nutmeg. Stir well and serve.

Clove Herbal Tea
(See Breakfast, Regular Track)

✳

LUNCH

Lamb Pâté with Plain Wheat Flour Tortillas

✳ SERVES 1

> 1–2 jars Beech-Nut Stage One Lamb
> 1/4 teaspoon ground rosemary
> Sea salt to taste

*1 large ripe fresh apple, washed, cored and sliced, but do
not peel*
*2 plain "commercial type" wheat flour tortillas heated (see
microwave directions below)*

Season lamb to taste with rosemary and salt. Spread lamb on apple slices and hot tortillas.

MW—To heat tortillas: Place tortillas on a microwave-safe plate and heat (H) 20–30 seconds.

Quick Carrot Soup

SERVES 1

2 jars Beech-Nut Stage One carrots
½ cup frozen sliced carrots
¼ cup plain carrot juice
Dash each nutmeg and sea salt
2 teaspoons honey
Water

Combine all ingredients except water in a saucepan and heat, stirring, until hot. Add water or additional carrot juice until soup is desired thickness. Correct seasoning with honey and salt.

MW—Combine all ingredients except water in a 2-cup microwave-safe measuring cup. Cover, leaving vent, and cook (H) until boiling, about 2 minutes. Stir, thin with water or carrot juice if desired and heat (H) until hot. Stir again, correct seasonings with honey and salt.

Fresh Apple

DINNER

One-Dish Lamb Chop Dinner

SERVES 1–2

2 teaspoons ground rosemary
2 shoulder lamb chops, 1–1½ inches thick
*1 teaspoon safflower oil plus 1 teaspoon additional oil, if
necessary*

½ cup each chopped frozen turnips and frozen sliced
carrots
1 cup frozen cranberries
½ teaspoon sea salt

Press rosemary into chops. Heat oil in a skillet over medium-high heat. Add chops and brown on both sides, about 5 minutes total cooking time. Lower heat slightly, add turnips, carrots and cranberries and continue to sauté until vegetables and berries are tender-crisp, about 5–7 minutes. (Add a teaspoon more oil to skillet if vegetables begin to stick.) Add salt. Arrange chops, vegetables and berries on a platter and serve.

Microwaved Baked Apple

✳   SERVES 1

1 large fresh baking apple
½ cup frozen cranberries or whole fresh cranberries
(washed and picked over)
1 teaspoon honey
1 teaspoon safflower oil
Nutmeg
1 (2-ounce) scoop Apple Sorbet (optional)

MW—Wash and core apple; do not pare. Place apple in a microwave-safe glass or ceramic baking dish. Fill with cranberries and drizzle with honey and oil. Sprinkle the apple lightly with nutmeg, cover it loosely with waxed paper and microwave (H) 4–5 minutes, until both cranberries and apple are tender when pierced with a fork. Serve warm or chilled with a scoop of Apple Sorbet. (See Night-Before Preparation Tips for Day Twelve).

NIGHT-BEFORE PREPARATION TIPS
FOR DAY 13

1. Make Banana Sorbet: Allowing 1 jar per serving, empty as many jars Beech-Nut Stage One bananas as you think you will need into a freezer container with a lid. Freeze overnight to use as instant sorbet in beverages or desserts. As dessert, allow to soften 15 minutes in the refrigerator before serving as sorbet.

2. Make soy milk: To make 1 quart soy milk, add 1 cup soy powder such as Fearn's brand to 4 cups water in a blender or shaker. Blend well to combine and chill overnight. To make an even smoother-tasting milk, mix soy powder and water as above, let stand at room temperature 2 hours, stirring occasionally. Cook in a double boiler over boiling water 20 minutes. Allow to cool. Strain through cheesecloth and refrigerate overnight. Shake well before using.

3. Make roast turkey breast: Rub a small turkey breast (about 2 pounds) with soy or Puritan oil and ground oregano. Roast in preheated 375°F. oven, allowing 20 minutes roasting time per pound of turkey. Wrap tightly in aluminum foil and refrigerate overnight.

DAY ✱ 13

THE REINTRODUCTION PHASE (SOY)

ALLOWED FOODS:
Soy, rice, bananas, blueberries, melon, broccoli, white kidney beans, spinach, yellow squash, turkey, thyme, cinnamon, dill, Puritan oil

MENU

	REGULAR	DIET EXPRESS
BREAKFAST	Hot or Cold Rice Cereal with Soy Milk and Bananas Blueberry-Rice Pancakes Cinnamon Stick Herbal Tea	Hot or Cold Rice Cereal with Soy Milk and Bananas Quick-Cooking Farina Cinnamon Stick Herbal Tea
SNACK	Fried Rice Sticks Blueberry-Banana Shake	Plain Rice Cakes or Crackers Quick Bean Dip Banana Cooler
LUNCH	White Bean Dip Toasted Rice Cakes Turkey Wingette Soup Blueberry-Banana Frozen Dessert Watermelon Cooler	Turkey Pâté Turkey Sandwich Quick Creamed Spinach Fresh Fruit Cup
DINNER	Turkey Florentine White or Brown Rice Spinach Salad Bean Dip Dressing Blueberry Crisp with Banana Sorbet	Turkey Stir-Fry Quick-Cooking Rice Fresh Spinach Salad Banana Sorbet with Blueberries

BULK AGENT: Rice bran

REGULAR TRACK

Note: Blueberries are used today for the first time on the diet. While blueberries are easily tolerated by most people, allergic reaction is possible. Make careful note of responses to today's menu. If sensitivity to blueberries is suspected or known, substitute melon for blueberries in today's recipes.

Note: Canned, water-pack turkey such as Swanson brand may be used in today's recipes calling for cooked turkey. Drain before using, reserving broth for making soups and gravies.

BREAKFAST

Hot or Cold Rice Cereal with Soy Milk and Bananas
✳
SERVES 4

Hot Cereal:

²/₃ cups water
²/₃ cup plain farina cereal
Dash salt
1 teaspoon soybean margarine or Puritan oil
1 cup soy milk (see Night-Before Preparation Tips for Day Thirteen)
2 ripe bananas, peeled
Heinz banana flakes to taste

Bring water to boil in saucepan. Stirring constantly, add cereal, salt and oil and reduce heat to low. Cook 5–10 minutes, stirring, until cereal is desired consistency. Serve with soy milk and peeled, sliced bananas. Sweeten to taste with Heinz banana flakes.

Cold Cereal:

Serve plain puffed rice cereal with soy milk, sliced bananas and Heinz banana flakes.

Blueberry-Rice Pancakes
✳
SERVES 4

2 cups crumbled plain ricecakes (about 4–5 large cakes)
1½ cups soft tofu

*

*1 tablespoon water or soy milk (see Night-Before
    Preparation Tips for Day Thirteen)
½ cup frozen blueberries (without syrup) or drained fresh
    blueberries (washed) plus additional blueberries for
    garnish (optional)
Puritan oil for greasing skillet
2 jars Beech-Nut Stage One bananas*

Mix the rice cake crumbs with tofu and water or soy milk until a thick batter is formed. Stir in the ½ cup blueberries. Grease a skillet with oil. Heat the skillet until hot but not smoking. Using ¼ cup for each pancake, pour batter onto the hot skillet. Spread with a spatula slightly or tip the pan to form a fairly thin cake. Cook pancake on one side until it is crisp and can be easily turned, 1–2 minutes. Turn and continue to cook until pancake is cooked through and crisp on the other side, about 2 minutes more. Spread hot pancakes with Beech-Nut bananas and sprinkle with additional blueberries if desired.

Cinnamon Stick Herbal Tea

*   SERVES 1

*1 cinnamon stick, broken into several pieces
4–5 fresh blueberries (washed)
6 ounces boiling water
Heinz banana flakes
Soy milk (optional)*

Place cinnamon and blueberries in a mug; add boiling water. Steep 2–5 minutes. Remove cinnamon stick pieces; eat or remove blueberries. Sweeten to taste with banana flakes and add soy milk, if desired.

SNACK

Fried Rice Sticks

*   SERVES 4

*1–2 cups Puritan oil
1 package (12 ounces or more) dry rice sticks
Sea salt to taste*

Pour oil into a fryer or deep, heavy skillet to the depth of 2 inches. Heat the oil until very hot, about 375°F. Drop rice sticks a handful at a time into hot oil. Sticks are cooked as soon as they puff up and become crisp. Remove them at once with a slotted spoon and drain on paper towels. Salt to taste with sea salt as a snack, or use them without salt as garnish on salads.

Note: Dry rice sticks are sold in the Chinese or ethnic food sections of most supermarkets.

Blueberry-Banana Shake

✻   SERVES 1

½ cup frozen blueberries (without syrup)
1 jar Beech-Nut Stage One bananas or 1 small, ripe banana,
    peeled
4 ounces soft tofu
Pinch ground cinnamon
Heinz banana flakes (optional)

Do not defrost blueberries. Place all ingredients except banana flakes in a blender. Blend on highest speed until creamy and smooth. Taste; if desired, blend in Heinz banana flakes to taste for additional sweetness.

LUNCH

White Bean Dip

✻   SERVES 4

1 cup drained, canned water-pack white kidney beans
¼ cup soft tofu
1 tablespoon Puritan oil or soybean margarine
1 teaspoon sea salt
½ teaspoon dill seed
1 cup broccoli florets (washed and trimmed)
1 large yellow squash, scrubbed, trimmed and cut into sticks

Place first five ingredients in a blender or processor. Blend on high power, scraping sides of container often, until dip is smooth. Remove dip to a bowl and correct seasoning with additional sea salt and dill. Cover and chill in refrigerator until ready to serve. Serve dip with Toasted Rice Cakes (see recipe below) and fresh vegetables.

✳

Toasted Rice Cakes

✳
SERVES 4

8 "mini"-size plain rice cakes
Soybean margarine

Preheat broiler.

Spread rice cakes lightly with margarine. Toast under a broiler 6 inches from heat until tops begin to brown. Cool slightly before serving.

Turkey Wingette Soup

✳
SERVES 4

4 turkey wingettes
3 cups water
1 teaspoon sea salt
2 teaspoons ground thyme
1 cup long-grain rice
1 tablespoon Puritan oil or soybean margarine, melted
2 tablespoons soy powder

Place wingettes and water in a large soup pot with a cover. Add salt and thyme and simmer, covered, until turkey meat is tender when pierced with a fork, about 1 hour. Remove wingettes from broth and set aside. Strain the broth through cheesecloth or a fine mesh strainer into a 4-cup measuring cup or pitcher. Clean the soup pot of scum, pour strained broth back into pot and bring to boil. Stir in rice, reduce heat to very low and simmer, covered, until rice is tender but still firm, about 15 minutes. Remove meat from wingettes and add to the broth and rice. In a cup, blend oil or margarine with soy powder until smooth. Stirring constantly, add the mixture to the soup and bring to boil, until soup is thickened. Remove from heat, correct seasoning with sea salt and serve.

Blueberry-Banana Frozen Dessert

✳
SERVES 4

10 ounces fresh or frozen blueberries (without syrup)
1–2 jars Beech-Nut Stage One bananas
1 cup soft tofu, well mashed

Rinse and drain blueberries if they are fresh. Toss with bananas until blueberries are thoroughly coated. (Bananas serve as sweetener;

Heinz banana flakes mixed with a little water can also be used.) Place fruit and tofu in a blender or processor. Blend until smooth. Freeze in an ice-cream freezer according to manufacturer's directions. To freeze in a home refrigerator-freezer, pour tofu-fruit blend into an ice-cube tray or plastic freezer container with a cover. (Covering protects flavor of dessert.) Freeze until almost firm. Break up with a fork, blend in blender once more, and freeze until firm.

Note: A small Donvier ice-cream freezer costs about $30. It can make this dessert in 20 minutes. Donvier freezers are available at most department stores.

Watermelon Cooler

✳   SERVES 1

   1½ cups seeded ripe watermelon chunks
   Pinch ground cinnamon (optional)
   Ice

Place watermelon chunks in a blender. Blend on highest power until melon liquefies. Add a pinch of cinnamon during blending, if desired, and serve over ice.

DINNER

Turkey Florentine

✳   SERVES 4–6

   3 tablespoons soybean margarine or Puritan oil
   1 tablespoon soy powder
   1 cup water or soy milk (see Night-Before Preparation Tips
      for Day Thirteen)
   2 cups soft tofu, mashed
   ½ teaspoon sea salt or to taste
   2 teaspoons ground thyme
   1 (20-ounce) bag frozen chopped spinach, defrosted and
      squeezed dry by hand
   Pinch ground cinnamon
   12–18 ounces (3 ounces per serving) sliced, cooked turkey
      breast (see Night-Before Preparation Tips for Day
      Thirteen)

Preheat broiler.
   Heat shortening in a saucepan, add powder and stir with a wire whisk until blended. Over medium-high heat add 1 cup water or soy milk and tofu, stirring slowly until thickened and very smooth just

✳

until boiling. (Thin with more water or soy milk if thinner sauce is desired.) Add sea salt and thyme. In a saucepan, combine spinach and ½ cup of the sauce. Add cinnamon and heat thoroughly, but do not boil. Spoon spinach onto warm heatproof platter and arrange turkey on top. Spoon remaining sauce over turkey. Brown lightly under broiler until sauce begins to brown and serve.

White or Brown Rice

✳   SERVES 4–6

2 cups water
Dash salt
1 cup white rice, brown rice or combination
1 teaspoon soybean margarine or Puritan oil

Over direct heat, bring water to boil in the top of a double boiler. Stir in salt, rice and margarine or oil. Cover and cook over moderately boiling water 20–30 minutes. Fluff with a fork and serve hot with additional soybean margarine if desired.

Spinach Salad

✳   SERVES 4–6

4 cups fresh spinach (washed, drained, trimmed and torn
    into bite-sized pieces)
6 ounces firm tofu
Bean Dip Dressing (recipe follows)

Place spinach in a salad bowl. Slice tofu into fairly thick slices. Press excess water from each slice by placing tofu between two pieces of waxed paper or plastic wrap and pressing gently against a flat, slanted surface set in the sink, allowing water to run off. Keep pressing until tofu is the texture of firm cheese. Cut the pressed tofu into squares and add to spinach. Pour Bean Dip Dressing over spinach and tofu and toss.

Bean Dip Dressing

✳   MAKES ¾ CUP

½ cup White Bean Dip (reserved from Lunch, Regular
    Track)
¼ cup soy milk (see Night-Before Preparation Tips for Day
    Thirteen) or Puritan oil
Sea salt and fresh minced dill to taste

Thin reserved bean dip with soy milk or Puritan oil; season to taste with salt and dill.

Blueberry Crisp with Banana Sorbet
✷   SERVES 4

> 2 cups fresh or frozen blueberries (without syrup)
> 1 tablespoon water
> 4 tablespoons Beech-Nut Stage One bananas
> ⅓ cup soybean margarine, melted
> 2–3 cups puffed rice cereal or 5 crumbed plain large
>   rice cakes
> 1 teaspoon ground cinnamon
> ⅓ cup Heinz banana flakes

Preheat oven to 350°F.

Rinse, drain and pick over berries if they are fresh. Place blueberries, water and bananas in a deep-dish (8-inch) pie plate and mix well. For topping, melt margarine in a saucepan and stir in cereal or rice-cake crumbs until coated. Sprinkle the mixture with cinnamon and Heinz banana flakes and stir until well combined. Spread topping over blueberries and press down. Bake pie until blueberries are bubbly and top is golden brown, about 15 minutes. Serve slices of pie with scoops of Banana Sorbet (see Night-Before Preparation Tips for Day Thirteen).

VARIATION: Preheat oven to 400°F. Prepare topping mixture as above. Spread over bottom and sides of an 8-inch pie plate and bake 5 minutes. Lower oven to 350°F. Cool shell, and fill with blueberry filling, prepared as above. Bake 15 minutes.

DIET EXPRESS

BREAKFAST

Hot or Cold Rice Cereal with Soy Milk and Bananas
(See Breakfast, Regular Track)
✷

Quick-Cooking Farina

SERVES 1

2 tablespoons quick-cooking farina
¾ cup water
Dash sea salt

MW—Stir 2 tablespoons quick-cooking farina with ¾ cup water in a microwave-safe bowl. Heat (H) to boiling, about 2 minutes. Stir, add salt and microwave (L) until cereal is desired consistency. Serve with soy milk (see Night-Before Preparation Tips for Day Thirteen) and/or bananas as described in Regular Track recipes.

Cinnamon Stick Herbal Tea
(See Breakfast, Regular Track)

SNACK

Plain Rice Cakes or Crackers

Quick Bean Dip

SERVES 1

½ cup drained, canned water-pack white kidney beans
½ cup soft tofu
1 teaspoon Puritan oil
¼ teaspoon dill seed
¼ teaspoon sea salt

Place all ingredients in blender or food processor fitted with a steel blade and blend until smooth. Spread on plain rice cakes or crackers.

Banana Cooler

SERVES 1

2 jars Beech-Nut Stage One bananas
1 ounce chilled soy milk (see Night-Before Preparation Tips
  for Day Thirteen)

*

1 ice cube, crushed
Dash ground cinnamon

Blend all ingredients in a blender 1 minute, until thick and smooth.

LUNCH

Turkey Pâté

*   SERVES 1

1 jar Beech-Nut Stage One turkey
1 teaspoon Puritan oil
Sea salt and ground thyme to taste

Blend all ingredients thoroughly and chill. Spread on plain rice crackers or rice cakes.

Turkey Sandwich

*   SERVES 1

1 jar Beech-Nut Stage One spinach
¼ teaspoon sea salt
1 teaspoon ground thyme
2 large plain rice cakes
4 leaves fresh spinach, washed, drained and trimmed
3 ounces cooked turkey breast, sliced (see Night-Before
*   Preparation Tips for Day Thirteen)*

Blend together the Beech-Nut spinach, salt and thyme; spread on rice cakes. Layer spinach leaves and turkey slices on one seasoned rice cake, press cakes together to make a "sandwich" and serve.

Quick Creamed Spinach

*   SERVES 1

1 jar Beech-Nut Stage One spinach
2 ounces soft tofu
¼ teaspoon sea salt
Dash ground cinnamon

Combine all ingredients in a small saucepan and heat over medium heat, stirring constantly, until hot.

✳

MW—Combine ingredients in a 2-cup microwave-safe measuring cup. Cook (H) 30 seconds. Stir, cook (M or L) until hot, about 1 minute more, stirring after 30 seconds.

Fresh Fruit Cup

✳
SERVES 1

¼ cup fresh blueberries (washed, drained and picked over)
½ small banana, peeled and sliced
½ cup bite-sized pieces honeydew or cantaloupe (rind removed)
½ teaspoon ground cinnamon
1–2 jars Beech-Nut Stage One bananas

Place fresh fruit in a bowl and sprinkle with cinnamon. Stir in Beech-Nut bananas until fresh fruit is coated. Serve.

DINNER

Turkey Stir-Fry

✳
SERVES 1–2

Puritan oil for greasing skillet
4 teaspoons soybean margarine
1 pound fresh turkey fillets, cut into julienne strips
Sea salt and thyme to taste
Dash ground cinnamon
1 cup fresh or frozen broccoli florets
1 cup sliced fresh or frozen yellow squash

Grease a skillet or wok with oil. Add 2 teaspoons margarine and heat until hot, but not browned. Add turkey, sprinkle with salt, thyme and a dash of cinnamon, and sauté, stirring, 2–3 minutes or until no longer pink. Remove from skillet and set aside. Add 1 more teaspoon margarine to the skillet and heat until hot. Add broccoli and squash, sprinkle lightly with salt and thyme and sauté, stirring, 2 minutes. Return turkey to skillet, add remaining margarine, and heat until hot. Correct seasoning with salt and thyme.

Quick-Cooking Rice

✳   SERVES 1–2

⅔ cup water
⅔ cup quick-cooking rice
Dash sea salt
1 teaspoon soybean margarine

In a saucepan with a cover, heat water to boil. Stir in rice, salt and margarine. Remove from heat, cover and allow to stand 5 minutes, until water is absorbed. Fluff with fork before serving.

Fresh Spinach Salad

✳   SERVES 1–2

2 cups fresh spinach (washed, dried and torn into bite-sized
    pieces)
½ cup firm tofu, cut into squares
¼ cup soft tofu, mashed
1 jar Beech-Nut Stage One spinach
1 tablespoon Puritan or soy oil
Sea salt, dill and ground thyme to taste

Place spinach and firm tofu squares in a bowl. Combine mashed tofu, Beech-Nut spinach and oil until thoroughly mixed. Season to taste with sea salt, dill and thyme; toss with spinach and firm tofu.

Banana Sorbet with Blueberries

✳   SERVES 1

½ cup frozen blueberries (without syrup)
½ cup Banana Sorbet (see Night-Before Preparation Tips
    for Day Thirteen)
Heinz banana flakes (optional)

Sprinkle blueberries over Banana Sorbet and serve. For additional sweetness, sprinkle dessert with Heinz banana flakes.

NIGHT-BEFORE PREPARATION TIPS
FOR DAY 14

1. Presoak kasha for quick, hot breakfast cereal and kasha for salad: Place 3½ cups raw, washed and picked over kasha in a large saucepan or bowl with a lid. Stir in 5½ cups boiling water, cover, and refrigerate overnight.

✳ ───────────────────────────────────

2. Roast beef for sandwiches: Preheat oven to 300°F. Place a small (4–5 pound) rolled rib roast fat side up on a rack in an open roasting pan. Rub with sea salt. Insert a meat thermometer in the thickest part of the roast. Roast, uncovered, 35 minutes per pound. Cook until medium-rare (about 150°F. on a meat thermometer). Cover and chill overnight.

DAY ✳ 14   REINTRODUCTION PHASE (MILK)

ALLOWED FOODS:
Milk, yogurt, cream, cottage cheese, sour cream, butter, kasha, chick-peas, peaches, bamboo shoots, cauliflower, celery, green beans, sweet potatoes, watercress, beef, sesame, ginger, summer savory, gelatin, maple syrup

MENU	REGULAR	DIET EXPRESS
BREAKFAST	Hot Kasha Cereal with Peaches Chick-pea Pancakes Cold Milk Ginger Herbal Tea	Microwaved Kasha Cereal with Peaches Milk Ginger Herbal Tea
SNACK	Yogurt with Peaches Tahini-Peach Clusters Peach Spritzer	Yogurt with Peaches Peach Shake
LUNCH	Cream of Watercress Soup Kasha-Beef Salad Tahini Dressing Frosted Peaches Peach Ice Cream	Hamburgers and Cottage Cheese Beef Pâté with Celery Sticks Peach
DINNER	Hamburger-Cauliflower Roll Rich Sweet Potatoes Vegetable Salad Sesame Dressing Peach Cheesecake	Sirloin Steak Stroganoff Creamed Sweet Potatoes Watercress Salad Instant Sorbet Peach Whip

BULK AGENT: None

R E G U L A R   T R A C K

BREAKFAST

Hot Kasha Cereal with Peaches

✳   SERVES 4

> 2 cups presoaked kasha (see Night-Before Preparation Tips
>   for Day Fourteen)
> Water
> 2 teaspoons butter
> Maple syrup or Heinz peach flakes to taste

Place presoaked kasha in a clean, large saucepan and stir in just
enough water to moisten. Too much water will result in mushy
texture. Add butter, heat to boiling and simmer, uncovered, until
kasha is tender but still firm, about 5 minutes. Sweeten with maple
syrup or Heinz peach flakes to taste. Serve with milk and sliced fresh
or frozen peaches. Refrigerate any leftover kasha for use later in the
day.

Note: If preparing unsoaked kasha, bring 2 cups water and ½ teaspoon
salt to boil in a large saucepan. As water boils, slowly add 1 cup raw,
washed and picked over kasha and 2 teaspoons butter. Lower heat
and simmer, stirring occasionally, 10–12 minutes.

Chick-pea Pancakes

✳   SERVES 4

> 1½ cups chick-pea flour*
> 1 tablespoon sesame oil plus oil for greasing skillet
> 1½–2 cups milk
> Dash ground ginger

Mix the chick-pea flour with oil and enough milk to make a thick but
pourable batter. Add ginger and blend until combined. Grease a skillet
with oil. Heat skillet until it is very hot, but not smoking. Using ½ cup
for each pancake, pour batter into hot skillet. Cook pancakes until
browned on one side, 2–3 minutes. Turn pancakes and brown on
other side about 1 minute, or until cooked through. Serve with butter
and maple syrup to taste.

✳

*Chick-pea flour can be found in health food stores, or you can make your own by grinding 2–3 (1 cup at a time) cups dry chick-peas in a processor. Be sure to sift the chick-pea flour well if smooth-textured pancakes are desired. Less sifting produces a grainier-textured pancake.

Cold Milk

✳

Ginger Herbal Tea

✳   SERVES 1

 2 teaspoons minced gingerroot
 6 ounces boiling water
 Milk and maple crystals or maple syrup to taste

Place gingerroot in the bottom of a mug. Add boiling water and steep root until tea is desired strength. Add milk and maple crystals or maple syrup to taste.

SNACK

Yogurt with Peaches

✳   SERVES 4

 2 large fresh peaches or 1 cup frozen sliced peaches
 1 jar Beech-Nut Stage One peaches
 1 teaspoon ground ginger
 1 pint plain yogurt*

Wash and chop the fresh peaches, leaving skins on, or use frozen peach slices, undefrosted. Combine with Beech-Nut peaches and ginger. Stir mixture into plain yogurt and serve cold.

*Read label to make sure yogurt is made with milk and milk derivatives only.

Tahini-Peach Clusters

✳ SERVES 4

1 cup tahini, mixed well to incorporate oil
1 cup nonfat dry milk
⅓ cup Beech-Nut Stage One peaches
½ cup maple syrup
1 teaspoon ground ginger
1 large fresh peach, washed and chopped, skin left on
Sesame seeds

Mix together the tahini, dry milk, Beech-Nut peaches, maple syrup and ginger until thoroughly combined. Fold in chopped peaches until completely mixed. Spread a generous amount of sesame seeds on a large sheet of waxed paper. Roll teaspoonfuls of tahini-peach mixture in seeds until each spoonful is completely coated. Place clusters in a single layer in a covered container or in an ice-cube tray lined with waxed paper and chill 1 hour or more.

Note: Clusters may be rolled in peach flakes instead of sesame seeds, if preferred.

Peach Spritzer

✳ SERVES 1

6 ounces strong Ginger Herbal Tea (see Breakfast, Regular
Track)
Ice cubes
1 jar Beech-Nut Stage One peaches
Dash ground ginger
2 teaspoons maple crystals or maple syrup
1–2 ounces sparkling mineral water

Pour tea over ice; stir in Beech-Nut Stage One peaches, ginger and maple crystals or syrup. Stir briskly to blend well. Add 1–2 ounces sparkling mineral water and serve.

LUNCH

Cream of Watercress Soup

✳ 4 SERVINGS

3 cups watercress (washed and stems removed)
2 cups water

✳

½ teaspoon each sea salt and summer savory
1 cup light cream
1 cup drained, canned water-pack bamboo shoots or fresh
*   bamboo shoots, rinsed and drained*

Simmer watercress in water 3–5 minutes. Transfer to the container of a blender or processor; add salt and savory. Cover and process on high speed. With motor running, remove cover and add the cream. When cream is blended into soup, pour mixture into a saucepan, add bamboo shoots and heat, stirring, over medium heat until hot. Do not boil. Correct seasoning with sea salt and savory. Pour hot soup into serving bowls and top each bowl with 1 tablespoon sour cream. If desired, chill soup in a covered container and serve cold.

Kasha-Beef Salad

✳   SERVES 4

12 ounces beef tenderloin, sliced into thin strips
½ teaspoon each sea salt, ground summer savory and
*   ground ginger*
1 tablespoon sesame oil plus oil for greasing skillet
½ cup water
1 quart watercress
1 cup presoaked kasha
2 cups drained, canned water-pack bamboo shoots or fresh
*   bamboo shoots (rinsed and drained)*
Tahini Dressing (recipe follows)

Rub tenderloin strips with salt, savory and ginger. Mix 1 tablespoon oil and water; pour over beef and marinate in the refrigerator 15–20 minutes. Meanwhile rinse watercress in cold water, drain it and remove stems; pat dry. Lightly grease a skillet with oil and stir-fry beef until meat is rare, about 2 minutes. Stir in kasha and bamboo shoots and heat until meat is medium-rare and mixture is hot, 1 minute. Divide watercress among 4 serving plates and spoon beef and kasha mixture on top. Dress with Tahini Dressing and sprinkle with sesame seeds.

Note: After combining beef with kasha and bamboo shoots, mixture can be refrigerated and served cold. Garnish before serving.

Tahini Dressing

*{: style="text-align:center"}

⅓ cup tahini, mixed well to incorporate oil
½ cup sour cream or plain yogurt
1 teaspoon each sea salt, ground ginger and ground
    summer savory
¼ cup whole milk

In a blender, combine tahini, sour cream or yogurt and seasonings; blend on medium power until smooth. With motor running, add milk until dressing is pourable, but still thick.

Frosted Peaches

1 pint plain cottage cheese
½ cup whole milk or half-and-half
4 large fresh peaches
Ground ginger

Beat cottage cheese with milk or half-and-half until smooth and fluffy. Peel peaches. Leaving peaches whole, remove pit so that peaches can be "stuffed" in the center. Fill peaches with cottage cheese mixture and then frost peaches all over with remaining cottage cheese mixture. Sprinkle lightly with ginger. Chill 15–20 minutes. Meanwhile, whip heavy cream until soft peaks form. Serve peaches topped with whipped cream; for added sweetness, sprinkle with Heinz peach flakes.

Peach Ice Cream

4 jars Beech-Nut Stage One peaches
1 (10 ounce) package frozen peaches, chopped
3 cups heavy cream
Pinch ground ginger (optional)

Combine all ingredients and freeze in an ice-cream freezer according to manufacturer's directions. If freezing in a home refrigerator-freezer, pour peach-cream mixture into a blender and blend on low power until mixture is combined but chunks of peach still remain. Pour mixture into an ice-cube tray or plastic freezer container, cover and freeze until almost firm. Break up with a fork, blend in a blender 1 minute or whip by hand with a wire whisk and freeze until firm.

DINNER

Hamburger-Cauliflower Roll

SERVES 4

Cauliflower:

> ½ medium head cauliflower, separated into florets, or 2 cups
>   frozen florets
> ½ cup sour cream
> 1½ tablespoons butter
> Sea salt to taste

Simmer cauliflower in water to cover until tender (10–15 minutes). Drain thoroughly. Slowly adding sour cream and butter, blend in a blender or mash by hand until smooth. Season to taste with salt and blend or beat until thoroughly combined. Set aside. (There should be 2 cups.)

Note: Cauliflower should be consistency of thickly mashed potatoes.

Hamburger:

> Butter for greasing 9 × 5 × 3-inch loaf pan
> 1 pound lean ground beef
> 1 cup cooked kasha (optional)
> 1 teaspoon butter
> ¼ teaspoon each sea salt and ground summer savory
> Sesame seeds
> ½ cup light cream

Heat oven to 350°F.

Grease a 9 × 5 × 3-inch loaf pan lightly with butter. In a mixing bowl, combine ground beef, kasha, if desired, butter and seasoning, and mix thoroughly. Sprinkle a piece of waxed paper with sesame seeds. Press meat out on seeds to make a rectangle about ½-inch thick. Spread "mashed" cauliflower on top of meat. Lifting one end of waxed paper, roll meat and cauliflower into a roll. Place in loaf pan. Bake roll 45 minutes, until brown. Remove from pan. Add light cream to drippings in the pan. Stir over very low heat until sauce is heated through. Season to taste with sea salt and savory. Pour over hamburger roll and serve.

Rich Sweet Potatoes

✳ SERVES 4–6

4 large sweet potatoes
3 cups heavy cream
¼ pound butter
Sea salt and ground summer savory to taste

Peel potatoes and grate in a medium grater or processor. Place the potatoes immediately in the top of a double boiler and pour heavy cream over them. Place butter on top. Cover and cook over boiling water 30 minutes. Stir potatoes, cover again, and cook over simmering water for 3 hours. Check water level in bottom of boiler occasionally; add water if necessary. Turn into a serving dish and season to taste with sea salt and savory.

Vegetable Salad

✳ SERVES 4–6

2 cups fresh or frozen cauliflower florets
2 cups fresh or frozen Italian green beans
Sesame Dressing (recipe follows)
2 cups watercress (washed and stems removed)

Place the cauliflower and green beans in boiling water for 2 minutes. Drain, rinse under cold water and toss with Sesame Dressing. Cover and chill several hours. Arrange watercress on serving plates and spoon vegetables on top. Sprinkle lightly with sesame seeds and serve.

Sesame Dressing

✳ MAKES 1 CUP

1 tablespoon tahini mixed with ¼ cup water
1 teaspoon sea salt
½ teaspoon ground ginger
1 teaspoon ground summer savory
¾ cup sesame oil

Place tahini and water, salt, ginger and savory in a blender. With motor running, gradually add sesame oil, until dressing is thick and smooth. Do not add all of sesame oil if dressing is becoming watery.

*

Peach Cheesecake

*

Crust:

> *1 cup raw kasha, washed, drained and picked over*
> *2 tablespoons butter, softened*

Preheat oven to 350°F.

Blend kasha with butter until kernels of kasha are completely coated. Press mixture in the bottom and sides of an 8-inch pie plate. Bake about 5–8 minutes, until kasha is crisp and browned. Set aside to cool before filling.

Note: Tahini can be substituted for butter if a peanut-flavored crust is desired.

Filling:

> *1 jar Beech-Nut Stage One peaches*
> *1 envelope Knox unflavored gelatin*
> *¾ cup boiling water*
> *1 pound cottage cheese (not low-fat) or whipped cream*
>   *cheese*
> *⅓ cup maple syrup*
> *1 teaspoon ground ginger*
> *3 large fresh peaches*
> *⅓ cup maple syrup*
> *1 pint heavy cream*
> *½ cup maple crystals or Heinz peach flakes (optional)*

Pour Beech-Nut peaches into a large bowl. Sprinkle gelatin on top and allow to soften 1 minute. Add boiling water and stir until gelatin is completely dissolved. Place mixture in a blender or in a food processor fitted with whipping blade. Blend on medium-high speed, slowly adding cottage or creamed cheese, maple syrup and ginger. Stop blender, scrape down sides of bowl and blend until smooth. Pour mixture into cooled crust and chill until firm, about 2 hours. Just before serving, peel and slice peaches and place them in a bowl. Add maple syrup and stir until peach slices are coated. Spread peaches on top of filling. Whip heavy cream until soft peaks form, adding maple crystals or Heinz peach flakes if sweetened cream is desired. Spread whipped cream over peaches and serve.

DIET EXPRESS

BREAKFAST

Microwaved Kasha Cereal with Peaches

✳ SERVES 1

> 1 cup water
> 1 teaspoon butter
> Dash each sea salt and ground ginger
> ½ cup raw kasha, picked over
> 2 teaspoons maple syrup
> ½ cup frozen sliced peaches or 1 fresh peach, washed and
>   sliced, skin left on

MW—Heat (H) water to boiling in a 2-cup microwave-safe bowl or casserole, about 2 minutes. Add butter, salt, ginger, and kasha. Stir well to combine. Cover and cook (H) 30 seconds. Stir. Uncover and cook (L) 4–8 minutes longer, until kasha is tender. Stir in maple syrup and peaches. Serve with milk or cream and additional maple syrup to taste.

Milk

✳

Ginger Herbal Tea
(See Breakfast, Regular Track)

✳

SNACK

Yogurt with Peaches
(See Snack, Regular Track)

✳

Peach Shake

✻ SERVES 1

¾ cup frozen sliced peaches
1 jar Beech-Nut Stage One peaches
Pinch ground ginger
½ cup light cream or half-and-half

Chop peach slices coarsely and toss them with Beech-Nut peaches until coated. Place in a blender with ginger, light cream or half-and-half; blend until thick and smooth.

LUNCH

Hamburgers and Cottage Cheese

✻ SERVES 1–2

½ pound chopped beef
1 teaspoon ground summer savory
½ teaspoon sea salt
2 teaspoons butter
1 cup cottage cheese

Shape beef lightly into 2 thick burgers. Sprinkle all sides of burgers with summer savory and press in. Sprinkle a heavy skillet with a light layer of sea salt. Place over high heat, and when salt begins to brown, add hamburgers. Cook 30 seconds over high heat. Turn, sear other side of burgers 30 seconds more. Lower heat to medium and cook until burgers are done to taste, 3–5 minutes more. Place a teaspoon of butter on each burger and serve each with a scoop of cottage cheese sprinkled lightly with ginger.

Beef Pâté with Celery Sticks

✻ SERVES 1

1 jar Beech-Nut Stage One beef
1 teaspoon sesame oil
¼ teaspoon each sea salt and ground summer savory
3 stalks fresh celery, scrubbed, ends trimmed and sliced into
*   sticks*

Combine beef, oil and seasonings. Chill or serve at room temperature with celery sticks.

Peach

✳

DINNER

Sirloin Steak Stroganoff

✳ SERVES 1–2

1 tablespoon sesame oil
1 tablespoon butter
1 (½-pound) sirloin steak, about ¼ inch thick
1 teaspoon each ground ginger and ground summer savory
5 ounces frozen french-cut string beans
1 stalk fresh celery, thinly sliced
5 ounces frozen cauliflower florets
½ teaspoon sea salt
½ cup sour cream

Heat oil and butter in a skillet or wok until very hot. Rub meat with ginger and savory and slice into thin slices or strips. Add to skillet and stir-fry just until brown, about 1 minute. Add a little more oil and butter to the skillet if meat sticks to pan, and add the vegetables. Sprinkle with sea salt and sauté 3 minutes more. Stir sour cream into meat and vegetables and heat but do not boil. Serve with Cooked Kasha (recipe follows).

Cooked Kasha

✳ MAKES 1 CUP

1 cup presoaked kasha (see Night-Before Preparation Tips
for Day Fourteen)
¼ cup water
Dash sea salt

Combine kasha, water and salt in a saucepan and heat to boil. Lower heat and simmer until water is absorbed, about 5 minutes.

Creamed Sweet Potatoes

✳ SERVES 1–2

2 jars Beech-Nut Stage One sweet potatoes
4 ounces light or heavy cream
Pinch ground ginger and sea salt

❋

Combine all ingredients and heat until hot but not boiling.

Note: Substitute 1 jar Beech-Nut Stage One peaches for one of the jars of sweet potatoes for a sweeter vegetable.

Watercress Salad

❋   SERVES 1–2

2 bunches watercress, washed, drained and stems removed
½ cup Sesame Dressing (see Dinner, Regular Track)
½ cup large-curd plain cottage cheese

Toss watercress with Sesame Dressing and cottage cheese until well combined.

Instant Sorbet

❋   SERVES 2

2 cups frozen sliced peaches
2 tablespoons Beech-Nut Stage One peaches
Pinch ground ginger

Place all ingredients in a blender. Blend until smooth and serve at once. Top with unsweetened whipped cream.

Peach Whip

❋   SERVES 2

1 pint heavy cream
1 cup frozen sliced peaches, chopped
1 jar Beech-Nut Stage One peaches
1 tablespoon maple syrup

Whip cream until fairly stiff peaks form. Fold in chopped peaches, Beech-Nut peaches and maple syrup until uniformly combined. Serve at once.

NIGHT-BEFORE PREPARATION TIPS
FOR DAY 15

1. Make Pear Sorbet: Allowing 1 jar per serving, empty as many jars Beech-Nut Stage One pears as you think you will need into a freezer container with a lid. Freeze overnight to use as instant sorbet in beverages or desserts. As dessert, allow to soften 15 minutes in the refrigerator before serving as sorbet.

2. Prepare lamb for Roast Marinated Leg of Lamb: Wipe 1 (6-pound) leg of lamb with damp paper towels. Using paring knife, make several small pockets in flesh of lamb, and insert basil leaves (4 teaspoons). Combine ½ cup sunflower oil and 2 cups red wine to make marinade. Place lamb in a large, shallow baking dish. Pour marinade over lamb. Refrigerate, covered, overnight. Turn lamb in the morning and keep refrigerated until cooking time (see Day Fifteen, Dinner, Regular Track).

3. Presoak black beans: Place 1 cup dry black beans in a bowl or pan with a cover. Cover with 2 cups boiling water, cool slightly and refrigerate, covered, overnight. Use on Day Fifteen for Basil and Bean Soup (see Lunch, Regular Track), if desired.

DAY
✳
15
THE REINTRODUCTION PHASE (VINEGAR/FERMENTATION PRODUCTS)

ALLOWED FOODS:
Oats, pears, dates, raisins, prunes, figs, white grape juice, beets, black beans, cucumbers, lettuce, mushrooms, olives, zucchini, lamb, vinegar, wine, beer, sunflower oil, basil, mint, nutmeg, white potatoes, yeast, vanilla, baking powder

MENU	REGULAR	DIET EXPRESS
BREAKFAST	Prune Juice	Prune Juice
	Pear and Oat Muffins	Oatmeal with Dates and
	Oatmeal with Dates and	Raisins
	Raisins	Mint Herbal Tea
	Oat Pancakes	
	Mint Herbal Tea	

✳

SNACK	Granola	White Grape Juice Spritzer
	White Grape Juice Spritzer	Crunchy Black Beans and
		Sunflower Seeds
LUNCH	Basil and Bean Soup	Lamb Pâté with Zucchini or
	Pickled Vegetables	Cucumber Sticks,
	Oat Bran Fruit Bars	Mushrooms and Olives
		Quick Borscht
DINNER	White Grape Aperitif	Broiled Lamb with Mint Sauce
	Roast Marinated Leg of Lamb	One-Dish Lamb Pie
	with Oat Stuffing	Pear Sorbet with Champagne
	Sunrise Salad with Herb Purée	
	Dressing	
	High-Nutrition Oat Bran Loaf	
	Drunken Pears	

BULK AGENT: Psyllium seed

R E G U L A R   T R A C K

Note: If you had an adverse reaction to oats on Day Ten, make the following changes in today's recipes:

1. Substitute barley flour (see Day Twenty-two, Barley Socca [Italian Flatbread], Breakfast, Regular Track) whenever recipes call for oat bran cereal.

2. Substitute Beech-Nut Stage One barley cereal for oatmeal in Oatmeal with Dates and Raisins, (Breakfast, Regular Track and Breakfast, Diet Express).

3. Substitute coarsely ground, *quick-cooking barley* for oatmeal in all other recipes calling for oatmeal.

BREAKFAST

Prune Juice

✳

Pear and Oat Muffins

✳   MAKES ABOUT 1 DOZEN

Sunflower oil for greasing muffin tins plus ¼ cup oil
1 cup water
½ cup plain pear juice or 1 jar Beech-Nut Stage One pears
¼ teaspoon pure vanilla extract
½ cup date sugar or Heinz pear flakes
1 cup plain oat bran cereal* (not flakes)
½ cup plain regular oatmeal (not quick-cooking)
½ cup potato starch flour
½ package (1 teaspoon) rapid-rising yeast

Preheat oven to 375°F.

Oil a 12-muffin baking tin lightly with sunflower oil. Beat together the water, pear juice or Beech-Nut pears, ¼ cup sunflower oil, and vanilla. Stir in date sugar or pear flakes. In a separate bowl, combine oat bran cereal, oatmeal, potato starch flour and yeast. Combine mixtures with minimal strokes. Divide into muffin tins and bake until golden brown on top, about 20–30 minutes. Test for doneness after 20 minutes by inserting a toothpick into center of muffin; if batter clings to toothpick, continue cooking 5–10 minutes more. Cool baked muffins 10 minutes and remove from tins.

*If you cannot find oat bran cereal, make a cup of oat flour as a substitute: Place 1 cup raw regular oatmeal in a blender or processor. Grind oatmeal into a coarse-textured flour and proceed with recipe.

Oatmeal with Dates and Raisins

✳   SERVES 4

4 cups water
Dash sea salt
1⅓ cups plain regular oatmeal (not quick-cooking)
½ cup raisins
½ cup dates, coarsely chopped

Bring water and salt to boil over high heat. Stir in oatmeal; immediately lower heat and simmer 3 minutes. Add raisins and dates and continue to cook, stirring occasionally, over low heat until oatmeal is desired thickness. Top with Beech-Nut pears.

Oat Pancakes

2 cups oat bran cereal (see above recipe for Pear and Oat
*   Muffins for substitute)*
2 cups (approximate) water
1 tablespoon sunflower oil plus oil for greasing skillet

Mix oat bran cereal, water and oil into a thick but pourable batter. Grease a skillet with oil. Heat the skillet until hot but not smoking. Using ½ cup for each pancake, pour batter onto hot skillet. Cook pancakes 1–2 minutes, until bubbles appear in surface. Turn the pancakes and cook them 1–2 minutes more, until they are cooked through and can be easily lifted from pan. Top with Beech-Nut pears.

Mint Herbal Tea

2–3 teaspoons mint flakes or 1 bag commercial mint herbal
*   tea*
4–5 raisins or 1 fresh fig, washed and chopped
6 ounces boiling water
Date or beet sugar to taste

If using mint flakes, place them in a tea ball or make a tea bag out of a piece of cheesecloth and thread. Steep tea bag and raisins or figs in boiling water 2–5 minutes, until tea is desired strength. Remove tea bag; eat or remove raisins or figs. Sweeten to taste with date or beet sugar.

SNACK

Granola

2 cups plain regular oatmeal (not quick-cooking)
3 tablespoons sunflower seeds
1 teaspoon nutmeg
3 tablespoons sunflower oil
½ cup each raisins, chopped dates and chopped figs
1 tablespoon date sugar or Heinz pear flakes

Preheat oven to 255°F.

In a bowl, mix all ingredients together, spread on a nonstick baking sheet and bake for 20 minutes. Stir frequently; remove from oven as soon as granola appears brown and crunchy.

MW—Prepare granola as above. Spread on a piece of waxed paper and cover with another piece of waxed paper or paper towel. Microwave (M) 5–8 minutes, until granola is dry and glazed with sweetened oil. Stir and check frequently to avoid burning. Granola crisps as it cools.

White Grape Juice Spritzer

SERVES 1

6 ounces white grape juice
2 ounces sparkling mineral water
Ice
1 (2-ounce) scoop Pear Sorbet (see Night-Before
Preparation Tips for Day Fifteen)
1 sprig fresh mint

Pour grape juice and water over ice. Add sorbet and garnish with mint.

LUNCH

Basil and Bean Soup

SERVES 4

1 tablespoon sunflower oil
½ pound ground lamb
½ cup presoaked and drained*, or dry black beans
2 medium zucchini, scrubbed and sliced
1 pound mushrooms, rinsed, dried and chopped
1 white potato, peeled and sliced
2 tablespoons chopped fresh basil
2 teaspoons sea salt
½ cup sherry
3½ cups water

Heat sunflower oil in a Dutch oven and sauté lamb until it is no longer pink. Add drained beans, zucchini, mushrooms, potato, seasonings, sherry and water. Bring to boil, lower heat, cover and cook until beans are tender, about 45–50 minutes.

✳

*See Night-Before Preparation Tips for Day Fifteen or quick-soak dry beans using the following method: Boil beans in water to cover 2 minutes. Cover and remove from heat; allow to cool at least 1 hour with lid on. Drain.

Pickled Vegetables

✳   MAKES ABOUT 4 CUPS

1 teaspoon sea salt
½ cup apple cider vinegar or wine vinegar
½ cup sherry
¼ cup white grape juice
1 tablespoon date sugar or Heinz pear flakes
2 tablespoons sunflower oil
2 leaves fresh basil
2 leaves fresh mint
1 cup chopped fresh mushrooms (rinsed and dried)
1 cup drained, canned water-pack beets
½ cup drained, canned water-pack olives
1 large zucchini, scrubbed, trimmed and sliced
1 large cucumber, scrubbed, trimmed and sliced

Heat first 8 ingredients in a large saucepan to boiling. Add vegetables and stir. Reduce heat, simmer, uncovered, 3 minutes. Transfer to a bowl and cool to room temperature. Set aside and refrigerate 1–2 cups cooled vegetables for use as condiment with Roast Marinated Leg of Lamb (see Dinner below).

Oat Bran Fruit Bars

✳   MAKES ABOUT 1 DOZEN

Sunflower oil for greasing pan plus 2 tablespoons oil
2¼ cups oat bran cereal (see Pear and Oat Muffins,
    Breakfast, Regular Track, for substitute)
¼ cup date sugar or Heinz pear flakes
1 tablespoon baking powder
Dash sea salt
¾ cup water
½ jar Beech-Nut Stage One pears
½ cup combination raisins and chopped dates, figs or
    prunes

Preheat oven to 425°F.
    Grease a medium-sized (about 8 × 11 inches) baking pan with oil. In a large mixing bowl, combine the oat bran cereal, date sugar,

baking powder and salt. Add the water, Beech-Nut pears and oil. Mix together just until dry ingredients are moistened. Add a little more water, if batter seems dry. Stir in the chopped fruit. Spread batter evenly in prepared baking pan and bake 15–17 minutes, until a toothpick comes out clean when inserted into batter. Cool about 5 minutes before serving. Cut into 12 bars.

DINNER

White Grape Aperitif
✳   SERVES 4

> *2 small fresh pears*
> *1 (liter) bottle sparkling white grape juice*
> *4 sprigs fresh mint, trimmed*

Peel and core pears; cut each in half. Place each half in a champagne glass and fill with grape juice. Garnish with a sprig of mint.

Roast Marinated Leg of Lamb
✳   SERVES 4–6

Lamb:

> *1 (6-pound) marinated leg of lamb with marinade (see*
> *Night-Before Preparation Tips, Day Fifteen)**

Preheat oven to 325°F.

Place lamb, fat side up, on rack in a shallow roasting pan. Insert meat thermometer in fleshy part, away from bone and fat. Roast, uncovered, and basting occasionally with marinade, 18 minutes per pound for well done (175°F. on a meat thermometer), 12 minutes for rare (140°F.). Let roast stand 20 minutes before carving. If desired, reserve marinade for oat stuffing (below).

*Marinating time for lamb may be reduced by having butcher bone leg of lamb. Add ½ cup wine vinegar to marinade and refrigerate 1–2 hours, turning lamb frequently.

Oat Stuffing:

> *¼ cup sunflower oil*
> *2 sprigs fresh basil, minced*

*

2 cups plain regular oatmeal (not quick-cooking)
1 cup white grape juice, water or marinade from lamb
½ teaspoon sea salt

Heat oil in a frying pan. Sauté basil and oatmeal; stir in liquid and salt. Bake in an ovenproof glass or ceramic baking dish, uncovered, last hour of roasting lamb. Stir every 15 minutes, adding more liquid if necessary to retain desired dryness or moistness of stuffing.

Serve lamb with oat stuffing and chilled Pickled Vegetables (reserved from Lunch above) as condiment. (Freeze leftover lamb for use on Day Nineteen.)

Sunrise Salad

*   SERVES 4–6

1 pound fresh mushrooms
1 bunch arugula*
1 head red leaf lettuce or radicchio
½ head romaine lettuce
Herb Purée Dressing (recipe follows)
¼ cup sunflower seeds (optional)

Rinse mushrooms, arugula, red leaf or radicchio and romaine lettuce under cold water; drain and pat dry with paper towels. Chop mushrooms coarsely and combine all vegetables in a salad bowl. Toss with Herb Purée Dressing and garnish with sunflower seeds, if desired.

*Also called "rocket" lettuce.

Herb Purée Dressing

*   MAKES 1½ CUPS

¼ cup wine vinegar
1 teaspoon salt
2 cups chopped fresh basil (rinsed and drained)
1 cup chopped fresh mint leaves (rinsed and drained)
2 tablespoons water
½ cup sunflower oil

In a blender or food processor, combine vinegar and salt; blend 30 seconds on medium power. Add basil, mint leaves and water; blend 30 seconds on high power. With motor running, gradually add oil; continue blending on high power until dressing is thoroughly combined and herbs are puréed. Serve at once or chill; shake well to combine before serving.

High-Nutrition Oat Bran Loaf

✳   SERVES 4–6

Sunflower oil for greasing pan plus ¼ cup oil
Oat bran cereal for dusting loaf pan plus 2½ cups
    (approximate) cereal (see Pear and Oat Muffins,
    Breakfast, Regular Track, for substitute)
1 (8-ounce) can water-pack black beans
¼ cup date sugar or Heinz pear flakes
1 teaspoon sea salt
2 teaspoons rapid-rising (not regular) yeast
½ cup white grape juice
½ cup water
Oat bran
½ cup chopped dates

Heat oven to 350°F.

Grease a 9 × 5 × 3-inch loaf pan with oil and dust it with oat bran cereal. Drain black beans and blend or process to make 1 cup bean purée. In a large bowl, combine 2½ cups oat bran cereal, date sugar or Heinz pear flakes, salt, and yeast. Heat grape juice, water and ¼ cup oil to lukewarm (about 120°F. on candy thermometer). Add the warm liquids to the dry ingredients; add the bean purée and mix just until dry ingredients are moistened. Add more oat bran or liquid as needed to make a thick batter the consistency of a quick-bread batter. Stir in the chopped dates. Spoon the batter into the loaf pan and bake 50–60 minutes, until golden brown on top and knife comes out clean when inserted in center of loaf.

Drunken Pears

✳   SERVES 4

2 large, ripe but firm fresh pears
¾ cup sherry or pink Catawba
⅘ pint chilled champagne
Fresh mint leaves

An hour or so before serving, wash and dry the pears, split them; remove stems and seeds. Freeze unpeeled pears in a plastic freezer container with a lid. Place one-half pear in each of 4 champagne glasses. Pour sherry over each pear, dividing wine equally among the glasses. Fill glasses with champagne and garnish with fresh mint leaves.

THE DIET EXPRESS

BREAKFAST

Prune Juice

❊

Oatmeal with Dates and Raisins

❊
SERVES 1

> 1 cup water
> ⅓ cup quick-cooking oatmeal
> ¼ cup each chopped dates and raisins
> Date sugar or Heinz pear flakes to taste

MW—Combine water and oatmeal in a microwave-safe bowl. Heat (H) until cereal begins to boil, about 1–2 minutes. Stir in dates and raisins, microwave (L) 1–2 minutes more, until cereal is desired consistency. Sprinkle with date sugar or Heinz pear flakes to taste; top with Beech-Nut pears.

Variation:

> 1 cup Beech-Nut Stage One oatmeal cereal
> 1 jar Beech-Nut Stage One pears
> ¼ cup (approximate) plain pear juice
> ¼ cup each chopped dates and raisins
> Date sugar or Heinz pear flakes to taste

Combine first 3 ingredients until cereal is desired consistency. Stir in dates and raisins; sprinkle with date sugar or Heinz pear flakes if extra sweetness is desired.

Mint Herbal Tea

❊

SNACK

White Grape Juice Spritzer
(See Snack, Regular Track)

❊

Crunchy Black Beans and Sunflower Seeds
✳   SERVES 1-2

1 (8-ounce) can water-pack black beans
½ cup sunflower seeds
Sea salt to taste

MW—Empty beans into a colander and drain; dry on paper towels.
Place beans and sunflower seeds on a dry microwave-safe paper towel;
cover with another towel. Microwave (H) 15–20 minutes, until beans
and seeds are crunchy. Watch carefully during cooking time to avoid
burning. Rotate beans and seeds halfway through cooking time, if
oven does not have a carousel. Taste; sprinkle with added sea salt if
desired.

LUNCH

Lamb Pâté with Zucchini or Cucumber Sticks, Mushrooms and Olives
✳   SERVES 1

1–2 jars Beech-Nut Stage One lamb
1 teaspoon wine vinegar
¼ teaspoon sea salt
1 teaspoon dried basil
1 teaspoon sunflower oil
1 small zucchini or cucumber, scrubbed, trimmed and cut
    into sticks
½ cup fresh mushrooms (rinsed and dried)
½ cup canned water-pack olives, drained

In a blender or by hand, blend lamb, vinegar, salt, basil and oil until
smooth and thoroughly mixed. Use as dip with mushrooms and olives.

Quick Borscht
✳   SERVES 1

1 jar Beech-Nut Stage One lamb
2 jars Beech-Nut Stage One beets
½ cup diced, drained, canned water-pack beets (reserve
    beet juice to thin soup)
½ cup diced, drained, canned water-pack white potato
¼ teaspoon apple cider vinegar

¼ *teaspoon dried basil*
½ *teaspoon sea salt*

Combine lamb, Beech-Nut beets and canned beets, potato, vinegar and basil. Heat, stirring constantly, in a saucepan until lamb and beets are blended and soup is hot, adding reserved beet juice until soup is desired thickness. Soup may also be served chilled.

DINNER

Broiled Lamb with Mint Sauce

SERVES 1–2

Lamb:

¼ *cup wine vinegar*
½ *cup sherry*
1 *tablespoon sunflower oil*
1 *teaspoon sea salt*
1 *teaspoon ground basil*
2 *lamb chops cut from the shoulder, about 1 inch thick*

Preheat broiler.
While broiler is heating, combine all ingredients except lamb and mix well. Add chops, prick them several times with a fork, and marinate at least 15 minutes, turning chops every few minutes.
Place chops on a rack in a broiling pan and broil 4 inches from heat, about 15 minutes total cooking time. Turn once during broiling, basting frequently with marinade. Place cooked chops on a heated platter (reserve ½ cup juices left from broiling chops) and allow to rest 5–10 minutes while making mint sauce.

Mint Sauce:

Reserved ½ *cup juices left from broiling chops*
½ *cup white grape juice*
1 *tablespoon dried mint*

Strain juices into a small saucepan, add grape juice and mint and bring to boil. Simmer until liquid is reduced by half, pour over chops and serve.

✳

One-Dish Lamb Pie

✳

Filling:

> 2 tablespoons sunflower oil
> ½ cup chopped fresh mushrooms (rinsed and dried)
> ½ pound ground lamb
> ¼ cup golden raisins
> ¼ cup (2–3 large olives) canned water-pack olives, pitted
>   and chopped
> 1 tablespoon apple cider vinegar or wine vinegar
> ½ teaspoon dried basil
> ¼ teaspoon sea salt

Heat oil in a large skillet over medium heat. Add mushrooms and sauté 1–2 minutes. Add lamb and sauté, breaking up meat with a spoon, until lamb is no longer pink, 3–5 minutes. Stir in remaining ingredients and remove from heat. Pour filling into a 2-cup shallow ovenproof casserole or small pie plate and top with crust.

Crust:

> 1 teaspoon rapid-rising yeast
> 1 cup plain regular oatmeal (not quick-cooking)
> 2 tablespoons sunflower oil
> ¼ cup warm water
> 1 teaspoon apple cider vinegar or wine vinegar
> ½ teaspoon sea salt
> ½ cup oat bran cereal (optional; see Pear and Oat Muffins,
>   Breakfast, Regular Track, for substitute)

Preheat oven to 400°F.

In a mixing bowl, stir yeast into oatmeal. Add oil, warm water, vinegar and salt; combine with a wooden spoon or your hands until dough holds together. Add oat bran if dough seems too moist or sticky. Place dough between large sheets of waxed paper and flatten it gently and quickly with your hands until it is roughly large enough to cover filling. Remove top sheet of waxed paper; lay uncovered dough on top of filling. Peel off other sheet of waxed paper. Bake 7–10 minutes, until crust is browned on top.

✳

Pear Sorbet with Champagne

✳
SERVES 1

1 (2-ounce) scoop Pear Sorbet (see Night-Before
  Preparation Tips for Day Fifteen)
Champagne or sparkling white grape juice
1 sprig fresh mint for garnish

Place sorbet in a champagne glass. Fill with champagne or sparkling
grape juice. Garnish with sprig of mint.

NIGHT-BEFORE PREPARATION TIPS
——————— FOR DAY 16 ———————

Make Apple Sorbet: Allowing 1 jar per serving, empty as many
jars Beech-Nut Stage One applesauce as you think you will need
into a freezer container with a lid. Freeze overnight to use as
instant sorbet in beverages or desserts. As dessert, allow to
soften 15 minutes in the refrigerator before serving as sorbet.

DAY
✳
16

THE REINTRODUCTION PHASE
(COFFEE/TEA)

ALLOWED FOODS:
Tapioca, arrowroot, amaranth, apples, pineapples,
avocados, bean sprouts, carrots, lentils, pumpkin, turnips,
tuna, salmon, whitefish, mustard, coffee, tea, safflower oil,
cinnamon, fennel, honey

MENU	REGULAR	DIET EXPRESS

BREAKFAST	Tapioca Pudding
	Amaranth Pancakes with
	  Pineapple Syrup
	Coffee or Tea
		Tapioca Pudding with
		  Applesauce
		Coffee or Tea

SNACK	Roasted Pumpkin Seeds Iced Tea Special Carrot-Pineapple Shake	Crunchy Lentils Iced Tea Special

LUNCH	Vegetable Soup
	Tuna-Pineapple Salad with
	  Mustard Dressing
	Apple Sorbet
	Coffee or Tea
		Brown-Bag Tuna (or Salmon)
		  Salad
		Quick Carrot Soup
		Coffee or Tea

DINNER	Swordfish with Fennel
	Pineapple-Mustard Purée
	Stuffed Turnips
	Bean Sprout Salad
	Caramelized Pineapple
	Pumpkin Pie Pudding
	Coffee or Tea
		Baked Whole Red Snapper
		Pumpkin Purée
		Hearty Lentil Salad with Apple
		  Juice Dressing
		Fruit Salad with Coffee-Honey
		  Sauce
		Coffee or Tea

BULK AGENT: None

REGULAR TRACK

Note: Pineapple is used for the first time today. If sensitivity is known or suspected, substitute plain unsweetened applesauce, plain apple juice, or fresh apple for pineapple in recipes.

BREAKFAST

Tapioca Pudding

✳   SERVES 4–6

> *2 cups plain apple juice*
> *½ cup unsweetened pineapple juice*
> *⅓ cup honey*
> *3 tablespoons granulated, quick-cooking tapioca*
> *1 cup chopped fresh pineapple* (rind removed)*

Combine apple juice, pineapple juice, honey and tapioca in a saucepan. Allow to stand 5 minutes. Stirring constantly, bring to a full boil over medium-high heat. Remove from heat and stir in chopped pineapple; pudding will thicken as it cools. Cool 20 minutes, stir and serve.

*Pineapple packed in its own juice (such as Dole, Empress, 3-Diamond and some generic brands such as Finast) can be substituted for fresh pineapple. Reserve juice for use in recipes.

Amaranth Pancakes with Pineapple Syrup

2 cups amaranth flour*
2 cups (approximate) water
1 tablespoon safflower oil plus oil for greasing skillet
Pineapple Syrup (recipe follows)

In a large mixing bowl, beat the flour, water and 1 tablespoon oil together until a smooth, thick but pourable batter is formed.

Grease a skillet with oil. Heat the skillet over medium-high heat until it is hot but not smoking. Using ½ cup for each pancake, pour the batter onto hot skillet. Cook pancakes on one side until bubbles appear and pancake is browned, about 1 minute. Turn pancake and cook until browned and cooked through, about 1 minute more. Serve with Pineapple Syrup.

*If you cannot find amaranth flour, grind 2 cups dry lentils in a processor until ground into flour. Sift the lentil flour twice before using to ensure a smooth-textured pancake. When you have ground and sifted dry lentils to make 2 cups, proceed with recipe as above.

Pineapple Syrup

½ cup canned crushed pineapple in its own juice
1 teaspoon safflower oil
⅓ cup honey
¼ teaspoon ground cinnamon

Combine all ingredients in a saucepan and bring to boil over medium-high heat. Stir constantly to make sure syrup does not burn, adding additional pineapple juice or water 1 tablespoon at a time if syrup seems too thick. Can be served hot or at room temperature.

Coffee or Tea

Select any coffee or tea that does not contain additional flavoring, spices, sweeteners or creamers. Prepare according to preference; sweeten with honey and a dash of cinnamon, if desired.

SNACK

Roasted Pumpkin Seeds

✳   SERVES 4

> 1 (2-pound) pumpkin
> 2 teaspoons safflower oil
> ½ teaspoon sea salt

Preheat oven to slow, 250°F.

Split the pumpkin and remove seeds; you should have about 2 cups seeds. (Refrigerate pumpkin in airtight bag or container for use later in the day.) Clean seeds completely of stringy material; dry with paper towels. In a skillet, heat seeds in oil and salt until seeds are coated. Remove from skillet. Bake in a baking tin 30–40 minutes, until browned and dry. Cool slightly; remove to paper towels until crisp and completely cooled.

Iced Tea Special

✳   SERVES 1

> 6 ounces strong plain tea, cooled
> Ice
> 4 ounces plain apple juice
> 1–2 teaspoons honey
> 2 ounces sparkling mineral water
> Pinch ground cinnamon

Pour tea over ice. Add remaining ingredients and stir to combine.

Carrot-Pineapple Shake

✳   SERVES 1

> 6 ounces plain carrot juice
> ½ cup undrained crushed pineapple in its own juice
> 1 ice cube, crushed
> 1 teaspoon honey
> Dash ground cinnamon

Combine all ingredients in a blender. Blend on highest speed until creamy. Serve at once.

LUNCH

Vegetable Soup

SERVES 4–6

*3 large, whole fresh carrots, pared and sliced or 3 cups
    frozen sliced carrots
1 large fresh turnip, pared and coarsely chopped or 1 cup
    frozen chopped turnips
1 cup coarsely chopped fresh pumpkin (rind removed;
    reserved from Roasted Pumpkin Seeds, Snack, Regular
    Track)
1½ cups fresh bean sprouts (rinsed and drained)
¼ cup safflower oil
2 cups water
1 cup plain carrot juice
1 teaspoon dry mustard
1–2 jars Beech-Nut Stage One carrots
½ cup diced peeled avocado
Sea salt to taste*

In a large soup pot, sauté carrots, turnips, pumpkin and sprouts in oil over medium heat 2 minutes. Add water, carrot juice, mustard and 1 jar Beech-Nut carrots. Bring to boil and simmer over very low heat 15–20 minutes. Just before serving, dice avocado and stir into soup. Thicken soup with remaining Beech-Nut carrots, if desired, and season to taste with sea salt. Serve hot or cold.

MW—Heat oil (H) 30 seconds in a large microwave-safe casserole. Stir in carrots, turnip, pumpkin, sprouts. Cover and cook (H) 1 minute. Stir. Add 1 cup water, ½ cup carrot juice, mustard and 1 jar Beech-Nut carrots. Cover and bring to boil (H), about 1 minute. Stir and cook (L) 5 minutes more. Stir in avocado, thicken soup with remaining Beech-Nut carrots. Salt to taste; serve hot or cold.

Tuna-Pineapple Salad

SERVES 4–6

*1 ripe fresh pineapple
2 (6-ounce) cans water-pack tuna, drained
8–10 fresh baby carrots, scrubbed and trimmed (do not
    pare)
1 cup fresh bean sprouts (rinsed and drained)
1 ripe avocado, peeled and diced*

½ cup Mustard Dressing (recipe follows)
Fennel seeds for garnish (optional)

Cut pineapple in half lengthwise. Cut out core and fruit, leaving shells; cut fruit into chunks. Toss pineapple, tuna, carrots, sprouts and avocado with ½ cup Mustard Dressing. Spoon into pineapple shells and sprinkle with seeds, if desired.

Mustard Dressing

✳   MAKES 1 CUP

2 teaspoons plain apple juice
2 tablespoons unsweetened pineapple juice
1 teaspoon dry mustard or 2 teaspoons freshly ground
    mustard seeds
2 leaves fresh fennel, minced
¼ teaspoon sea salt
¾ cup safflower oil

In a blender or by hand with a wire whisk, beat together the juices, mustard, fennel and salt. Blend or whisk in oil until dressing is thick and smooth. Set aside and refrigerate ½ cup dressing to use in Bean Sprout Salad (see Dinner, Regular Track).

Apple Sorbet
(See Night-Before Preparation Tips for Day Sixteen)

✳

Coffee or Tea
(See Breakfast, Regular Track)

✳

DINNER

Swordfish with Fennel

✳   SERVES 4–6

4 (6 ounces each) swordfish steaks, about 1½ inches thick
4 tablespoons safflower oil
Sea salt
4 cups (approximate) fresh fennel (rinsed and trimmed)
Pineapple-Mustard Purée (recipe follows)

✳

Preheat broiler.

Rinse fish in cold water and pat dry with paper towels. Brush steaks with oil and sprinkle lightly with salt. Lay half the fennel on an oiled broiling pan or foil, place fish on top. Cover with remaining fennel. Broil 4 inches from heat 10–20 minutes, until fish flakes easily with a fork and is opaque. Do not turn fish. Serve with Pineapple-Mustard Purée.

MW—Remove skin from fish. Rub steaks with oil, but do not salt. Lightly oil a microwave-safe baking dish and line it with half the fennel. Place fish on top. Cover with remaining fennel. Cover with waxed paper. Cook (M) or (H) with a microwave-safe glass of water placed in oven during cooking, 12 minutes. Let stand 5 minutes and salt to taste.

Pineapple-Mustard Purée

✳
MAKES 1 CUP

2 teaspoons dry mustard
2 teaspoons coarsely ground mustard seeds
1 teaspoon water
1 tablespoon safflower oil
½ teaspoon sea salt
¾ cup undrained crushed pineapple packed in its own juice

Mix dry mustard, ground seeds, water and oil to make a thick paste (add more or less dry mustard until mixture is consistency of a good-quality, whole-grain prepared mustard). Stir in salt. Combine mustard mixture with pineapple in a blender or food processor and blend until thick and fairly smooth, about 1 minute.

Stuffed Turnips

✳
SERVES 4

4 large fresh turnips
Safflower oil
¾ cup plain unsweetened chunky-style applesauce
1 jar Beech-Nut Stage One carrots
2 teaspoons honey

Preheat oven to 400°F.

Scrub and dry turnips. Rub the skins with oil, prick with a fork and bake 45–60 minutes, until turnips are tender when pierced with a fork. Combine applesauce, Beech-Nut carrots and honey in a bowl. Remove a thin slice from the top of each turnip. Scoop out the inside of each turnip, leaving a shell. Add turnip to carrot-applesauce mixture, tossing to mix well. Spoon lightly into turnip shells, mounding high. Place in a shallow baking pan and return to oven for a few minutes until filling is hot.

Bean Sprout Salad

SERVES 4

2 small, ripe avocados, peeled and sliced
2½ cups fresh bean sprouts (rinsed and drained)
½ cup Mustard Dressing (reserved from Mustard Dressing, Lunch, Regular Track)

Toss all ingredients together and serve.

Caramelized Pineapple

SERVES 4

1 teaspoon safflower oil or safflower oil margarine*
4 tablespoons honey
8 slices fresh pineapple, cut in rings

In a heavy-bottomed enamel pot, heat oil or margarine, honey and pineapple over very low heat, turning slices occasionally, until pineapple is golden brown and softened, and sauce is formed. Serve with Pumpkin Pie Pudding (recipe follows) or with a scoop of Apple Sorbet (see Night-Before Preparation Tips for Day Sixteen).

*Pure safflower oil margarine can be found in many health food stores.

Pumpkin Pie Pudding

SERVES 4

2 cups unsweetened pineapple juice
1 tablespoon arrowroot
1 cup canned, unsweetened pumpkin
1 teaspoon ground cinnamon
¼ cup honey

In a small saucepan, combine juice and arrowroot; whisk together until arrowroot is completely dissolved. Stirring constantly, heat almost to boiling; arrowroot thickens before boiling. Remove from heat, stir in pumpkin, cinnamon and honey. Taste and add more honey if sweeter pudding is desired. Cool. Top with Caramelized Pineapple (see recipe above), or fresh pineapple chunks.

Coffee or Tea
(See Breakfast, Regular Track)

✳

DIET EXPRESS

BREAKFAST

Tapioca Pudding with Applesauce
✳   SERVES 1–2

>   *⅓ cup plain unsweetened chunky-style applesauce*
>   *1 tablespoon granulated quick-cooking tapioca*
>   *1 cup plain apple juice*
>   *¼ teaspoon ground cinnamon*

In a small saucepan, combine applesauce, tapioca, juice and cinnamon. Allow to stand 5 minutes. Stirring constantly, bring to boil over medium-high heat. Remove from heat and cool 10 minutes before serving.

Coffee or Tea
(See Breakfast, Regular Track)

✳

SNACK

Crunchy Lentils
✳   SERVES 1–2

>   *1 (8-ounce) can water-pack lentils, drained*

MW—Spread drained lentils on paper towels and pat dry. Place a dry sheet of microwave-safe paper towel on a heavy microwave-safe dish or platter; spread lentils on top in a single layer. Cover lentils with another paper towel. Cook (H) 8–12 minutes, until lentils are dry and crisp. Watch carefully to avoid burning. Cool completely before serving.

Iced Tea Special
(See Snack, Regular Track)

✳

LUNCH

Brown-Bag Tuna (or Salmon) Salad

✳ SERVES 1–2

½ cup undrained crushed pineapple packed in its own juice
1 teaspoon safflower oil
Freshly ground mustard seeds
Sea salt
½ cup drained canned bean sprouts
1 (6-ounce) can water-pack tuna or salmon, drained
1 fresh unpeeled apple, rinsed and patted dry
1 small, ripe avocado

Mix pineapple and oil. Layer salad in the following order in a thermal container, sprinkling each layer with freshly ground mustard and a dash of sea salt: crushed pineapple and oil; bean sprouts; tuna or salmon. Chill until ready to eat. Leave apple and avocado whole, and pack them separately. Just before serving, slice avocado in half, remove pit. Slice apple and toss with chilled salad; stuff mixture into avocado halves and serve.

Quick Carrot Soup

✳ SERVES 1–2

2 jars Beech-Nut Stage One carrots
⅓ cup frozen sliced carrots
⅓ cup honey
½ teaspoon sea salt
Dash ground cinnamon
½ cup plain apple juice

MW—Combine Beech-Nut carrots, frozen carrots, honey, salt and cinnamon in a microwave-safe covered soup dish. Stir and cook (H) until hot, 1–2 minutes. Stir in apple juice; reheat until hot, about 1 minute. Do not boil. Soup may also be refrigerated and served chilled.

❄

Coffee or Tea
(See Breakfast, Regular Track)

❄

DINNER

Baked Whole Red Snapper

❄   SERVES 1–2

1 whole red snapper, approximately 1 pound
2 teaspoons fennel seeds
1 teaspoon sea salt
1 tablespoon safflower oil for greasing pan plus 2–3
   tablespoons oil

Have fish cleaned and scaled, leaving on the head and tail.
   Preheat oven to 350°F.
   Sprinkle cavity and outside of fish with fennel seeds and salt. Grease
a baking pan with 1 tablespoon safflower oil; place fish in pan. Drizzle
remaining oil over fish. Bake for 25 minutes or until fish flakes easily
with a fork.
   Serve with Pineapple-Mustard Purée (see Swordfish with Fennel,
Dinner, Regular Track, for directions.)

Pumpkin Purée

❄   SERVES 1–2

1½ cups canned, unsweetened pumpkin
¼ cup honey, or to taste
¼ teaspoon freshly ground mustard seeds
Dash each ground cinnamon and sea salt

Combine ingredients, heat and serve.

Hearty Lentil Salad with Apple Juice Dressing

❄   SERVES 1–2

1 large fresh carrot
½ cup drained, canned water-pack lentils
⅓ cup drained, canned water-pack bean sprouts
½ ripe avocado
Apple Juice Dressing (recipe follows)

Pare, trim and shred the carrot; place in a salad bowl. Add lentils and bean sprouts. Peel and slice avocado, add to salad with Apple Juice Dressing. Toss gently and serve.

Apple Juice Dressing

✻   MAKES ¾ CUP

1 teaspoon dry mustard
1 teaspoon water
¼ cup plain apple juice
¼ teaspoon sea salt or to taste
⅓ cup safflower oil

Mix dry mustard with water until smooth. In a small mixing bowl, whisk together the mustard paste, apple juice, salt and oil until well combined.

Fruit Salad with Coffee-Honey Sauce

✻   SERVES 1–2

1 large unpeeled apple, washed, cored, and cut into slices
    or chunks
1½ cups drained, canned pineapple in its own juice,
    (reserve juice for making sauce)
⅓ cup pineapple juice reserved from canned pineapple
¾ cup honey
Hot coffee

Place apple and drained pineapple in a heatproof serving bowl. Combine honey and ⅓ cup reserved pineapple juice in a small saucepan and heat slowly, adding hot coffee just until sauce is the consistency of rich chocolate syrup. Pour over fruits and serve.

Coffee or Tea
(See Breakfast, Regular Track)

✻

✻

NIGHT-BEFORE PREPARATION TIPS
FOR DAY 17

1. Make Banana Sorbet: Allowing 1 jar per serving, empty as many jars Beech-Nut Stage One bananas as you think you will need into a freezer container with a lid. Freeze overnight to use as instant sorbet in beverages or desserts. As dessert, allow to soften 15 minutes in the refrigerator before serving as sorbet.

2. Cooked chicken: Poach or microwave 2 pounds chicken thighs or breast pieces according to the following guides:
Poach: Place chicken pieces in water to cover on top of stove, bring to boil, lower heat and simmer 10 minutes per pound.

MW—remove skin from chicken pieces; place in a shallow micro-wave-safe casserole and cook (H), loosely covered, 4 minutes per pound. Rotate casserole after every minute if you do not have a carousel.
On Day Seventeen use cooked chicken for Chicken Salad, Lunch, Regular Track.

3. Prepare coconut milk: In a small saucepan, place 1 cup unsweetened shredded coconut or finely chopped Fresh Coconut (See Day Two, Breakfast, Regular Track) and 3 teaspoons super-fine cane sugar in 2 cups water. Bring to boil, turn off heat, cover and allow to cool. Purée in a blender until creamy and smooth, adding a little more water if thinner milk is desired. Adjust sweetening to taste with cane sugar. Refrigerate overnight and shake well before using, to recombine. (Unblended coconut milk may be left to cool overnight in refrigerator, covered. Blend in the morning just before using.)

DAY 17
※

THE REINTRODUCTION PHASE
(CANE SUGAR)

ALLOWED FOODS:
Rice, lima beans, bananas, coconut, cranberries, celery, endive, spinach, chicken, ginger, olive oil, nyafat, thyme, light brown sugar, cane sugar, unsulphured light molasses, carob

MENU

	REGULAR	DIET EXPRESS
BREAKFAST	Hot Farina with Bananas, Milk and Sugar Lima Bean Pancakes Sugar Syrup Carob Cocoa Banana Crème	Puffed Rice Cereal with Bananas, Milk and Sugar Banana Crème Carob Cocoa
SNACK	Sweet Ginger Herbal Tea Rice Cakes with Berry Spread	Sweet Ginger Herbal Tea Rice Cakes with Bananas, Brown Sugar and Coconut
LUNCH	Chicken Salad Cranberry Relish No-Bake Coconut Clusters Carob-Banana Soda	Cream of Spinach Soup Chicken Sandwich with Ginger Butter or Chicken Pâté with Rice Crackers and Celery Sticks Banana Sorbet
DINNER	Lima Bean and Chicken Bake Wild Rice Fruit Cobbler with Hard Sauce	Quick Creamy Soup Broiled Breast of Chicken Quick-Cooking Rice Spinach Salad with Spinach Dressing Caramelized Bananas

BULK AGENT: Rice bran

REGULAR TRACK

Note: If you had no adverse reaction to cow's milk on Day Fourteen, you may use whole or low-fat cow's milk in today's recipes. If you cannot use cow's milk, substitute Coconut Milk (see Night-Before Preparation Tips for Day Seventeen) or Banana Crème (see Breakfast, Regular Track) when milk is called for.

✳

Note too, that only commercial light brown sugar and unsulphured light molasses are allowed. Dark brown sugars usually contain artificial coloring, and sulphured (dark) molasses contain sulfites used during processing. Confectioners' sugar also usually contains cornstarch to prevent caking. Read ingredients on the labels to be sure the cane sugar product you are buying is additive-free.

BREAKFAST

Hot Farina with Bananas, Milk and Sugar

✳ SERVES 4

3 cups water
Dash sea salt
¾ cup regular farina
1 teaspoon ground ginger
2 small bananas, peeled and sliced
Nyafat
Milk and white or light brown cane sugar to taste

In a saucepan, bring water and salt to boil. Stirring constantly, add farina and reduce heat; cook over low heat 2–5 mintues, until cereal is desired consistency. Serve with sliced bananas, nyafat, milk and sugar to taste.

Lima Bean Pancakes

✳ SERVES 4

1 (10-ounce) package frozen lima beans (do not defrost)
Sunflower oil for greasing skillet plus 1 teaspoon oil
1 cup (approximate) water
Nyafat

Empty the lima beans into a blender or processor and process until they resemble cornmeal in texture, about 1 minute. Scrape ground limas into a bowl. Grease a skillet thoroughly with oil. Heat the skillet until it is hot (beads of water will dance on a properly heated skillet). Add 1 teaspoon oil and the water to ground limas until batter is pourable but still thick. Using 2–3 tablespoons for each pancake drop batter onto the hot skillet. Cook pancakes until lightly browned on one side, 2–3 minutes. Turn pancakes and brown on other side until cooked through. Top with nyafat, unsulphured light molasses or Sugar Syrup (recipe follows) to taste.

Sugar Syrup

✳   MAKES 2 CUPS

>   2 cups cane sugar
>   2 cups water
>   ½ teaspoon ground ginger

In a heavy saucepan, combine sugar, water and ginger. Stirring constantly, cook over low heat until sugar and ginger are completely dissolved. Allow to cool slightly before serving. (Refrigerate leftover syrup for recipes later in the day.)

Carob Cocoa

✳   SERVES 1

>   1 teaspoon (scant) carob powder (use carob sparingly as it
>   has a slightly bitter taste)
>   2 heaping teaspoons cane sugar, unsulphured light
>   molasses or Sugar Syrup (see recipe above)
>   6 ounces milk or Banana Crème (recipe follows)
>   Dash ground ginger (optional)

Combine the carob and sugar in a cup or mug. Add 2 teaspoons cold milk and stir until smooth. Heat remaining milk until hot; fill cup and add a dash of ginger, if desired. Correct sweetness to taste with cane sugar.

Banana Crème

✳   MAKES ¾ CUP

>   1 jar Beech-Nut Stage One bananas
>   2 ounces water

Whisk together the bananas and water until consistency of light cream.

✳ ─────────────────────────────────────

───

SNACK

───

Sweet Ginger Herbal Tea

✳   SERVES 1

> 2 teaspoons minced gingerroot
> 4–5 whole fresh cranberries (washed and picked over)
> 6 ounces boiling water
> Cane sugar and milk to taste

In a mug, steep gingerroot and cranberries in boiling water 2–5 minutes. Remove gingerroot; eat or discard cranberries. Add sugar and milk to taste.

Rice Cakes with Berry Spread

✳   SERVES 4

> 4 large plain rice cakes
> ½ cup Berry Spread (recipe follows)

Spread each rice cake with 1 tablespoon Berry Spread.

Berry Spread

✳   MAKES ABOUT 1 CUP

> ¾ cup whole fresh cranberries (washed and picked over) or
>   frozen cranberries
> 2 tablespoons cane sugar
> Water (approximately 1½ cups)
> ¾ cup nyafat

In approximately 1½ cups water to cover, heat cranberries and 1 tablespoon sugar to boiling. Simmer until skins of berries pop. Remove from heat and allow to cool. Drain berries. Reserve and chill 1½ cups juice to use in Cranberry Relish (Lunch, Regular Track). Place drained berries, remaining 1 tablespoon sugar and nyafat in a blender and blend until combined, or mash mixture together by hand until thoroughly blended. Serve with rice cakes. (Shape any remaining spread into a log, cover with waxed paper or plastic wrap and chill for snacks later in the day, if desired).

LUNCH

Chicken Salad

✳ SERVES 4

> 2 (7-ounce) cans canned water-pack chicken or 1 pound
>   cooked chicken (see Night-Before Preparation Tips for
>   Day Seventeen)
> 4 heads Belgian endive, halved lengthwise
> 2 cups cooked rice, prepared according to package
>   directions using sea salt and nyafat
> Cranberry Relish (recipe follows)

Drain canned chicken and pick over carefully for skin and bones; remove skin and bones from cooked chicken and cut meat into chunks. Set aside. Place endive in ice water 15 minutes to crisp. Dry gently with paper towels. Divide endive among 4 salad plates and arrange chicken and rice (cold) on top. Pour Cranberry Relish to taste over salads. Serve with plain rice crackers or plain rice cakes.

Cranberry Relish

✳ MAKES ABOUT 2½ CUPS

> 12–16 ounces whole fresh cranberries (rinsed, drained and
>   picked over)
> 2 cups cane sugar
> 1 cup water
> ½ cup sliced fresh celery
> ½ cup cranberry juice (reserved from Berry Spread,
>   Breakfast, Regular Track) or water

Combine all ingredients in a saucepan and cook until skins of berries pop, about 10 minutes. Skim foam from surface, cool. Reserve and refrigerate any leftover relish for No-Bake Coconut Clusters.

No-Bake Coconut Clusters

✳ SERVES 4

> 1½ cups shredded Fresh Coconut (shell removed; see Day
>   Two, Breakfast, Regular Track)
> 3 teaspoons superfine cane sugar
> ¼ cup nyafat
> ½ cup light brown sugar

*

½ cup whole fresh cranberries (rinsed, drained and picked
    over)
¼ cup reserved Cranberry Relish (see recipe above),
    unsulphured light molasses or Sugar Syrup (see
    Breakfast, Regular Track)
1 tablespoon water
1½ cups crumbled puffed rice cereal or 4 large plain rice
    cakes, crumbled

In a large bowl, toss coconut with superfine sugar and set aside. In a
saucepan, melt nyafat and add sugar, cranberries, relish and 1 tablespoon water. Bring to boil, lower heat and cook 2 minutes. Stir in
cereal or rice cakes until mixture holds together in tablespoonfuls.
Drop by tablespoonfuls into sweetened coconut. Roll to coat completely. Cool on a sheet of waxed paper.

Carob-Banana Soda

✳   SERVES 1

1 teaspoon (scant) carob powder (use carob sparingly as it
    has a slightly bitter taste)
2 teaspoons Sugar Syrup (see Breakfast, Regular Track) or
    unsulphured light molasses
2 teaspoons cold water or milk
1 jar Beech-Nut Stage One bananas
1 (2-ounce) scoop Banana Sorbet (see Night-Before
    Preparation Tips for Day Seventeen)
Chilled sparkling mineral water

Combine carob, syrup or molasses and cold water or milk together in
a soda glass. Stir until smooth. Stir in Beech-Nut Stage One bananas
until thoroughly combined. Add scoop of sorbet and fill glass with
sparkling water.

DINNER

Lima Bean and Chicken Bake

✳   SERVES 4

1 tablespoon olive oil
1 (4-pound) roasting chicken, cut into 8 pieces, excess fat
    removed
1 cup chicken livers (optional)
1 tablespoon nyafat

1 teaspoon ground ginger
2 teaspoons crushed fresh thyme leaves or 1 teaspoon
   ground thyme
¼ cup firmly packed light brown sugar
2 jars Beech-Nut Stage One chicken
1 (10-ounce) package frozen lima beans
1 cup water
½ teaspoon sea salt or to taste

Preheat oven to 350°F.

In a deep skillet or Dutch oven, heat oil over medium-high heat; brown chicken pieces on all sides, 15–20 minutes. Add chicken livers last 5 minutes if used, and sauté. Remove chicken and livers and drain fat from pan. Rinse pan of any burned bits clinging to the bottom; dry and return to stove top. Melt nyafat over low heat; add remaining ingredients and stir well to combine. Return chicken and livers to pan; cover and bake 15 minutes. Stir; add a little more water if necessary to prevent burning. Cover and bake 15 minutes more. Stir well, correct seasoning with sea salt and thyme. To serve, remove chicken pieces to a deep serving dish. Over low heat on top of the stove, stir limas and gravy until thoroughly combined, scraping up browned bits from bottom of pan. Pour over chicken and serve.

Wild Rice

✳ SERVES 4

1½ cups wild rice*
Boiling water
½ teaspoon sea salt or to taste
1 teaspoon nyafat

In a colander, rinse rice in cold water and drain. Place rice in a bowl or pot, stir in 4 cups boiling water. Cover pot or bowl and allow to stand 20 minutes. Repeat three times or more, using fresh boiling water each time, until rice is tender and fluffy. Add salt and nyafat last time. Serve with additional nyafat if desired.

*You may also use a whole-grain brown rice such as Uncle Ben's. Prepare according to package directions, using water, nyafat and sea salt.

Fruit Cobbler with Hard Sauce

SERVES 4

20 ounces whole fresh or frozen cranberries
1 cup water
½ cup light brown sugar or to taste
1 teaspoon ground ginger
1 cup milk or Banana Crème (see Breakfast, Regular Track,
    for directions)
2 tablespoons quick-cooking farina or Beech-Nut Stage One
    rice cereal
2 bananas, peeled
½ cup shredded Fresh Coconut (shell removed, see Day
    Two, Breakfast, Regular Track)

If using fresh cranberries, rinse, drain and pick over. In a small saucepan, combine water and cranberries and heat to boiling. Stir, lower heat to simmer and add sugar, ginger and milk. Sprinkle in cereal and cook over very low heat 2 minutes, stirring, until sauce is thick and smooth. Slice bananas and spread them in an 8-inch round baking dish. Pour cranberry mixture over bananas; sprinkle top of cobbler with shredded coconut, if desired. Cover and chill or serve warm. Pass Hard Sauce (recipe follows) separately and serve with cobbler.

Hard Sauce

MAKES ABOUT 1 CUP

1 cup nyafat
1 cup superfine cane sugar
¼ cup milk or Banana Crème (see Breakfast, Regular
    Track, for directions)
1 teaspoon ground ginger or to taste

Cream nyafat and sugar together until well combined. Add milk a few drops at a time and beat until fluffy. Add ginger to taste and chill.

DIET EXPRESS

BREAKFAST

Puffed Rice Cereal with Bananas, Milk and Sugar

✳ SERVES 1

> *1 cup puffed rice cereal*
> *1 small banana, peeled and sliced*
> *Milk and sugar to taste*
> *Dash ground ginger (optional)*

Pour cereal into a bowl. Top with bananas, milk, sugar and ginger, if desired.

Variation:

> *⅓ cup Beech-Nut Stage One rice cereal*
> *Banana Crème (see below) to taste*
> *Sugar and gound ginger to taste*

Pour cereal into a bowl. Blend Banana Crème with cereal until smooth and of desired consistency; add sugar and ginger to taste. Heat before mixing with cereal if hot cereal is desired.

Banana Crème
(See Breakfast, Regular Track)
✳

Carob Cocoa
(See Breakfast, Regular Track)
✳

SNACK

Sweet Ginger Herbal Tea
(See Breakfast, Regular Track)
✳

Rice Cakes with Bananas, Brown Sugar and Coconut

SERVES 1

2 large plain rice cakes
1 jar Beech-Nut Stage One bananas
Light brown sugar to taste
¼ cup shredded Fresh Coconut (shell removed; see Day
*   Two, Breakfast, Regular Track)*

Spread rice cakes with bananas; sprinkle with light brown sugar and coconut.

LUNCH

Cream of Spinach Soup

SERVES 1

4 ounces frozen chopped spinach
1 jar Beech-Nut Stage One chicken
Sea salt to taste
Dash ground ginger
¼ cup (approximate) milk or water

MW—Place frozen spinach in a shallow microwave-safe soup bowl. Set microwave oven to defrost setting and cook, loosely covered, 3–5 minutes, until spinach is defrosted. Do not drain. Stir in chicken, salt and ginger until uniformly combined; cover and cook (H) until hot, about 2 minutes. Stir, add milk or water until soup is desired thickness, reheat (H) 15–30 seconds and serve.

Chicken Sandwich with Ginger Butter

SERVES 1

2 large plain rice cakes
Ginger Butter (recipe follows)
4 fresh leaves spinach, washed and patted dry
5 ounces drained, canned water-pack chicken

Spread rice cakes with Ginger Butter. Alternating layers, arrange spinach and chicken on 1 rice cake, top with second and serve.

Ginger Butter

✳ MAKES ¼ CUP

¼ cup nyafat
2 teaspoons ground ginger
1 teaspoon ground thyme
¼ teaspoon sea salt

Cream all ingredients together until smooth and uniformly combined.

Chicken Pâté with Rice Crackers and Celery Sticks

✳ SERVES 1

2 stalks fresh celery, trimmed.
1 jar Beech-Nut Stage One chicken
¼ teaspoon each sea salt and thyme or to taste
Plain rice crackers

Slice celery into thin sticks. Blend chicken, salt and thyme until completely combined and seasoned to taste. Spread on celery sticks and rice crackers.

Banana Sorbet
(See Night-Before Preparation Tips for Day Seventeen)

✳

DINNER

Quick Creamy Soup

✳ SERVES 1

½ cup (approximate) milk or water
1 jar Beech-Nut Stage One chicken
Ground thyme and sea salt to taste

In a small saucepan, stir milk or water into chicken over medium heat until soup is desired consistency. Season to taste with thyme and salt.

Broiled Breast of Chicken

SERVES 1

2 boneless chicken breast halves, skins on
2 teaspoons nyafat
1 teaspoon minced fresh thyme
Sea salt to taste

Preheat broiler.

Dot chicken breasts with nyafat, sprinkle them with thyme and salt. Broil 4 inches from heat 3–4 minutes each side, until skins are crisped and brown. Serve with Quick-Cooking Rice.

Quick-Cooking Rice

Make any brand, plain precooked rice according to package instructions for 1–2 servings, using nyafat, sea salt and water.

Spinach Salad with Spinach Dressing

SERVES 1

½ pound fresh spinach, washed, trimmed and patted dry
¼ cup frozen cranberries
¼ cup shredded fresh coconut
Spinach Dressing (recipe follows)

Tear spinach leaves into bite-sized pieces and place in a salad bowl. Add undefrosted cranberries; toss with Spinach Dressing and serve.

Spinach Dressing

MAKES ABOUT ¾ CUP

1 tablespoon water or cranberry juice (reserved from Berry
    Spread, Breakfast, Regular Track)
¼ teaspoon each cane sugar and ground ginger
1 jar Beech-Nut Stage One spinach
3 tablespoons olive oil

In a small, deep bowl, whisk together the water or juice, sugar and ginger. Continue whisking, adding Beech-Nut spinach and oil until dressing is smooth and well combined.

Caramelized Bananas

✳   SERVES 1

2 tablespoons nyafat
2 tablespoons light brown sugar or unsulphured light
*   molasses*
1 firm, slightly underripe banana, peeled and sliced
Pinch ground ginger

Melt nyafat in a small skillet over medium heat. Add sugar and stir until dissolved and syrup is smooth. Add sliced bananas and ginger and cook over low heat, turning slices occasionally until bananas are brown and sugar is dark brown and caramelized, about 10 minutes.

NIGHT-BEFORE PREPARATION TIPS
FOR DAY 18

> Make Peach Sorbet: Allowing 1 jar per serving, empty as many jars Beech-Nut Stage One peaches as you think you will need into a freezer container with a lid. Freeze overnight to use as instant sorbet in beverages or desserts. As dessert, allow to soften 15 minutes in the refrigerator before serving as sorbet.

DAY ✳ 18   THE REINTRODUCTION PHASE (CHOCOLATE)

ALLOWED FOODS:
Corn, cherries, peaches, asparagus, beets, pink beans, rhubarb, zucchini, veal, mint, nutmeg, dill, maple syrup, unsweetened cocoa (chocolate), gelatin, baking soda

MENU	REGULAR	DIET EXPRESS
BREAKFAST	Hasty Pudding Corn Tortillas Corn Cracker-Bread Hot Chocolate	Puffed Corn Cereal with Peaches Quick-Cooking Grits Hot Chocolate
SNACK	Chocolate Truffles Cocoa Nuts Mint Herbal Tea	Fresh Microwave Popcorn Mint Herbal Tea

❋

LUNCH	Veal Patties	Veal Pâté with Tortillas and
	Corn Shortbread	Zucchini Sticks
	Rhubarb Salad	Peaches or Cherries with
	Dill Dressing	Chocolate-Maple Sauce
	Chocolate Spritzer	
DINNER	Veal Chops with Peaches	Veal Piccata with Rhubarb
	Corn on the Cob	Corn on the Cob
	Asparagus with Dill	Asparagus with Dill
	Vinaigrette	Vinaigrette
	Rhubarb-Cherry Pie	Quick Chocolate Fondue

BULK AGENT: Corn bran

R E G U L A R   T R A C K

B R E A K F A S T

Hasty Pudding

❋   SERVES 4

¾ cup yellow cornmeal
3 cups water
½ teaspoon sea salt
Maple syrup

Mix cornmeal with 1 cup water. Bring 2 cups water to boil, add salt. Stir in cornmeal mixture, lower heat, and cook 10–15 minutes, stirring frequently. Serve warm with maple syrup to taste. (Pudding may be started in the top half of a double boiler, then covered and placed over boiling water and steamed for half an hour. This eliminates need for frequent stirring.)

Corn Tortillas

❋   MAKES ABOUT 1 DOZEN

2 cups corn flour plus flour for dusting
2 cups water (approximate)
1 tablespoon pure corn oil

Combine flour and water in a large bowl until dough is firm but not dry. Keep dough covered with a clean, damp cloth while making tortillas. On a large piece of waxed paper dusted with corn flour, place

1 heaping tablespoonful of dough and cover it with another piece of waxed paper. With a rolling pin or thick, smooth-sided glass, flatten the ball of dough into a thin circle, as near to ⅛-inch thickness as possible. When tortilla is formed, carefully remove top piece of waxed paper. Heat oil in heavy skillet until medium-hot. Place tortilla in hot skillet, paper side up. Allow tortilla to cook a few seconds, then peel paper off. Cook tortilla about 1 minute on first side. Turn and cook other side about 1 minute more. Tortilla is done when dry around the edges. Remove tortilla when cooked to a clean cloth towel. Repeat procedure until all the dough is used, stacking cooked tortillas on top of one another in the cloth towel. When all tortillas are cooked, wrap them in the towel until they are cool enough to eat. Spread with Beech-Nut Stage One peaches, if desired. (Refrigerate or freeze any leftover tortillas for use later on in the day.)

Corn Cracker-Bread
(See Day Eight, Lunch, Regular Track)

✳

Hot Chocolate

✳   SERVES 1

> *1 heaping teaspoon unsweetened cocoa such as Hershey's brand*
> *2 heaping teaspoons maple crystals or maple syrup or beet sugar*
> *2 teaspoons cold water*
> *Hot water*

Combine cocoa and sugar in a cup or mug. Stir in cold water until smooth. Fill cup with hot water. Use more or less sweetener to taste. Serve with a sprig of fresh mint, if desired.

SNACK

Chocolate Truffles

✳   MAKES 1–2 DOZEN, DEPENDING ON SIZE

> *1 jar Beech-Nut Stage One peaches*
> *¾ cup unsweetened cocoa such as Hershey's brand*
> *½ cup chopped, pitted fresh or frozen cherries*

✳

1½ cups (approximate) crushed puffed corn cereal
1 tablespoon pure corn oil
3 tablespoons (approximate) maple syrup

In a large mixing bowl, combine peaches and ¼ cup of the cocoa until evenly blended. Stir in cherries, puffed corn cereal, oil and syrup; mix well, adjusting ingredients until mixture holds together. (Add more crumbs if mixture is too moist; add maple syrup if it is too dry.) Cover and chill 1 hour. Spread the remaining cocoa on a sheet of waxed paper. Scoop up truffle mixture 1 tablespoon at a time, forming the tablespoonfuls into balls. Roll the balls in cocoa and serve. (Chill any remaining truffles on waxed paper in a covered container.)

Cocoa Nuts

✳   SERVES 4

1 cup drained, patted dry, canned water-pack pink beans
1 tablespoon pure corn oil plus oil for greasing baking sheet
4 tablespoons maple crystals or beet sugar
3 tablespoons unsweetened cocoa such as Hershey's brand

Preheat oven to 250°F.
In a skillet over medium heat, sauté beans in 1 tablespoon oil; stir until all beans are coated. Remove from heat. Combine sugar and cocoa in a mixing bowl; toss beans with mixture until coated. Lightly oil a baking sheet; bake beans until dry and crunchy but not burned, about 20 minutes.

Mint Herbal Tea

✳   SERVES 1

3–4 leaves fresh mint, washed, patted dry and trimmed
2–3 cherries, washed, pits removed and chopped
¾ cup boiling water
Maple crystals or maple syrup or beet sugar to taste

Place mint leaves and cherries in a mug or cup, add boiling water and steep until tea is desired strength. Remove and discard mint leaves; eat or discard cherries. Sweeten to taste with sugar.

LUNCH

Veal Patties

✳   SERVES 4

1 pound ground fresh veal
¼ teaspoon sea salt
1 tablespoon minced dill weed
½ cup (approximate) cornmeal
1 tablespoon pure corn oil

Combine veal, salt and dill. Shape meat into patties, flatten slightly and coat with cornmeal. Heat oil in a skillet until hot and fry patties 2–4 minutes each side (depending on thickness of patties). Serve with Corn Shortbread (recipe follows) or Corn Tortillas (see Breakfast, Regular Track).

Corn Shortbread

✳   MAKES ABOUT 1½ DOZEN PIECES

Pure corn oil for greasing pan plus ½ cup oil
½ cup maple crystals or beet sugar or ⅓ cup maple syrup
1 cup cornmeal
½ cup corn flour
½ teaspoon sea salt
1 teaspoon baking soda

Preheat oven to 350°F.

Lightly grease an 8- or 9-inch-square baking pan with oil. Combine ½ cup oil and sweetener and beat well. Sift together cornmeal, corn flour, salt and baking soda; add to oil-sugar mixture. Blend thoroughly; dough should be firm but not dry. Press mixture into prepared pan and prick surface with a fork. Mark sixteen to twenty squares, cutting about halfway through the dough. Bake until firm when pressed gently in the center, about 50 minutes. Shortbread will look toasted, but not brown. Cool bread in the pan; to serve, cut squares where marked.

Rhubarb Salad

✳   SERVES 4

½ cup thinly sliced frozen rhubarb or 2 stalks fresh
    rhubarb, scrubbed, trimmed and sliced
½ cup water

*

Dash sea salt
2 small zucchini
1 cup canned water-pack beets
Dill Dressing (recipe follows)

Place rhubarb in a small saucepan and cover with ½ cup water and salt. Bring to boil, remove from heat and allow to stand a few minutes while assembling salad. Scrub, trim and slice the zucchini and place them in a salad bowl. Drain beets, chop them and add to zucchini. Drain rhubarb, reserving rhubarb "vinegar" and add to salad. Toss vegetables with dressing and serve.

Dill Dressing

*   MAKES ABOUT 2 CUPS

1 envelope unflavored gelatin
¼ cup rhubarb "vinegar" (reserved from Rhubarb Salad
  [see recipe above]), chilled
⅓ cup (approximate) pure corn oil
½ teaspoon sea salt or to taste
1 tablespoon minced dill weed

In a small, deep saucepan, sprinkle gelatin over cold rhubarb "vinegar"; allow gelatin to soften 1 minute. Beating constantly with an electric beater, bring mixture to a boil over medium-high heat. Remove from heat as soon as mixture boils and gelatin begins to foam and increase volume. Continue to beat, adding pure corn oil a drop at a time until dressing is consistency of mayonnaise. Correct seasoning to taste with salt and add dill, mixing well to combine.

Chocolate Spritzer

*   SERVES 1

1 heaping teaspoon unsweetened cocoa such as Hershey's
  brand
3 heaping tablespoons maple crystals or maple syrup or
  beet sugar or Heinz peach flakes
6 ounces chilled sparkling mineral water
1 (2-ounce) scoop Peach Sorbet (see Night-Before
  Preparations for Day Eighteen)
1 sprig fresh mint for garnish

Combine cocoa and sweetener in a tall glass. Mix well, adding 2 ounces cold mineral water and stirring until smooth. Add sorbet and fill glass with remaining mineral water. Garnish with a sprig of fresh mint.

DINNER

Veal Chops with Peaches

✳ SERVES 4

4 veal chops (1 inch thick), cut from leg or shoulder
½ cup (approximate) cornmeal
½ teaspoon sea salt
2 tablespoons pure corn oil
1 cup chopped frozen peaches or 2 peaches, washed and
    chopped but not peeled
1 jar Beech-Nut Stage One peaches
½ cup water

Rinse chops and pat dry. Combine cornmeal and salt in a mixing bowl or paper bag; add chops one at a time and coat lightly with cornmeal. Heat oil in a skillet large enough to hold chops in one layer. Add chops and brown, turning frequently until chops are crisp and brown on both sides, about 10 minutes. Drain chops on paper towels; drain excess fat and any burned bits from skillet. Return skillet to stove and add chopped peaches, Beech-Nut Stage One peaches and water; stir over low heat until combined. Return chops to the skillet, cover and cook over very low heat 15–20 minutes, until chops are tender and cooked through.

MW—Coat chops with cornmeal as described above. Heat (H) a microwave browning dish 4 minutes. Add corn oil to cover bottom of the dish, add chops and brown (H) 1 minute. Turn and cook (H) 1 minute more. Stir together ¼ cup water, chopped peaches and Beech-Nut peaches; stir into chops. Cover and cook (L) or roast setting 5–10 minutes. Rearrange chops after half cooking time, moving inside chops to outside of dish. After cooking, correct seasoning with sea salt.

Note: If you do not have a microwave browning dish, brown chops as directed in regular recipe and finish cooking in the microwave in a covered microwave-safe casserole.

Corn on the Cob

✳ SERVES 4

4 ears frozen corn on the cob or fresh corn, husked and
    washed
Cold water
Dash sea salt

Place the corn in large saucepan with a cover. Fill pan with enough cold water so that corn can float freely. Add a dash of salt. Bring water to boil, immediately turn off heat. Cover pan and allow corn to stand in cooling water at least 10 minutes. Drain. Serve with salt and pure corn oil to taste.

MW—Wrap shucked ears of corn in waxed paper or plastic wrap. Cook (H) 2–3 minutes (approximate) per ear of corn. Season to taste after cooking with salt and pure corn oil.

Asparagus with Dill Vinaigrette

SERVES 4

1 (10-ounce) package frozen asparagus spears or 6–8 stalks
    fresh asparagus or 1 (12-ounce) can water-pack white
    asparagus, drained
Pinch sea salt
Dill Vinaigrette (recipe follows)

Defrost frozen asparagus by placing it in a colander and rinsing it with hot water until thawed. If using fresh asparagus, scrub stalks thoroughly and cut off tough white bottoms of stems. Place asparagus in a large pan of cold water, add a pinch of sea salt and bring to boil. Parboil 3 minutes; remove from pan and drain on paper towels. Cut each stalk of asparagus in half; divide equally among 4 salad plates. Drizzle with Dill Vinaigrette and serve.

Dill Vinaigrette

MAKES 1 CUP

¼ cup rhubarb "vinegar" (reserved from Rhubarb Salad,
    Lunch, Regular Track)
½ teaspoon sea salt
2 teaspoons minced dill weed
¾ cup pure corn oil

In a blender or small deep bowl, blend or whisk together the rhubarb "vinegar", salt and dill. Whisking or blending steadily, add oil until dressing is thoroughly combined.

hubarb-Cherry Pie

✳

Crust:

2 cups crushed puffed corn cereal
⅓ cup pure corn oil

Preheat oven to 400°F.

Combine crushed corn puff cereal and oil until mixture holds together. Press into an 8- or 9-inch pie plate and bake 5 minutes. Cool while preparing filling.

Filling:

2 cups frozen cherries or fresh cherries* (rinsed and patted dry)
½ cup maple crystals or beet sugar or maple syrup
2 teaspoons cornstarch
¼ cup cold water
1 stalk fresh rhubarb, scrubbed, trimmed and chopped
2 jars Beech-Nut Stage One peaches

Remove pits from cherries and slice in half. Sprinkle cherries with sugar or drizzle with syrup; stir to coat and set aside. In a measuring cup, stir cornstarch into cold water and blend until smooth. Place sweetened cherries, rhubarb and peaches in a saucepan and heat until boiling, stirring constantly and adding cornstarch-water mixture in a stream. Remove from heat as soon as filling comes to boil and thickens. Taste; add additional sugar or syrup for greater sweetness. Pour into prepared crust; serve warm or chilled with scoops of Peach Sorbet (see Night-Before Preparation Tips for Day Eighteen).

*Fresh or frozen peaches may be substituted for cherries.

DIET EXPRESS

BREAKFAST

Puffed Corn Cereal with Peaches

✳

1 cup puffed corn cereal
½ cup frozen sliced peaches or 1 fresh peach, washed and sliced

✳

1 jar Beech-Nut Stage One peaches
Dash ground nutmeg
Heinz peach flakes to taste

Pour corn puffs into a bowl. Place sliced peaches on top; pour Beech-Nut peaches over all, sprinkle lightly with nutmeg and mix to combine. Sprinkle with Heinz peach flakes for added sweetness.

Quick-Cooking Grits

✳   SERVES 1

1 cup water
¼ cup quick-cooking grits
Dash each sea salt and nutmeg

MW—Combine water, grits, salt and nutmeg in a microwave-safe 2-cup cereal or soup bowl. Cook (H), uncovered, until boiling, 1–2 minutes. Stir, cook (L) 2–3 minutes more, until grits are desired consistency. Top with fresh or frozen sliced peaches, Beech-Nut peaches and peach flakes to taste.

Hot Chocolate
(See Breakfast, Regular Track)

✳

SNACK

Fresh Microwave Popcorn
(See Day Eight, Snack, Diet Express)

✳

Mint Herbal Tea
(See Snack, Regular Track)

✳

LUNCH

Veal Pâté with Tortillas and Zucchini Sticks

✳ SERVES 1

2–3 corn tortillas (commercial)*
1 small zucchini, scrubbed, trimmed and sliced into sticks
Sea salt for salting zucchini
1–2 jars Beech-Nut Stage One veal
¼ teaspoon each sea salt and minced dill weed
1 teaspoon pure corn oil
½ cup well-drained, canned water-pack minced beets
  (optional)

Heat oven to moderate, 350°F.

Place tortillas on a baking pan or piece of aluminum foil and heat briefly in oven while preparing zucchini and pâté. Sprinkle zucchini lightly with salt and set aside. Mix together the veal, ¼ teaspoon salt, ¼ teaspoon dill and oil until thoroughly combined. Spread veal on warm tortillas and top with beets, if desired. Fold tortillas and serve with salted zucchini sticks.

*Fresh, corn-flour-and-water-only tortillas can be found in the freezer section of most markets. One good brand is Patio.

Peaches or Cherries with Chocolate-Maple Sauce

✳ SERVES 1

1 cup frozen pitted cherries or peaches (not in syrup)
2 teaspoons unsweetened cocoa such as Hershey's brand
⅓ cup maple syrup
Dash ground nutmeg

Sprinkle undefrosted fruit with cocoa, syrup and nutmeg. Stir until cocoa is dissolved and fruit is coated with syrup.

✳ ─────────────────────────────

DINNER

Veal Piccata with Rhubarb

✳   SERVES 1–2

½ cup (approximate) cornmeal
1 teaspoon sea salt
2 teaspoons ground nutmeg
4 slices veal scallopine, or cutlets, pounded very thin
4 teaspoons (approximate) pure corn oil for brushing veal
    plus 2 tablespoons oil
½ cup chopped frozen rhubarb

In a large bowl, combine cornmeal, salt and nutmeg. Brush veal slices all over with oil, then dip in cornmeal, coating completely. In a large skillet, heat remaining 2 tablespoons oil until hot; brown veal until breading is crisp, turning frequently, about 10 minutes. Remove veal from skillet, drain briefly on paper towels, and keep warm. Add frozen rhubarb to juices in skillet; sauté 2–4 minutes, scraping up browned bits in pan and stirring until rhubarb is tender-crisp. Spoon rhubarb and sauce over veal and serve.

Corn on the Cob
(See Dinner, Regular Track)

✳

Asparagus with Dill Vinaigrette
(See Dinner, Regular Track)

✳

Quick Chocolate Fondue

✳   SERVES 1

½ cup plus 1 tablespoon unsweetened cocoa, such as
    Hershey's brand
1 tablespoon pure corn oil
¼ cup hot water
½ cup beet sugar*
½ cup water
1 teaspoon crushed fresh mint (optional)
1 cup frozen sliced peaches or frozen cherries

In a measuring cup, mix together cocoa, oil and hot water until smooth. In a small saucepan over low heat, cook sugar and water, stirring constantly, until sugar is completely dissolved. Gradually add cocoa-oil mixture and mint to sugar syrup, stirring constantly; simmer over very low heat 1 minute. Cool slightly and pour into a bowl. Dip frozen fruit into hot syrup.

*If you cannot find beet sugar, substitute ½ cup light Karo syrup for corn oil and hot water. Light Karo corn syrup contains vanilla, however; do not use it if you had a reaction to ferments on Day Fifteen. Instead, substitute ½ cup Heinz peach flakes for beet sugar and proceed as above.

NIGHT BEFORE PREPARATION TIPS
FOR DAY 19

1. Make Apple Sorbet: Allowing 1 jar per serving, empty as many jars Beech-Nut Stage One applesauce as you think you will need into a freezer container with a lid. Freeze overnight to use as instant sorbet in beverages or desserts. As dessert, allow to soften 15 minutes in the refrigerator before serving as sorbet.

2. Presoak kasha: Place 1 cup raw, washed and picked over kasha in a casserole with a cover. Pour 2 cups boiling water over kasha, cool slightly. Cover and refrigerate overnight. Use on Day Nineteen for Diet Express breakfast, Quick Hot Kasha with Applesauce, or in cold salads.

3. Remove leftover Roast Marinated Leg of Lamb cooked on Day Fifteen (see Dinner, Regular Track) from the freezer. Place in the refrigerator to thaw overnight. Use on Day Nineteen for Cold Lamb Salad (Lunch, Regular Track) and, if desired, for Stuffed Tomato (Lunch, Diet Express).

DAY 19

THE REINTRODUCTION PHASE (TOMATO)

ALLOWED FOODS:
Kasha, chick-peas, apples, papayas, pineapple, cucumber, lettuce, sweet potato, tomatoes, lamb, sesame, cinnamon, mace, oregano, tapioca

MENU	REGULAR	DIET EXPRESS
BREAKFAST	Herbed Tomato Juice Hot Kasha Cereal with Apples Chick-pea Pancakes Cinnamon Stick Herbal Tea	Herbed Tomato Juice Quick Hot Kasha with Applesauce Cinnamon Stick Herbal Tea
SNACK	Crunchy Chick-peas Papaya-Pineapple-Apple Shake	Pineapple Juice Mock "P&J" on Apple Slices
LUNCH	Tomato Soup Cold Lamb Salad Tomato Dressing	Quick Tomato Soup Stuffed Tomato Apple Sorbet

DINNER	Lamb Shanks
	Buckwheat Pasta or
	Hot Kasha
	Cucumber Salad with
	  Tahihi Dressing
	Apple Whip
		Lamb Chop Broil
		Yam Noodles with Tomato
		  Sauce
		Ten-Minute Sweet Potatoes
		Soft-Serve Sesame Ice Cream

BULK AGENT: Psyllium seed

REGULAR TRACK

BREAKFAST

Herbed Tomato Juice

SERVES 4

1 quart plain tomato juice
1 teaspoon sea salt
1 tablespoon ground oregano
Ice

Pour tomato juice into a pitcher; add salt and oregano and stir well to combine. Serve over ice.

Hot Kasha Cereal with Apples

SERVES 4

4 cups water
2 cups raw, washed and picked over kasha
1 large fresh unpeeled apple, cored and chopped
2 teaspoons ground cinnamon
1 teaspoon tahini or sesame oil
½ cup (approximate) plain apple juice

In a large saucepan, bring water to a boil and stir in kasha. Lower heat to simmer, add apple, cinnamon, and tahini and cook 15 minutes, stirring occasionally. Add apple juice and continue cooking until kasha is tender and cereal is desired thickness. Serve warm with plain apple butter or plain unsweetened applesauce for added sweetness.

Chick-pea Pancakes

SERVES 4

2 cups chick-pea flour*
2 cups (approximate) water
1 tablespoon sesame oil plus oil for greasing skillet
½ teaspoon sea salt

In a large mixing bowl, blend the flour with water, 1 tablespoon oil and salt to make a thick but pourable batter. Lightly grease a skillet with oil; heat skillet until it is very hot, but not smoking. Using ½ cup for each pancake, pour batter into hot skillet. Cook pancakes until browned on one side, 1–2 minutes. Turn and brown on other side about 1 minute, or until cooked through. Serve with a choice of plain apple butter, or tahini (for peanut butter-like taste) as topping.

*Chick-pea flour can be found in many health food stores, or you can make your own by grinding 2–3 cups dry chick-peas in a processor. Be sure to sift the chick-pea flour well if smooth-textured pancakes are desired. Less sifting produces a grainier-textured pancake.

Cinnamon Stick Herbal Tea

SERVES 1

1 cinnamon stick, broken into pieces
2 tablespoons chopped apple peel from a fresh, washed
    apple

✳

6 ounces boiling water
2 teaspoons Heinz apple flakes

Place cinnamon and apple peel in a mug or cup. Add boiling water and allow to steep 2–5 minutes, according to strength desired. Remove cinnamon; eat or discard apple peel. Sweeten to taste with apple flakes.

SNACK

Crunchy Chick-peas

✳   MAKES 1 CUP PEAS

Sesame oil for greasing pan
1 cup drained, canned water-pack chick-peas (patted dry)

Preheat oven to moderate, 350°F.
   Lightly grease a baking pan with sesame oil. Spread dry chick-peas on pan in a single layer and bake until crisp, about 20 minutes. Stir occasionally during cooking. Cool completely before serving.

Papaya-Pineapple-Apple Shake

✳   SERVES 1

1 ripe fresh papaya, peeled, seeded and cut into chunks or
   ½ cup undrained, canned crushed pineapple packed in
   its own juice
¼ cup plain apple juice
Dash ground cinnamon
1 ice cube, crushed
1 cinnamon stick for garnish

Place papaya or pineapple in a blender or food processor fitted with a steel blade. Add apple juice, cinnamon and crushed ice; process on high power until smooth. Pour into a goblet and garnish with a cinnamon stick.

✳

LUNCH

Tomato Soup

✳

> *2 tablespoons sesame oil*
> *1 small cucumber, peeled and chopped*
> *1 quart undrained, canned tomatoes packed in their own*
> *   juice*
> *1 tablespoon minced fresh oregano or ½ tablespoon ground*
> *   oregano*
> *2 teaspoons sea salt*
> *Dash mace*
> *1 tablespoon granulated, quick-cooking tapioca or 1*
> *   tablespoon buckwheat flour mixed with ¼ cup cold*
> *   water until smooth*

Heat oil in a large soup pot or saucepan and sauté cucumber until just slightly brown. Add tomatoes with juice, oregano, salt and mace. Lower heat and simmer 15–20 minutes, uncovered, stirring occasionally. Strain the soup to remove tomato and cucumber seeds, return to soup pot and bring to boil, gradually adding tapioca or buckwheat flour. Cook over low heat until soup is slightly thickened. Correct seasoning with salt. Serve hot or cold.

Cold Lamb Salad

✳

> *1 small head lettuce, washed and patted dry*
> *1 (8-ounce) can yam noodles or threads, drained*
> *1 pound cooked roast lamb, thinly sliced (see Night-Before*
> *   Preparation Tips, for Day Nineteen)*
> *½ cup precooked kasha (see Night-Before Preparation Tips*
> *   for Day Nineteen)*
> *4 Italian tomatoes, washed and sliced or 1 (12-ounce) can*
> *   sliced tomatoes packed in their own juice, drained**
> *Tomato Dressing (recipe follows)*

Divide lettuce among 4 salad plates and arrange yam noodles or threads on top. In a bowl, combine lamb, kasha, tomatoes and Tomato

*

Dressing. Toss gently to combine and spoon on beds of noodles or threads. Sprinkle with sesame seeds.

*Reserve juice for use in Tomato Dressing.

Tomato Dressing

* MAKES ABOUT 1 CUP

⅓ cup plain tomato juice
½ teaspoon sea salt or to taste
2 teaspoons minced fresh oregano or 1 teaspoon ground
    oregano
¾ cup sesame oil

In a blender or a small bowl, blend or whisk together the tomato juice, salt and oregano. Whisking or blending constantly, add oil in a stream, until dressing is thoroughly blended.

DINNER

Lamb Shanks

* SERVES 4

4 lamb shanks, rinsed and patted dry with paper towels
2 tablespoons minced fresh oregano or 1 tablespoon ground
    oregano
1 teaspoon sea salt
3 tablespoons sesame oil
1 (6-ounce) can plain tomato paste
1 quart undrained, canned tomatoes packed in their own
    juice

Preheat oven to low, 225°F.

Rub shanks all over with oregano and salt. Heat oil in a Dutch oven or heavy skillet with a cover until hot. Add shanks and brown on all sides over medium-high heat, about 20 minutes. Add tomato paste and tomatoes with juice; stir until smooth. Lamb shanks should be at least half-covered with sauce. Bring sauce to boil, cover and bake 1–1½ hours, until shanks are very tender. Check level of sauce occasionally during cooking, adding more tomato juice if needed. Correct seasoning with salt. Serve with Buckwheat Pasta or Hot Kasha (recipes follow).

Buckwheat Pasta

SERVES 4

2 quarts water plus 1 cup cold water
1 tablespoon sesame oil
7 ounces plain buckwheat pasta

Bring 2 quarts water to boil in a large pan. Add oil and pasta. Return to boil; immediately add 1 cup cold water and lower heat to avoid boil-over. Cook pasta over medium heat 5 minutes, stirring gently while noodles cook to prevent them from sticking together. Taste; continue to cook until noodles are tender but still firm. Drain noodles and rinse under cold running water.

Hot Kasha

SERVES 4

4 cups water
2 cups raw, washed and picked over kasha
1 teaspoon sea salt
1 tablespoon sesame oil

Bring water to boil in a large saucepan. Stir in kasha, salt and oil, reduce heat to very low. Cover and cook 7–12 minutes, until kasha is tender.

Cucumber Salad with Tahini Dressing

SERVES 4

1 small head lettuce, washed and patted dry
2 large cucumbers, pared and thinly sliced
½ pint cherry tomatoes, washed and cut in halves or 1 (10-
*   ounce) can sliced tomatoes packed in their own juice,*
*   drained*
Tahini Dressing (recipe follows)

Tear lettuce into bite-size pieces and place in a salad bowl. Add cucumbers and tomatoes, toss with Tahini Dressing and serve.

✳

Tahini Dressing

✳

⅓ cup tahini, mixed well to incorporate oil
⅓ cup water
1 tablespoon minced fresh oregano or 2 teaspoons ground
    oregano
½ teaspoon sea salt

Combine all ingredients and blend until smooth.

Apple Whip

✳

2 cups plain apple juice
3 tablespoons granulated, quick-cooking tapioca
1 jar Beech-Nut Stage One applesauce
½ teaspoon ground cinnamon

Combine juice and tapioca in a saucepan. Allow to stand 5 minutes. Stirring constantly, bring to boil. Reduce heat to low and simmer, still stirring, 1–2 minutes. Stir in applesauce and cinnamon. Remove from heat; cool 10 minutes. Place mixture in the bowl of a processor and whip on highest power until mixture is four times its original volume. Spoon into serving goblets or bowls and refrigerate up to 2 hours. Top the whip with chopped fresh papaya or pineapple.

DIET EXPRESS

BREAKFAST

Herbed Tomato Juice
(See Breakfast, Regular Track)

✳

Quick Hot Kasha with Applesauce

✳

⅓ cup presoaked kasha (see Night-Before Preparation Tips
    for Day Nineteen)

Dash ground cinnamon
½ cup plain unsweetened smooth or chunky-style
    applesauce
Heinz apple flakes to taste

MW—In a microwave-safe bowl, combine kasha, cinnamon and apple-sauce. Cook (H) until hot, about 1 minute. Stir and test kasha for tenderness; cook (L) 1–2 minutes more, if desired. Sweeten to taste with Heinz apple flakes. (Reserve any leftover kasha for Quick Tomato Soup, Lunch, Diet Express.)

Cinnamon Stick Herbal Tea
(See Breakfast, Regular Track)

✳

SNACK

Pineapple Juice
✳

Mock "P&J" on Apple Slices
✳   SERVES 1

1 large fresh unpeeled apple, washed, cored and sliced
Tahini
Plain apple butter

Spread apple slices first with tahini, then with apple butter for a mock peanut butter and jelly snack.

LUNCH

Quick Tomato Soup
✳   SERVES 1

1 cup plain tomato juice
1 tablespoon plain tomato paste
½ teaspoon sea salt or to taste
1 teaspoon ground oregano

✳ ————————————————————————————————

Combine all ingredients and heat over medium-high heat until smooth and hot. Add more tomato juice if a thinner soup is desired.

Note: If you reserved cooked kasha from Quick Hot Kasha with Applesauce (see Breakfast, Regular Track), add to soup for greater heartiness.

Stuffed Tomato

✳   SERVES 1

1 large, firm fresh beefsteak tomato, washed, patted dry
*   and cut in half*
4 ounces cooked roast lamb, cut in julienne strips (see
*   Night-Before Preparation Tips for Day Nineteen) or 1*
*   jar Beech-Nut Stage One lamb*
1 teaspoon ground oregano
Sea salt to taste
1 tablespoon sesame oil
½ small cucumber, pared and diced
Sesame seeds (optional)
2–3 leaves lettuce, washed and patted dry

Scoop tomato pulp from each half, leaving shells intact. Dice tomato pulp. Combine lamb, oregano and salt to taste; blend in sesame oil. Gently fold diced cucumber and tomato pulp into seasoned lamb. Stuff tomato shells with mixture; sprinkle with sesame seeds, if desired. Place stuffed tomato halves on lettuce leaves and serve.

Apple Sorbet
(See Night-Before Preparation Tips for Day Nineteen)

✳

DINNER

Lamb Chop Broil

✳   SERVES 1–2

1 large fresh beefsteak tomato, washed and patted dry
2 loin lamb chops
Sesame oil
Ground oregano
Sea salt to taste

Preheat broiler to very hot.

Halve the tomato and arrange, cut side up in a shallow, heatproof dish. Sprinkle cut side of tomatoes and both sides of chops with sesame oil; place lamb chops on same platter with tomatoes and sprinkle all with ground oregano. Broil 3 inches from heat about 10 minutes, turning lamb chops once during cooking time. Tops of tomato will be brown and chops will be rare. Remove tomato and chops to a plate. Scrape up browned bits and tomato juice from broiling platter and spoon over chops. Season to taste with sea salt.

Yam Noodles with Tomato Sauce

✳   SERVES 1–2

> 1 (10-ounce) can water-pack yam noodles, drained
> Tomato Sauce (recipe follows)

Place yam noodles in a large bowl. Toss gently with hot Tomato Sauce and serve.

Tomato Sauce

✳   MAKES ABOUT 1½ CUPS

> 3 ounces plain tomato paste
> ½ cup plain tomato juice
> 1 cup water, depending on desired thickness of sauce
> 1 teaspoon ground oregano or 2 teaspoons minced fresh
>   oregano
> ½ teaspoon sea salt or to taste

Combine all ingredients in a small saucepan. Heat, stirring until hot.

Ten-Minute Sweet Potatoes

✳   SERVES 2

> 2 sweet potatoes
> 4 teaspoons each tahini and plain apple butter
> Dash ground cinnamon

MW—Scrub sweet potatoes and pat dry. Prick them twice with a fork and cook (H) on high power 8–10 minutes, until tender when pierced with a fork. While potatoes are cooking, blend together the tahini, apple butter and cinnamon. Split cooked potatoes; top each with 2 teaspoons tahini-apple butter.

✳

Soft-Serve Sesame Ice Cream

✳   SERVES 1–2

12 ounces frozen unsweetened apple juice concentrate
½ cup (approximate) tahini, mixed well to incorporate oil
1 teaspoon ground cinnamon

Place all ingredients in a blender or food processor and blend just until mixture is smooth and mounds lightly when spooned, about 20 seconds. Serve immediately.

NIGHT-BEFORE PREPARATION TIPS
FOR DAY 20

1. Make Banana Sorbet: Allowing 1 jar per serving, empty as many jars Beech-Nut Stage One bananas as you think you will need into a freezer container with a lid. Freeze overnight to use as instant sorbet in beverages or desserts. As dessert, allow to soften 15 minutes in the refrigerator before serving as sorbet.

2. Presoak peas: Cover 1½ cups dried split peas with water and refrigerate overnight for tomorrow's pea soup recipe.

3. Presoak millet: Heat 1 tablespoon peanut oil in a saucepan and add 1 cup millet; sauté until grain is lightly browned. Add 2 cups boiling water and 1 teaspoon sea salt, stir and remove from heat. Cool slightly, cover and refrigerate overnight.

DAY ✳ 20 THE REINTRODUCTION PHASE (PEAS AND PEANUTS)

ALLOWED FOODS:
Millet, amaranth, bananas, coconut, cranberries, melon, alfalfa sprouts, carrots, green beans, lentils, peas, peanuts, snow peas, spinach, water chestnuts, pork, whitefish, tuna, salmon, ginger, summer savory

MENU	REGULAR	DIET EXPRESS
BREAKFAST	Fresh Melon or Fresh Coconut Carrot Juice Hot Millet with Bananas Amaranth Pancakes Ginger Herbal Tea	Fresh Melon or Fresh Coconut Carrot Juice Puffed Millet with Bananas Ginger Herbal Tea
SNACK	Roasted Peanuts Melon-Banana Cooler	Microwave-Roasted Peanuts
LUNCH	Pea Soup Pork Burgers Peanut Butter Clusters	Superquick Soup Salmon Salad Ginger Dressing Sliced Bananas with Peanut Butter
DINNER	Stuffed Sole Fillets Snow-Pea Salad with Ginger Dressing Caramelized Bananas	Microwaved Fish Fillets Spinach Sauce Hot Millet Three-Pea Salad Banana Split with Peanut Butter Sauce

BULK AGENT: None

REGULAR TRACK

BREAKFAST

Fresh Melon
✳

Fresh Coconut
(See Day Two, Breakfast, Regular Track)
✳

✳

Carrot Juice
(See Breakfast, Diet Express)

✳

Hot Millet with Bananas

✳   SERVES 4

1 teaspoon peanut oil
1 cup raw millet
Dash sea salt
2 teaspoons ground ginger
2 cups water
2 jars Beech-Nut Stage One bananas

Heat oil in a heavy saucepan with a cover. Add millet and sauté over medium heat until millet is lightly browned, about 3 minutes. Stir in salt, ginger and water and bring to boil. Lower heat, cover and simmer 20–30 minutes, or until millet is tender. Add Beech-Nut bananas and heat, stirring, until hot. Spoon cereal into serving bowls. Top with sliced bananas and Heinz banana flakes to taste.

Amaranth Pancakes

✳   SERVES 4

2 cups amaranth flour*
2 cups (approximate) water
1 tablespoon peanut oil plus oil for greasing skillet

Follow directions for Amaranth Pancakes on Day Sixteen, Breakfast, Regular Track, substituting peanut oil for safflower oil and omitting Pineapple Syrup. Serve pancakes today with Beech-Nut Stage One bananas as topping.

*See amaranth flour in list of ingredients for Amaranth Pancakes, Day Sixteen.

Ginger Herbal Tea

✳   SERVES 1

2 teaspoons minced gingerroot
6 ounces boiling water
Heinz banana flakes to taste

Place gingerroot in a mug or cup and add boiling water. Steep 2–5 minutes; sweeten to taste with banana flakes.

SNACK

Roasted Peanuts

✳   SERVES 4

> 2 teaspoons peanut oil
> 2 cups shelled raw peanuts*
> 1 teaspoon sea salt
> 1 teaspoon ground ginger

Preheat oven to 375°F.

Heat oil in a heavy skillet; add peanuts, salt and ginger and sauté 1 minute, until peanuts are coated. Remove peanuts from oil with a slotted spoon; arrange peanuts in a single layer on a nonstick baking sheet. Bake 10–15 minutes, stirring often, until browned. Transfer to a bowl and cool.

*Peanuts are perishable foods and can become rancid if left at room temperature too long. Buy them fresh and refrigerate them in an airtight container.

Melon-Banana Cooler

✳   SERVES 1

> 1 cup chopped, seeded,* chilled watermelon (rind
>   removed) or 1 (2-ounce) scoop Banana Sorbet (see
>   Night-Before Preparation Tips for Day Twenty)
> 1 small, very ripe banana, peeled
> 1 ice cube, crushed
> Pinch ground ginger

Combine all ingredients in a blender. Blend until smooth and serve.

*You do not have to remove the white seeds.

LUNCH

Pea Soup

✳   SERVES 4

> 1½ quarts water
> 1 teaspoon sea salt
> 1½ pounds pork neck bones or meaty spareribs

1½ cups rinsed, drained, presoaked dried split peas (see
    Night-Before Preparation Tips for Day Twenty)
2 large fresh carrots, pared and sliced
2 teaspoons crumbled fresh summer savory

In a large saucepan, bring water and salt to boil. Add pork bones, lower heat and simmer, covered, 20–30 minutes, until meat is no longer pink. Remove bones, strain broth. Cut meat from bones and set aside. Return broth to a clean saucepan. Add peas, carrots, savory and salt to taste; bring to boil. Lower heat and simmer, uncovered, 1 hour, stirring occasionally. Purée soup in batches in blender or food processor and return to pot. Add meat and correct seasonings. Serve hot.

MW—Place bones and 1 cup water in a large, shallow microwave-safe casserole. Cover and cook (H) 10 minutes. Rearrange bones in casserole after half cooking time, for even cooking. Remove bones, strain broth. Cut meat from bones and set aside. To strained broth, add enough water to make 1½ cups broth. Return broth to clean casserole, add presoaked peas (rinsed and drained), carrots and savory. Stir well to combine. Cover and cook (H) 5 minutes. Stir and cook (H) 5 minutes more, covered, or until peas are tender. Purée soup in blender. Add cooked pork and season to taste with sea salt and savory.

Pork Burgers

SERVES 4

Sea salt
2 teaspoons ground summer savory
1 pound ground pork
4 teaspoons natural-pack* peanut butter (optional)

Sprinkle a large, heavy skillet lightly with sea salt and heat it to very hot. Mix savory into ground pork; shape into 4 thick burgers. Place burgers in hot skillet and cook about 4 minutes each side until pork is fully cooked. If desired, put 1 teaspoon peanut butter on top of each burger before serving.

*"Natural-pack" means peanut butter has been packed in its own oil, without added ingredients. Many commercial peanut butters remove peanut oil during processing and replace it with vegetable oil. Some butters are also sweetened with corn syrup. Read label before buying. There are a number of natural-pack brands in most markets. Mix peanut butter to reincorporate oil; natural-pack butters separate in containers and must be mixed before using.

Peanut Butter Clusters

✳   MAKES ABOUT 2 DOZEN CLUSTERS

1 cup chunky-style natural-pack* peanut butter
1 canister Heinz banana flakes
1 cup puffed millet cereal
½ cup frozen cranberries, defrosted (optional)
1 teaspoon ground ginger
Shredded (fresh or dried) unsweetened coconut or puffed
    millet cereal for coating clusters

Mix peanut butter to reincorporate oil. Mix in banana flakes, millet, cranberries and ginger. Drop peanut-banana mixture by teaspoonfuls into shredded coconut or puffed millet (puffed millet does not have to be crushed). Roll to coat completely. Place clusters on waxed paper and chill 20 minutes or longer before serving.

*See natural-pack peanut butter in list of ingredients for Pork Burgers (see recipe above).

DINNER

Stuffed Sole Fillets

✳   SERVES 4

Peanut oil for greasing baking dish
4 large sole fillets, about 6 ounces each
12 whole fresh green beans, rinsed and trimmed
1 large fresh carrot, pared and cut in thin sticks
½ cup cooked millet*
½ cup crushed raw peanuts
2 teaspoons peanut oil
1 teaspoon each ground ginger and ground summer savory
½ teaspoon sea salt

Preheat oven to 400°F.
    Grease a baking dish with peanut oil. Lay 2 fillets in dish and divide green beans, carrots, millet and half the peanuts between the 2 fillets. Spread filling almost to the edges of fillets. Drizzle with peanut oil, sprinkle with ginger, savory and salt. Cover "stuffing" with remaining 2 fillets. Scatter remaining peanuts on top and drizzle lightly with additional peanut oil. Bake 10–12 minutes, or until fish flakes easily and is browned on top.

*Prepare raw millet according to package directions, using peanut oil, water and sea salt.

✳

Snow-Pea Salad with Ginger Dressing

✳

> *3 cups fresh spinach (washed, patted dry and torn into bite-*
> *size pieces)*
> *1 (10-ounce) package frozen snow peas or 2 cups fresh*
> *snow peas (rinsed and stringed)*
> *1 (10-ounce) package frozen water chestnuts or 1 cup*
> *drained, canned water-pack water chestnuts*
> *1 cup fresh alfalfa sprouts (washed and drained)*
> *1 cup frozen cranberries*
> *½ cup coarsely chopped raw peanuts*
> *Ginger Dressing (recipe follows)*

Combine spinach, snow peas, water chestnuts, alfalfa sprouts and cranberries in a mixing bowl. Toss with Ginger Dressing, sprinkle with peanuts and serve.

Ginger Dressing

✳

> *1 jar Beech-Nut Stage One spinach*
> *2 teaspoons ground ginger*
> *2 teaspoons minced summer savory*
> *1 teaspoon sea salt*
> *¾ cup peanut oil*

In a blender or in a small mixing bowl, blend or whisk together the Beech-Nut spinach, ginger, savory and salt. Blending or whisking constantly, add oil in a stream; blend until dressing is thoroughly combined.

Caramelized Bananas

✳

> *1 teaspoon peanut oil plus oil for greasing baking dish*
> *1 tablespoon Heinz banana flakes*
> *4 tablespoons water*
> *4 small, very ripe bananas*
> *1 teaspoon ground ginger*

Preheat oven to 350°F.
   In a saucepan, heat 1 teaspoon oil, banana flakes and water until hot; lower heat and cook until smooth and caramelized, about 2 minutes. Peel bananas, slice them in half lengthwise and place them

in a baking pan lightly greased with peanut oil. Sprinkle bananas with ginger; pour sauce over them and bake 5 minutes, until golden brown and glazed on top.

DIET EXPRESS

BREAKFAST

Fresh Melon
✳

Fresh Coconut
(See Day Two, Breakfast, Regular Track)
✳

Carrot Juice
✳   SERVES 1

> *6 ounces plain carrot juice*
> *Dash ground ginger*
> *Heinz banana flakes to taste*

Pour carrot juice into a tall glass; add ginger and stir. Sweeten to taste with Heinz banana flakes.

Puffed Millet with Bananas
✳   SERVES 1

> *1½ cups puffed millet cereal*
> *1 small banana, peeled and sliced*
> *1 jar Beech-Nut Stage One bananas*

Place cereal in a bowl; top with sliced banana and Beech-Nut bananas and serve.

Ginger Herbal Tea
(See Breakfast, Regular Track)
✳

✳ ──────────────────────────────────────

SNACK

Microwave-Roasted Peanuts

✳   MAKES 1 CUP

1 tablespoon peanut oil
1 cup shelled peanuts
Sea salt

MW—Place oil in a shallow microwave-safe dish and heat (H) in a
microwave oven until hot, 30 seconds to 1 minute. Add peanuts; stir
until all are coated with hot oil. Return to oven; cook (H) 1 minute.
Stir and cook (H) 30 seconds more, until peanuts are browned and
hot, but not burned. Remove from oven; sprinkle lightly with sea salt.
Drain peanuts on a paper towel and allow to cool before serving.

LUNCH

Superquick Soup

✳   SERVES 1

4 ounces ground pork
1 tablespoon water
½ cup sliced frozen carrots
1 jar Beech-Nut Stage One peas
1 jar Beech-Nut Stage One spinach
¼ cup water
1 teaspoon ground summer savory
Sea salt to taste
Water or carrot juice (optional)

MW—Combine pork and water in a shallow microwave-safe soup
bowl; microwave (H) until pork is no longer pink, about 1 minute. Add
carrots, stir, and cook (H) 1 minute more, until carrots are hot and
tender. Add peas, spinach, water and savory. Stir and cook (H) until
hot, about 1 minute. Season to taste with sea salt and thin with a little
water or carrot juice, if desired. Reheat (H) a few seconds until hot.

Salmon Salad

✳   SERVES 2

½ cup frozen cranberries
½ cup water
6 ounces canned water-pack salmon, drained and flaked

½ cup frozen green peas
½ cup fresh alfalfa sprouts (washed and drained)
½ cup frozen snow peas, defrosted
2 ounces drained, canned water-pack water chestnuts or
*   frozen water chestnuts*
6 whole fresh green beans, washed and trimmed
Ginger Dressing (recipe follows)
1 cup fresh whole-leaf spinach (washed, trimmed, patted
*   dry and torn into bite-size pieces)*
⅓ cup coarsely chopped shelled peanuts

MW—Place the cranberries in a 2-cup microwave-safe measuring cup or bowl; add ½ cup water and microwave (H) 2–3 minutes, until mixture comes to a full boil. Remove from oven and allow to stand at least 5 minutes. In a salad bowl, combine salmon, peas, alfalfa sprouts, snow peas, water chestnuts and green beans. Drain cranberries, reserving juice for Ginger Dressing, and add to salad. Put the spinach on 2 plates. Toss vegetables and cranberries with Ginger Dressing and spoon onto spinach leaves. Sprinkle with peanuts and serve.

Ginger Dressing

*   MAKES ABOUT ¾ CUP

¼ cup cranberry juice (reserved from Salmon Salad [see
*   recipe above])*
2 teaspoons ground ginger
1 teaspoon ground summer savory
½ teaspoon sea salt or to taste
½ cup peanut oil

In a blender or in a small bowl, blend or whisk juice, ginger, savory and salt together until combined. Constantly blending or whisking, add oil in a stream. Process until thoroughly blended.

Sliced Bananas with Peanut Butter

*   SERVES 2

2 firm bananas
*2 tablespoons (approximately) natural-pack peanut butter**

Peel bananas and slice into thick slices. Spoon 1 tablespoon peanut butter on each of 2 dessert plates and serve sliced bananas on the side. Spread banana slices with peanut butter and sprinkle with ginger, if desired.

✳

*See natural-pack peanut butter in list of ingredients for Pork Burgers (see Lunch, Regular Track).

DINNER

Microwaved Fish Fillets

✳   SERVES 1

Peanut oil for greasing casserole plus 1 teaspoon oil
1 (6-ounce) whitefish fillet such as flounder or perch, skinned
1 teaspoon each ground summer savory and ground ginger
¼ cup shelled peanuts, crushed
Spinach Sauce (recipe follows)

MW—Grease a shallow microwave-safe casserole with oil and lay fillet in dish. Sprinkle fillet with savory, ginger and peanuts. Drizzle with 1 teaspoon oil, cover loosely with plastic wrap and cook (H) until fish is opaque, about 3 minutes, depending on thickness of fillet. Remove cooked fillet to a plate and allow to stand while preparing Spinach Sauce. Pour hot sauce over fish and serve.

Spinach Sauce

✳   MAKES ABOUT ½CUP

1 jar Beech-Nut Stage One spinach
1 teaspoon each ground ginger and ground summer savory
1 teaspoon peanut oil
Sea salt to taste

MW—In a microwave-safe bowl or cup, whisk together all ingredients and heat (H) until hot, 1–2 minutes.

Hot Millet

✳   SERVES 1

⅓ cup presoaked millet (see Night-Before Preparation Tips
    for Day Twenty)
⅓ cup boiling water
1 teaspoon peanut oil
Dash sea salt

MW—Remove presoaked millet from soaking dish with a slotted spoon into a microwave-safe 2-cup bowl or cup. Add boiling water, oil and salt; stir to combine. Cover loosely, cook (M) 5–10 minutes, stirring every few minutes, until millet is tender and water is absorbed.

Three-Pea Salad
✻   SERVES 1

> ½ cup frozen black-eyed peas
> ½ cup frozen sweet green peas
> ½ cup frozen snow peas
> ¼ cup water
> 1 teaspoon each ground summer savory and ground ginger
> 2 tablespoons peanut oil
> 1 tablespoon plain carrot juice
> Sea salt to taste
> 1 cup fresh whole-leaf spinach (washed, trimmed, patted
>   dry and torn into bite-size pieces)

Combine peas and water in a small saucepan and bring to boil over medium heat. Sprinkle with savory and ginger and cook until crisp-tender, stirring frequently, about 2 minutes. Remove from heat and drain. Put the spinach on a plate. In a bowl, toss peas with peanut oil and carrot juice. Add sea salt to taste; toss again and spoon onto spinach leaves. Sprinkle with puffed millet cereal for crouton-like crunch.

Banana Split with Peanut Butter Sauce
✻   SERVES 1

> Peanut oil for greasing bowl
> 1 small, ripe banana
> 1 teaspoon ground ginger
> 2 heaping teaspoons chunky-style or smooth natural-pack*
>   peanut butter
> 1 large scoop Banana Sorbet (see Night-Before Preparation
>   Tips for Day Twenty)

MW—Grease a shallow microwave-safe bowl very lightly with peanut oil. Peel the banana, split it lengthwise in half and lay both halves in the dish. Sprinkle bananas evenly with ginger; top each half with a heaping teaspoon of peanut butter. Cook (H) the bananas 2 minutes, or until peanut butter on each banana half melts and bananas are tender and hot. Top with a scoop of Banana Sorbet and serve.

*See natural-pack peanut butter in list of ingredients for Pork Burgers (see Lunch, Regular Track).

✳

NIGHT-BEFORE PREPARATION TIPS
—————— FOR DAY 21 ——————

1. Make Pear Sorbet: Allowing 1 jar per serving, empty as many jars Beech-Nut Stage One pears as you think you will need into a freezer container with a lid. Freeze overnight to use as instant sorbet in beverages or desserts. As dessert, allow to soften 15 minutes in the refrigerator before serving as sorbet.

2. Make turkey stock for Onion Soup: Place 2 turkey legs and 1 sliced yellow onion in a large saucepan, sprinkle the turkey with dry mustard and add 5 cups water. Bring water to boil, lower heat, and simmer until turkey is tender, 1½ hours. Allow to cool and refrigerate, covered, overnight.

DAY 21
✳

THE REINTRODUCTION PHASE
(ONION AND CHIVES)

ALLOWED FOODS:
Oats, mangoes, peaches, pears, rose hips, artichokes, chives, garlic, leeks, lima beans, onions, parsley, white potatoes, squash, watercress, zucchini, turkey, mustard, mint, sunflower oil, sunflower seeds, nutmeg, poppy seeds, sweet basil, thyme, honey, arrowroot, pignoli (pine) nuts

MENU	REGULAR	DIET EXPRESS
BREAKFAST	Plain Pear Juice Hot Oatmeal with Pears Oatmeal Pancakes Mint or Rose Hip Herbal Tea	Plain Pear Juice Quick-Cooking Oatmeal with Pears Mint or Rose Hip Herbal Tea
SNACK	Crunchy Limas Mango-Pear Frappe Pignoli (Pine nuts) and Sunflower Seeds	Crunchy Limas Pear Spritzer
LUNCH	Potato Soup or Onion Soup Herb Burgers with Smothered Onions Honey-Dipped Pears	Brown-Bag Turkey Salad Honey-Dipped Pears

DINNER	Stuffed Turkey Breast with	Quick Squash Soup
	Onion Broth	Glazed Turkey
	Chutney	Turkey Sauté
	Potatoes with Pesto	Watercress and Artichoke
	Watercress and Artichoke	Salad
	Salad	Poached Mangoes and Pears
	Poppy Seed Dressing	with Oatmeal Topping
	Sautéed Pears	

BULK AGENT: Rice bran

REGULAR TRACK

Note: If you had an adverse reaction to oats on Day Ten, follow recipes for Day Two (Elimination Stage) instead, making the following additions to Day Two recipes:

Potato Pancakes (Breakfast, Regular Track): Add ½ cup yellow onion, peeled and minced, to pancake batter before frying.

Autumn Soup (Lunch, Regular Track): Add 1 yellow onion, peeled and sliced, when adding other vegetables to soup.

Vealburgers (Lunch, Regular Track): Add ½ cup yellow onion, peeled and minced, or ½ cup leeks or green onion, washed and minced, to veal and sage before frying.

Veal Chops with Jerusalem Artichokes (Dinner, Regular Track, and Dinner, Diet Express): Add 3 cloves garlic, peeled and crushed, when sautéing artichokes in oil. Remove garlic after chops are cooked and discard.

"Mayo" Dressing (Dinner, Regular Track): Stir in 1 teaspoon frozen minced chives when adding rhubarb "vinegar" and salt.

Veal Pâté on Rice Cakes (Lunch, Diet Express): Stir in 1 teaspoon green onion, washed and minced when combining ingredients for pâté.

Note: Canned, water-pack turkey such as Swanson brand may be used in today's recipes calling for cooked turkey. Drain before using, reserving broth for making soups and gravies.

BREAKFAST

Plain Pear Juice

✳

Not nectar; pure juice such as After the Fall brand.

✳

Note: If you cannot find pure pear juice for today's recipe, thin 1 jar Beech-Nut Stage One pears with 4 ounces water as a substitute (yield: 8 ounces pear juice).

Hot Oatmeal with Pears

✳ SERVES 4

3½ cups water
¼ teaspoon sea salt
1⅓ cups plain regular oatmeal (not quick-cooking)
Plain pear juice (optional)
1 large fresh pear, washed, cored and chopped, but not
    peeled
1 teaspoon ground nutmeg

Bring water and salt to a boil. Stir in oatmeal and reduce heat, simmering cereal until it is desired consistency, about 5 minutes. Add more water or pear juice, if needed. Add chopped pear and nutmeg; stir until combined. Serve with honey to taste.

Oatmeal Pancakes

✳ SERVES 4

1 cup oat bran cereal
½ cup quick-cooking oats
1 teaspoon sunflower oil plus oil for greasing griddle
1 teaspoon nutmeg
¾–1 cup (approximate) water or plain pear juice

In a mixing bowl, combine oat bran cereal, oats, 1 teaspoon oil, nutmeg and ¾ cup water or pear juice. Mix vigorously until batter is thick but pourable and you have beaten in some air to give the pancakes as light a texture as possible. If thinner pancakes are desired, beat in remaining ¼ cup water or pear juice. Lightly grease a griddle or frying pan with sunflower oil and heat over medium-high heat until hot. Using ¼ cup for each pancake, pour batter onto hot griddle; cook on one side until browned and dry. (Air holes will appear in the surface of pancake as it begins to brown and dry.) Turn and brown on other side until pancakes are cooked through. Serve hot with honey or Beech-Nut Stage One pears.

Mint or Rose Hip Herbal Tea

✳   SERVES 1

*1 bag commercial rose hip tea or 2–3 teaspoons dried mint
    leaves and 2 tablespoons chopped peel from a fresh,
    washed pear (optional)
6 ounces boiling water
Honey to taste*

To make mint herbal tea, place mint and pear peel, if desired, in a tea ball or bind them into a small square of cheesecloth with plain white thread. Place the "tea bag" in a mug or cup. Add boiling water and steep until tea is desired strength, about 5 minutes. Sweeten to taste with honey.

Note: Commercial rose hip herbal tea is also allowed today. Brew to desired strength and sweeten to taste with honey.

SNACK

Crunchy Limas
(See Day One, Snack, Diet Express)

✳

Mango-Pear Frappe

✳   SERVES 1

*1 ripe mango or 1 cup frozen sliced peaches
1 small ripe fresh pear, peeled, cored and chopped or 1 jar
    Beech-Nut Stage One pears
Dash nutmeg
1 tablespoon honey or to taste
1 ice cube, crushed
¼ cup plain pear juice (optional)*

Place mango or peaches, pears, nutmeg and honey in a blender or food processor fitted with a steel blade and purée on highest power, 1 minute. Add ice and continue to purée until thick and smooth. Thin with pear juice during processing if a thinner frappe is desired.

✻

Pignoli (Pine Nuts) and Sunflower Seeds

✻

LUNCH

Potato Soup

✻   SERVES 4–6

4 cups turkey stock (see Night-Before Preparation Tips for
*   Day Twenty-One)*
¼ cup sunflower oil
1 large clove garlic, peeled and crushed
3 leeks, white part only, cleaned and julienned
1 yellow onion, peeled and sliced
5 medium white potatoes, peeled and thinly sliced
2 teaspoons sea salt
½ cup frozen chopped chives or chopped fresh chives
*   (rinsed) for garnish*

Remove turkey legs from broth. Refrigerate turkey. Skim broth and set aside. Heat oil in a deep kettle or soup pot and sauté the garlic, leeks and onion until soft and translucent but not brown. Remove garlic clove and discard. Add the potatoes, reserved broth and salt and bring to boil. Lower heat and simmer 35 minutes, or until vegetables are very tender. Purée in a blender or food processor fitted with a steel blade. Return puréed soup to pot and heat until hot, correcting seasoning with sea salt to taste. Serve garnished with fresh or fresh-frozen chopped chives.

Note: Soup can also be chilled after puréeing and served cold. Garnish just before serving with chopped chives.

MW—Heat (H) oil in a 2-quart microwave-safe casserole until hot, about 1 minute. Stir in garlic, leeks and onion, cover, and cook (H) 30 seconds. Stir and cook 20 seconds more, or until vegetables are tender but not burned. Add potatoes and 2½ cups broth (omit salt). Cover and cook (H) 15 minutes, stirring every 5 minutes, until potatoes are very tender. Purée soup as above, adding remaining broth. Return to casserole, cover and cook (H) until hot, about 5 minutes, stirring after 2 minutes. Season to taste with sea salt and garnish with chives.

Onion Soup
✳   SERVES 4–6

Sunflower oil for greasing broiling pan plus ½ cup oil
2 medium zucchini or summer squash,* scrubbed, trimmed
*   and cut in half lengthwise*
1 teaspoon each sea salt and freshly ground mustard seeds
½ teaspoon nutmeg
4 cups turkey stock (see Night-Before Preparation Tips for
*   Day Twenty-One)*
4 medium yellow onions, peeled and thinly sliced

Preheat broiler to hot, 500°F.

Grease a broiling pan and place zucchini or summer squash in pan, cut sides up. Brush the cut sides with 2 teaspoons sunflower oil and sprinkle them lightly with salt, mustard and nutmeg. Broil 3 inches from source of heat until surfaces are toasted brown (about 2 minutes). Set aside while preparing soup. Reduce oven temperature to 400°F. Remove turkey legs from broth. Refrigerate turkey. Skim broth and set aside. Heat remaining oil in a heavy skillet until hot. Add onions and sauté until golden brown. Add stock and bring to boil. Lower heat and simmer 10 minutes, stirring every few minutes. Season to taste with sea salt and freshly ground mustard seeds. Place the toasted zucchini or squash in 1 large or 4 small heatproof casseroles, add the soup and bake until zucchini or squash are tender and golden brown, about 5 minutes.

*Potato slices may be substituted for zucchini or squash in the following manner: Bake a large, scrubbed white potato until it is tender but still firm when pierced with a fork, about 35–40 minutes at 400°F. in a regular oven, or 4 minutes (H) in a microwave oven. Leaving the skin on the potato, slice it in 4 slices of equal thickness, about ¼–½-inch thick. Brush the slices on one side with sunflower oil, season them lightly with sea salt, nutmeg and mustard, and broil them until toasted as directed for zucchini or squash. Add to soup and bake as above.

Herb Burgers with Smothered Onions
✳   SERVES 4

2 large yellow onions, peeled and sliced
2 large cloves garlic, peeled and crushed
1 cup water

*

2 tablespoons sunflower oil
1 teaspoon honey
¼ teaspoon sea salt
1 pound ground turkey
1 teaspoon each ground thyme, freshly ground mustard
    seeds, chopped chives and sea salt
½ teaspoon ground nutmeg

Place onions and garlic in a saucepan, add water and bring to boil. Cover and simmer until tender, about 20 minutes. Drain the onions, reserving the broth, and set onions aside; discard garlic cloves. (Refrigerate reserved onion broth for use in Regular Track dinner recipe, Stuffed Turkey Breast.) Heat half the oil in a heavy skillet, add the drained onions and honey, sprinkle with salt and cook slowly, shaking pan or turning onions until they are light golden brown. Set skillet aside and keep warm. Combine turkey, thyme, mustard seeds, chives, nutmeg and salt and shape into 4 burgers. Heat remaining oil in a clean skillet and heat until hot. Sear burgers on one side 2 minutes. Turn, add a bit more oil if burgers are sticking to pan, and cook 2–3 minutes more, reducing heat slightly to prevent burning. Spoon smothered onions onto serving plates; place burgers on top.

Honey-Dipped Pears

*
SERVES 4–6

1½ cups plain oatmeal (regular or quick-cooking)
1 cup pignoli (pine nuts), finely crushed
1 teaspoon ground nutmeg
1 cup (approximate) honey
4 medium, firm fresh pears, peeled

In a shallow bowl, combine oatmeal, pine nuts and nutmeg. Pour honey into a second bowl. Stand pears upright and slice carefully into long, thick slices. Dip pear slices first in honey and then oatmeal-nut mixture until thoroughly coated. Serve at once, or place on waxed paper in a covered container and chill.

Note: Pears can also be served as a frozen dessert. Prepare pears as above. Wrap coated slices separately in waxed paper and freeze in a covered container. Serve frozen. Drizzle with extra honey, if desired, or pour Beech-Nut Stage One pears over frozen slices as sauce.

✳

DINNER

Stuffed Turkey Breast with Onion Broth

✳   SERVES 4–6

1 (4–5 pound) fresh turkey breast
1½ cups plain regular oatmeal
1 teaspoon minced garlic
¼ cup each chopped fresh parsley and chopped fresh
    chives (rinsed and trimmed)
¼ cup coarsely chopped pignoli (pine nuts) or sunflower
    seeds (optional)
1 teaspoon each sea salt and dry mustard
1 teaspoon ground thyme
½ cup onion-garlic broth (reserved from Herb Burgers with
    Smothered Onions, Lunch, Regular Track) or Onion
    Broth (recipe follows)
2 teaspoons sunflower oil
1 tablespoon sunflower oil mixed with 2 teaspoons dry
    mustard and 1 teaspoon ground thyme until smooth
¼ cup water (omit for microwave version)

Preheat oven to 350°F.

Have butcher prepare turkey breast for stuffing or cut a large pocket in the breast with a sharp knife. Combine oatmeal, garlic, parsley, chives, nuts or seeds, sea salt, mustard and thyme with broth. Stir in 2 teaspoons oil; stuffing should be barely moist. Brush 1 tablespoon seasoned oil over turkey breast and place it in a roasting pan. Roast, uncovered, 20 minutes. Add ¼ cup water to pan, baste breast with drippings and roast 30–45 minutes more, or until a meat thermometer inserted in the thickest part registers 160°. Remove breast to platter and stir juices in pan until combined. Serve with slices of stuffed turkey breast and Chutney (see recipe below).

MW—Bone turkey breast and remove skin, as it will not brown. Grease a large microwave-safe glass baking dish with sunflower oil. Prepare pocket and stuffing as above, omitting salt. Stuff turkey breast. Prepare seasoned oil as above and spread on top of breast. Cook the breast, loosely covered with a waxed paper "tent," on roast setting or on (M) 15 minutes. (If you do not have medium or roast settings, place a microwave-safe glass of water in the oven with the turkey and cook [H].) Rotate dish one quarter turn if you do not have a carousel, and roast 15 minutes more. Allow cooked breast to rest 10 minutes before slicing. Serve with Chutney (see recipe below).

Onion Broth

MAKES ¾ CUP

½ tablespoon sunflower oil
½ yellow onion, peeled and diced
⅛ cup diced fresh parsley (washed)
¼ teaspoon sea salt or to taste
⅛ teaspoon ground thyme
¾ cup water

Heat oil in a skillet until hot. Add onion, parsley, salt and thyme and sauté until the onion is translucent and tender but not browned, about 5 minutes. Stir in water and simmer, partially covered, until onion flavor is fully rendered, about 15 minutes. Purée in a blender, or leave diced vegetables whole for a more textured broth.

Chutney

MAKES 2–3 CUPS

2 ripe fresh mangoes, peeled, seeded and chopped or 2
    cups frozen sliced peaches
1 fresh pear, peeled, cored and chopped
¼ cup sweet onion, peeled and chopped
⅓ cup honey
¼ cup water
1 teaspoon freshly ground mustard seeds
½ teaspoon salt
1 teaspoon ground nutmeg

In a 2-quart saucepan, combine mangoes or peaches, pears, onions, honey and water; cook over medium-low heat, stirring, 5 minutes. Add remaining ingredients and bring to boil, stirring constantly. Reduce heat and simmer over very low heat, uncovered, about 20 minutes, or until chutney is thickened. Stir frequently and check to make sure heat is low enough to prevent scorching. Cool; serve chilled or at room temperature.

MW—Combine mangoes or peaches, pears, onions, honey and water in a 2-quart microwave-safe casserole. Stir and cook (H) to boiling, about 2 minutes. Stir in remaining ingredients, cover loosely and cook (L) 7–10 minutes, stirring every 3 minutes, until chutney is thickened.

Potatoes with Pesto

✳   SERVES 4

1 pound new potatoes
Cold water to cover
Dash sea salt
2 tablespoons sunflower oil
4 tablespoons Pesto (recipe follows)

Scrub the potatoes and place them in a large saucepan in water to cover. Add salt, bring to boil, lower heat and simmer until tender, about 15 minutes. Drain, and when cool enough to handle but still warm, cut each potato into quarters. Place potatoes in a bowl and sprinkle with sunflower oil. Add Pesto and toss gently, coating potatoes with sauce. Serve at once or at room temperature.

Pesto

✳   MAKES ABOUT 1½ CUPS

2 bunches fresh parsley, rinsed, trimmed and chopped
½ cup fresh sweet basil, rinsed, trimmed and chopped
½ cup minced fresh or frozen chives
3 cloves garlic, peeled and crushed
1 teaspoon sea salt
½ cup pignoli (pine nuts)
½–¾ cup sunflower oil

Place all ingredients except oil in a blender or processor fitted with a steel blade. Add 2 tablespoons of the oil and process on high power 1 minute, scraping down the sides of the container after 30 seconds. Gradually add remaining oil until sauce is the consistency of mayonnaise. Pour into a jar and chill.

Note: Pesto can also be spread on slices of fresh zucchini or squash toasted as for Onion Soup (see Lunch, Regular Track) or fried in sunflower oil.

Watercress and Artichoke Salad

✳   SERVES 4

1 (10-ounce) package frozen artichoke hearts
Sea salt
Water
2 bunches watercress
Poppy Seed Dressing (recipe follows)
Sunflower seeds or pignoli (pine nuts) (optional)

✳

Cook artichoke hearts according to package directions, using sea salt and water. Drain and set aside to cool. Wash watercress and pick over for brown edges and stems. Pat dry with paper towels. Toss reserved hearts and watercress with Poppy Seed Dressing, top with seeds or nuts, if desired, and serve.

Poppy Seed Dressing

✳   MAKES ABOUT 1 CUP

¼ cup minced, peeled sweet onion
1 teaspoon dry mustard
1 teaspoon sea salt
⅓ cup plain pear juice or ¼ cup Beech-Nut Stage One pears
  mixed with enough water to make ⅓ cup
¾ cup sunflower oil
1 teaspoon poppy seeds

Put all ingredients except oil in a blender or food processor fitted with a steel blade. Adding oil a little at a time, process until thoroughly blended.

Sautéed Pears

✳   SERVES 4

1 tablespoon sunflower oil
3 large, firm fresh pears, washed, cored and sliced, but not
  peeled
1 teaspoon ground nutmeg
⅓ cup honey
4 (2-ounce) scoops Pear Sorbet (see Night-Before
  Preparation Tips for Day Twenty-One)

Heat oil in a large skillet. Add pears to skillet in a single layer, sprinkle with nutmeg and cook over low heat 5 minutes. Turn pear slices carefully, stir in honey and heat until sauce is hot. Serve warm over scoops of Pear Sorbet.

MW—Heat (H) oil in a 2-quart microwave-safe casserole until hot, about 10 seconds. Add pears and nutmeg; stir and cook (H) 1–2 minutes, until pears are tender when pierced with a fork. Stir in honey and heat (L) just until hot, 1 minute more.

⁜

DIET EXPRESS

BREAKFAST

Plain Pear Juice
(See Breakfast, Regular Track)

⁜

Quick-Cooking Oatmeal with Pears
⁜

SERVES 1

> ³/₄ cup water
> ¹/₃ cup quick-cooking oatmeal
> 1 fresh pear, washed, cored and sliced, but not peeled or ¹/₂
>   cup frozen sliced peaches
> Dash nutmeg
> Honey to taste

MW—Combine water and oatmeal in a microwave-safe bowl and heat (H) until mixture boils, 1–2 minutes. Stir in pear or peach slices and nutmeg, cook (L) 2–3 minutes more, until cereal is desired consistency. Serve with honey to taste.

Variation:

> ¹/₂ cup Beech-Nut Stage One oatmeal cereal
> 1 jar Beech-Nut Stage One pears
> ¹/₄ cup plain pear juice
> ¹/₂ cup chopped fresh unpeeled pears (washed and cored)
> Dash nutmeg
> Honey to taste

In a cereal bowl, mix cereal with Beech-Nut pears and pear juice until cereal is consistency desired. Stir in chopped pears and nutmeg; sweeten to taste with honey.

Mint or Rose Hip Herbal Tea
(See Breakfast, Regular Track)

⁜

SNACK

Crunchy Limas
(See Day One, Snack, Diet Express)

*

Pear Spritzer
*

SERVES 1

> 4 ounce Mint or Rose Hip Herbal Tea (see Breakfast, Regular
>   Track) cooled
> 4 ounces plain pear juice,* chilled
> 2 ounces sparkling mineral water, chilled
> Honey to taste
> 1 (2-ounce) scoop Pear Sorbet (see Night-Before
>   Preparation Tips for Day Twenty-One)

Combine tea, pear juice, and mineral water. Sweeten to taste with honey and add sorbet.

*Substitute 3 ounces Beech-Nut Stage One pears mixed with 1 ounce water, if preferred.

LUNCH

Brown-Bag Turkey Salad
*

SERVES 1

Sweet and Sour Dressing:

> 2 ounces plain pear juice or Beech-Nut Stage One pears
> 1 teaspoon water
> 1 teaspoon dry mustard
> 1/4 teaspoon ground thyme
> 1/4 cup sunflower oil

In a small bowl, whisk all ingredients together until thoroughly combined. Pour dressing into a 4-cup container with a lid.

Salad:

> ¼ cup thinly sliced, peeled sweet red onion
> Sea salt
> 1 small zucchini, scrubbed, trimmed and sliced
> 1 small summer squash, scrubbed, trimmed and sliced
> 4 ounces canned water-pack turkey, drained
> 1 small bunch watercress, washed and trimmed
> 1 tablespoon pignoli (pine nuts) (optional)

Layer onions on top of Sweet and Sour Dressing in container and sprinkle with salt. Layer zucchini on top; sprinkle with salt. Repeat layering with squash and turkey, sprinkling each lightly with salt. Cover turkey with watercress; sprinkle pignoli over all. Do not sprinkle watercress and nuts with salt. Cover container and chill. Toss just before serving.

Honey-Dipped Pears
(See Lunch, Regular Track)

✳

DINNER

Quick Squash Soup

✳   SERVES 1–2

> 1 teaspoon sunflower oil
> ½ small yellow onion, peeled and diced
> ½ teaspoon dry mustard
> ½ cup water
> 2 jars Beech-Nut Stage One squash
> Sea salt to taste

MW—Place oil in a shallow microwave-safe bowl and heat (H) until hot, about 5 seconds. Add onion, stir and cook (H) 30 seconds more or until onion is translucent, but not browned. In a measuring cup, mix mustard and water until smooth; stir into onion and cook (L) 1 minute. Add squash, stir, and cook (H) until hot, about 1 minute more. Add salt to taste and serve.

Glazed Turkey

SERVES 1–2

Sunflower oil for greasing pan plus 1 tablespoon
 (approximate) oil
½ fresh mango, peeled and chopped or ½ cup chopped
 frozen sliced peaches*
¼ cup water
¼ teaspoon dry mustard
¼ teaspoon ground nutmeg
2 tablespoons honey
½ pound fresh turkey tenderloin, sliced about ½ inch thick
Sea salt to taste

Preheat broiler to hot.

Grease a broiling pan with sunflower oil. In a small bowl, combine mangoes or peaches, water, mustard, nutmeg and honey until blended. Lay turkey slices in prepared pan and brush them all over with 1 tablespoon sunflower oil. Broil 3–4 inches from heat 2 minutes; turn slices and broil 2 minutes more. Brush turkey slices with glaze. Broil 2 minutes on one side, turn, and brush other side with glaze. Broil again until turkey is done, about 5 minutes total cooking time, brushing each few minutes with glaze. Salt to taste after cooking.

*1 jar Beech-Nut Stage One peaches may be substituted for frozen peaches; omit water.

Turkey Sauté

SERVES 1–2

3 tablespoons sunflower oil plus 1 teaspoon additional oil, if
 needed
1 small yellow onion, peeled and thinly sliced
1 tablespoon chopped frozen chives
1 teaspoon dry mustard mixed with 1 tablespoon water
 until smooth
¾ cup (approximate) oat bran or quick-cooking oatmeal
1 teaspoon ground thyme
½ pound fresh turkey tenderloin, sliced ½ inch thick
1 large white potato, scrubbed, but not peeled, and thinly
 sliced
½ teaspoon each dry mustard and sea salt

Heat 1 tablespoon oil in a heavy skillet, add onion and chives and sauté 5 minutes over medium heat, until onion is translucent but not browned. Stir in mustard and water mixture and sauté 1 minute more. Remove from heat and keep warm. In a small bowl, combine oat bran or oatmeal, thyme and salt. In a clean skillet, heat 2 tablespoons oil until hot. Rinse turkey slices briefly in water and shake dry until they are moist, but not dripping. Dip turkey slices in seasoned oats until they are coated. Add to hot oil and fry about 5 minutes each side, until turkey slices are crisp and browned and no longer pink in the middle. Remove turkey to a warm plate. Add 1 teaspoon additional oil to the skillet if needed and heat again until hot, scraping up browned bits left from turkey. Add potatoes and cook in a single layer about 5 minutes, sprinkling with mustard and salt. Turn potatoes and cook on other side until tender and browned, about 5 minutes more. Stir onion-chive mixture into potatoes and heat until hot. Serve with turkey slices and Beech-Nut Stage One pears as condiment.

Watercress and Artichoke Salad
(See Dinner, Regular Track)

✳

Poached Mangoes and Pears with Oatmeal Topping
✳   SERVES 1–2

2 ripe fresh mangoes, peeled, seeded and chopped or 1 cup
    frozen sliced peaches
1 small firm fresh unpeeled pear, washed, cored and
    chopped
1 teaspoon ground nutmeg
½ cup water
⅓ cup honey or to taste
Pear Sorbet (see Night-Before Preparation Tips for Day
    Twenty-One)
Oatmeal Topping (recipe follows)

MW—Combine mangoes or frozen peaches, pears, nutmeg and water in a microwave-safe casserole with a cover. Stir, cover and heat (H) to boiling, 2–3 minutes. Stir in honey and cook (L) until fruits are tender, 5–8 minutes more, stirring after 3 minutes. Cool slightly; spoon over scoops of Pear Sorbet and sprinkle with Oatmeal Topping.

Note: Fruits can also be poached in a saucepan on the stove. Stir fruits into ½ cup water and sprinkle with nutmeg. Bring to boil, reduce heat and simmer, uncovered, until tender, 10–15 minutes. Add honey, stir and simmer until very tender, about 5 minutes more.

✳

Oatmeal Topping

✳   MAKES ABOUT 1½ CUPS

Sunflower oil for greasing baking sheet
1 cup plain regular oatmeal (not quick-cooking)
½ cup coarsely chopped combination sunflower seeds and
    pignoli (pine nuts)
1 teaspoon ground nutmeg
¼ cup (approximate) sunflower oil

Heat oven to 350°F.

Grease a baking sheet with oil. Combine oatmeal, seeds, nuts and nutmeg with enough sunflower oil barely to moisten. Bake on prepared baking sheet about 5 minutes, until browned and crisp. Stir mixture after 3 minutes, checking to make sure topping does not burn. Cool slightly; drain on paper towel until crisp and completely cooled.

DAY 22 ✳   THE REINTRODUCTION PHASE (RECOVERY DAY)

ALLOWED FOODS:
Barley, plums, apricots, mammees, chestnuts, hearts of palm, collards, kale, eggplant, white kidney beans, wax beans, rabbit, frogs' legs, marjoram, sorrel, anise, Puritan oil, arrowroot, palm sugar, barley malt sugar, gelatin

MENU	REGULAR	DIET EXPRESS

BREAKFAST	Fresh Mammees
	Barley Cereal with Fruit
	Barley Socca (Italian
	   Flatbread)
	Plum Herbal Tea
		Fresh Mammees
		Instant Barley Cereal with
		   Fruit
		Plum Herbal Tea

SNACK	Crunchy Bean Nuts Plum or Apricot Spritzer	Microwave-Roasted Chestnuts Plum or Apricot Spritzer
LUNCH	Creamy Chestnut Soup Eggplant Caviar Fresh Fruit Mousse	Brown-Bag Salad Sorrel Vinaigrette Fresh Apricots

DINNER   Frogs' Legs with Herbs   Quick Stir-Fry with Quick
Rabbit with Plums or Apricots   White Beans
Baked Barley   Broiled Rabbit and Eggplant
Stir-Fried Collards   Quick Fruit Compote
Hearts of Palm Salad
Plum Vinegar Dressing
Barley Pudding

BULK AGENT: None

REGULAR TRACK

Note: Barley malt sugar or syrup is made from grain steeped in water and allowed to germinate; enzymes involved in the process may cause adverse reactions. Palm sugar is a safer choice. It is sold in many shops specializing in Asian cuisine.

BREAKFAST

Fresh Mammees*

✳   SERVES 4

2 mammees
Barley malt sugar to taste

Rinse and cut mammees in half; cut fruit into bite-size sections, leaving skins intact. Serve with sugar to taste.

*Mammees are a large, brown-skinned fruit with a soft, smooth, orange flesh and sweet flavor. If you can't find mammees, kiwi fruit may be substituted.

Barley Cereal with Fruit

✳   SERVES 4

3 cups water
1 cup quick-cooking barley
1 teaspoon Puritan oil
3 fresh purple plums or fresh apricots, washed, pits
    removed and chopped
Barley malt sugar or palm sugar to taste

✳

Over direct heat, bring water to boil in the top of a double boiler. Stir in barley, oil and fruit and place over moderately boiling water. Cover and cook until cereal is thick and creamy, 20–30 minutes. Stir occasionally; add more water if needed. Serve with sugar to taste.

Barley Socca (Italian Flatbread)

✳   SERVES 4

> 1 cup barley flour*
> 1 cup (approximate) water
> 1 tablespoon Puritan oil plus oil for greasing baking sheet
> Sea salt

Preheat broiler.

Combine flour with water and 1 tablespoon oil. Beat well by hand or blend in food processor on high power using a steel blade until a smooth, waffle-like batter is formed. Spread batter on prepared baking sheet; sprinkle lightly with sea salt. Place bread in center of oven. Broil 3–5 minutes, until bread starts to brown at the edges. Serve hot or wrap in foil or plastic wrap and refrigerate. Serve with Eggplant Caviar at lunch.

*To make barley flour, place 2 cups (approximate) raw pearl barley (not quick-cooking) in a food processor fitted with a steel blade and process on highest speed, 10–15 minutes, until flour is ground. Sift and regrind if necessary, until sifted flour measures 1 cup.

Note: Barley flour is sold in some health food and natural food stores.

Plum Herbal Tea

✳   SERVES 1

> 1 small purple plum, washed
> ¼ teaspoon whole anise seeds
> 10 ounces boiling water
> Barley malt sugar or palm sugar to taste

Peel the plum (eat the fruit or refrigerate it in an airtight container for use later in the day). Chop peel coarsely and place it with anise seeds in a small, clean teapot. Add water and allow tea to steep 2–5 minutes; 5 minutes produces a strong-flavored tea. Stir and pour tea into a cup. Sweeten to taste with sugar.

SNACK

Crunchy Bean Nuts

✻   MAKES ABOUT 1½ CUPS

*1 (12–16-ounce) can water-pack white kidney beans with
    liquid
Puritan oil for greasing baking sheet*

Preheat oven to 400°F.

Drain the beans, reserving liquid (refrigerate for later use). Spread beans on a paper towel and pat dry. Oil a baking sheet with Puritan oil; spread beans in a single layer on prepared pan. Bake until beans are roasted and crisp, about 20 minutes. Stir after 10 minutes; do not allow to overbrown. Cool slightly; spread beans on absorbent paper to cool completely before serving.

Plum or Apricot Spritzer

✻   SERVES 1

*4 ounces Plum Herbal Tea (see recipe above, Breakfast,
    Regular Track)
1 tablespoon Sugar Syrup (recipe follows)
Ice
2 ounces mineral water
1 ripe fresh apricot or small fresh purple plum, peeled, pit
    removed and cut in half*

In a large goblet or soda glass, combine tea and Sugar Syrup. Stir well to blend; add ice and sparkling water and stir again, until very cold. Remove ice and float plum or apricot on top.

Sugar Syrup

✻   MAKES 1 CUP

*1 cup barley malt sugar or palm sugar
1 cup water*

Combine sugar and water in a small, heavy saucepan and bring to boil. Reduce heat, and simmer, stirring constantly, until sugar is completely dissolved. Cool; stir again before using.

✳

LUNCH

Creamy Chestnut Soup

✳
                                                    SERVES 4

¾ pound Roasted Chestnuts (recipe follows)
3 cups (approximate) water
1 teaspoon dried marjoram
1 can (12–16-ounce) water-pack white kidney beans with
    liquid
1 teaspoon Puritan oil
Sea salt to taste

Place the chestnuts in a large soup pot. Fill the pot with enough water to cover nuts to the depth of 2 inches. Add marjoram and bring to boil. Cover and simmer over low heat until chestnuts are tender, about 30 minutes. Drain the nuts and place them in a blender or food processor fitted with a steel blade. Add the kidney beans with liquid from can; pureé the mixture until smooth. Return purée to a clean saucepan, add oil and reheat to hot, stirring and adding water until soup is desired consistency. Salt to taste and serve.

Roasted Chestnuts

✳
                                        MAKES ABOUT 2 CUPS NUTS

¾ pound raw chestnuts
1 teaspoon Puritan oil

Preheat oven to 350°F.
   With a sharp knife, make a slash in the flat side of each chestnut. Place the nuts in a bowl and toss them with oil until coated. Spread the nuts on a nonstick baking pan and roast until shells and inner skins can be easily removed, about 15 minutes. Wrap nuts in a clean dish towel and allow them to cool. Using the towel as aid, rub off shells and skins.

Eggplant Caviar

✳
                                                    SERVES 4–6

Puritan oil for greasing broiling pan plus 3 tablespoons oil
1 medium eggplant

*

1 teaspoon sea salt or to taste
⅓ cup finely minced fresh sorrel (washed)
½ cup drained, water-pack white kidney beans

Preheat broiler.

Grease pan with oil and broil eggplant, 5–6 inches from heat, turning often, for 30–45 minutes or until skin is blackened and pulp is very tender. Wrap the hot eggplant in a clean dish towel; cool it completely. Peel and mince the eggplant pulp and place it in a large bowl. Add 3 tablespoons oil, salt and sorrel; stir until combined. Place the kidney beans in a blender or food processor fitted with a steel blade; purée or blend until smooth. Add puréed beans to eggplant mixture, stir gently to combine and refrigerate 2–3 hours. Serve with Barley Socca (reserved from Breakfast, Regular Track).

MW—Pare eggplant and cut it into strips. Place in a shallow microwave-safe dish, add ¼ cup water and cook (H), loosely covered, until eggplant is tender, 5–8 minutes. Stir after half cooking time. Cool and mince, and proceed with recipe as above.

Note: Another quick method of cooking eggplant is to steam the pared eggplant strips in a colander or vegetable steamer over boiling water until tender, about 7–10 minutes. Cool and mince.

Fresh Fruit Mousse

*   SERVES 4

2 cups chopped ripe fresh plums or fresh apricots (washed
*   and pitted)*
⅔ cup water plus 2 tablespoons (approximate) cold water
⅓ cup barley malt sugar or palm sugar plus 1 tablespoon
*   barley malt sugar or palm sugar*
¼ teaspoon arrowroot mixed with 1½ teaspoons water
1 envelope Knox unflavored gelatin

Combine fruit, ⅓ cup water and ⅓ cup sugar in a saucepan and bring to boil. Reduce heat to low and simmer until sugar is completely dissolved. Whisk in arrowroot mixture and cook 3 minutes more over low heat. Set aside to cool. Place ⅓ cup water and 1 tablespoon sugar in a small saucepan and sprinkle gelatin on top. Allow gelatin to soften 1 minute. Beating constantly with a hand electric mixer, bring to boil over direct heat. Remove from heat when gelatin is dissolved and continue to whip, adding cold water a few drops (about 2

✳

tablespoons) at a time, until gelatin stands in soft peaks. Fold in cooked fruits with syrup and serve at once or chill in individual serving dishes until ready to eat. Gelatin rises to the top of this pudding and serves as a whipped topping when set.

DINNER

Frogs' Legs with Herbs

✳
SERVES 4

  4 jumbo frogs' legs, trimmed
  4 cups (approximate) water
  4 tablespoons Puritan oil for brushing frogs' legs plus ½ cup
      oil
  1 cup barley flour (see Barley Socca, Breakfast, Regular
      Track) or Beech-Nut Stage One barley cereal* for
      dredging
  ¼ cup minced fresh sorrel (washed)
  Sea salt to taste

Soak frogs' legs in water 2 hours. Drain and dry well. Brush each frog's leg lightly with oil and dredge with flour. Add ½ cup oil to a skillet to the depth of ¼ inch and heat until hot. Add frogs' legs and fry, turning frequently, 6–8 minutes, until browned and cooked through. Transfer frogs' legs to a hot platter, sprinkle with minced sorrel and sea salt and serve.

Note: A quick method of soaking frogs' legs is to place them in water to cover and bring to boil. Remove from heat and allow to cool. Drain and dry well.

*Beech-Nut Stage One barley cereal contains soy oil. If sensitivity to soy is known or suspected, do not use.

Rabbit with Plums or Apricots

✳
SERVES 4

  4 pieces rabbit*
  ½ teaspoon sea salt
  1 teaspoon ground marjoram

*4 fresh purple Italian plums or 4 large fresh apricots,
    washed, pits removed and chopped*
¼ teaspoon anise seeds
2 tablespoons water, if needed

Preheat oven to 350°F.

Arrange rabbit pieces in a baking dish, sprinkle lightly with salt and marjoram and bake 20 minutes, basting often with juices rendered during cooking. Add fruit and anise seeds; add water if all liquid in the pan has cooked away. Bake 20–25 minutes longer.

*Frozen domestic rabbit such as Pel-Freeze brand is recommended. Domestic rabbit tastes much like chicken, and because it is tender, does not have the "gamey" flavor of wild rabbit.

Baked Barley

✳   SERVES 4

1 cup raw pearl barley (not quick-cooking)
3 cups water
1 teaspoon sea salt
1 tablespoon Puritan oil

Preheat oven to slow, 300°F.

Place barley in a heavy casserole. Add half the water, oil and the salt. Stir, cover tightly and bake 45 minutes. Add remaining water, cover and bake 45 minutes longer, or until barley is tender.

Stir-Fried Collards

✳   SERVES 4

2 tablespoons Puritan oil
*4 cups chopped fresh or frozen collard greens (washed and
    trimmed)*
½ teaspoon sea salt
1 teaspoon ground marjoram
1 tablespoon water

Heat oil in a skillet until hot, add collards and sprinkle with sea salt and marjoram. Add water and stir-fry over medium heat until collards are wilted and tender-crisp, about 5 minutes. Correct seasoning and serve.

Hearts of Palm Salad

SERVES 4

1 (12-ounce) can water-pack hearts of palm, rinsed and
    drained
Plum Vinegar Dressing (recipe follows)
12 leaves fresh kale or fresh collard greens, washed,
    trimmed and patted dry

Place hearts of palm in bowl and toss with Plum Vinegar Dressing.
Arrange greens on salad plates and spoon hearts of palm on top.

Plum Vinegar Dressing

MAKES ABOUT ¾ CUP

1 fresh purple plum
¼ cup boiling water
¼ teaspoon each sea salt and ground marjoram
¼ cup minced fresh sorrel (washed)
½ cup Puritan oil

Wash and peel the plum. Reserve the peel. Remove and discard pit;
chop the fruit coarsely and set aside. To make plum "vinegar," place
reserved peel in a glass measuring cup and pour boiling water on top.
Steep 5 minutes; remove peel and discard. In a blender or small bowl,
whisk or blend together the plum "vinegar," salt, marjoram, sorrel
and oil until thoroughly combined. Stir in chopped plum just before
adding to salad. (Reserve 1 tablespoon, if desired, to use in Sorrel
Vinaigrette, Lunch, Diet Express.)

Barley Pudding

SERVES 4–6

1 cup raw pearl barley (not quick-cooking)
3½ cups water
1 teaspoon ground marjoram
⅓ cup palm sugar or barley malt sugar plus ½ cup sugar
1 tablespoon Puritan oil
8 large fresh Italian purple plums or 8 fresh apricots,
    washed, pitted, but not peeled

Preheat oven to slow, 300°F.
    Place the barley in a heavy casserole and add 1½ cups water. Stir,
cover tightly and bake 45 minutes. Add additional 1½ cups water,

✳

marjoram, ⅓ cup sugar and oil. Stir, recover and bake 45 minutes longer. Stir occasionally and cool after cooking. Place cooled barley in a large bowl or food processor fitted with a steel blade. Mash by hand or process until barley is the texture of rice pudding. Spoon into a serving bowl, cover and chill. Place fruit in a saucepan with remaining ½ cup water and remaining ½ cup sugar. Bring to a boil, stirring. Lower heat and continue to cook over low heat, stirring constantly, until sugar is completely dissolved and fruit is tender, about 10 minutes. Cool slightly, pour over barley. Cover and chill 1 hour or more. Spoon pudding and fruit compote sauce from glass bowl.

MW—Place 1 cup quick-cooking barley and 2 cups water in a large casserole. Cook (H) until mixture boils, about 4 minutes, stirring after 2 minutes. Cover and cook 10 minutes longer (L), stirring after 5 minutes. Stir in marjoram, sugar and oil, and cook (L) covered 5 minutes more, or until barley is creamy and tender. Add ¼ cup additional water during last 5 minutes of cooking if barley seems dry. Allow cooked barley to cool to room temperature and proceed with recipe as above.

Note: Cooking regular pearl barley in a microwave oven is not recommended.

DIET EXPRESS

BREAKFAST

Fresh Mammees
(See Breakfast, Regular Track)

✳

Instant Barley Cereal with Fruit

✳

SERVES 1

½ cup Beech-Nut Stage One barley cereal*
3 teaspoons palm sugar or barley malt sugar
1 fresh purple plum or 2 fresh apricots, washed, pits
removed and chopped
¾ cup boiling water

✳

Combine all ingredients in a large cereal bowl and mix until smooth.

MW—For extra creaminess and fuller flavor, combine all ingredients in a microwave-safe bowl and microwave (L) 2–3 minutes after mixing.

*Beech-Nut Stage One and Gerber barley cereals both contain soy oil. If sensitivity to soy is known or suspected, substitute Barley Cereal with Fruit (see Breakfast, Regular Track) instead of Beech-Nut cereal.

Plum Herbal Tea
(See Breakfast, Regular Track)

✳

SNACK

Microwave-Roasted Chestnuts

✳   SERVES 1

> 1 cup drained, canned water-pack chestnuts

MW—Spread chestnuts on a paper towel and pat dry. Place another paper towel on a microwave-safe dish and arrange chestnuts on dish in a single layer. Cover with another paper towel and microwave (H) 5–10 minutes, until chestnuts are roasted, but not burned. Cool slightly, and serve.

Plum or Apricot Spritzer
(See Lunch, Regular Track)

✳

Prepare spritzer according to Regular Track directions. Omit Sugar Syrup, if desired, and substitute 2–3 teaspoons sugar or barley malt sugar.

LUNCH

Brown-Bag Salad

½ cup drained, canned water-pack wax beans
½ cup drained, canned water-pack white kidney beans
1 cup chopped fresh collard greens (washed and trimmed)
1 cup drained, canned water-pack chestnuts
Sorrel Vinaigrette (recipe follows)

Combine all ingredients and toss well. Chill in a covered container until ready to eat.

Sorrel Vinaigrette

MAKES ABOUT ⅔ CUP

1 tablespoon water or plum "vinegar" (see Plum Vinegar
    Dressing, Dinner, Regular Track, for directions)
½ teaspoon sea salt or to taste
⅓ cup snipped fresh sorrel leaves (washed and trimmed)
⅓ cup Puritan oil

In a blender or small bowl, blend or whisk together the water or "vinegar" and salt. Blending or whisking constantly, add sorrel and oil; blend until completely combined.

Fresh Apricots

DINNER

Quick Stir-Fry

SERVES 1–2

3 large frogs' legs*
3 cups water
1 tablespoon Puritan oil
½ cup minced fresh sorrel (washed and dry patted)
½ teaspoon sea salt
1 cup frozen or drained, canned water-pack wax beans

✻ ───

In large saucepan, place frogs' legs in water and bring to boil. Boil 2 minutes, remove from heat and allow to cool in water. Remove frogs' legs from water and pat dry with paper towels. Heat oil in a heavy skillet until hot. Add frogs' legs and fry, turning frequently until evenly browned, 6–8 minutes. Add sorrel to skillet and sprinkle frogs' legs and sorrel with sea salt; sauté 1 minute, until sorrel is wilted but not browned. Add beans and stir-fry until hot. Transfer frogs' legs and vegetables to a platter and serve at once. Serve with Quick White Beans (recipe follows).

*Substitute 2–3 pieces rabbit, cut into strips, for frogs' legs, if desired. Increase stir-frying time to 10 minutes for rabbit.

Quick White Beans

✻   SERVES 1–2

1½ cups undrained, canned water-pack white kidney beans
1 teaspoon Puritan oil
⅓ cup chopped fresh sorrel leaves (washed)
1 teaspoon ground marjoram
Sea salt to taste

In a saucepan, heat beans in liquid from can until hot. Drain, stir in remaining ingredients and heat until hot. Serve with Quick Stir-Fry (see recipe above).

Broiled Rabbit and Eggplant

✻   SERVES 1–2

*2–3 pieces rabbit**
Seasoned Oil (recipe follows)
2 cups pared eggplant

Preheat broiler to hot, 500°F.
Brush rabbit with Seasoned Oil. Broil 6 inches from heat 10 minutes; turn and broil 10 minutes more. Continue to broil rabbit and brush it with oil, turning every few minutes to prevent burning of skin, 25–30 minutes, until rabbit pieces are golden brown and juice from meat runs clear when meat is pierced with a fork. Brush eggplant strips with oil and add to rabbit during last 5 minutes of broiling time, turning once.

*See rabbit in list of ingredients for Rabbit with Plums or Apricots, Dinner, Regular Track.

Seasoned Oil

✳ MAKES ½ CUP

½ teaspoon sea salt
1 tablespoon ground marjoram
½ cup Puritan oil

In a small bowl, whisk all ingredients together until thoroughly combined.

Quick Fruit Compote

✳ SERVES 1–2

4 large fresh Italian purple plums or fresh apricots, washed,
*   pits removed and cut in half*
½ cup palm sugar or barley malt sugar
½ cup water
¼ teaspoon anise seeds

Place fruit in a saucepan with sugar, water and anise seeds. Stirring constantly, bring to boil. Lower heat and cook, stirring, until sugar is completely dissolved. Remove from heat, cool slightly, and spoon into shallow dessert bowls.

Appendix

For readers interested in a more in-depth look at the scientific underpinnings of *The Allergy Discovery Diet,* the following material provides a complete description of the underlying hypotheses and experimental work.

What Do We Mean by Allergy?

There have been many definitions of allergy since the term was first used by Von Pirquet in 1906. However, the most useful definition has been that of Dr. B. Robert Feldman: "Allergy is simply an abnormal response of the body to a substance that is ordinarily harmless for most people."[14] For the most part, the allergic reactions that will concern us are produced by the effects of antibodies. The nature of antibodies and how they vary, the ways in which different antibodies combine with antigens, other antibodies and various cells to produce many types of biological reactions are the substance of this discussion. There is, however, another whole category of important allergic reactions that are produced by certain types of cells (lymphocytes) without the intervention of antibodies. The relation of these reactions to food is still too uncertain to be included in our discussion.

An antibody is a protein which has a region which can recognize the special features of a particular substance. You can think of this as the way a gelatin mold would "recognize" gelatin that had come from another mold of the identical sort. The antibody is able to fit together with the region of the antigen to which it corresponds. Antigen is a technical name for the substance which stimulates the production of a specific antibody. Another name for antigen is sometimes "allergen," the substance to which a person is allergic.

Antibodies are produced by special cells called plasma cells, which can be found in the bone marrow, lymph nodes or along the lining of the lung, sinuses, intestinal or genital tracts. The antigen must first be picked up by a scavenger cell called a "macrophage." The macrophage then processes the antigen and with the help of certain lymphocytes (T-cells) activates the plasma cell (B-cell) to secrete the proper antibody. This is a very quick description of a very complicated sequence of events. However, a more detailed description would not help further our understanding of the allergic reactions. Readers who want to pursue this can consult the bibliography at the end of the book.

The antibody has two ends. The one end contains the "gelatin mold" area. This determines the specificity of the antibody. That is, a particular antibody is specific for a uniquely shaped area on the antigen or allergen against which the antibody is directed. An antigen may have many different areas against which different antibodies may be directed. Each of these antibodies would be said to have a different specificity even though they might all be antibodies against strepto-coccus or polio or wheat. Although each of these antibodies is different, there could be regions on dissimilar antigens which resem-ble each other. The antibody could become "confused" and an antibody that is supposed to be directed against a bacterium could cross-react with human tissue.

Of course, some antigens are similar and may share certain regions in common. Antibodies that are made against one of the antigens may very appropriately cross-react with the other antigens. A common example of this is the cross-reactivity between cow's milk and goat's milk. There would be considerably less overlap between giraffe's milk and whale's milk. This overlap can be important because patients who have an allergy to a particular food may have related allergic reactions to other foods in the same family group, even if they have never been directly exposed to that specific food.

The other end of the antibody defines the class of the antibody. There are five major classes of antibody. Each class appears to have a different role in the protection of the body. For the most part, each antibody is made by a different class of plasma cell, which may have a preference for the location in the body where it secretes its antibody product. It is rare to find plasma cells in the bloodstream and most of them appear to do their work at specific tissue sites. The five classes of antibody are IgA (for immunoglobulin A), IgD, IgE, IgG and IgM. IgA and IgG appear to have subclasses but a difference in function of the subclasses is not yet clear.

When a person is exposed to a virus or bacteria, the first class of antibody that is made is IgM. This is a very large molecule which is found both in the blood and in the secretions such as saliva, sputum and the digestive juices. However, this antibody is rather short-lived and in about a week another antibody to the bacteria or virus appears which may be either an IgG- or IgA-class antibody.

IgG is the primary antibody in the blood. This antibody is made in the bone marrow, the spleen and in the lymph nodes. It is the "gamma globulin" which you may have received to protect you against expo-sure to an infectious disease or before traveling to some remote or unhygienic place. In the early days of the study of immunology, it was thought that IgG was the only antibody. Now we know that the mature

*

antibody response in the blood is by IgG antibodies and the mature antibody response in the secretions is by IgA antibodies. In fact, we can date the time of past exposure to an infection such as hepatitis by measuring whether the antibody to the hepatitis virus is IgM or IgG.

IgA is the major mature antibody in secretions. This makes it the antibody of most interest here because it is the antibody that first makes contact with foods to which a person may have an allergy. Secretory IgA (SIgA), which is the form of IgA found in the secretions, is a large molecule formed by hooking together two single (monomer) IgA molecules.

There is a very small amount of SIgA found in the blood, but most of the IgA found in the blood is in the monomeric form. There are two subclasses of monomeric IgA in the blood, but there is no information about what role they play there or why there should be two different kinds. Our real interest will be directed to the SIgA which protects our internal body surfaces.

The mystery antibody is IgD. It is present in the blood in very small amounts and although it was first discovered twenty years ago, its function is still unclear. It appears to have some role in regulating the amount of other types of antibody that is secreted by the plasma cells. How this may be done is not known and whether there are other roles that it plays is similarly unknown. It is in fact only recently that the speculation that IgD has a role in antibody regulation has been conceived.[8]

The antibody that most people, including doctors, think of when discussing allergy is IgE. This is the antibody most often involved in the production of hay fever, hives and the kind of immediate-onset asthma which some people get when they come into close contact with cats or horses. This is the antibody whose presence and strength was originally measured by the familiar skin tests. Now it is possible to measure levels of IgE antibodies by very sophisticated blood tests.

A number of mysteries surround IgE even though allergists have been working with it for almost a century. It is not at all understood why some allergens should provoke IgE antibodies and other allergens provoke IgA or IgG. The pollen of ragweed and the antigens of intestinal parasites are very much more likely to provoke IgE antibodies than any other. It is not clear in what way the antigens may be processed differently by the scavenger macrophage. Another mystery is how the injection of small amounts of antigens can "desensitize" a patient's allergic response. There has been clear and reproducible evidence that the allergist's "shots" do help but we have no real information about the mechanism.

To summarize, antibodies can exist in either the secretions along the internal surfaces of the body or in the blood itself. The former work to prevent the absorption of the "foreign" antigens into the body. They block them at the surface and by joining several antibody molecules together hasten their removal. The antibodies in the blood circulate freely waiting to come in contact with their corresponding antigens. These are the antibodies that protect us from "blood poisoning" or the entrance and circulation of bacteria in the bloodstream. If you get a boil on your arm or pneumonia or a bladder infection, bacteria are constantly being absorbed from the infected area into the bloodstream. If these bacteria were allowed to circulate, the infection could spread to the brain or bones or elsewhere as they do if the patient's "defense mechanisms" are not up to par. The blood antibodies, primarily IgG, localize at the site of the infection and help immobilize the bacteria so the scavenger cells can engulf them. The engulfed bacteria are then killed by special systems inside the cells. This is the way bacterial illnesses have been fought off for the millions of years before the advent of antibiotics. Even now, with very powerful antibiotics, we have learned that if the patient's immune system is not able to respond, antibiotics alone are often not able to eradicate infection.

We have been discussing the effects of antibodies working directly against antigens. There is another and very exciting way that antibodies can work and amplify their effects. We know that IgE is able to produce its effects because it is able to activate a special class of allergic cell called a mast cell. The IgE does this because its "class specific" end, as opposed to its "antigen specific" (gelatin mold) end, binds to a receptor on the surface of the mast cell. In effect, all of the IgE antibody molecules bound to the surface of the mast cell "arm" it for battle. When the specific antigen binds to the IgE antibody on the surface of the mast cell it activates a mechanism. When the concentration of antigens is high enough to activate a critical percentage of the IgE dependent mechanisms the cell is activated and liberates all of the irritating chemicals inside it. These chemicals include a substance called histamine, which is the principal agent of the sneezing and eye tearing of hay fever. Anti-histamines do not prevent the activation of the mast cell but they do reduce or prevent the effect of the main chemical liberated by this activation.

There are other examples of cell membrane-associated antibodies. The technical name for the class specific end of the antibody molecule is the Fc end. This comes historically from the manner in which antibodies were first analyzed chemically. One would digest various parts of them with enzymes and then see what functions were associated with what remaining fragments. Since the class specific end of the antibody is referred to as the Fc end, the receptor to which it attaches on the cell membrane is referred to as the Fc receptor. The Fc receptor on the surface of the mast cell is specific for IgE.

*

There are Fc receptors on the surfaces of red blood cells and platelets which are specific for IgG. Some scientists have thought they have found Fc receptors on platelets for other classes of antibody, but there is no general agreement on this. However, Fc receptors for IgA have been found on certain kinds of liver cells.[39, 41] These appear to have an important role in the removal of immune complexes containing IgA.

Based on experimental findings in other mammals, there also appears to be a diversity of mast cells. It is possible that different classes of mast cells might carry Fc receptors for different immunoglobulins. The point of this discussion is that the body has a great diversity of antibodies. There is a diversity of antigen specificity and there is a diversity of cell membrane-associated antibodies. The body is able to mount a variety of different responses to a single antigen. It is also able to respond to different stimulating antigens with a single response. The antibody system has a "language" of its own with which it can respond to the world around it with a complexity and variation that mirrors the possibilities in that world.

Despite the power of the antibody system, not all reactions to the environment are produced by antibody-mediated allergic reactions. In particular, we know that there are several food reactions that are clearly not allergic in origin. Examples of this class of reaction are lactose intolerance and aspirin sensitivity.

Lactose is the principal carbohydrate of milk. It is composed of two simple sugars that have to be chewed apart in order to be absorbed by the digestive system. The enzyme lactase does this separation. Virtually all infants have this enzyme. In some ethnic groups, however, the concentration of this enzyme in the intestinal tissue shows a marked decline at puberty. If a person is missing the lactase enzyme and he drinks milk, he will get a reaction. The lactose does not get broken down in the small intestine where it can be absorbed but travels to the colon. There the lactose is fermented by the bacteria and yeasts which normally inhabit that part of the body. The effect of fermenting lactose is to produce "gas" and acid. The patient experiences this as flatulence, abdominal cramps and, frequently, diarrhea. The patient is clearly sensitive to milk but there is no antibody involved and one would not be correct in attributing this to an "allergy" to milk. The end result is the same in the sense that the solution to the patient's discomfort is to avoid milk. However, by attempting to understand precisely the nature of the sensitivity, a way has been found to allow patients with lactose intolerance to enjoy milk products. An enzyme similar to the one missing from the intestine has been purified and can be added to milk before using so that the lactose is degraded into its constituent parts before it is ingested. This enzyme additive has no effect on the ability to drink milk by patients who have symptoms caused by immune complexes containing milk antigens.

Another example of nonallergic sensitivity which masquerades as allergy is the production of hives and asthma by aspirin. This is a more subtle situation than the lactose example because aspirin causes a nonallergic activation of the mast cell. The end result here looks very much like an allergic reaction biochemically. Yet there are features which allow one to distinguish between them. There are some medicines that block the production of allergic reactions rather than just block the products of allergic reactions as do the antihistamines. One of these medicines is called cromolyn sodium. This works at mucosal surfaces to block the activation of mast cells by IgE-antigen combination.[29] Mucosal surfaces are those tissues other than the skin where the body comes in contact with "foreign" substances. They typically secrete mucus. Examples are the nose, sinuses, lungs, gastrointestinal and genital surfaces, all the surfaces which elaborate IgA. If a patient is sensitive to the inhaling of cat dander, he can inhale the cromolyn before coming into contact with the cat dander and it will block the asthmatic reaction. As was mentioned above antibodies vary in their specificity and intensity, so it may be that in some patients not enough cromolyn can be delivered to the lungs to completely block the reaction. But the principle of mucosal block still holds. Similarly, there are patients who will begin to wheeze in response to something that they may have eaten.[2, 6, 10, 11, 33] Cromolyn has been shown to block this reaction but only if it is taken by mouth. Cromolyn is not appreciably absorbed. It attaches to the mast cells that line the gut and prevents them from being activated by the ingested allergen. When antibody-mediated reactions are considered, inhaling cromolyn has no effect on an ingested allergen and swallowing cromolyn has no effect on an inhaled allergen.

Cromolyn also seems to have a role in nonantibody-mediated reactions such as some aspirin-related reactions. What makes the situation with aspirin curious is that the reaction to swallowed aspirin cannot be prevented by oral cromolyn.[11] However, the reaction can be prevented in some patients by inhaling cromolyn before ingesting aspirin.[2] This is the chemical activation of the mast cell by a nonallergic means.

Most of the diet reactions have not yet been proved to be specifically allergic or nonallergic. Often, it is not clear whether a reaction is due to the food or to an associated preservative. For the most part we refer to reactions as "sensitivity." This is meant to emphasize our lack of precise information about mechanisms. It will not detract from the benefit of *The Allergy Discovery Diet*, which is based on very practical considerations. In fact, *The Allergy Discovery Diet* is more

*

accurate than any single type of test could be. If an accurate food antibody test were available, it would not tell us about reactions that were caused by nonantibody mechanisms. You would still have to try a dietary elimination and then a reintroduction regimen to assess all of your reactions. As more information becomes available we will be able to categorize each reaction more accurately.

How Could Allergy Produce Disease?

Now that we are familiar with antibodies, their structure and some of their differences, it is time to examine the ways in which they might cause disease. There are three mechanisms by which antibodies cause disease: immune complex formation, cell-mediated immune reactions and immune complex adherence to cells. This formidable statement really breaks down into a pretty simple restatement of what we began to discuss in the last section.

An immune complex is a substance formed when an antibody combines with the specific allergen against which it has been directed. It is the combination of the gelatin and the gelatin mold. Immune complexes come in all sorts of sizes and shapes. Rarely would we be dealing with a single antibody combining with a single antigen. More likely there would be some multiple of antibodies combining with some other multiple of allergens. The antibodies do not have to be all of the same specificity or class. It is possible that some antigen areas would be covered by an IgG antibody and another adjacent area complexed with an IgM antibody. This allows a combination of different antibodies with a single antigen.[44]

There is a lot of evidence that these immune complexes can cause much biological mischief when they become deposited in various tissues.

KIDNEY FAILURE

The situation that is best known is that of the kidney. The kidneys serve to filter the blood and excrete the waste products that are formed by the metabolism of the body. There are special capillary blood vessels in the glomeruli of the kidney which have pores through which these wastes can pass. When there is a great excess of immune complexes, they can effectively plug up these pores and prevent the filtering of the blood. In addition, the presence of these complexes stuck in the capillaries of the glomerulus excites an inflammatory reaction by macrophages and other white cells. This causes more swelling of the area where the immune complexes have been deposited. The kidneys' function is further reduced and the blood flow to parts of the kidney may be closed off. This is called kidney failure and

                                                                    ✳

leads to what used to be referred to as "uremic poisoning." This is
certainly not the only cause of kidney failure but it is a well-known
cause.

ARTHRITIS

Another type of immune complex disease is arthritis. While we are
still unsure about what stimulates the appearance of immune complexes in the various types of arthritis, there is little argument that
immune complexes participate in the joint inflammation that is seen.
There is evidence that many different antigens may contribute to the
immune complex. There have been associations with viruses such as
rubella (German measles) and hepatitis B, drugs such as penicillin
and foods such as milk.[34, 35] The types of arthritis we have been
discussing are referred to as inflammatory arthritis to distinguish them
from the "wear and tear" type of arthritis, which is called degenerative
or osteo-arthritis.

RASHES AND SKIN PROBLEMS

The skin is a frequent site of immune complex attack. Many of the
rashes that are seen in the course of the various childhood diseases
are caused by the deposition of complexes created by combining the
infecting virus or bacteria and the antibodies being made against it.
Measles is one dramatic example. The rashes of allergic reactions to
drugs are another example. Here the body has begun to make an
antibody against a medicine that the patient is taking. When the two
combine, and are filtered through the blood vessels in the skin and
deposited there, the same scavenger cells come to ingest the immune
complex and produce the inflammation that is seen clinically.

GASTROINTESTINAL DISEASE

Two additional areas of immune complex deposition that are less
well understood are the gastrointestinal tract and the blood vessels.
There have been few descriptions of circulating immune complex
deposition in the gut tissue[1, 25] and little confirmed human disease.[5] It
may be that that condition has not yet been adequately investigated
with the appropriate medical tools because there are many classes of
colitis and gastritis which remain very mysterious in their cause.

VASCULITIS

The condition of immune complex vasculitis is well known to
physicians but not widely familiar to patients. Examples have affected
blood vessels of every size and conceivable location in the body.

＊

The purpose of this description of the variety of sorts of immune complex disease is to demonstrate that everyone has come into contact with examples. We are not discussing rare diseases. Although you may not have been aware of the physiology behind measles and penicillin rashes, everyone has seen someone with them. What we will point out subsequently is the relationship of these mechanisms to other diseases that have not yet been thought of as caused by immune complexes.

Before we go on to this, there are still two additional types of allergic mechanisms that rely on antibodies. The most easily recognized type is "the cell-mediated reaction." This was mentioned in the previous section when we discussed hay fever. You may remember that the IgE antibody made against the ragweed pollen attached to the mast cell via an Fc receptor. This "armed" the mast cell so that if it came into contact with sufficient pollen antigens a reaction could be triggered. By this means all the chemicals in the mast cell are discharged into the adjacent tissues causing fluid accumulation and stimulation of the delicate nerves which results in itching or sneezing. A similar reaction takes place in hives and immediate-onset asthma. While we have historically thought of mast cells as representing a single category of cell, this is probably not true.[4] In other species, several different categories of mast cells have been observed as well as a difference of mast cells in the circulation from those lodged in tissues.[21, 42] This represents quite a spectrum of cell types, each of which could respond to a different antibody with a specific response.

While the antibody-mast cell reaction is the one with which most people will have had experience, there are other cell-antibody reactions which are well documented. There is the adherence of IgG to platelets via an Fc receptor.[12] Platelets are usually thought of in terms of blood coagulation. However, they really have many other interesting functions in the body. Within their membrane coats lie a complicated package of enzymes and chemicals which can initiate all sorts of reactions. Some of these participate in migraine headaches, some in asthma and some in menstrual cramps. There are undoubtedly many similar reactions which have not yet been described.

An area of uncertainty is whether platelets have Fc receptors for antibodies other than IgG.[13] Some scientists have thought they have found them while others deny it. There is less controversy about the ability of both IgA and IgG to "arm" lymphocytes against bacteria.[43] While there is not yet a description of this particular mechanism participating in any of the "allergic" diseases, it may be expected as we learn more about these reactions. There are also reports of IgA Fc receptors on liver cells[39, 41] which appear to have a role in immune complex removal from the circulation.

The final antibody-related allergic mechanism to be touched on is of great importance. This is the adherence to cells and platelets of already formed immune complexes. Experiments have shown this in both red blood cells[46] and platelets.[12, 13] The effect of the attachment of immune complexes to the surface of platelets is to produce aggregation (clumping) and activation of the platelets.[38] This activation of the platelets liberates such chemicals as serotonin, prostaglandins and leukotrienes, among others. These chemicals have demonstrated roles in hives, migraine headaches and asthma. Many other factors have been found in platelets and their roles in allergic disease remain to be investigated. The attachment of already formed immune complexes to red blood cells does not have any obvious allergic function. However, it serves to show that this type of attachment is not a rare situation and may well be seen with other more "interesting" allergic cells as further experiments are performed.

As we are building our understanding of how the "antibody arm" of the immune system functions by first learning about antibody formation and then about how antibodies participate in allergic diseases, it is now time to put this information together. In the next section we see where all of this is going and then how our knowledge can help us escape from the effects when this system is stimulated by normal features of our environment.

An Integrated Theory of Mucosal Immunity

We have been working up from the antibody molecules to the combinations of antibody and allergen. Now we have to consider how the system operates which results in putting the antibody at the surface where it can meet virus, bacteria or food particle. As we shall see, there is a beautiful symmetry in the way this system works together.

The insight which permitted development of knowledge in this area was provided by a team studying maternal immunity that could be passed to infants by nursing.[17] This group of scientists developed ways of isolating the secretory IgA (SIgA) antibody from colostrum (mother's milk). They were able to isolate enough of it that they could study the specificity of the antibodies against the bacteria of various types of dysentery. From this others surmised that there was some mechanism that the body had of taking antigens internally by mouth and processing them so that antibodies could be produced in the colostrum. They tried to test this mechanism by attempting to immunize nursing rabbits[32] against pneumococcus by giving them an extract from killed pneumococcal bacteria by mouth. They then kept measuring the antibody level in the secreted colostrum to see if and when the antibody to the pneumococcus might appear. Happily, the experiment worked and opened up an entire area of research in the functioning of what is called the mucosal immune system.

Mucosal refers to the type of tissue which is able to secrete mucus. These tissues occur at the interface of the body with the outside world. It is easy to understand this when we talk about the lung and tonsils, which come into direct contact with the inhaled and exhaled air that we breathe. However, it also refers to the lining tissue of the sinuses, the whole gastrointestinal tract and the genital tract. These are topographically outside the body even though we usually think of them as being inside us. It may be helpful to think of the hole in a doughnut. The hole is not inside the substance of the doughnut, which is made up of flour and sugar and egg and water. If you think of the human body for the moment as an elongated cylindrical dough-nut, you can see that the gastrointestinal tract has the same relation to the substance of the body as does the hole to the doughnut.

A lot of effort went into studying the types of cells that were necessary to pick up the antigens at the gut surface and then carry them to certain cells in the lymph nodes of the intestine.[45] There special B-cells become activated to secrete antibodies against the specific antigens. However, when the B-cell which is activated is one which is prepared to secrete IgA it does not stay in the lymph node where it was activated. Curiously, it migrates into the circulation and ends up being deposited at a mucosal surface somewhere. This activated IgA B-cell need not end up only at the mucosal surface from which the antigen was scavenged, it could end up at any other mucosal surface.[3] This provides a very convenient method of ensuring that each surface has the same potential to produce protective antibodies.[45]

An important link in this theory was the demonstration that the appearance of specific antibody in the colostrum was not a freak but an instance of a more general immune response. This proof was very difficult because the amount of antibody secreted at the other muco-sal surfaces was either very dilute or quickly destroyed by enzymes and other factors also found at these surfaces. However, using tech-niques which were very sophisticated in their technology and imagi-native in their conception, a number of scientists were able to demonstrate that priming the system in one part of the gastrointesti-nal tract resulted in antibody not only in colostrum but in bronchial secretions,[31] saliva,[30] and in the secretions of the gastrointestinal tract which had been physically excluded from any direct contact with the priming antigen.[23]

An additional feature to be worked out was how different parts of this system might communicate with each other. All the cells secreting SIgA are like individual sentries on guard. They are able to shoot their antibodies at specific invaders with which they come in contact. This is fine as long as there are only a few antigens, but what happens if there is a massive invasion. The sentries on guard duty need a way to alert their colleagues and their backups that more help is needed. There needs to be a recruitment and activation of additional B-cells to provide more antibodies against pneumococcus or salmonella or whatever.

How the body performs this recruitment is still a mystery. It would appear to be the result of some hormonal mechanism. By hormonal is meant only that there must be some circulating chemical messenger which carries the message to the potential antibody-producing cells wherever they may be. This circulatory method is necessary because the cells are physically dispersed. Rarely are they next to each other, so the message cannot spread directly from one to the next. (This mechanism is used in the heart muscle, for instance, when a contraction takes place.) Nor are these cells at the end of nerves, so that one cannot use a nervous system-mediated mechanism as when the brain causes you to move your fingers when you type or causes the secretion of adrenalin from either the adrenal medulla or the sympathetic nerve endings.

The type of "hormone" that the body uses for this messenger could be any of a large variety of substances. Among the possibilities are interferons, prostaglandins, leukotrienes and immune complexes. Since these are all substances which might be found in the circulation at any time, it is hard to determine what other effects they might have. It should be made clear that these are not the only possible messengers. There may be others as yet undiscovered or unthought of. The advantage of the ones named was that in the early days of this hypothesis when I was most concerned with understanding asthma, all these substances could cause asthma if present in high enough concentration.

The basic scientific outline of how this mucosal immune system works together can be demonstrated practically. Before we can review this evidence, it will be necessary to discuss a phenomenon referred to as the biphasic asthmatic response (for a more complete discussion see Reference 36). Asthma is the reversible spasm or closure of the bronchial (breathing) tubes in the lungs. Many studies of this reaction have shown that there are two components. There is an initial, rapid onset reaction. This is of limited duration and responds completely to adrenalin injection. However, this does not always end the asthmatic response. There is a late response which may have its onset three to four hours after the immediate response. This is also a long-lasting response which may continue for hours after it begins. Furthermore, the response of this phase of the reaction to adrenalin

✳ ——————————————————————————————————

is partial and transient. Adrenalin may improve breathing temporarily but as its blood level declines the bronchospasm returns as if the adrenalin had never been injected.

There is a particular importance of this two-part response to understanding the general workings of the mucosal immune system. Not only can this biphasic response be produced by inhaling an allergen to which the patient is sensitive,[37] it has also been produced by the ingestion of an allergen.[10] The characteristic time course of the resulting lung response is identical whether the avenue of stimulus was through the gut or via the lung. Furthermore, the response can be blocked by the same method in each case. There is a medicine that has been available for over fifteen years called sodium cromolyn (Intal). If it is inhaled in appropriate concentration before the allergen is inhaled, it blocks all lung reaction. However, inhaling the medicine will not block the dual response initiated by ingestion of an allergen. If, on the other hand, sufficient cromolyn is taken by mouth before ingesting the allergen, then the cromolyn does prevent the development of the lung response. In other words, the allergic response can be triggered at either the lung surface or the gut surface but it can be blocked only at the surface where it started. What has been so puzzling is that when the doctor examines the patient he cannot tell whether the wheezing that he hears is a response to something that the patient has inhaled or to something that he has eaten.

Most doctors feel that the immediate phase of the asthmatic response is due to antibodies of the IgE class. The abrupt onset and the similarly abrupt response to adrenalin are characteristics of the childhood-type asthmatic response seen so often in patients who are sensitive to cats and horses. In these patients the specificity and severity of the allergic response is very highly correlated with the skin tests and the blood tests which measure IgE antibodies. There are many allergists who have believed that the second phase of the reaction is also due to IgE because if the first phase of the reaction is prevented by pretreatment with cromolyn, then the second phase will not occur.

I do not believe that the evidence favors this opinion. Not all asthmatic responses show this two-phased character. There are many which are only immediate onset without the late phase and similarly there are those which demonstrate only the late phase and are missing the early phase.[22, 28] It is not necessary for both to appear together.[37] This suggests that different mechanisms may be involved. In addition, although both phases are similarly responsive to prevention by pretreatment with cromolyn, the phases respond differently to other interventions. As mentioned earlier, the effect of adrenalin is complete in the early phase and temporary in the late phase. Another important difference is the effect of cortisone and its steroid derivatives on the responses. The cortisone drugs have no effect on the early response. However, cortisone pretreatment is very effective in preventing the late phase even if the early phase has occurred.

The differences between the early and late phases of the asthmatic response indicate that the old ideas of IgE mediated allergy are not sufficient to explain the complexity of the observed responses. A newer and better explanation is required. None has yet been proved. However, the characteristics of the dual allergic response have been sought in other areas that might provide a clue to the mechanisms involved. Finally, a similar response was recorded. Circulating immune complexes were sought in the blood of food-allergic patients who were exposed to the specific foods to which they were allergic. Not only were the immune complexes able to be measured, their appearance in the blood followed a two-phased time course that was identical to the asthmatic response we have discussed.[33]

This observation provided that last necessary theoretical link in the hypothesis. There was now a measurable intermediary between the observed clinical behavior and the inciting stimulus. This also explained some other puzzling features of the patient with asthma. Often it would appear that the provoking stimuli for an attack were additive. A patient would appear to be food allergic in some instances only if he also had a "cold." "Doctor, why is it that if I drink milk when I have a cold, I wheeze, but I can usually drink a glass of milk without any trouble?" Responses would also appear to be dose-related: small amounts were tolerable but larger amounts were not. Furthermore, even in patients demonstrated to be allergic to a particular food, if they were otherwise in a quiet state from the standpoint of their asthma, they might be able to eat a small amount of the food as long as they did not try it every day.

All of this makes the allergic or asthmatic response appear to be additive. There appears to be a certain cumulative amount of stimulation that is necessary to achieve a "threshold" before symptoms appear. This observation has been discussed for many years but no mechanism was able to explain it. With the measurement of the circulating immune complexes correlating in time and appearance with the allergic symptoms, an explanation is at hand. It has long been recognized that the body has mechanisms for disposal of immune complexes.[15] These disposal mechanisms can be overwhelmed and then act as a way for immune complex-mediated responses to be perpetuated. If only a small number of immune complexes are generated, then they are disposed of quickly. If more are generated, the total amount might for a period of time push through the threshold of symptoms until the clearance mechanisms

*

are able to reduce the concentration. In more severe cases, the concentration of immune complexes may last for days or longer because the clearance systems behave as if they are a clogged drain that needs flushing.

Although much has been learned about immune complex handling and clearance by the body, there is much more still to be learned. Some portion of this clearance occurs via the liver,[39] some by the kidneys and some by the spleen.[15] Other methods will probably be discovered in the future. However, there is proof that blockade of either the liver or the kidney[7] does result in the persistent elevation of circulating immune complexes. The types of circulating immune complexes are determined both by the antibodies and allergens as well as the particular clearance mechanism that may be blocked. Each mechanism has a preference for a specific size or immunoglobulin content of the immune complex.

There are two specific mechanisms by which the threshold effect of stimulation by allergic reactions are produced. The first is demonstrated by the mast cells "armed" with IgE antibodies. The adherence of one antigen molecule to an IgE molecule on the surface of the mast cell is not sufficient to trigger the activation of the mast cell. There is, however, some number of antigen molecules which is sufficient to trigger activation of the mast cell with resulting liberation of the inflammation-producing chemicals stored inside. The Fc receptors for IgE on the surface of the mast cells do not "care" what may be the antibody specificity of the other end of the IgE molecule. The "armed" mast cell is not armed only with antibodies of a single specificity. The specificities of the adherent antibodies parallel those of the antibodies of the class for which the particular cell has Fc receptors. If there are very few antibodies with a particular specificity, such as for rutabaga, then one would be able to eat quite a lot of rutabaga without running any risk that there would be a critical number of rutabaga antigen molecules attached to the "armed" mast cell. On the other hand, if one ate rutabaga along with kiwis and there were some number of anti-kiwi antibodies distributed on the surface of the mast cell, then there might be a point at which the addition of the activated anti-rutabaga antibodies to the activated anti-kiwi antibodies on the mast cell surface would be sufficient to trigger liberation of histamine from the cell. This is an example of the additive effect of low-level allergies reaching a threshold beyond which the clinically observable allergic reaction takes place.

While the distribution of antibodies on the surface of mast cells provides one example of how a threshold effect can be produced, there is another way as well. The concentration of immune complexes in the circulation determines the amount of immune complex adherent to the Fc receptors on the surfaces of the various cells (and cell

✳

fragments such as platelets) which have Fc receptors. Again just as there is a critical number of antigen molecules to activate the surface antibodies of the mast cell, there is a critical number of adherent immune complexes necessary to activate the other types of allergic effector cells. The production of the allergic reaction is a function of the creation of immune complexes by the absorption of antigens, the removal of immune complexes by the various clearance mechanisms and the sensitivity of the several allergic effector cells to activation by the adherence of the circulating immune complexes.

By starting with an elimination phase, *The Allergy Discovery Diet* allows the level of circulating immune complexes to decline. The choice of generally nonreactive foods means that new food-related immune complexes will not be created during this phase. The decline of immune complex concentration in the extracellular fluids also means less fluid accumulation in joints, around eyes and in tissues generally. The patient will find his joints more flexible and less painful, fewer pouches under the eyes and a marked tendency to lose *fluid* weight or "bloat." In addition, the marked reduction of food-related circulating immune complexes means that during the reintroduction phase, the food-allergic person will respond more dramatically to an increase in immune complexes produced by exposure to an allergic food. This has an important implication: If there has been a long-standing exposure to an allergic food and a large buildup of circulating immune complexes, it may take longer than six days for the overburdened immune complex clearance mechanism to reduce the level satisfactorily. That is the reason behind advising the reader to repeat the elimination phase of the diet if he has had a partial or inadequate response, so that there may be a further decline in the level of circulating immune complexes.

How Can the Allergic Response Be Countered?

We have seen the way in which the body's interaction with the allergens in the environment produces the various types of allergic reactions. Now attention needs to be turned to the ways in which we can prevent, contain or reverse these reactions. There can be no doubt that the most effective way of preventing the sequence of events culminating in the allergic reaction is to remove the allergen from the patient's environment. *The Allergy Discovery Diet* is one way to obtain the information to allow you to do this. However, there may be a number of allergens to which there are low-grade antibodies. It may be difficult to analyze the extent of allergy to these allergens because of this low intensity and the reaction may only occur when several of these low-intensity allergens are encountered together. It may not be possible to avoid all contact with allergens in the environment be-

*

cause there may be mold spores in the air which may not be anticipated before coming in contact with them. The additive effect of these invisible allergens to whatever dietary allergens may have been ingested can result in allergic reactions of varying severity. Because it is frequently difficult to avoid allergens even if we know what we are allergic to, it is important to consider the alternatives.

The first point of intervention is at the contact of the antigen with the mucosal surface. We have seen that the use of cromolyn can block the reaction at both the respiratory surface and the gastrointestinal surface. This apparently occurs because although the reaction of the antigen and the antibody still occurs, cromolyn blocks the mechanism by which this activates the allergic cell. It can work only on allergic cells that occur at mucosal surfaces. It is not absorbed across mucosal surfaces in quantities that would allow it to be effective against allergens that might be generated within the body itself. Nor can it be effective against allergens that get absorbed and combine with circulating nonmucosal antibodies. Cromolyn has been effective at other surface sites such as the eyes, where it can prevent the expression of hay fever.

A second way of reducing the allergic reaction if we cannot eliminate allergen contact is to reduce the quantity of antibody. There are two general ways of accomplishing this. The most common approach is through the use of cortisone and its derivatives. These drugs affect allergic reactions not just by reducing antibody levels as we shall see later. An additional way of reducing antibody levels is by the use of certain "immunosuppressants," which were originally used as drugs against cancer. Some of these are being used or have been tried against arthritis, asthma, colitis and psoriasis. Again these drugs have multiple effects which are not limited to the reduction of antibody levels. The side effects of cortisone derivatives and immunosuppressants are so considerable that one is justified in using them only in the most severe and advanced conditions.

Once the allergen has gained access to the body and there is a sufficient quantity of antibody available, the reaction will take place unless we can keep the immune complex concentration under the "threshold" of clinical expression. We are more familiar with ways to reduce immune complex clearance than to increase it. Cortisone derivatives have been shown to retard the ability of the clearance system to remove immune complexes,[19] Similarly, there appears to be a "clogging" effect,[20][39] so that after a certain point of immune complex creation the mechanism for removal breaks down and the immune complex levels go up.[9] The only way that is currently known to reduce immune complex levels is by plasmapheresis.[27] This means that blood is withdrawn, the blood cells are spun off and returned to the body and the proteins in the plasma, including the immune complexes, are removed. This may sound simple enough in concept; however, there are many problems in practice. A major problem is that in addition to what may be toxic immune complexes being removed, there are many good and important proteins removed as well. Most notable among these good proteins are the clotting factors which are necessary to keep us from hemorrhaging to death. Another problem is the malnutrition and body fluid retention that can occur if too much of the body's albumin is removed. This is the most abundant single protein in the blood. It is made by the liver and if it is removed at a rate faster than the liver can synthesize it the total level will go down. Nevertheless, there are some reports about the benefit of plasmapheresis in progressive life-threatening asthma[16] and in the improvement of patients with multiple sclerosis[24] as well as some with lupus erythematosus.[27]

If we have not been able to prevent the encounter of antigen and antibody and if we have no way of accelerating the removal of the complex from the circulation, we may still be able to reduce the intensity of the allergic response. This is one of the main uses of the cortisone derivatives in the allergic diseases. The trick is to use the cortisone in a way, at a level and for a length of time that will skirt the major side effects while allowing the suppression of the allergic response. This is an art but there may be no real way of doing this safely and great caution must be used whenever cortisone is considered.

Another way of reducing the intensity of the allergic response is the result of some exciting new experiments with certain types of fish oils. The production of the allergic response is due in part to the preformed mediators already in the effector cell and in part to the mediators that are made as a consequence of the activation of the effector cell. The platelets that we discussed earlier contain quantities of serotonin stored in granules. These are ready to be discharged into the circulation or tissues when the platelet is activated.

However, there is another powerful mechanism of allergic activation. The membranes of cells and platelets contain both fatty acids and the enzymes to break down the fatty acids into other compounds.[26] Many of these compounds are extraordinarily powerful provokers of allergic reactions such as leukotrienes and prostaglandins. Many studies have been done exploring the supplementation of diet in humans with various types of fatty acids. The most exciting have been those using fats from cold-water ocean fish, the omega-3 fatty acids: eicosapentaenoic (EPA) and docosahexaenoic (DHA). These acids are very effective in substituting for arachidonic acid in cell membranes including red blood cells, white blood cells and platelets. When the cell is activated by an allergic stimulus and the enzymes in the cell membrane are supposed to break down the fatty acids into irritating chemicals, everything suddenly goes in slow motion. The EPA and DHA substitute for the arachidonic acid in the enzymes as well as in the membranes and the products of this reaction are very much less irritating than the natural products. It is possible that dietary supplementation with omega-3 fatty acids will attenuate the allergic response.

While the biochemistry that we have just reviewed is on firm ground, it does not appear to be the whole story. There are two documented situations in which the fish oils have been therapeutic that do not require the interference with arachidonic acid metabolism. During the course of a trial of the benefits of fish oils in preventing heart disease which was being conducted at the University of Cincinnati Medical School, the researchers were struck by the number of patients who reported that while on the oil their migraine headaches got very much better. This suggestion was unexpected and without explanation. The usual procedure would have been to note it down and forget it. Instead, these doctors decided to see if they could reproduce the findings in a group of patients who suffered from intractable migraines that did not respond to any other treatment.

They did just such an experiment utilizing a "double blind cross-over" study.[18] This means that neither the doctor assessing the treatment nor the patient receiving the treatment knew which oil was being used when. In addition, after a predetermined period of time the oil was switched from the "test" oil to the "control" oil. This is the best type of experimental design although it is often difficult to accomplish in other clinical situations with sick patients. The results of this test showed that after a lag time of two weeks, three quarters of the patients on the fish oil had a dramatic improvement in their headaches and that the improvement appeared to coincide with the alteration of the fatty acid content of the cell membrane.

The problem with this is that we are more inclined to look at migraine as the result of serotonin liberation into the circulation than as a result of the products of arachidonic acid metabolism. If this is so, then the fish oil replacement in the cell membrane must be having some other effect on the activation of platelets. This has not been proved by the usual tests of platelet aggregation in clotting, despite the observation that at higher doses a bleeding tendency does develop. The two possibilities that come to mind are that in some way the fish oil makes the platelet membrane "stronger" so that it will not disrupt as easily in response to a stimulus or that in some other way the replacement of the usual fatty acid with the fish oil prevents the adherence of stimulus (immune complex?) to the platelet membrane. In either case there is a loosening of the connection between biologic stimulus and response and a reduction in headache. These are questions that have an answer which will hopefully be forthcoming in the future.

Another observation that is intriguing in this regard was made in an inbred mouse colony that had a very high incidence of immune complex kidney failure.[40] For reasons not reported, there was a switch in the source of oil used as a food supplement with the result that the mice lived longer. This was explored in a formal scientific experiment which demonstrated unequivocally that the addition of fish oil reduced by three quarters the death rate from kidney disease in this mouse strain. Again there does not appear to be any obvious connection with arachidonic acid metabolism and the mystery mechanism would appear to have more in common with the migraine experiment.

Investigation into the mechanisms of immune complex formation and clearance and the ways in which immune complexes interact with cells will provide us with new methods of avoidance and treatment in the future. Unfortunately, we have to try to relieve symptoms and prevent disease with current incomplete knowledge. The drugs available frequently are expensive or toxic or both. By achieving an understanding of and mastery over our diet we should be able to keep the drugs to a minimum. *The Allergy Discovery Diet* has the advantage of uncovering food sensitivities of a nonallergic origin as well as those that are antibody mediated. Furthermore, its structure and sequence follow from our understanding of antibody secretion, immune complex creation and clearance. The complexity of antibody responses to food antigens is so great that even when a method for determining secretory antibody specificity is available, it will take many years to verify the validity of these tests. The dietary approach will remain the standard until this occurs and *The Allergy Discovery Diet,* unique in its structure and flexibility, is the most palatable and detailed illustration of this approach.

References for Appendix

1. Accinni, L., J. Brentjens, et al. (1978): Deposition of Circulating Antigen-Antibody Complexes in the Gastrointestinal Tract of Rabbits with Chronic Serum Sickness. Digestive Diseases 23:1098–1106.
2. Basomba, A., A. Romar, et al. (1976): The Effect of Sodium Cromoglycate in Preventing Aspirin Induced Bronchospasm. Clin. Allergy 6:269–75.
3. Bienenstock, J. (1980): Bronchus Associated Lymphoid Tissue and the Source of Immunoglobulin Containing Cells in the Mucosa. Environ. Health Perspec. 35:39–42.
4. Bienenstock, J., and A. D. Befus (1980): Mucosal Immunology. Immunology 41:249–70.
5. Brentjens, J., E. Ossi, et al. (1977): Disseminated Immune Deposits in Lupus Erythematosus. Arthritis Rheumat. 20:962–68.
6. Breslin, A. B. X., D. J. Hendrick, and J. Pepys (1973): Effect of Disodium Cromoglycate on Asthmatic Reactions to Alcoholic Beverages. Clin. Allergy 3:71–82.
7. Cairns, S. A., A. London, and N. P. Mallick (1981): Circulating Immune Complexes Following Food: Delayed Clearance in Idiopathic Glomerulonephritis. J. Clin. Lab. Immunol. 6:121–26.
8. Calvert, J. E. (1986): A Function for IgD. Immunology Today 7:136–37.
9. Coppo, R., B. Basolo, et al. (1985): Immunological Monitoring of Plasma Exchange in Primary IgA Nephropathy. Artificial Organs 9:351–60.
10. Dahl, R. (1978): Disodium Cromoglycate and Food Allergy: The Effect of Oral and Inhaled Disodium Cromoglycate in a Food Allergic Patient. Allergy 33:120–24.
11. Dahl, R. (1981): Oral and Inhaled Sodium Cromoglycate in Challenge Test with Food Allergens or Acetyl Salicylic Acid. Allergy 36:161–65.
12. Endresen, G. K. M., and O. Forre (1982): Studies on the Binding of Immunoglobulins and Immune Complexes to the Surface of Human Platelets. Int. Archs. Allergy Appl. Immun. 67:33–39.
13. Endresen, G. K. M., and O. Forre (1985): Studies on the Binding of Proteins to the Human Platelet Surface. Thromb. Haemostasis 53:360–65.
14. Feldman, B. Robert (1986): The Complete Book of Children's Allergies. New York: Times Books, p. 3.

15. Frank, M. M. (1983): Immunoglobulin G Fc Receptor Mediated Clearance in Autoimmune Diseases. Ann. Int. Med. *98*:206–18.
16. Gartman, J., P. Grob, and M. Frey (1978): Plasmapheresis in Severe Asthma. Lancet *ii*:40.
17. Gindrat, J. J., L. Gothefors, et al. (1972): Antibodies in Human Milk Against E. Coli of Serogroups Most Commonly Found in Neonatal Infections. Acta Paediatra Scand. 61:587–90.
18. Gleuck, C. J., T. McCarren, et al. (1986): Amelioration of Severe Migraine with Omega-3 Fatty Acids: A Double-Blind Placebo Controlled Clinical Trial (Abstract). Am. J. Clin. Nutr. *43*:710.
19. Haakenstad, A. O., J. B. Case, and M. Mannik (1975): Effect of Cortisone on the Disappearance Kinetics and Tissue Localization of Soluble Immune Complexes. J. Immunol. *114*:1153–60.
20. Haakenstad, A. O., and M. Mannik (1974): Saturation of the Reticuloendothelial System with Soluble Immune Complexes. J. Immunol. *112*:1939–48.
21. Haig, D. M., T. A. McKee, et al. (1982): Generation of Mucosal Mast Cells Is Stimulated *in vitro* by Factors Derived from T Cells of Helminth Infected Rats. Nature *300*:188–90.
22. Johnson, T. F., R. E. Reisman, and C. E. Arbesman (1975): Late Onset Asthma Due to Inhalation of *Aspergillus niger.* Clin. Allergy *5*:397–401.
23. Keren, D. F., S. E. Kern, et al. (1982): Direct Demonstration in Intestinal Secretions of an IgA Memory Response to Orally Administered *Shigella flexneri* Antigens. J. Immunol. *128*:475–79.
24. Khatri, B. O., M. P. McQuillen, et al. (1985): Chronic Progressive Multiple Sclerosis: Double Blind Controlled Study of Plasmapheresis in Patients Taking Immunosuppressive Drugs. Neurology *35*:312–19.
25. Kirkham, S., K. J. Bloch, et al. (1986): Immune Complex Induced Enteropathy in the Rat. Digestive Diseases and Sciences *31*:737–43.
26. Lee, T. H., and J. P. Arm (1986): Prospects for Modifying the Allergic Response by Fish Oil Diets. Clin. Allergy *16*:89–100.
27. Low, A., A. Hotze, et al. (1985): The Nonspecific Clearance Function of the Reticuloendothelial System in Patients with Immune Complex Mediated Diseases Before and After Therapeutic Plasmapheresis. Rheumatol. Int. *5*:69–72.
28. Malo, J. L., A. Cartier, et al. (1985): Isolated Late Asthmatic Reaction Due to Nickel Sulphate without Antibodies to Nickel. Clin. Allergy *15*:95–99.
29. Mazurek, N., G. Berger, and I. Pecht (1980): A Binding Site on Mast Cells and Basophils for the Anti-Allergic Drug Cromolyn. Nature *286*:722–23.
30. Mestecky, J., J. R. McGhee, et al. (1978): Selective Induction of an Immune Response in Human External Secretions by Ingestion of Bacterial Antigen. J. Clin. Invest. *61*:731–37.

31. Montgomery, P. C., K. M. Connelly, et al. (1978): Remote Site Stimulation of Secretory IgA Antibodies Following Bronchial and Gastric Stimulation. Adv. Exp. Med. Biol. *107:*113–22.

32. Montgomery, P. C., B. R. Rosner, and J. Cohn (1974): The Secretory Antibody Response. Anti-DNP Antibodies Induced by Dinitrophenylated Type III Pneumococcus. Immunol. Commun. *3:*143–56.

33. Paganelli, R., R. J. Levinsky, et al. (1979): Immune Complexes Containing Food Proteins in Normal and Atopic Subjects After Oral Challenge and Effect of Sodium Cromoglycate on Antigen Absorption. Lancet *i:*1270–72.

34. Panush, R. S., R. M. Stroud, and E. A. Webster (1986): Food Induced (Allergic) Arthritis. Arthritis Rheumat. *29:*220–26.

35. Parke, A. L., and G. R. V. Hughes (1981): Rheumatoid Arthritis and Food: A Case Study. Br. Med. J. *282:*2027–29.

36. Pepys, J. (1976): Chapter 17: Nonimmediate Asthmatic Reactions. *In* Bronchial Asthma: Mechanisms and Therapeutics, Weiss, E. B., and M. S. Segal, eds. Boston: Little, Brown and Co., pp. 231–56.

37. Pepys, J., C. A. C. Pickering, et al. (1972): Asthma Due to Inhaled Chemical Agents—Tolylene Di-Isocyanate. Clin. Allergy *2:*225–36.

38. Pfueller, S. L., S. Weber, and E. F. Luscher (1977): Studies of the Mechanism of the Human Platelet Release Reaction Induced by Immunologic Stimuli. J. Immunol. *118:*514–24.

39. Rifai, A., and M. Mannik (1984): Clearance of Circulating IgA Immune Complexes Is Mediated by a Specific Receptor on Kupffer Cells in Mice. J. Exp. Med. *160:*125–37.

40. Robinson, D. R., J. D. Prickett, et al. (1985): The Protective Effect of Dietary Fish Oil on Murine Lupus. Prostaglandins *30:*51–75.

41. Sancho, J., E. Gonzalez, and J. Egido (1986): The Importance of the Fc Receptors for IgA in the Recognition of IgA by Mouse Liver Cells. Immunology *57:*37–42.

42. Stallman, P. J., S. S. Wagenaar, et al. (1977): Cell Bound IgE on Human Mast Cells and Basophilic Granulocytes in Atopic and Non-Atopic Subjects. Int. Archs. Allergy Appl. Immunol. *54:*443–50.

43. Tagliabue, A., L. Nencioni, et al. (1983): Antibody Dependent Cell Mediated Antibacterial Activity of Intestinal Lymphocytes with Secretory IgA. Nature *306:*184–86.

44. Wager, O., K. K. Mustakallio, et al. (1968): Mixed IgA-IgG Cryoglobulinemia. Am. J. Med. *44:*179–87.

45. Walker, W. A., and K. J. Isselbacher (1977): Intestinal Antibodies. New Engl. J. Med. *297:*767–73.

46. Waxman, F. J., L. A. Hebert, et al. (1986): Differential Binding of Immunoglobulin A and Immunoglubulin G1 Immune Complexes to Primate Erythrocyte *in vivo.* J. Clin. Invest. *77:*82–89.

General References

Food Allergy, A Practical Approach to Diagnosis and Management, ed. by Lawrence T. Chiaramonte, Arlene T. Schneider and Fima Lifshitz, Clinical Pediatrics, Vol. 5. New York: Marcel Dekker, Inc., 1988.

Food Allergy, ed. by Eberhardt Schmidt, Nestle's Nutrition Workshop Series, Vol. 17. New York: Nestec, Ltd., Vevey/Raven Press, Ltd., 1988.

Handbook of Food Allergies, ed. by James C. Breneman, Immunology Series, Vol. 29. New York: Marcel Dekker, Inc., 1987.

Index

Abdominal pain, 6
See also Gastrointestinal tract;
  Stomach; Stomachache
Additives, 5, 17, 19–20, 45, 65, 66,
  67
  chart of, 40
  defined, 39
  and Allergy Discovery Diet, 39–
  41, 66–67
  hidden, 11–12, 17, 23, 25, 36
Albumin, 27
Alcohol, 31, 32–35, 44
See also Fermentation products
Allergens, 26
See also Antigens; Environmental allergens
Allergic reactions (non-food), 7,
  25
  and threshold effect, 7, 17
Allergy (general), 4, 15, 22, 36
See also Food allergy/sensitivity
Allergy Discovery Diet
  benefits of, 8–9, 12, 14, 22, 23,
  39
  common sense basis of, 19–20
  described, 8, 12, 13, 18–19
  how to use, 42–60, 61–65, 75.
    See also Elimination Phase;
    Reintroduction Phase
  menu choices, 61, 75
  precautions, 8, 23, 38, 49, 75
  preparing for, 42–45

  purpose of, 8–9
  scientific basis of, 15–16
  shopping lists for, 65–66,
  69–72
Allergy Discovery Diet Cookbook,
  76–338
  and baby foods, 45, 66–67
  description of, 63, 75
  how to shop for, 65–66, 67–68
  recipe choices, 61–62, 75
  specialty foods for, 68
Allergy Discovery Diet Food Chart,
  53–59
  Elimination Phase, 53
  mention of, 44
  Reintroduction Phase, 54–59
Anaphylactic reactions, 7
Antibodies, 15, 16, 17, 21, 24, 28,
  38
  and cross-reactions, 17
  and food allergies, 8–9, 16–17
  and threshold effect, 17, 21
See also IgA; IgE
Antigens, 8, 15, 16, 17, 25, 28, 34,
  36, 42, 49–50
  and cross-reactions, 17, 37–38
  and food allergies, 16–17
  and threshold effect, 17
See also Allergens
Arthritis, 5, 18, 25, 34
See also Joint pain
Asthma, 5, 9, 22–23, 25

B-cells, 16
See also Blood cells
Backaches, 4
Bacteria, 24–25, 27, 31
Bacterial infections (and food al-
lergies), 17
Baking powder, 23
Beer, 31, 40, 44
and Allergy Discovery Diet, 44
See also Fermentation products
Beet sugar, 65
Bisulfites, 32, 41
Bloating, 4–5, 6
Blood cells, 16, 18
See also B-cells
Blood cholesterol, 44
See also Cholesterol; LDL cho-
lesterol
Blood tests (for food allergies), 9
See also Diagnosis; Tests
Brain (and alcohol), 34
Brand names (and Allergy Discov-
ery Diet), 65–66
Bronchial problems, 6, 22, 25, 26,
27
See also Bronchitis; Coughs
Bronchitis, 10
See also Bronchial problems;
Coughs
Butter. *See* Milk

Caffeine, 35
Cane sugar, 35–36, 51, 62
recipes featuring, 262–74
substitutes for, 35, 66
See also Sugar
Canker sores, 3, 5, 6
Cardiovascular system (and food
allergies), 5
See also Heart disorders
Cell-mediated reactions, 19

Cheese, 14, 23, 29, 32, 36
and Allergy Discovery Diet, 29–
31
See also Cottage cheese; Dairy
products; Fermentation
products; Milk
Chemicals, 11, 18, 19, 20, 32, 36,
39
See also Additives
Chest pains, 5
See also Cardiovascular system;
Heart disorders
Chicken, 5, 24–25, 51, 62, 65, 67
and cross-reactions, 25
and Allergy Discovery Diet, 24–
25, 51, 62
recipes featuring, 165–74
and salmonella, 24–25, 27
Children (and Allergy Discovery
Diet), 44–45
Chives, 51, 62
See also Onion/chives
Chocolate, 10–12, 22, 25, 36, 62
and Allergy Discovery Diet, 51,
62
recipes featuring, 274–86
Cholesterol, 26, 27, 30–31
and Allergy Discovery Diet, 44
See also Blood cholesterol
Circulation problems, 18
See also Cardiovascular system;
Heart disorders
Citrus, 22–23, 51, 62
and Allergy Discovery Diet, 51,
62
recipes featuring, 142–52
Coffee/tea, 31, 35, 51, 62
recipes featuring, 249–61
See also Fermentation products;
Tea leaves
Constipation, 5, 43
and Allergy Discovery Diet, 43

*

Corn, 3, 23–24, 42, 43, 51, 62
  as hidden additive, 11–12, 14, 24
  recipes featuring, 152–65
Corn bran, 43
  See also Laxatives
Cornstarch, 11
Cottage cheese, 29, 65
  recipes featuring, 223–36
  See also Dairy products; Milk
Coughs, 5, 6
  See also Bronchial problems;
    Bronchitis
Cramps, 5, 6, 18, 24
  See also Dysmenorrhea
Cream. *See* Milk
Cross-reactions, 17, 32, 37–38
Cytotoxic testing, 9

Dairy products, 12, 14, 28, 29–30,
    32, 36
  recipes featuring, 223–36
  See also Milk
Diabetes, 42
Diagnosis (of food allergy), 4, 47
  Allergy Discovery Diet question-
    naire, 6
  See also Blood tests; Tests
Diarrhea, 3, 4, 5, 22, 23, 24, 26
Diet Express (of Allergy Discovery
    Diet), 45, 61, 75
Dietetic Therapy of Urticaria, the,
    13
Digestion, 18
Drugs, 5, 22, 33, 35
  prescriptions and Allergy Dis-
    covery Diet, 42–43
Dysmenorrhea, 4, 29
  See also Cramps; Menses; Men-
    strual cramps

Eczema, 25
  See also Skin problems

Eggs, 18, 22, 24, 26–27, 51, 62
  and cross-reactions, 25
  as hidden additive, 26
  recipes featuring, 184–98
  replacements for in cooking, 27
  and salmonella infection, 27
Elimination diets, 13, 19, 22
Elimination Phase (of Allergy Dis-
    covery Diet), 18, 23, 35,
    36, 38, 43, 49–51, 60, 62,
    64, 65
  how to use, 49–51
Endometriosis, 4, 29
Environmental allergens, 7
  See also Allergens
Eyes, 3, 4, 14, 18, 19, 35

Fatigue, 4, 5, 33, 35
  and caffeine, 35
Fermentation products, 14, 31–32,
    43, 51, 62
  recipes featuring, 236–49
Food additives. *See* Additives
Food allergic reactions
  mechanics of, 9
  mention of, 5, 16, 21–22, 26, 32,
    38, 42
  severe (and Allergy Discovery
    Diet)
    during Elimination Phase, 50
    during Reintroduction Phase,
      64–65. *See also* Recovery
      Day
  symptoms of, 5, 6, 25, 66
    symptom questionnaire, 6
  tests for, 9
  timing of, 9
Food allergy/sensitivity
  as cause of illness, 4, 17–19, 50
  defined, 4–5
  described, 8, 12, 13, 17–19, 25

Food allergy/sensitivity (*cont.*)
  vs. non-food allergy, 5, 15–16,
    25
  See also Allergy
Food diary
  example of, 48–49
  how to keep, 45–49, 52
  questionnaire, 46–47
  reason for, 52
Food intolerance, 5
Food toxicity, 5
Foods
  and antigens, 15–16
  associated with allergy. *See* Hy-
    perallergenic foods; Hy-
    poallergenic foods
  and cross-reactions. *See* Cross-
    reactions
  and hidden additives, 23. *See
    also* Additives; Hidden ad-
    ditives

Garlic, 38
  See also Onions/chives
Gas, 38
  See also Gastroenteritis; Gastro-
    intestinal tract
Gastroenteritis, 24–25
Gastrointestinal tract
  and food allergies, 3, 4, 14, 18,
    23–24, 27–28, 39. *See also*
    Gas; Gastroenteritis
  and mucosal immune system,
    27–28

Hay fever, 9
Headaches, 4, 5, 7, 9, 10, 11, 16,
    24, 29, 31, 32, 35, 39
  See also Migraine headaches
Heart (and alcohol), 34
Heartburn, 3, 5, 23, 38

Heart disorders
  and Allergy Discovery Diet, 42
  as symptom of food allergy, 5, 6
  See also Cardiovascular system
Hidden additives, 17, 25, 27, 36,
    39, 40, 42
  See also Additives
Histamine, 18, 27
Hives, 5, 26, 34
Hyperallergenic foods, 22, 51, 64
  list of, 51
Hypoallergenic foods, 13, 30, 65,
    75
  list of, 49

IgA (antibody), 16, 38
  See also Antibodies
IgE (antibody), 7
  See also Antibodies
Illness (and Allergy Discovery
    Diet), 42
Immune complex, 18, 20
  defined, 17–18
Immune system, 4, 7, 8, 15, 17–18,
    19, 21–22, 25, 31, 38, 39,
    42, 51
  and neuropeptides, 21
Indigestion, 5, 6, 26, 38
  See also Gastrointestinal tract
Itching, 5, 18, 25

Joint pain, 4, 5, 11, 25, 33, 34
  See also Arthritis

Kidney disorders, 18

Lactose intolerance, 5
Laxatives (and Allergy Discovery
    Diet), 43

✳

Leeks, 38
  See also Onions/chives
Legumes (food family), 37
Lily (food family), 38
Lungs, 27–28

Medicines, 42
  See also Drugs
Menses, 6
  See also Dysmenorrhea; Menstrual cramps
Menstrual cramps, 30
  See also Cramps; Dysmenorrhea; Menses
Menus (Allergy Discovery Diet)
  mention of, 43, 45, 61
Migraine headaches, 26, 32–33, 36
  See also Headaches
Milk, 5, 7, 14, 18, 29–30, 62, 51
  See also Dairy products
Mold, 31, 37
Mucosal immune system, 27–28
Muscle aches/spasms, 5, 25, 29

Nasal congestion, 5
  See also Stuffy nose
Nausea, 6, 26, 30
Nonimmunologic reactions, 5, 39
Nose problems
  and histamine, 18
  as symptom of food allergy, 5, 6, 7
  See also Nasal congestion; Rhinitis; Stuffy nose

Oat bran, 43
Oats, 25–26, 51, 62
  recipes featuring, 174–83, 236–49, 309–25
Onions/chives, 38–39, 51, 62
  recipes featuring, 309–25

Peanuts, 7, 17, 51, 62
  recipes featuring, 298–309
  See also Peas/peanuts
Peas/peanuts, 37–38, 51, 62
  recipes featuring, 298–309
Pharmacologic reactions, 5
Pollen, 7, 16, 17
Potassium, 40, 43
Pregnancy (and Allergy Discovery Diet), 44–45
Prescribed diets (and Allergy Discovery Diet), 42
Preservatives, 39, 40, 42
  See also Additives; Hidden additives
Processed foods, 17, 19, 22, 26, 28, 34, 35, 39, 45, 65
  and Allergy Discovery Diet, 45, 50
Prostate pain, 6
Psoriasis, 3, 5, 14, 30–31, 36
Psychoneuroimmunology, 21
Psyllium seed, 43
  See also Laxatives

Rashes, 3, 9, 18, 25
  See also Skin problems
Reintroduction (of foods)
  and Allergy Discovery Diet, 13, 19
  natural, 20
  precautions, 8, 19–20, 23, 38, 51–52
  See also Reintroduction Phase
Reintroduction Phase (of Allergy Discovery Diet), 22, 23, 24, 38, 43, 51–52, 60, 62, 64
  how to use, 51–52
  precautions, 8, 23, 38, 51, 52
Recipes. *See* Allergy Discovery Diet Cookbook

Recovery Day (of Allergy Discovery Diet), 23, 50, 64–65
how to use, 50, 64–65
during Elimination Phase, 50
during Reintroduction Phase, 23, 64–65
recipes for, 325–38
Regular Track (of Allergy Discovery Diet)
described, 63
Respiration (and food allergy), 5, 18
See also Asthma; Bronchial problems; Bronchitis; Coughs
Rhinitis, 26
See also Nose problems
Rice bran, 43
Rotary Diversified Diet, 13
Rotation (of foods)
and Allergy Discovery Diet, 8, 13, 19–20, 45, 51, 62–63, 64
how to rotate substitute foods, 62–63, 64–65
history of, 13, 20

Salicylates, 5
Salmonella bacteria, 24–25, 27
Salt, 11, 19, 42
and Allergy Discovery Diet, 42
and laxatives, 43
Scratch tests (for food allergies), 9
Shopping lists (for Allergy Discovery Diet), 65–66, 68, 69–72
special foods, 68
staple foods, 69–72
Sinuses, 5, 10–11
Sinus headaches, 39
See also Headaches

Skin problems, 4, 5, 18, 19, 26, 30, 35
See also Eczema; Rashes
Skin tests (for food allergies), 9
Soy, 14, 19, 22, 28–29, 51, 62
recipes featuring, 211–23
Stomach, 3, 14, 30, 31, 34, 36, 38
See also Abdominal pain; Gastrointestinal tract; Stomachache
Stomachache, 4, 5, 30, 36
See also Abdominal pain; Gastrointestinal tract; Stomach
Stuffy nose, 5, 8, 10, 22
See also Nasal congestion; Nose problems
Substituting foods (and Allergy Discovery Diet)
how to, 62–63, 64–65
Sugar, 32, 35, 51, 62, 66
cane sugar (and Allergy Discovery Diet), 35, 51, 62, 66
recipes featuring, 262–74
and fermentation, 31–32
as hidden additives, 11–12, 36, 42, 43
See also Cane sugar
Sulfites, 40, 42
Symptoms (of allergies)
to chemicals, 40 (chart)
to foods, 4, 6, 7, 9, 26, 42, 49–50, 52, 66
list of, 5, 6
primary, 8
questionnaire, 6
secondary, 8. See also Food allergic reactions; Food allergy/sensitivity
general, 15. See also Allergy to impurities, 26

Tea. *See* Coffee/tea
Tea leaves, 31
    See also Fermentation products
Tests (for food allergies), 9
    Allergy Discovery Diet test, 22
Threshold effect, 17, 21
Tofu, 27
    See also Soy
Tomatoes, 14, 36–37, 51, 62
    recipes featuring, 287–97

Ulcer, 30
Under-eye pouches, 3, 4
    See also Eyes
Uremic poisoning, 18
Urinary problems, 5, 6

Vanilla beans, 31
    See also Fermentation products
Vinegar, 14, 31
    See also Fermentation products

Viral infection, 7, 17, 42
    and Allergy Discovery Diet, 42
Vitamins, 27, 43
    and Allergy Discovery Diet, 43–44
Vomiting, 24, 26, 36

Weight loss
    and Allergy Discovery Diet, 30, 44
Welts, 5, 6
    See also Skin problems
Wheat, 8, 14, 19, 27–28, 42, 51, 62
    recipes featuring, 198–211
Wheat bran, 43
Wheezing, 6, 23
Wine, 9, 14, 31, 44.
    See also Fermentation products

Yeast, 19, 22, 31, 32, 43
    as hidden additive, 19
    See also Fermentation products

ABOUT THE AUTHORS

DR. JOHN POSTLEY is a Manhattan allergist and Assistant Clinical Professor of Medicine at Columbia University. He lives in New York City with his wife and son.

JANET BARTON, who developed the recipes for this diet, has an M.A. in Special Education from American University. She lives with her husband and twin sons on Long Island.

BOOK MARK

The text of this book was composed in
the typeface ITC Cheltenham Book
with display typography in ITC Cheltenham Book
by Folio Graphics Company, Inc.,
New York, New York

Printing of this book is
by Berryville Graphics,
Berryville, Virginia

BOOK DESIGN BY STANLEY S. DRATE,
FOLIO GRAPHICS COMPANY, INC.